COLLEGE CLASSICS IN ENGLISH

General Editor

NORTHROP FRYE

FRANCIS BACON

A SELECTION OF HIS WORKS

Edited by
SIDNEY WARHAFT
University of Manitoba

Essayes, 1597
Essaies, 1612
The Essayes or Counsels, Civill and Morall, 1625
The Proficience and Advancement of Learning
The Wisdom of the Ancients
The Great Instauration
The New Organon
Of the Dignity and Advancement of Learning
New Atlantis
Letters

THE ODYSSEY PRESS · NEW YORK

Published in the United States by
THE ODYSSEY PRESS
A Division of Western Publishing Company, Inc.

© *The Macmillan Company of Canada Limited 1965*

Library of Congress Catalogue Card No. 65-20259

Printed in the United States of America

Contents

THE PROFICIENCE AND ADVANCEMENT OF LEARNING

THE WISDOM OF THE ANCIENTS

THE GREAT INSTAURATION

THE NEW ORGANON

OF THE DIGNITY AND ADVANCEMENT OF LEARNING

LETTERS

Francis Bacon

A Selection of His Works

Introduction

Francis Bacon was one of those capacious men of the Renaissance who crammed several careers into one lifetime. Though rather frail and often sickly, he was an outstanding jurist, courtier, and parliamentarian, as well as a great writer and philosopher. In a famous letter of 1592 to his uncle Lord Treasurer Burghley, he revealed that he had both public and private ambitions: he desired to dedicate his abilities both to his "excellent Sovereign" and to "vast contemplative ends". And although he is best remembered for his contribution to the realm he loved best, that of contemplation, his achievements in the world of action were hardly less remarkable. In both areas he sought "commandment of more wits than a man's own", for he always felt it his calling to lead men's thoughts as well as their actions into new and better ways.

The offspring of learned and illustrious parents, Francis was almost born into public service. His father, Sir Nicholas Bacon, Lord Keeper of the Great Seal and Lord Chancellor, was a principled jurist whose counsels Elizabeth heard with respect. His mother, Ann, daughter of Edward VI's tutor and sister of Lady Burghley, was also an erudite and upright person, of an intense piety that could not but have had some effect on her sensitive son. At the age of twelve Francis went to Trinity College, Cambridge, where he learned to question the authority of Aristotle. Four years later he was admitted to Gray's Inn to study law, but it was not until he became a Bencher in 1586 that he was entitled to practise. In the meantime, his father had died, leaving him with such a "narrow portion" as to give him serious concern over ways and means of sustaining himself and his ambitions in the world. In November 1584, he embarked on what was to be a long and honourable career in Parliament. At much the same time he looked to the Court, but his uncle Lord Burghley seemed hesitant to advance him, and Queen Elizabeth was soon angered by Bacon's opposition in Commons to a money-raising measure of hers that he considered improper. To be sure, the Queen later relented and made him her Learned Counsel Extraordinary, but the position was not an official one and brought in little recognition or reward. So it was that, in spite of considerable service and much suing, Bacon found himself waxing "somewhat ancient" in "the meanness" of his estate when he wrote his appeal to his uncle in 1592.

Unfortunately, he was to wax even more ancient before the meanness was to abate. For it was not until James I had come to the throne and Burghley's son, Lord Salisbury, had taken over the position of Lord Treasurer that any considerable portion came Bacon's way. The story of his advancement after his being knighted in 1603 has been summed up in his own words. In a letter of 1621 written to King James to thank him for the title of Viscount of St. Albans, Bacon says, "You found me of the Learned Counsel, Extraordinary, without patent or fee; a kind of *individuum vagum*. You established me, and brought me into ordinary. Soon after you placed me Solicitor, where I served seven years. Then your Majesty made me your Attorney or Procurator General. Then a Privy Councillor, while I was Attorney; a kind of miracle of your favour, that had not been in many ages. Then Keeper of your Seal: and because that was a kind of planet and not fixed, Chancellor. And when your Majesty could raise me no higher, it was your grace to illustrate me with beams of honour; first making me Baron Verulam, and now Viscount of St. Albans." Almost as these words were being penned, however, Bacon's political career was coming to an abrupt end, and the disgraced public man was about to be released to return to his private thoughts and studies.

Such a bald recital of the facts hardly discloses the drama and the accomplishment behind them. Bacon's contribution to the common weal was a solid one. In fact, although he has been severely censured for helping to prosecute his one-time patron the Earl of Essex for treason, and although he has been condemned for the corruption of which the House of Lords found him guilty in 1621, there is reason to believe that in both of these events he was sacrificing himself for the good of the state.[1] Nor does it seem fair to think of him as a shameless sycophant completely dedicated to self-advancement. There is no doubt that he worked hard at seeking positions commensurate with his genius, but there is little indication that his contemporaries condemned such efforts. Almost all of the evidence, in fact, is on the other side. His chaplain Dr. Rawley, his apothecary, his friends, his servants, and even many of his enemies respected him. Ben Jonson seems to have summed up a widespread sentiment: "I have, and do reverence him for the greatness that was only proper to himself, in that he seemed to me ever, by his work, one of the greatest men, and most worthy of admiration, that had been in many ages. In his adversity I ever prayed that God would give him strength: for greatness he could not want." And to add to this is John Aubrey's tribute: "All that were great and good loved and honoured him."

Whatever Bacon's personal attributes were, there can be no doubt about the respectability of his public service. His dedication to his sovereign, his attempts to revise and codify the laws of his country, his opposition to excessive taxation, his encouragement of a generous colonial policy, and his efforts to weld Great Britain into a unity, all of these are matters of record whose worth posterity has vindicated. To both of the sovereigns he served under he gave shrewd counsel on the handling of both internal and external religious threats to England. In treatises like *A Brief Discourse touching the Happy Union of the Kingdoms of England and Scotland* and his *Discourse of the Plantation in Ireland* he evinced enlightened concern over the welfare of Britain as a whole. His works on the law were undertaken in the profound hope of reforming legal theory and practice. Many more examples of his dedicated patriotism could easily be cited, but further demonstration

---

[1] It is impossible to examine here the full details of Bacon's aims and character and the conditions under which these sought fulfillment. For a balanced treatment see Anderson, *Francis Bacon, His Career and His Thought* (in Bibliography).

hardly seems needed. Courageously facing every obstacle (including the King himself as well as Parliament) that would prevent Britain from becoming a great "Monarchy in the West", he surely deserves Rawley's estimation as "the glory of his age and nation".

Such was Bacon's endowment, however, that his glory was destined to shine even brighter in the fields of letters and thought. For as he himself put it in his *Gesta Grayorum*, a masque written for Queen Elizabeth, "the monuments of wit survive the monuments of power". His treatises on religious matters played no small part in the history of toleration; his legal tracts are still consulted; and his *History of Henry VII* remains a classic of its kind. But it is mainly such monuments as his *Essays*, his *Advancement of Learning*, *The Great Instauration* (which includes *The New Organon*), and *New Atlantis* that have survived his works as a statesman.

Like so much else in his life, Bacon's essays derive from his feeling that it was his mission to help his fellow man. In his dedication of the first edition (1597), he declares that his volume is "medicinable", having nothing in it repugnant to religion or manners. For Bacon medicinable meant useful, and useful meant containing honest and realistic instruction on what men are and do in this world. Immediately popular, the original edition of ten essays was revised and augmented to thirty-eight in 1612, and finally to fifty-eight in 1625.

The style in which the truth about the facts of life is conveyed is not accidental. Thoroughly grounded in problems of communication, Bacon believed that usefulness in knowledge was best realized through what he called, in the *De Augmentis Scientiarum*, the Initiative method as opposed to the Magistral. "The magistral method teaches; the initiative intimates. The magistral requires that what is told should be believed; the initiative that it should be examined." Much the same distinction is drawn between the methodical and aphoristic delivery of knowledge. Methods pretend to completeness, aim to win consent, and in "carrying the show of a total, make men careless, as if they were already at the end". Aphorisms, however, which challenge the writer to avoid being ridiculous or shallow, aim at quite the opposite. Imitating the dispersed actions of life, they are not arranged in any significant order; and representing fragments of knowledge, they invite men to inquire further. The importance Bacon attached to aphorisms may be measured not only by his life-long practice of keeping commonplace books, recording apophthegms, and collecting sentences for his own use, but also by his efforts to make up for deficiencies of such collections in the *De Augmentis*. To fill the gap, he furnishes his Promptuary or Preparatory Store with sophisms, colours of good and evil, antitheses of things, and the like, all useful "intimations" or invitations to "expectant inquiry".

The meaningful relationship between these and the *Essays* emerges clearly in Bacon's discussion of Antitheses. Here he recommends that the writer always have commonplaces ready at hand, "in which the question is argued and handled on either side". He wants "in short all topics which there is frequent occasion to handle . . . studied and prepared beforehand; and not only so, but the case exaggerated both ways with the utmost force of the wit, and urged unfairly, as it were, and quite beyond the truth". Such commonplaces should be contracted into aphorisms or "acute and concise sentences", ready for use as needed. Of the forty-seven instances of his Antitheses of Things in the *De Augmentis*, many contain the germs of his essays. The following, for example, casts light on Essays XVI and XVII, *Of Atheism* and *Of Superstition*:

Superstition

For

They that err from zeal, though we cannot approve them, yet we must love them.

Mediocrities belong to matters moral; extremities to matters divine.

The religious man is called superstitious. I had rather be-

Against

As the likeness of an ape to a man makes him all the more ugly, so does the likeness of superstition to religion.

Look how hateful affectation is in human affairs, so hateful is superstition in divine.

Better have no opinion of

lieve the most monstrous fables that are to be found in any religion, than that this world was made without a deity.

God at all than an injurious one.

It was not the Epicureans but the Stoics that troubled the ancient states.

There is no such thing as a mere atheist in opinion; but great hypocrites are the true atheists, who are ever handling holy things without reverencing them.

This practice of presenting both sides of a question in curt, aphoristic form has often been misunderstood by readers of the *Essays*. The aim of initiating examination called for provocative technique. Hence it was not meanness that led Bacon to avoid committing himself on ethical issues in the *Essays*, but rather the intent to reveal to the reader, in a challenging way, the objective truth about such issues. Dealing with such universal matters as truth, death, revenge, adversity, friendship, ambition, and the vicissitudes of things, his "brief notes" were supposed to be medicinable for all civilized men. They are about "topics which there is frequent occasion to handle", and they are handled in the initiative or aphoristic mode deliberately to stimulate thought. But it is the development in terms of antitheses that most strongly challenges the reader. Not only is the question "argued and handled on either side", but it is also wittily and often unfairly "exaggerated both ways". As theorizing or speculation is kept to a minimum, and as the antitheses are faithfully explored, rarely is any attempt made to reach a conclusion. Instead of being lulled into acceptance, the intellect is incited to analysis and evaluation, a process further aided and quickened by the curt phraseology and uneven movement of the aphoristic treatment. In describing the value of apophthegms, Bacon might have been describing his own sentences: they are " 'words which are as goads', words with an edge or point, that cut and penetrate the knots of business and affairs". Thus it is hard to sympathize with, say, Blake's view of the *Essays* as "Good advice for Satan's kingdom". If making an unsentimental survey of both sides of a fundamental matter is bad counsel, and if Satan's kingdom is identified with human business and affairs, then Blake was not far off the mark. But it should not be forgotten that Bacon uncovers the ideal as well as the practical. Consequently, if an exciting challenge to examine the worldly together with the unworldly is valid, the palm must go to Bacon.

As the essays were reissued, Bacon "enlarged them", not only in number but also in weight. Whether the author felt that "in profit and in popular estimation wisdom yields to eloquence", whether he had begun to regard himself as an oracle who must be believed, or whether his aims regarding the essays changed over the years,[2] the revisions as well as the additions became more and more magistral. Transitions were smoothed; illustrations, figures, and proverbs were added; the style generally was made more concrete; and the organization received more care. It should be noted, moreover, that the style always tended to the magistral when the topic was of public concern, particularly when it was of contemporary application. Thus such essays as *Of Unity in Religion, Of Seditions and Troubles,* and *Of Plantations,* which dealt with problems directly involving the welfare of the state, are more eloquent, more fully connected and amplified than those on more abstract matters. None the less, rarely is there that copiousness, that "round and clear composition . . . , and . . . sweet falling of the clauses" which Bacon so deplored. The over-all effect remains one of brevity, curtness, and cool provocation.

The impressive achievement of the essays, however, is more than a matter of following rhetorical principles. Certainly Bacon was master of the techniques he recommended, but he brought to these a knowledge of the world, an understanding of the ways of men, a profound and richly furnished mind, and a feeling for the rhythms and nuances of language without which the techniques would have remained barren. Derived from a unique experience and wisdom, Bacon's "dispersed meditations" are

[2] It is likely that he thought of the essays as satisfying some of the deficiencies noted in *The Advancement.* See Crane and Zeitlin in the Bibliography.

often disturbing, always stimulating. The noblest sentiments jostle the most mundane. Shortly after this penetrating statement, "Truth may perhaps come to the price of a pearl, that showeth best by day, but it will not rise to the price of a diamond or carbuncle, that showeth best in varied lights," comes this one: "Clear and round dealing is the honour of man's nature." Similarly, "He that hath wife and children hath given hostages to fortune" is followed by "Certainly wife and children are a kind of discipline of humanity." Many an observation teases one into mazes of thought: "I cannot call riches better than the baggage of virtue," and "Virtue is like a rich stone, best plain set." As many of these quotations prove, the imagery is often brilliant and strikingly apt. And consider the relevance of the figures in these: "A man that studieth revenge keeps his own wounds green." "Beauty is as summer fruits, which are easy to corrupt, and cannot last." Such great sentences, with their subtle rhythms, evocative images, and stinging diction, although eminently memorable and quotable, are often beyond analysis. How, for instance, is one to get at the ultimate effect of the cadences and language of a triumph like this: "Certainly virtue is like precious odours, most fragrant when they are incensed or crushed: for prosperity doth best discover vice, but adversity doth best discover virtue." Whether one always agrees with their sentiments or not, Bacon's *Essays* cannot be denied greatness. Their thought is still fresh, their phraseology still alive. Truly they give body to Ezra Pound's dictum that literature is news that stays news.

The other great monuments of Bacon's wit, his philosophical writings, have also remained news. Certainly their influence on western culture is still being felt. For Bacon was nothing less than the spokesman for and leader of the scientific view of modern times. In that famous letter to Burghley he declared he wanted to take all knowledge as his province, for he hoped, he said, to "bring in industrious observations, grounded conclusions, and profitable inventions and discoveries". This is Bacon's essential aim, repeated with many variations in almost all of his philosophical works. The goal of knowledge, he says in *The New Organon*, is "that human life be endowed with new discoveries and powers". He is concerned with "the real business and fortunes of the human race"; he wants knowledge to be directed to "the benefit and use of life", the "profit and dignity of mankind", "the welfare of man". As the Father of Salomon's House sums it up in the *New Atlantis*, "The End of our Foundation is the knowledge of Causes and secret motions of things, and the enlarging of the bounds of Human Empire, to the effecting of all things possible."

To achieve this conquest of nature, what is needed is "a total reconstruction of the sciences, arts, and all human knowledge raised upon the proper foundation". This is the Great Instauration, an immense plan of renewal which Bacon evolved over the years "for the interest of the present and future generations". Of the six parts of this plan that he envisaged, only three ever approached completion. The first part, *The Divisions of the Sciences*, which he described as a "summary or general description of the knowledge which the human race at present possesses", was to include not only an inspection of things known but also a survey of things deficient, that is, of things "omitted which ought to be there". The requirements of this part are outlined in *The Advancement of Learning* and more fully discussed in the expanded Latin version of this work, the *De Augmentis*. The second part of the plan, *The New Organon*, contains the directions on how to interpret nature. Significantly set out in aphorisms, this is an exposition of that inductive method which is to equip the intellect to pass beyond the present store of human knowledge.

These first two parts are the most fully developed and the most interesting of the six that made up Bacon's design. Of the last four, the third, which he called *The Phenomena of the Universe; or a Natural and Experimental History for the Foundation of Philosophy*, was intended to provide the investigator with a sufficient body of data from which he might derive axioms or principles for a foundation to build philosophy upon. This body Bacon himself managed partially to provide in three of the six "histories" planned for this part: the *Sylva Sylvarum; or a Natural History* (hurriedly compiled, it is a vast, dreary, and remarkably unoriginal collection of "scientific" facts, scraps, and observations), *The Natural History of Winds* (complete), and *The History Natural and Experimental of Life and Death* (complete); of the other three, *The History of Density and Rarity*, *The History of Heavy and Light*, and *The History of Sympathy and Antipathy of Things*, there appeared only quite fragmentary "entrances" or prefaces. As for the rest, the fourth part, *The Ladder of the Intellect*, was to provide illustrations or demonstrations of the inductive process, but it never got past an introduction; the fifth, *The Forerunners; or Anticipations of the New Philosophy*, was to be a record of what might be achieved by common sense working directly on nature; it too is limited to a preface; finally, the sixth part, *The New Philosophy; or Active Science*, "to which the rest is subservient and ministrant", was to set forth Bacon's true philosophy. Its completion had to be left to the future and fortune of the human race.

Generally speaking, the method central to this huge undertaking is empirical and inductive, as opposed to the prevailing scholastic method, which was deductive and syllogistic. Whereas the Aristotelian Schoolmen argued from established major premises (taken from past authority and the revelations of religion), Bacon wanted to shift and reverse the perspective. His plan (which bypassed authorities and religion entirely) was to go from the observation of particulars to general principles. As his new organon was to replace the old *Organon* of Aristotle, Bacon contrasted his way with Aristotle's:

> There are and can be only two ways of searching into and discovering truth. The one flies from the senses and particulars to the most general axioms, and from these principles, the truth of which it takes for settled and immovable, proceeds to judgment and to the discovery of middle axioms. And this way is now in fashion. The other derives axioms from the senses and particulars, rising by a gradual and unbroken ascent, so that it arrives at the most general axioms last of all. This is the true way, but as yet untried.

The true way contains three distinct steps. First comes the immersion in the facts: limited by "enclosures of particularity", the mind is required to "analyse experience and take it to pieces". He desires, Bacon says, to lead men to particulars themselves, "while men on their side must force themselves for awhile to lay their notions by and begin to familiarize themselves with facts". On the basis of this familiarization, there follows "due process of exclusion and rejection", that is, elimination from the collection of facts of all that are not relevant to the matter being examined. At the same time (this Bacon seems to have discovered through practice) affirmative or "prerogative" instances must not be neglected. Mere tabulation and rejection can hardly arrive at the grounded truths and principles that are the last stage of the process. Nor is this stage to be gained in a straight line. The investigator must first pause carefully at lesser axioms and test these by returning to the facts: only then may he go on to greater generality. At every step upward he must check his principles with the particulars and the lesser principles subtending them. Moreover, from the new light cast by axioms new particulars may be found: the "road does not lie on a level, but ascends and descends, first ascending to axioms, then descending to works". Finally, the investigator might arrive at a knowledge of the highest and most general principles, "but the middle are the true and solid and living axioms, on which depend the affairs and fortunes of men".

The pyramidal structure of this whole approach may be discerned in concrete terms in the *New Atlantis*. The first measure taken by the College of Six Days Works is to gather information, to collect data of all kinds through their Merchants of Light, their Depredators, and their Mystery Men. Following this, Pioneers or Miners try new experiments (apparently, as recommended in the fifth part of the Great Instauration, *The Forerunners*, on the basis of common sense in touch with empirical fact). Next Compilers arrange and classify these experiments, which are then examined by the Dowry Men or Benefactors for their usefulness both for human benefits and scientific theory. Toward the end comes the entry into the true philosophy: the

Lamps "direct new experiments of a higher light more penetrating into nature than the former"; the Inoculators execute these experiments and report them; and finally the Interpreters of Nature enunciate new general axioms or principles derived from their study of these reports. The process is a slow one, requiring many years and the co-operation of many men for its fruition. Through particulars, as Bacon might have said, men could eventually raise themselves up to generalities and so "to the effecting of all things possible".

The exposition of the new method had three main parts: refutation, classification, and reassurance. What was useless or dangerous in past knowledge had to be exposed and set aside; the rest had to be put into usable categories; and men's feelings had to be made secure in the face of the sweeping reform.

In his survey and praise of learning in *The Advancement*, Bacon had to deliver it first from "the discredits and disgraces which it hath received, all from ignorance, but ignorance severally disguised, appearing sometimes in the zeal and jealousy of divines, sometimes in the severity and arrogancy of politiques, and sometimes in the errors and imperfections of learned men themselves". Since the first two refutations are relatively straightforward and deal with prejudices more than with practices, it is not necessary to elaborate them here. Similarly the treatment of the indifferent fortunes and manners of learned men needs only to be mentioned. Far more nearly basic to Bacon's needs was a criticism of "those errors and vanities which have intervened amongst the studies themselves of the learned". As Bacon sees it, there are three vanities or "distempers" in studies which have been hurtful to knowledge: "the first, fantastical learning; the second, contentious learning; and the last, delicate learning; vain imaginations, vain altercations, and vain affections". In reverse order, the first of these is the "study of words and not matter". Although eloquence is not entirely to be disdained, magistral copiousness has been too much sought after. Men have been more interested in stylistic finish and flourish than in "weight of matter, worth of subject, soundness of argument, life of invention, or depth of judgment".

The second distemper, vain matter, is worse than vain words. Here the Schoolmen are most to blame, for from a minimum of material and an "infinite agitation of wit" they have spun out laborious and flimsy webs of learning. Both their subjects and their manner of handling them are suspect: they concentrate on involved, "vermiculate questions" and unrealistic inventions, and they break these down into minute fragments, "through particular confutations and solutions of every scruple, cavillation, and objection, breeding for the most part one question as fast as it solveth another".

The third vice of learning is the deceit in the imposture of authors and the credulity of learners. Credulity particularly has been detrimental to knowledge: it has resulted in such fantastic beliefs and given so great a credit to authors that new ideas receive no quarter. Thus Aristotle has been made into a dictator beyond whose pronouncements men have been loath to venture.

In addition to these primary diseases of learning, there are eleven secondary "peccant humours" or unhealthy conditions, which are somewhat easier to cure. The first of these is the attraction to either of the two extremes, antiquity or novelty. Admiration for the past especially has prevented progress, since men who look backward must neglect "new additions". The next two weaknesses are related to the first in their assumptions that all possible intellectual discoveries were made long ago, and that the best of these have prevailed. The fourth and fifth peccant humours deal with the faulty management of knowledge itself. On the one hand is the premature reduction of knowledge into arts and methods so that no room is left for expansion; on the other is the abandonment of universality or *philosophia prima*, that set of highest principles which would apply to all knowledge.

The following three errors have to do with the mind and attitudes of the investigator. The sixth is a too great reverence for the human understanding, a reverence which has resulted in a withdrawal of contemplation from nature to the mind and its conceits. The seventh is a distortion of vision caused by personal preference for some limited ideas or system. Plato and

Aristotle in the past, the alchemists and William Gilbert more recently, all went astray in that they built up false philosophies from one restricted position. As for the eighth error, it is "an impatience of doubt". Even when the mind does dwell objectively on things, it is allowed to rush on to conclusions, without the "due and mature suspension of judgment" needed to arrive at certainty.

Following the ninth peccant humour, which is mainly a rephrasing of the first vanity, namely that the delivery of knowledge has been too magistral, the last two deal with the mistaken goals set for knowledge. The immediate ends that individuals seek are improper, and, most important of all, the last or furthest end of knowledge is misplaced. Men strive in the former case to attain personal success, and in the latter to satisfy curiosity, to entertain themselves, or to gain recognition, and the like, but "seldom sincerely to give a true account of their gift of reason to the benefit and use of man; as if there were sought in knowledge a couch, whereupon to rest a searching and restless spirit; or a terrace, for a wandering and variable mind to walk up and down with a fair prospect; or a tower of state, for a proud mind to raise itself upon; or a fort or commanding ground, for strife and contention; or a shop, for profit and sale; and not a rich storehouse, for the glory of the Creator and the relief of man's estate".

As a number of these vanities and errors reveal, Bacon entertained considerable reservations about the ability of the mind to arrive at truth. "For the mind of man is far from the nature of a clear and equal glass, wherein the beams of things should reflect according to their true incidence; nay, it is rather like an enchanted glass, full of superstition and imposture, if it be not delivered and reduced." As he grew more and more aware of the necessity of refuting these impostures, Bacon slowly developed his famous concept of the Idols. These false notions or phantoms that possess the understanding must be exposed and where possible destroyed if men are to be led "to the particulars themselves". In *The New Organon*, where they receive their most detailed analysis, Bacon distinguishes four classes of Idols:

of the Tribe, of the Cave, of the Market Place, and of the Theatre. The first three of these are innate; that is, they have their foundation in the human condition itself: the first in the nature of the race as a whole, the second in the character of individual men, and the third in the intercourse and association of men with each other. The Idols of the Theatre are adventitious: they come to man from without, moving into the mind from philosophical dogma and wrong laws of demonstration. These may with care be eliminated; the others can only be avoided or controlled.

The Idols of the Tribe are the many natural tendencies to distort experience. The mind is prone to impose order where none is, and to relate the unrelated. It is inclined to interpret things in the light of its favourite beliefs, blindly allowing itself to be convinced by affirmations of its judgments while disregarding exceptions and inconsistencies. It is also unquiet, restlessly seeking comprehension of absolutes that are really beyond its grasp. Not only is it swayed by the sudden and unusual, but it is also coloured by the will and affections. Worst of all, it tends to put its trust in the senses, despite their "dulness, incompetency, and deceptions". Finally, even when the understanding does confront substance and reality (see the eighth peccant humour), it is disposed to hurry on prematurely to the highest generalities instead of resting patiently in matter.

The sources of the Idols of the Cave are education, environment, special training and interests, and "the peculiar constitution, mental or bodily, of each individual". Every man has a den or cave of his own from which he views the world. Thus the mind is marked by excessive predilections in one direction or another: the predominance, as with the logic of Aristotle or the magnetism of Gilbert, of a favourite subject (the seventh peccant humour); too great an admiration for antiquity or novelty (the first peccant humour); or the immoderate tendency either to compare or to distinguish (to synthesize or analyse). It is consequently wise for the student of nature to hold in suspicion "whatever his mind seizes upon with peculiar satisfaction".

Idols of the Market Place, the most troublesome of all, are the fallacies caused by the obscuring of the intellect by words. Invented by the vulgar, words do not allow for greater acuteness and more precise communication than are found in their crude origins. Because of the limitations of language, advanced discussions often end in disputes about definitions; but even if the definitions came first, they could not help much in dealing with nature, for they too consist of words, and words only beget words. There are two kinds of idols imposed by words on the understanding. The first are names of things, such as Fortune, Prime Mover, and Element of Fire, which do not exist; the second are names of things, such as humidity, which do exist but which are "yet confused and ill defined, and hastily and irregularly derived from realities".

The Idols of the Theatre are false systems of philosophy and perverted rules of demonstration established, like stage plays, without much regard to reality. Most systems derive either a great deal from a few things, or a very little from many things, so that in both instances they are too narrowly based. For example, the Rational or Sophistical school, of which Aristotle is the conspicuous representative, fails to consult experience sufficiently before coming to its conclusions. The Empirical philosophers do even worse. Like the alchemists and Gilbert, they have founded their systems not on common notions but on very few experiments, "wresting all other facts in a strange fashion to conformity" with their dogma. Finally, there is the Superstitious school, consisting of those who mix their philosophy with theology to the detriment of both. This widespread practice is most pernicious, as it flatters the understanding into the unjustified belief that it comprehends the most lofty matters.

That these Idols were not simply fabrications of Bacon's fancy may be seen from the following example, which illustrates not only the Idol of the Theatre but other of the vanities and errors of learning as well and represents a well-established way of thought. Shortly after Galileo published the account in 1610 of his discovery of the four moons of Jupiter, a respectable representative of the old school refuted him with this argument:

There are seven windows given to animals in the domicile of the head, through which the air is admitted to the tabernacle of the body, to enlighten, to warm, and to nourish it. What are these parts of the *microcosmos*? Two nostrils, two eyes, two ears, and a mouth. So in the heavens, as in a *macrocosmos*, there are two favourable stars, two unpropitious, two luminaries, and Mercury undecided and indifferent. From this and many other similarities in nature, such as the seven metals, etc., which it were tedious to enumerate, we gather that the number of the planets is necessarily seven. Moreover, these satellites of Jupiter are invisible to the naked eye, and therefore would be useless, and therefore do not exist. Now, if we increase the number of the planets, this whole and beautiful system falls to the ground.

For the mind to be "delivered and reduced" from all such fallacies and impostures Bacon recommended many remedies. Foremost amongst these was his own method: "The formation of ideas and axioms by true induction is no doubt the proper remedy to be applied for the keeping off and clearing away of idols." To form axioms by true induction required first that men see and accept the necessity of purging their understanding. Then they had carefully to make use of various helps to the senses and to the memory that Bacon provided. At the same time they were constrained to keep their reason fixed on particulars, to hang their understanding with the weights of experiments and data to keep it from flying. Only through these patient procedures could the mind be cleansed and a line and race of inventions developed "that may in some degree subdue and overcome the necessities and miseries of humanity".

As part of his great plan, Bacon had to reorganize knowledge as well as refute its errors. Like his method, the reclassification was to supersede Aristotle's and make new discoveries possible. In its broadest terms, Bacon's arrangement was based on the human faculties and completely excluded fundamental matters of faith. Thus he placed all aspects of history under memory, of poetry under imagination, and of philosophy under reason. Although this division was not without far-reaching implications, some of which will be mentioned later, it was his exclusion of theology from natural philosophy that held the greatest significance for the future. Arguing on behalf of his inductive method, he could not allow the deductive practice of applying (as in the example of the refutation of Galileo cited above) revealed axioms or the highest principles derived from faith to the facts of nature. First causes and final causes, he insisted, can have no part in the inquiry into natural phenomena. Although the truths of science do not contradict the truths of religion, they must not be confounded, for seeking the one in the other is like seeking the dead among the living, and "from this unwholesome mixture of things human and divine there arises not only a fantastic philosophy but also a heretical religion". Thus we must render unto faith only that which is faith's, and soberly restrict philosophy to rational investigation.

It is difficult to exaggerate the effect of the application, which Bacon so insistently prescribed, of this principle to all areas of human thought. Everything that was not indisputably faith's became with one stroke a concern of natural philosophy. Thus Bacon not only redefined metaphysics so as to make of it a branch of physics, but he also placed traditional (ideal) ethics and politics directly under divinity and so out of bounds for prying curiosity. The doctrine of religion, he said, "as well moral as mystical, is not to be attained but by inspiration and revelation from God". It must be noted, however, that he also separated divinity into a natural part and a revealed part, allowing investigation only of the first, that is, of the practical aspects of ethics and politics, which were themselves divorced from each other. In his discussion of these natural phenomena of human behaviour his approach is dispassionate and honest. Just as in his essays he realistically confronts the issue of how to negotiate in the real world, or of how to proceed "if you would work any man", so in his *De Augmentis* he faces squarely the fact that men in politics do not always act altruistically. Untiringly concerned with the failure of his predecessors to distinguish the actual from the ideal, and very much intent on laying down the categories within which his new philosophy might operate, he observes with detached objectivity: ". . . Moral philosophy propounds to itself to imbue and endow the mind with internal goodness; but civil knowledge requires only an external goodness, for that suffices for society." In the light of such detachment, which can still shock today, it becomes clear that it was no simple reclassification of knowledge that Bacon envisaged.

The last important requirement for the establishment of Bacon's instauration was reassurance. Men had to be convinced that his plan was good as well as productive, a need that called for a revolution in human feelings about the objective world. The prevailing attitude in his day was a gloomy one. Most people would have agreed with John Donne's opinions that man and the world were depraved and decaying, that they had been decaying since and because of the Fall of man, and that "the whole frame of the world and every piece thereof" were nearing their end. The common centre to all of creation, Donne says in his tenth Meditation, "is decay, ruin. . . . The heavens have had their dropsy, they drowned the world; and they shall have their fever, and burn the world". All their training, religious and classical, had taught Bacon's generation to look upon change as ominous and to suspect time (the partner of change) as an enemy. As conscious inheritors of original sin, they believed that their sole concern in this existence was to prepare for salvation in the next. History was not to them an accidental process stretching indefinitely into the future, but a meaningful development divinely ordered toward a definable end. The natural world, which had fallen along with man, appeared to them as a tangle of deceptive snares always ready to pull down the unwary. It too was mutable and so was destined soon to be cleansed along with man in the apocalyptic fire.

In the face of such views, Bacon invited men to hope: "I am now therefore to speak touching Hope, especially as I am not a dealer in promises, and wish neither to force nor to ensnare men's judgments, but to lead them by the hand with their good will." Although he believed that the only hope for progress lay in a reconstruction of the sciences, it was no less true that the only chance for such a reconstruction lay in hope. Progress was impossible without the desire for it and the belief in it, and these Bacon did his best to foster. Specifically, what was involved was a reversal of the traditional views of nature and time. This reversal of views is actually contained in Bacon's classification, where the isolation of the worldly from the divine implied the freeing of the human milieu from supernatural direction, but reassurance demanded more direct tactics. How Bacon undertook the task of rehabilitating nature and establishing it in men's minds as divine instead of Satanic has been competently demonstrated by Basil Willey,[3] but a glance at how the reformer managed the problem of redeeming time might be useful.

Bacon attacks the matter of time from a number of different positions, basic to which is the removal of history from heavenly dispensation. Once time is seen as something other than a series of moments darkened by sin and directed from above, once history in other words is viewed as something different from the inescapable working out of God's will, change and advancement in time become not only possible but also desirable. The process leading toward the new outlook roughly follows that of establishing the new science. First comes the denial that the past is superior to the present. The ancients were not better endowed nor more intelligent than the moderns, Bacon argues again and again, and even if they were, the moderns have the advantage over them because, like pygmies on the backs of giants, they can see farther and more clearly because of their predecessors. But men have in any case long deceived themselves about the true meaning of antiquity: "For the old age of the world is to be accounted the true antiquity; . . . which, though in respect of us it was the elder, yet in respect of the world it was the younger." Accompanying this denial is the refutation. Bacon will not allow that time has made the best prevail and that therefore the judgment of generations past must be accepted without question. It is in fact quite certain that we have lost a good deal of the knowledge of discoveries made and attempted heretofore. And it is even more certain, he observes in one of his favourite images, that only those things that are light and puffed up have been

[3] See Chapter II of *The Seventeenth Century Background* (in Bibliography).

brought down to us by the river of time, "while those which are weighty and solid have sunk".

Once this (logically indefensible) attack has been made, however, a more affirmative position is called for. If from one point of view time is a destroyer, from another it is a deliverer. From being a movement away from man's innocence, it must become a movement toward it. Thus the new philosophy is called upon to change the direction of man's history since the Fall, and, by reversing the effects of God's curse, to allow man to aspire anew to paradise. "For man by the fall fell at the same time from his state of innocency and from his dominion over creation. Both of these losses however can even in this life be in some part repaired; the former by religion and faith, the latter by arts and sciences." The true end of knowledge is not fame nor gain, but a "restitution and reinvesting (in great part) of man to the sovereignty and power (for whensoever he shall be able to call the creatures by their true names he shall again command them) which he had in his first state of creation". At the beginning of his Great Instauration Bacon argues in much the same way, suggesting that with the helps he intends to provide for the intellect "commerce between the mind of man and the nature of things . . . might . . . be restored to its perfect and original condition, or if that may not be, yet reduced to a better condition than that in which it now is".

Moreover, Bacon's "great work" was not a matter for any single individual to finish off but a product of the years, requiring the co-operation of many men through many generations. He has sown the seeds for forthcoming ages, he says, and with the assent and help of the present and the future his labours will prove fruitful. Thus time through his pleading becomes a power filled with expectation, not only the disciple of the past instead of its servant, but also "the author of authors" making possible an infinity of progress in the future. So too the closed outlook, which foresaw the imminent end of the world, is changed into an endless prospect of benefits on earth and good things to men. Co-operation with time, "the greatest innovator", makes all things possible, for the advancement of learning and the future of humanity go hand in hand, much as Adam and Eve might make their way back to the Garden.

Some of the implications in Bacon's reconstruction have been much criticized, and it must be admitted that, in his need to cleanse away the useless and in his desire to establish his own views, he slighted much that was worth while. Oriented as his philosophy was to materially useful things, it tended to detract from the value of everything not physical in man: the mind, the emotions, and the soul. The whole realm of the moral, the subjective, and the spiritual was either set apart as unexaminable because dependent upon divine revelation or dismissed as untrustworthy because emanating from the Idols.

As L. C. Knights has demonstrated,[4] if Bacon did not originate he strongly represented, even in his style and images, that seventeenth-century dissociation of sensibility – that split between thought and sensation, between reason and feeling – from which T. S. Eliot says we have never recovered. Certainly he helped relegate imagination and its products to an inferior place in the cultural hierarchy. As imagination is not tied to the laws of matter and so may make whatever "matches and divorces of things it pleases", it can hardly be useful in any practical sense. In matters of faith, however, imagination must be allowed its place, for there it is a power above reason, an instrument of illumination or revelation, "which is the reason why religion ever sought access to the mind by similitudes, types, parables, visions, dreams".

As for the major secular product of the imagination, poetry, it was a thing of words and an issue of the lawless fancy and feelings – hardly substantial or profitable. Not that poetry is without value in the Baconian canon: suspect as a thing in itself, it is nevertheless useful in communicating moral lessons and in depicting human nature in a pleasant, palatable fashion. This feigned history, as Bacon called poetry, gives "some shadow of satisfaction to the mind of man in those points wherein the nature of things doth deny it" (that is, it seems – apparently without much justification – to satisfy the human yearning for

4 See entry in Bibliography.

the ideal in an actually imperfect world), and in so doing appears to serve and confer "to magnanimity, morality, and delectation". But since in this respect poetry "was ever thought to have some participation of divineness, because it doth raise and erect the mind, by submitting the shows of things to the desires of the mind", it can have at best but an uneasy place in the realm that has been rendered unto Caesar. In that realm just the reverse obtains: there "reason doth buckle and bow the mind unto the nature of things" – a function that Bacon finds it considerably more comfortable to contemplate. Thus poetry is regarded as a handmaid of morality and a kind of ornament in or diversion from the more exacting and comprehensible "nature of things". Instead of being an expression of the whole man, it is, as an effect of the imagination, cut off from reason and to all intents and purposes placed in an inferior position to it. Its reality and hence its usefulness can hardly be demonstrated; and besides, since it has "some participation in divineness", whatever truth it has is inaccessible to rational evaluation anyway.

Also divorced from reason was everything in the realm of theology not reducible to material fact: "Sacred Theology ought to be derived from the word and oracles of God, and not from the light of nature, or the dictates of reason." Thus all rational consideration of such problems as deity, the after-life, and the ends of creation is relegated to faith, where "the more discordant . . . and incredible the Divine mystery is, the more honour is shown to God in believing it". What was left was completely neutralized and secularized. Hence what Bacon called meta-physics, which he made a part of "the doctrine concerning nature", was for him an independent science concerned strictly with the examination of the physical side of man. Under such restrictions, all objective discussion of the rational soul becomes impossible. Knowledge of this faculty, which was breathed into man by God, Bacon places beyond reason, because (the one great defence never falters) it "must be drawn from the same divine inspiration from which that substance first proceeded".

Similarly with politics and ethics. As politics is released from moral considerations and as ethics is limited to a knowledge of "how to frame and subdue the will of man" to the revealed moral law, one is led farther and farther away from the ideal in thought and behaviour. Thus where politics in the Christian-humanistic view of the Renaissance was indissolubly connected with the common weal and the good life, for Bacon it became the science of exercising power and of manipulating the public. The politic man changes from the virtuous citizen whose informed reason is "the state's best strength" (as a friend of Bacon's, the poet and statesman Fulke Greville, put it), to the self-seeking person "politic for his own future". It was much the same with ethics. The venerable ideal of self-knowledge, for example, a fundamental part of the Christian-humanistic morality, undergoes considerable transformation in the practical Baconian context. What had long been held as a universal obligation in the achieving of humility, wisdom, and knowledge of one's relationships to God, appears in the *De Augmentis* as a function of informed opportunism, treated under "Architecture of Fortune", a branch of "Negotiation". Instead of examining himself in preparation for a virtuous life and salvation, a person should "take an impartial view" of his own abilities and virtues in order to ascertain how his nature conforms with his times and acquaintances, and so determine how best to make his way in the world. Inevitably spurning the contemplative principle with its other-worldly goals, Bacon retranslated the ancient precept of "Know Thyself" into a set of pragmatic recommendations concerned with the advancement of the individual in control and power. Thus in both public and private terms the outlines of a new ethic appear, an ethic founded on "what men do, and not [on] what they ought to do".[5]

This split on almost every human level between the ideal and the actual, the subjective and the empirical, which Bacon so expressed as to make reconciliation through the ordinary human will impossible, has troubled many. It is true that Bacon often repeated that his instauration was to be undertaken in humility

[5] See my article "Bacon and the Renaissance Ideal of Self-Knowledge", *The Personalist*, XLIV, 4 (Autumn 1963), pp. 454-71, from which I here borrow by kind permission of the editor, Dr. W. H. Werkmeister.

and charity, but his open materialism had really little to do with these virtues, and he left them rather vaguely to providence. It is further true that he insisted that the investigation and control of nature were to be limited by religion and "referred to use and action". The uses to which men put their findings are after all of ethical significance, and so if knowledge "be severed from charity, and not referred to the good of men and mankind, it hath rather a sounding and unworthy glory than a meriting and substantial virtue". But Bacon tends to define the "good of mankind" in terms of practical benefits, with the result that once again man is caught in a materialistic circle from which he can hardly escape. Finally, the possibility of sheer neglect of the subjective realm and its values in Bacon's reconstruction should not be ignored. The more that interest is shifted from contemplation to investigation, from understanding to power, whatever the beauty of the rationale behind the shift, the less heed is paid to the inner life.

Such criticisms, however, should not be allowed to obscure Bacon's immense achievement as a writer and moulder of the modern spirit. His essays and his rhetorical ideas made a powerful impact on the generations that followed him; indeed, the clear, functional style of writing that had come into vogue by the end of the seventeenth century owed much to him. His influence upon science was also swift and enormous. Although his own scientific theory was fragmentary and imperfect and his practice even weaker, he gave to the scientific movement the full weight of his prestige and the moving power of his eloquence. Sir Thomas Browne's *Pseudodoxia Epidemica; or, Enquiries into Vulgar Errors* was written to fill up one of the deficiencies Bacon had noted in his survey of knowledge. The founding of the Royal Society was inspired in great part by his recommendations. And experimenting and gathering of facts for the advancement of learning were all the rage by 1700. Probably more than any other single individual, Bacon helped to free the understanding from its idols and to direct the mind to a "sober inquiry of truth" and to a dispassionate contemplation of "the Nature of Things".

Above all he induced men to believe that material progress

was not only possible but also legitimate. By providing men with solid "grounds . . . for putting away despair", he was able to lead them "by the hand with their good will" to the edge of the land of promise. Cowley's picture of him, drawn in a poem of congratulation to the Society that he helped engender, represents him as a prophet:

> *Bacon* like *Moses*, led us forth at last,
> The barren Wilderness he past,
> Did on the very Border stand
> Of the blest promis'd Land,
> And, from the Mountain's Top of his exalted Wit,
> Saw it himself, and shew'd us it.

This is in fact the way Bacon preferred to think of himself: something like the herald of that spirit of modern civilization of which science is only a part. In the *De Augmentis*, he places himself in the company of those sacred men of whom Homer speaks: "Hail, trumpeters, messengers of Jove and men!" As trumpeter of the new time, he announced the end of the reign of the irrational in the world's affairs; he convinced men to replace despair with hope, and depravity with innocence; and he inspired them to believe that the life of New Atlantis could be theirs.

Note on the Text

The text is essentially that of the definitive edition of the *Works*, edited by James Spedding, R. L. Ellis, and D. D. Heath (7 vols. London, 1857-59). The letters are from James Spedding's *The Letters and Life* (7 vols. London, 1861-74; sometimes numbered as volumes VIII-XIV consecutive to the *Works*). Other editions have also been consulted, often closely consulted, but (except in one or two instances where first editions have provided superior readings) Spedding has remained the ultimate authority. The essays of 1597 and 1612 have been deliberately reproduced without change (outside of a few minor emendations), simply to give the reader some idea of their original appearance and flavour. The letters are printed pretty well as Spedding prints them. In the rest, the punctuation, the spelling, and many of the translations of foreign words and phrases have been considerably modernized.

The Notes and Glossary supply only that information not available in an ordinary college dictionary. As their briefness often indicates, they are intended not as comprehensive teaching aids but rather as guides to further reading and study. An asterisk (*) after an expression means that the expression has already been commented on and its meaning may henceforward be found in the Glossary.

Unfortunately, but with Bacon inevitably, it was not possible to provide a complete text of every work in this edition; the following had to be omitted: *Essayes*, 1597: 6 essays; *Essaies*, 1612: 31 essays; *The Advancement*: all of Book II after "To the King" (but see the selection from *De Augmentis* – a Latin revision of *The Advancement*); *The Wisdom of the Ancients*: 25 chapters; *The New Organon*: Book I: several aphorisms; Book II: several parts and aphorisms as indicated in the text; *De Augmentis*: Book I: all (see *The Advancement*); Book II: Chapters 6-12; Book III: Chapters 2-6; Books IV-IX.

Francis Bacon

BIOGRAPHICAL DATA

Dates in parentheses are those of first publication. A question mark in parentheses means that the date of writing is uncertain. Years given are new style (N.S.), that is, with January 1 taken as the beginning of the year; before 1752 it had been the practice to consider the year as beginning on March 25.

1561 January 22. Born at York House, London.

1573 Entered Trinity College, Cambridge.

1576 Admitted to Gray's Inn.

1577 Joined the suite of the Ambassador to France in Paris.

1579 Returned to London on the death of his father, Sir Nicholas Bacon.

1582 Admitted as utter barrister. *Temporis Partus Maximus* (?) [see 1608].

1584 Elected Member of Parliament for Melcombe Regis. (He remained a member representing various constituencies for thirty-six years.)

1588 Elected Reader at Gray's Inn.

1589 Made Clerk in the council of the Star Chamber.

1594 Admitted M.A. at Cambridge.

1596 Appointed Queen's Counsel Extraordinary about this time.

1597 *Essayes. Religious Meditations* [*Meditationes Sacrae*]. *Places of perswasion and disswasion* [*Of the Coulers of Good and Evill*].

1600 Appointed Double Reader at Gray's Inn.

1601 *A Declaration of the Practises and Treasons attempted and committed by Robert late Earl of Essex, &c.*

1603 Knighted by James I. *A Brief Discourse touching the Happy Union of the Kingdoms of England and Scotland.*

1603 *Valerius Terminus of the Interpretation of Nature* (?) (1734).

1604 Appointed King's Counsel.

1605 *The Proficience and Advancement of Learning.*

1606 Married Alice Barnham.

1607 Appointed Solicitor General. *Cogitata et Visa* (1653).

1608 Appointed Clerk of the Star Chamber. *Inquisitio Legitima de Motu* (1653). *Calor et Frigus* (1734). *Historia Soni et Auditus* (1658). *Temporis Partus Masculus* (?) (1653).

1609 *De Sapientia Veterum.*

1612 Second edition of the *Essays. Thema Coeli* (?) (1653).

1613 Appointed Attorney General.

1616 Made a Member of the Privy Council. *Proposition to His Majesty touching the Compiling and Amendment of the Laws of England. De Fluxu et Refluxu Maris* (?) (1653).

1617 Made Lord Keeper.

1618 Made Lord Chancellor. Created Baron Verulam.

1619 English translation of *De Sapientia Veterum* by Sir A. Gorges.

1620 *Novum Organum.*

1621 Created Viscount St. Alban. Sentenced by the House of Lords for accepting bribes.

1622 *Historia Naturalis et Experimentalis. Advertisement touching an Holy War* (1629). *The History of the Reign of King Henry the Seventh.*

1623 *De Augmentis Scientiarum libri ix. The History of the Reign of King Henry the Eighth. Sylva Sylvarum* (?) (1627).

1624 *Considerations touching a War with Spain* (1629). *New Atlantis* (1627). *Apophthegms. Translation of Certain Psalms into English Verse.*

1625 Third edition of the *Essays.*

1626 April 9. Died at Highgate, near London.

1627 *New Atlantis published posthumously.*

Essayes

1597

The Epistle Dedicatorie

To M. Anthony Bacon
his deare Brother

Louing and beloued Brother, I doe nowe like some that haue an Orcharde il neighbored, that gather their fruit before it is ripe, to preuent stealing. These fragments of my conceites were going to print; To labour the staie of them had bin troublesome, and subiect to interpretation; to let them passe had been to advē-ture the wrong they mought receiue by vntrue Coppies, or by some garnishment, which it mought please any that should set them forth to bestow upon them. Therefore I helde it best discreation to publish them my selfe as they passed long agoe from my pen, without any further disgrace, then the weaknesse of the Author. And as I did euer hold, there mought be as great a vanitie in retiring and withdrawing mens conceites (except they bee of some nature) from the world, as in obtruding them: So in these particulars I haue played my selfe the Inquisitor, and find nothing to my vnderstanding in them contrarie or infectious to the state of Religion, or manners, but rather (as I suppose) medicinable. Only I disliked now to put them out because they will be like the late new halfe-pence, which though the Siluer were good, yet the peeces were small. But since they would not stay with their Master, but would needes trauaile abroad, I haue preferred them to you that are next myself, Dedicating them, such as they are, to our loue, in the depth whereof (I assure you) I sometimes wish your infirmities translated uppon my selfe, that her Maiestie mought haue the seruice of so actiue and able a mind, & I mought be with excuse confined to these contemplations & studies for which I am fittest, so commende I you to the preseruation of the diuine Maiestie. From my Chamber at Graies Inne, this 30. of Ianuarie. 1597.

Your entire Louing brother.

Fran. Bacon.

[1.] OF STUDIES

STUDIES serue for pastimes, for ornaments and for abilities. Their chiefe vse for pastime is in priuatenes and retiring; for ornamente is in discourse, and for abilitie is in iudgement. For expert men can execute, but learned men are fittest to iudge or censure.

¶ To spend too much time in them is slouth, to vse them too much for ornament is affectation: to make iudgement wholly by their rules, is the humour of a Scholler. ¶ They perfect *Nature*, and are perfected by experience. ¶ Craftie men contemne them, simple men admire them, wise men vse them: For they teach not their owne vse, but that is a wisedome without them: and aboue them wonne by observation. ¶ Reade not to contradict, nor to belieue, but to waigh and consider. ¶ Some bookes are to bee tasted, others to bee swallowed, and some few to bee chewed and disgested: That is, some bookes are to be read only in partes; others to be read, but cursorily, and some few to be read wholly and with diligence and attention. ¶ Reading maketh a full man, conference a readye man, and writing an exacte man. And therefore if a man write little, he had neede haue a great memorie, if he conferre little, he had neede haue a present wit, and if he reade little, hee had neede haue much cunning, to seeme to know that he doth not. ¶ Histories make men wise, Poets wittie: the Mathematickes subtle, naturall Phylosophie deepe: Morall graue, Logicke and Rhetoricke able to contend.

[3.] OF CEREMONIES AND RESPECTES

HE that is onely reall had need haue exceeding great parts of vertue, as the stone had neede be rich that is set without foyle. ¶ But commonly it is in praise as it is in gaine. For as the prouerbe is true, *That light gaines make heauie Purses*: Because they come thicke, wheras great come but now and then, so it is as true that smal matters winne great commendation: because they are continually in vse and in note, whereas the occasion of any great vertue commeth but on holy-daies. ¶ To attaine good formes, it sufficeth not to despise them, for so shal a man observe them in others, and let him trust himselfe with the rest: for if he care to expresse them hee shall leese their grace, which is to be naturall and vnaffected. Some mens behauiour is like a verse wherein euery sillable is measured. How can a man comprehend great matters that breaketh his minde too much to small obseruations? ¶ Not to vse Ceremonies at all, is to teach others not to vse them againe, and so diminish his respect; especially they be not to bee omitted to straungers and strange natures. ¶ Among a mans Peires a man shall be sure of familiaritie, and therefore it is good a little to keepe state; amongst a mans inferiours one shall be sure of reuerence, and therefore it is good a little to be familiar. ¶ Hee that is too much in any thing, so that he give another occasion of satietie, maketh himselfe cheape. ¶ To applie ones selfe to others is good, so it be with demonstration that a man doth it upon regard, and not vpon facilitie. ¶ It is a good precept generally in seconding another: yet to adde somewhat of ones owne; as if you will graunt his opinion, let it be with some distinction, if you wil follow his motion, let it be with condition; if you allow his counsell, let it be with alleadging further reason.

[6.] OF EXPENCE

RICHES are for spending, and spending for honour and good actions. Therefore extraordinarie Expence must bee limited by the worth of the ocasion; for voluntarie vndoing may bee as well for a mans countrie as for the kingdome of heauen. But ordinarie expence ought to bee limited by a mans estate, and gouerned with such regard, as it be within his compasse, and not subiect to deceite and abuse of seruants, and ordered to the best shew, that the Bils maye be lesse then the estimation abroad. ¶ It is no basenes for the greatest to descend and looke into their owne estate. Some forbeare it not vpon negligence alone, but doubting to bring themselues into Melancholy in respect they shall finde it broken. But *woundes cannot bee cured without searching.* ¶ He that cannot looke into his owne estate, had neede both choose well those whom he imployeth, yea and change them often. For new are more timerous and lesse subtle. ¶ In clearing of a mans estate hee may as well hurt himselfe in being too suddaine, as in letting it runne on too long, for hastie selling is commonly as disaduantageable as interest. ¶ He that hath a state to repaire may not despise small things; and commonly it is lesse dishonourable to abridge pettie charges then to stoupe to pettie gettings. ¶ A man ought warily to begin charges, which once begunne must continue. But in matters that returne not, he may be more magnificent.

[9.] OF FACTION

MANIE have a newe wisedome, indeed, a fond opinion; That for a Prince to gouerne his estate, or for a great person to governe his proceedings according to the respects of Factions, is the principal part of pollicie. Whereas contrariwise, the chiefest wisedome is either in ordering those things which are generall, and wherein men of severall Factions doe neuerthelesse agree, or in dealing with correspondence to particular persons one by one. But I say not that the consideration of Factions is to be neglected.

¶ Meane men must adheare, but great men that haue strength in themselues were better to maintaine themselues indifferent and neutrall; yet euen in beginners to adheare so moderatly, as he be a man of the one Faction, which is passablest with the other, commonly giveth best way. ¶ The lower and weaker

Faction is the firmer in conjunction. ¶ When one of the Factions is extinguished, the remaining subdiuideth which is good for a second Faction. It is commonly seene that men once placed, take in with the contrarie faction to that by which they enter. ¶ The traitor in Factions lightly goeth away with it, for when matters have stucke long in ballancing, the winning of some one man casteth them, and hee getteth al the thankes.

Essaies

1612

The Epistle Dedicatorie

To my Loving Brother, Sir Iohn Constable Knight

MY last Essaies I dedicated to my deare brother *Master Anthony Bacon,* who is with God. Looking amongst my papers this vacation, I found others of the same Nature: which if I my selfe shall not suffer to be lost, it seemeth the World will not; by the often printing of the former. Missing my Brother, I found you next; in respect of bond both of neare alliance, and of straight friendship and societie, and particularly of communication in studies. Wherein I must acknowledge my selfe beholding to you. For as my businesse found rest in my contemplations; so my contemplations euer found rest in your louing conference and iudgement. So wishing you all good, I remaine

> *Your louing brother and friend,*
> Fra. Bacon.

1. OF RELIGION

THE quarrels, and diuisions for *Religion*, were euils vnknowne to the Heathen: and no maruell; for it is the true God that is the iealous God; and the gods of the Heathen were good fellowes. But yet the bonds of religious vnity, are so to be strengthened, as the bonds of humane society be not dissolued. *Lucretius* the Poet, when hee beheld the act of *Agamemnon*, induring and assisting at the sacrifice of his daughter, concludes with this verse;

Tantū relligio potuit suadere malorum.

But what would hee haue done, if he had knowne the massacre of *France*, or the powder treason of *England*? Certainly he would haue beene seuen times more Epicure and Atheist then he was. Nay, hee would rather haue chosen to be one of the Madmen of *Munster*, then to haue beene a partaker of those Counsels. For it is better that Religion should deface mens vnderstanding, then their piety and charitie; retaining reason onely but as an *Engine*, and *Charriot driuer* of cruelty, and malice. It was a great blasphemie, when the Diuell said; *I will ascend, and be like the highest*: but it is a greater blasphemie, if they make God to say; *I will descend, and be like the Prince of Darknesse*: and it is no better, when they make the cause of *Religion* descend, to the execrable accions of murthering of Princes, butchery of people, and firing of States. Neither is there such a sinne against the person of the holy Ghost, (if one should take it literally) as in stead of the likenes of a *Doue*, to bring him downe in the likenesse of a *Vulture*, or *Rauen*; nor such a scandall to their Church, as out of the Barke of Saint *Peter*, to set forth the flagge of a Barke of *Pirats* and *Assassins*. Therefore since these things are the common enemies of humane society; *Princes* by their power; *Churches* by their Decrees; and all learning, Christian, morall, of what soeuer sect, or opinion, by their *Mercurie* rod; ought to ioyne in the damning to Hell for euer, these facts, and their supports: and in all Counsels concerning Religion, that Counsel of the Apostle, would be prefixed, *Ira hominis non implet iustitiam Dei.*

7. OF NOBILITY

IT is a reuerend thing to see an ancient castle or building not in decay; or to see a faire timber tree sound & perfect: how much more to behold an ancient Noble familie, which hath stood against the waues and weathers of time. For new Nobility is but the act of power; but ancient Nobility is the act of time. The first raisers of *Fortunes* are commonly more vertuous, but lesse inno- cent, then their descendents. For there is rarely rising, but by a commixture of good and euil Arts. But it is reason the memorie of their vertues remain to their posterities, and their faults die with themselues. *Nobilitie* of Birth commonly abateth industrie: and hee that is not industrious, enuieth him that is: Besides noble persons, cannot goe much higher: And he that standeth at a stay when others rise, can hardly auoid motions of enuie. On the other side Nobility extinguisheth the passiue enuie in others towards them; because they are in possession of *Honour*: and Enuy is as the sunne beames, that beate more vpon a rising ground, then vpon a leuell. A great *Nobilitie* addeth maiesty to a *Monarch*, but diminisheth power: and putteth life and spirit into the people; but presseth their fortunes. It is well when nobles are not too great for *Soueraigntie*, nor for *Iustice*; and yet maintained in that height, as the insollency of inferiours may be broken vpon them, before it come on too fast vpon the maiestie of *Kings*. Certainely *Kings* that haue able men of their Nobility, shal find ease in imploying them; and a better slide in their businesse: For people naturally bend to them, as borne in some sort to command.

13. OF FRIENDSHIP

THERE is no greater desert or wildernes then to bee without true friends. For without friendship, society is but meeting. And as it is certaine, that in bodies inanimate, vnion strengthneth any naturall motion, and weakeneth any violent motion; So amongst men, friendship multiplieth ioies, and diuideth griefes. Therefore whosoeuer wanteth fortitude, let him worshippe *Friendship*. For the yoke of *Friendship* maketh the yoke of *fortune* more light. There bee some whose liues are, as if they perpetually plaid vpon a stage, disguised to all others, open onely to themselues. But perpetuall dissimulation is painfull; and hee that is all *Fortune*, and no *Nature* is an exquisite *Hierling*. Liue not in continuall smother, but take some friends with whom to communicate. It will vnfold thy vnderstanding; it will euaporate thy affections; it will prepare thy businesse. A man may keepe a corner of his minde from his friend, and it be but to witnesse to himselfe, that it is not vpon facility, but vpon true vse of friendship that hee imparteth himselfe. Want of true friends, as it is the reward of perfidious natures; so is it an imposition vpon great fortunes. The one deserue it, the other cannot scape it. And therefore it is good to retaine sincerity, and to put it into the reckoning of *Ambition*, that the higher one goeth, the fewer true friends he shall haue. Perfection of friendship, is but a speculation. It is friendship, when a man can say to himselfe, I loue this man without respect of vtility. I am open hearted to him, I single him frō the generality of those with whom I liue; I make him a portion of my owne wishes.

18. OF EXPENCES

RICHES are for spending, and spending for honour & good actions. Therefore extraordinary expence must bee limited by the worth of the occasion, for voluntary vndoing may bee aswell for a mans Countrey, as for the kingdome of *Heauen*. But ordinarie expence, ought to be limitted by a mans estate and gouerned with such regard, as it be within his compasse, and not subiect to deceit, and abuse of seruants; and ordered to the best shew, that the bils may be lesse then the estimation abroad. It is no basenesse for the greatest to descend and looke into their owne estates. Some forbeare it not vpon negligence alone, but doubting to bring themselues into malancholy in respect they shall find it broken. But wounds cannot bee cured without searching. Hee that cannot looke into his owne estate at all, had neede both choose well those whom he imploieth, and change them often: for new are more timorous, and less subtill. He that can looke into his estate but seldom, had need turne all to certainties. In cleering of a mans estate, hee may aswell hurt himselfe in being too sudden, as in letting it run on to long. For hasty selling is commonly as disaduantageable as interest. Besides, he that cleeres at once will relapse: For finding himself out of straights, he wil reuert to his customes. But hee that cleereth by degrees, induceth an habite of frugality, and gaineth aswell vpon his minde as vpon his estate. Certainly who hath a state to repaire may not despise small things; and commonly it is lesse dishonourable to abridge pettie charges, then to stoope to petty gettings. A man ought warily to begin charges, which once begun must continue. But in matters that return not, he may bee more magnificent.

29. OF STUDIES

STUDIES serue for Delight, for Ornament, and for Ability; their cheife vse for delight, is, in priuatnesse, and retiring; for ornament, is in discourse, and for abilitie, is in iudgement. For expert men can execute, but learned men are fittest to iudge or censure. To spend too much time in them, is *Sloth*; to vse them too much for ornament, is *affectation*; to make iudgement wholly by their rules, is the *humour of a Scholer*. They perfect *Nature*, and are perfected by Experience. Crafty men contemne them, simple men admire them, and wise men vse them. For they teach not their owne vse, but that is a wisdome without them, and aboue them, wonne by obseruation. Read not to contradict, nor to beleeue, but to weigh and consider. Some bookes are to bee tasted, others to bee swallowed, and some few to be chewed and digested. That is, some bookes are to be read only in parts; other to bee read, but not curiously; and some few to bee read wholly, and with diligence and attention. Reading maketh a full man, Conference a ready man, and writing an exact man. And therefore if a man write little, hee had neede haue a great memory; if he confer little, hee had neede haue a present wit, and if he read little, hee had neede haue much cunning, to seeme to know that hee doth not. *Histories* make men wise, *Poets* wittie, the *Mathematickes* subtill, Naturall *Philosophie* deepe, *Morall* graue, *Logicke* and *Rethoricke* able to contend. *Abeunt studia in mores.* Nay, thear is no stond or impediment in the wit, but may be wrought out by fit studies: like as diseases of the body may haue appropriate exercises. Bowling is good for the Stone and Raines; Shooting for the longs & breast; gentle walking for the stomacke; riding for the head: and the like. So if a mans wit be wandring, let him study the *Mathematiks*; if his wit be not apt to distinguish, or find difference, let him study the Schoolemen; if it bee not apt to beat ouer matters and to find out resemblances, let him study Lawyers cases. So euerie defect of the mind may haue a speciall receit.

30. OF CEREMONIES AND RESPECTS

HEE that is onely reall, had need haue exceeding great parts of vertue: as the stone had neede to be rich that is set without foile. But commonly it is in praise, as it is in gaine: For as the prouerbe is true, *That light gaines make heauie purses*, because they come thicke, whereas great come, but now and then: so it is true, that small matters winne great commendation, because they are continually in vse, and in note. Whereas the occasion of any great vertue, commeth but on holie daies. To attaine good formes, it sufficeth not to despise them: for so shall a man obserue them in others: And let him trust himself with the rest. For if he care to expresse them, hee shall lose their grace, which is to be naturall and vnaffected. Some mens behauiour is like a verse wherein euery sillable is measured; how can a man comprehend great matters, that breaketh his mind to much to small obseruation? Not to vse Ceremonies at al, is to teach others not to vse them againe; & so diminisheth respect: especially they bee not to be omitted to strangers, & formall natures. Amongst a mans Peeres, a man shall be sure of familiarity; and therefore it is good a little to keep state: amongst a mans inferiours one shal be sure of Reuerence; and therefore it is good a little to bee familiar. Hee that is too much in any thing, so that hee giueth another occasion of satietie, maketh himself cheap. To apply ones selfe to others is good; so it be with demonstration that a man doth it vpon regard, and not vpon facility. It is a good precept, generally in seconding another, yet to adde somewhat of ones owne; as if you will grant his opinion, let it be with some distinction; if you will follow his motion; let it be with condition; if you allow his counsell, let it be with alleging further reason. Men had neede beware how they be too perfit in complements. For be they neuer so sufficient otherwise, their enuiers will bee sure to giue them that attribute to the disaduantage of their greater vertue. It is losse also in businesse to be too full of respects, or to be to curious in obseruing times and oportunities. *Salomon* saith *He that considereth the wind shall not sowe, and hee that looketh to the clowdes, shall not reape.* A wise man will make more opportunities than he findes.

34. OF FACTION

MANY haue an opinion not wise; That for a Prince to gouerne his estate, or for a great person to gouerne his proceedings, according to the respect of factions, is the principall part of pollicy: whereas contrariwise, the chiefest wisdome is either in ordering those things which are generall, and wherein men of seuerall factions doe neuerthelesse agree, or in dealing with correspondence to particuler persons, one by one. But I say not, that the consideration of factions is to be neglected. Meane men must adhere, but great men that haue strength in themselues were better to maintaine themselues indifferent, and neutrall. Yet euen in beginners to adhere so moderatly, as he be a man of the one faction, which is passablest with the other, commonly giueth best way. The lower and weaker faction is the firmer in coniunction. When one of the factions is extinguished, the remaining subdiuideth: which is good for a second. It is cōmonly seene, that men once placed, take in with the contrary factiō to that, by which they enter. The Traitor in factions lightly goeth away with it: for when matters haue stucke long in balancing, the winning of some one man casteth them and he getteth all the thankes. The euen carriage betweene two factions, proceedeth not alwaies of moderation, but of a truenesse to a mans selfe, with end to make vse of both. Certainely in *Italie* they hold it a little suspect in Popes, when they haue often in their mouth *Padre Commune*, & take it to a signe of one that meaneth to referre all to the greatnesse of his own house.

The

Essayes or Counsels

Civill and Morall

1625

The Epistle Dedicatory

To the Right Honourable my very good Lo.
the Duke of Buckingham his Grace,
Lo. High Admiral of England.

Excellent Lo.

SALOMON says, *A good name is as a precious ointment*; and I assure myself, such will your Grace's name be with posterity. For your fortune and merit both have been eminent. And you have planted things that are like to last. I do now publish my Essays; which, of all my other works, have been most current; for that, as it seems, they come home to men's business and bosoms. I have enlarged them both in number and weight; so that they are indeed a new work. I thought it therefore agreeable to my affection and obligation to your Grace, to prefix your name before them, both in English and in Latin. For I do conceive that the Latin volume of them (being in the universal language) may last as long as books last. My Instauration I dedicated to the King; my History of Henry the Seventh (which I have now also translated into Latin), and my portions of Natural History, to the Prince; and these I dedicate to your Grace; being of the best fruits that by the good encrease which God gives to my pen and labours I could yield. God lead your Grace by the hand.

> *Your Grace's most obliged and*
> *faithful servant,*

> Fr. St. Alban.

I. OF TRUTH

What is Truth? said jesting Pilate, and would not stay for an answer. Certainly there be that delight in giddiness,[1] and count it a bondage to fix a belief, affecting[2] free will in thinking, as well as in acting. And though the sects of philosophers[3] of that kind be gone, yet there remain certain discoursing wits which are of the same veins,[4] though there be not so much blood in them as was in those of the ancients. But it is not only the difficulty and labour which men take in finding out of truth, nor again that when it is found it imposeth upon[5] men's thoughts, that doth bring lies in favour, but a natural though corrupt love of the lie itself. One of the later school of the Grecians[6] examineth the matter, and is at a stand to think what should be in it, that men should love lies, where neither they make for pleasure, as with poets, nor for advantage, as with the merchant, but for the lie's sake. But I cannot tell: this same truth is a naked and open daylight, that doth not show the masks and mummeries and triumphs of the world, half so stately and daintily as candle-lights. Truth may perhaps come to the price of a pearl, that showeth best by day; but it will not rise to the price of a diamond or carbuncle, that showeth best in varied lights. A mixture of a lie doth ever add pleasure. Doth any man doubt, that if there were taken out of men's minds vain opinions, flattering hopes, false valuations, imaginations as one would, and the like, but it would leave the minds of a number of men poor shrunken things, full of melancholy and indisposition, and unpleasing to themselves? One of the Fathers, in great severity, called poesy *vinum dæmonum*,[7] because it filleth the imagination, and yet it is but with the shadow of a lie. But it is not the lie that passeth through the mind, but the lie that sinketh in and settleth in it, that doth the hurt; such as we spake of before. But howsoever these things are thus in men's depraved judgments and affections, yet truth,

---

[1] inconstancy of opinion.
[2] aiming at, striving for.
[3] probably the Sceptics.
[4] rambling or talkative minds that are of the same inclinations.

[5] makes an impression on.
[6] perhaps Lucian, in *The Lover of Lies, or The Doubter*, I.
[7] "the wine of devils"; perhaps from St. Augustine, *Confessions*, I.16.

which only doth judge itself, teacheth that the inquiry of truth, which is the love-making or wooing of it, the knowledge of truth, which is the presence of it, and the belief of truth, which is the enjoying of it, is the sovereign good of human nature. The first creature of God, in the works of the days, was the light of the sense, the last was the light of reason; and his sabbath work ever since is the illumination of His Spirit. First He breathed light upon the face of the matter or chaos; then He breathed light into the face of man; and still He breatheth and inspireth light into the face of his chosen. The poet[8] that beautified the sect that was otherwise inferior to the rest saith yet excellently well: *It is a pleasure to stand upon the shore, and to see ships tossed upon the sea; a pleasure to stand in the window of a castle, and to see a battle and the adventures[9] thereof below; but no pleasure is comparable to the standing upon the vantage ground of Truth* (a hill not to be commanded,[10] and where the air is always clear and serene), *and to see the errors, and wanderings, and mists, and tempests, in the vale below;* so[11] always that this prospect be with pity and not with swelling or pride. Certainly it is heaven upon earth to have a man's mind move in charity, rest in providence, and turn upon the poles of truth.

To pass from theological and philosophical truth to the truth of civil business, it will be acknowledged even by those that practise it not that clear and round[12] dealing is the honour of man's nature; and that mixture of falsehood is like allay[13] in coin of gold and silver, which may make the metal work the better, but it embaseth it. For these winding and crooked courses are the goings of the serpent, which goeth basely upon the belly and not upon the feet. There is no vice that doth so cover a man with shame as to be found false and perfidious, And therefore Montaigne saith prettily, when he inquired the reason, why the word of the lie should be such a disgrace and such an odious charge? Saith he, *If it be well weighed, to say that a man lieth, is as much to say, as that he is brave towards God and a coward towards men.*[14] For a

---

[8] Lucretius, *On the Nature of Things*, II.1-13.
[9] perils.
[10] dominated, overtopped.
[11] provided.
[12] honest and straightforward.
[13] alloy.
[14] *Essays*, II.18.

lie faces God and shrinks from man. Surely the wickedness of falsehood and breach of faith cannot possibly be so highly expressed, as in that it shall be the last peal to call the judgments of God upon the generations of men, it being foretold that when Christ cometh, *he shall not find faith upon the earth.*[15]

II. OF DEATH

MEN fear Death, as children fear to go in the dark; and as that natural fear in children is increased with tales, so is the other. Certainly the contemplation of death, as the wages of sin and passage to another world, is holy and religious, but the fear of it, as a tribute due unto nature, is weak. Yet in religious meditations there is sometimes mixture of vanity and of superstition. You shall read in some of the friars' books of mortification, that a man should think with himself what the pain is if he have but his finger's end pressed or tortured, and thereby imagine what the pains of death are, when the whole body is corrupted and dissolved; when many times death passeth with less pain than the torture of a limb, for the most vital parts are not the quickest of sense. And by him that spake only as a philosopher and natural man, it was well said, *Pompa mortis magis terret, quam mors ipsa.*[1] Groans and convulsions, and a discoloured face, and friends weeping, and blacks, and obsequies, and the like show death terrible. It is worthy the observing that there is no passion in the mind of man so weak, but it mates and masters the fear of death; and therefore death is no such terrible enemy when a man hath so many attendants about him that can win the combat of him. Revenge triumphs over death; Love slights it; Honour aspireth to it; Grief flieth to it; Fear preoccupateth[2] it; nay we read, after Otho the emperor had slain himself, Pity (which is the tenderest of affections) provoked many to die out of mere compassion to their sovereign, and as the truest sort of followers.[3]

---

[15] See Luke 18:8.

[1] "The circumstances surrounding death are more terrifying than death itself." Perhaps suggested by a passage in Seneca, *Epistles*, XXIV.14.

[2] anticipates, viz. by suicide.

[3] See Tacitus, *History*, II.49; Plutarch, *Otho*, 17. Otho: Roman emperor who committed suicide when his army was defeated in A.D. 69.

Nay Seneca adds niceness[4] and satiety: *Cogita quamdiu eadem feceris; mori velle, non tantum fortis, aut miser, sed etiam fastidiosus potest.*[5] A man would die, though he were neither valiant nor miserable, only upon a weariness to do the same thing so oft over and over. It is no less worthy to observe how little alteration in good spirits the approaches of death make, for they appear to be the same men till the last instant. Augustus Cæsar died in a compliment: *Livia, conjugii nostri memor, vive et vale;*[6] Tiberius in dissimulation, as Tacitus saith of him: *Jam Tiberium vires et corpus, non dissimulatio, deserebant;*[7] Vespasian in a jest, sitting upon the stool: *Ut puto Deus fio;*[8] Galba with a sentence: *Feri, si ex re sit populi Romani,*[9] holding forth his neck; Septimius Severus in despatch: *Adeste si quid mihi restat agendum.*[10] And the like. Certainly the Stoics bestowed too much cost upon death, and by their great preparations made it appear more fearful. Better saith he, *qui finem vitæ extremum inter munera ponat naturæ.*[11] It is as natural to die as to be born; and to a little infant, perhaps, the one is as painful as the other. He that dies in an earnest pursuit is like one that is wounded in hot blood, who, for the time, scarce feels the hurt; and therefore a mind fixed and bent upon somewhat that is good doth avert the dolours[12] of death. But above all, believe it, the sweetest canticle is, *Nunc dimittis;*[13] when a man hath obtained worthy ends and expectations. Death hath this also, that it openeth the gate to good fame, and extinguisheth envy. *Extinctus amabitur idem.*[14]

---

[4] fastidiousness.

[5] *Epistles,* LXXVII.6. Here, as often elsewhere, Bacon quotes with variations from the original; he also follows his frequent practice of translating in the following lines.

[6] "Mindful of our marriage, Livia, live and farewell." See Suetonius, *Octavius Augustus,* 99.

[7] "His physical powers were deserting Tiberius, not his powers of dissimulation." *Annals,* VI.50.

[8] "I think I am becoming a god." Suetonius, *Vespasian,* 23.

[9] "Strike, if it be for the good of the Roman people." Tacitus, *History,* I.41.

[10] "Make haste, if anything remains for me to do." Dion Cassius, LXXVII.17.

[11] "who deems the end of life one of the blessings of nature". Juvenal, *Satires,* X.358.

[12] pains.

[13] "Now lettest thou thy servant depart." Luke 2:29.

[14] "The same man [envied when alive] will be loved when dead." Horace, *Epistles,* II.i.14.

III. OF UNITY IN RELIGION

RELIGION being the chief band of human society, it is a happy thing when itself is well contained within the true band of Unity. The quarrels and divisions about religion were evils unknown to the heathen. The reason was, because the religion of the heathen consisted rather in rites and ceremonies than in any constant belief. For you may imagine what kind of faith theirs was, when the chief doctors[1] and fathers of their church were the poets. But the true God hath this attribute, that he is a *jealous God*, and therefore his worship and religion will endure no mixture nor partner. We shall therefore speak a few words concerning the Unity of the Church: what are the Fruits thereof; what the Bounds; and what the Means.

The Fruits of Unity (next unto the well pleasing of God, which is all in all) are two: the one towards those that are without the church, the other towards those that are within. For the former, it is certain that heresies and schisms are of all others the greatest scandals; yea, more than corruption of manners.[2] For as in the natural body a wound or solution of continuity is worse than a corrupt humour,[3] so in the spiritual. So that nothing doth so much keep men out of the church, and drive men out of the church as breach of unity. And therefore, whensoever it cometh to that pass that one saith *Ecce in deserto*, another saith *Ecce in penetralibus;*[4] that is, when some men seek Christ in the conventicles of heretics, and others in an outward face of a church, that voice had need continually to sound in men's ears, *Nolite exire* – *Go not out*. The Doctor of the Gentiles[5] (the propriety[6] of whose vocation drew him to have a special care of those without) saith, *If an heathen come in, and hear you speak with several tongues, will he not say that you are mad?* And certainly it is little better, when atheists and profane persons do hear of so

---

[1] learned men.

[2] morals.

[3] i.e., an imbalance or other disturbance in the four constituents (fluids) of the body. solution of continuity: cut, wound, fracture.

[4] "Behold, he is in the desert, . . . Behold, he is in the secret chambers." Matt. 24:26.

[5] i.e., St. Paul. See I Cor. 14:23.

[6] peculiarity.

many discordant and contrary opinions in religion; it doth avert them from the church, and maketh them *to sit down in the chair of the scorners*.[7] It is but a light thing to be vouched[8] in so serious a matter, but yet it expresseth well the deformity. There is a master of scoffing,[9] that in his catalogue of books of a feigned library sets down this title of a book, *The Morris-Dance of Heretics*. For indeed every sect of them hath a diverse posture or cringe by themselves, which cannot but move derision in worldlings and depraved politics,[10] who are apt to contemn holy things.

As for the fruit towards those that are within, it is peace which containeth infinite blessings. It establisheth faith. It kindleth charity. The outward peace of the church distilleth into peace of conscience. And it turneth the labours of writing and reading of controversies into treaties[11] of mortification and devotion.

Concerning the Bounds of Unity, the true placing of them importeth exceedingly. There appear to be two extremes. For to certain zelants[12] all speech of pacification is odious. *Is it peace, Jehu? What hast thou to do with peace? turn thee behind me*.[13] Peace is not the matter, but following and party. Contrariwise, certain Laodiceans and lukewarm persons think they may accommodate points of religion by middle ways, and taking part of both, and witty[14] reconcilements, as if they would make an arbitrement[15] between God and man. Both these extremes are to be avoided, which will be done, if the league of Christians penned by our Saviour himself were in the two cross clauses thereof soundly and plainly expounded: *He that is not with us is against us;* and again, *He that is not against us is with us;*[16] that is, if the points fundamental and of substance in religion were truly discerned and distinguished from points not merely[17] of faith but of opinion, order, or good intention. This is a thing

[7] Cf. Psalms 1:1.
[8] quoted as evidence.
[9] François Rabelais, *Pantagruel*, II.7.
[10] politicians.
[11] treatises.
[12] zealots.

[13] Cf. II Kings 9:18, 19.
[14] clever, ingenious.
[15] settlement, arbitration.
[16] See Matt. 12:30; Mark 9:40; Luke 9:50.
[17] entirely, completely.

may seem to many a matter trivial, and done already. But if it were done less partially, it would be embraced more generally.

Of this I may give only this advice, according to my small model. Men ought to take heed of rending God's church by two kinds of controversies. The one is when the matter of the point controverted is too small and light, not worth the heat and strife about it, kindled only by contradiction. For as it is noted by one of the fathers, *Christ's coat indeed had no seam, but the church's vesture was of divers colours;* whereupon he saith, *In veste varietas sit, scissura non sit:*[18] they be two things, Unity and Uniformity. The other is when the matter of the point controverted is great, but it is driven to an overgreat subtilty and obscurity, so that it becometh a thing rather ingenious than substantial. A man that is of judgment and understanding shall sometimes hear ignorant men differ, and know well within himself that those which so differ mean one thing, and yet they themselves would never agree. And if it come so to pass in that distance of judgment which is between man and man, shall we think that God above, that knows the heart, doth not discern that frail men in some of their contradictions intend the same thing, and accepteth of both? The nature of such controversies is excellently expressed by St. Paul in the warning and precept that he giveth concerning the same, *Devita profanas vocum novitates, et oppositiones falsi nominis scientiæ.*[19] Men create oppositions which are not, and put them into new terms so fixed, as whereas the meaning ought to govern the term, the term in effect governeth the meaning. There be also two false peaces or unities: the one, when the peace is grounded but upon an implicit ignorance, for all colours will agree in the dark; the other, when it is pieced[20] up upon a direct admission of contraries in fundamental points. For truth and falsehood in such things are like the iron and clay in the toes

---

[18] "Let there be variety in the garment, but no division." The Latin is quoted from St. Augustine, Commentary on Psalm 44[45]:24, but it does not refer to Christ's coat. In several passages of St. Bernard is found the same fanciful interpretation. [Northup] See also John 19:23.

[19] "Avoid profane novelties of terms and the oppositions of what is falsely called knowledge." I Timothy 6:20.

[20] patched.

of Nebuchadnezzar's image: they may cleave, but they will not incorporate.[21]

Concerning the Means of procuring Unity, men must beware that in the procuring or muniting[22] of religious unity they do not dissolve and deface the laws of charity and of human society. There be two swords amongst Christians, the spiritual and temporal, and both have their due office and place in the maintenance of religion. But we may not take up the third sword, which is Mahomet's sword, or like unto it; that is, to propagate religion by wars or by sanguinary persecutions to force consciences, except it be in cases of overt scandal, blasphemy, or intermixture of practice[23] against the state; much less to nourish seditions, to authorise conspiracies and rebellions, to put the sword into the people's hands, and the like, tending to the subversion of all government, which is the ordinance of God. For this is but to dash the first table against the second; and so to consider men as Christians, as we forget that they are men. Lucretius the poet, when he beheld the act of Agamemnon, that could endure the sacrificing of his own daughter, exclaimed:

Tantum Religio potuit suadere malorum.[24]

What would he have said, if he had known of the massacre in France or the powder treason of England? He would have been seven times more Epicure and atheist than he was. For as the temporal sword is to be drawn with great circumspection in cases of religion, so it is a thing monstrous to put it into the hands of the common people. Let that be left unto the Anabaptists and other furies. It was great blasphemy when the devil said, *I will ascend and be like the Highest*,[25] but it is greater blasphemy to personate God, and bring him in saying, *I will descend, and be like the prince of darkness;* and what is it better, to make the cause of religion to descend to the cruel and execrable actions of murthering princes, butchery of people, and subversion of states and governments? Surely this is to bring down the Holy Ghost,

---

[21] See Daniel 2:33, 41.
[22] strengthening.
[23] intrigue.

[24] "So many evils could religion induce." *On the Nature of Things,* I.95.
[25] Isaiah 14:14.

instead of the likeness of a dove, in the shape of a vulture or raven, and set out of the bark of a Christian church a flag of a bark of pirates and assassins. Therefore it is most necessary that the church by doctrine and decree, princes by their sword, and all learnings, both Christian and moral, as by their Mercury rod,[26] do damn and send to hell for ever those facts and opinions tending to the support of the same, as hath been already in good part done. Surely in counsels concerning religion, that counsel of the apostle would be prefixed, *Ira hominis non implet justitiam Dei.*[27] And it was a notable observation of a wise father, and no less ingenuously confessed, *that those which held and persuaded*[28] *pressure of consciences were commonly interessed*[29] *therein themselves for their own ends.*

IV. OF REVENGE

REVENGE is a kind of wild justice, which the more man's nature runs to, the more ought law to weed it out. For as for the first wrong, it doth but offend the law, but the revenge of that wrong putteth the law out of office. Certainly in taking revenge, a man is but even with his enemy, but in passing it over, he is superior, for it is a prince's part to pardon. And Salomon, I am sure, saith, *It is the glory of a man to pass by an offence.*[1] That which is past is gone and irrevocable, and wise men have enough to do with things present and to come; therefore they do but trifle with themselves that labour in past matters. There is no man doth a wrong for the wrong's sake, but thereby to purchase himself profit, or pleasure, or honour, or the like. Therefore why should I be angry with a man for loving himself better than me? And if any man should do wrong merely* out of ill nature, why, yet it is but like the thorn or briar, which prick and scratch because they can do no other. The most tolerable sort of revenge is for those

---

[26] the caduceus, by which Mercury summoned the souls of the dead to the world below. Cf. Virgil, *Aeneid,* IV.242f.

[27] "The wrath of man worketh not the righteousness of God." James 1:20.

[28] inculcated.

[29] interested.

[1] Cf. Prov. 19:11.

wrongs which there is no law to remedy, but then let a man take heed the revenge be such as there is no law to punish; else a man's enemy is still beforehand,[2] and it is two for one. Some, when they take revenge, are desirous the party should know whence it cometh. This the more generous. For the delight seemeth to be not so much in doing the hurt as in making the party repent. But base and crafty cowards are like the arrow that flieth in the dark. Cosmus, Duke of Florence,[3] had a desperate saying against perfidious or neglecting friends, as if those wrongs were unpardonable: *You shall read* (saith he) *that we are commanded to forgive our enemies; but you never read that we are commanded to forgive our friends.* But yet the spirit of Job was in a better tune: *Shall we* (saith he) *take good at God's hands, and not be content to take evil also?*[4] And so of friends in a proportion. This is certain, that a man that studieth revenge keeps his own wounds green, which otherwise would heal and do well. Public revenges are for the most part fortunate, as that for the death of Cæsar, for the death of Pertinax, for the death of Henry the Third of France,[5] and many more. But in private revenges it is not so. Nay rather, vindictive persons live the life of witches, who, as they are mischievous, so end they infortunate.[6]

V. OF ADVERSITY

IT was a high[1] speech of Seneca (after the manner of the Stoics), *that the good things which belong to prosperity are to be wished, but the good things that belong to adversity are to be admired. Bona rerum secundarum optabilia; adversarum mirabilia.*[2] Certainly if miracles be the command over nature, they appear most in adversity. It is yet a higher speech of his than the other (much

---

[2] i.e., ahead of him, has the advantage over him.

[3] Cosimo de' Medici (1519-74), known as Cosimo the Great.

[4] Job 2:10.

[5] The references here are to Augustus (avenger of Julius Caesar), Septimius Severus (avenger of Pertinax, Roman emperor of the second century), and Henry IV (avenger of Henry III), all of whom prospered.

[6] unfortunate.

---

[1] presumptuous.

[2] *Epistles*, LXVI.29.

too high for a heathen), *It is true greatness to have in one the frailty of a man and the security of a God. Vere magnum habere fragilitatem hominis, securitatem Dei.*[3] This would have done better in poesy, where transcendences[4] are more allowed. And the poets indeed have been busy with it, for it is in effect the thing which is figured in that strange fiction of the ancient poets, which seemeth not to be without mystery, nay, and to have some approach to the state of a Christian, that *Hercules, when he went to unbind Prometheus* (by whom human nature is represented), *sailed the length of the great ocean in an earthen pot or pitcher,*[5] lively describing Christian resolution, that saileth in the frail bark of the flesh thorough the waves of the world. But to speak in a mean:[6] the virtue of Prosperity is temperance, the virtue of Adversity is fortitude, which in morals is the more heroical virtue. Prosperity is the blessing of the Old Testament; Adversity is the blessing of the New, which carrieth the greater benediction and the clearer revelation of God's favour. Yet even in the Old Testament, if you listen to David's harp,[7] you shall hear as many hearse-like airs as carols, and the pencil of the Holy Ghost hath laboured more in describing the afflictions of Job than the felicities of Salomon. Prosperity is not without many fears and distastes,[8] and Adversity is not without comforts and hopes. We see in needleworks and embroideries, it is more pleasing to have a lively work upon a sad and solemn ground than to have a dark and melancholy work upon a lightsome ground; judge therefore of the pleasure of the heart by the pleasure of the eye. Certainly virtue is like precious odours, most fragrant when they are incensed[9] or crushed, for Prosperity doth best discover vice, but Adversity doth best discover virtue.

---

[3] Seneca, *Epistles*, LIII.12.
[4] flights of the imagination.
[5] Apollodorus, *On the Origins of the Gods*, II.5.
[6] moderately.

[7] i.e., the Book of Psalms. See also I Kings 3:10.
[8] annoyances.
[9] burned.

VI. OF SIMULATION AND DISSIMULATION

DISSIMULATION is but a faint kind of policy or wisdom, for it asketh a strong wit and a strong heart to know when to tell truth, and to do it. Therefore it is the weaker sort of politics* that are the great dissemblers.

Tacitus saith, *Livia sorted[1] well with the arts of her husband and dissimulation of her son*, attributing arts or policy to Augustus, and dissimulation to Tiberius. And again, when Mucianus encourageth Vespasian to take arms against Vitellius, he saith, *We rise not against the piercing judgment of Augustus, nor the extreme caution or closeness of Tiberius.*[2] These properties, of arts or policy and dissimulation or closeness, are indeed habits and faculties several, and to be distinguished. For if a man have that penetration of judgment as he can discern what things are to be laid open, and what to be secreted, and what to be showed at half lights, and to whom and when (which indeed are arts of state and arts of life, as Tacitus[3] well calleth them), to him a habit of dissimulation is a hindrance and a poorness. But if a man cannot obtain to that judgment, then it is left to him generally to be close and a dissembler. For where a man cannot choose or vary in particulars, there it is good to take the safest and wariest way in general, like the going softly by one that cannot well see. Certainly the ablest men that ever were have had all an openness and frankness of dealing, and a name of[4] certainty and veracity; but then they were like horses well managed,[5] for they could tell passing well when to stop or turn; and at such times when they thought the case indeed required dissimulation, if then they used it, it came to pass that the former opinion spread abroad of their good faith, and clearness[6] of dealing made them almost invisible.

There be three degrees of this hiding and veiling of a man's self. The first, Closeness, Reservation, and Secrecy, when a man

---

[1] suited, fitted. See *Annals*, V.1.

[2] Tacitus, *Hist.*, II.76. Mucianus: Governor of Syria and Roman consul of the first century. Aulus Vitellius (*c*. A.D. 15-69): Roman consul and emperor for one year.

[3] *Agricola*, 39.

[4] reputation for.

[5] trained.

[6] openness.

leaveth himself without observation or without hold to be taken, what he is. The second, Dissimulation, in the negative, when a man lets fall signs and arguments that he is not that he is. And the third, Simulation, in the affirmative, when a man industriously[7] and expressly feigns and pretends to be that he is not.

For the first of these, Secrecy, it is indeed the virtue of a confessor. And assuredly the secret man heareth many confessions. For who will open himself to a blab or babbler? But if a man be thought secret, it inviteth discovery,[8] as the more close air sucketh in the more open; and as in confession the revealing is not for worldly use, but for the ease of a man's heart, so secret men come to the knowledge of many things in that kind,[9] while men rather discharge their minds than impart their minds. In few words, mysteries are due to secrecy. Besides (to say truth) nakedness is uncomely, as well in mind as body, and it addeth no small reverence to men's manners* and actions, if they be not altogether open. As for talkers and futile[10] persons, they are commonly vain and credulous withal. For he that talketh what he knoweth will also talk what he knoweth not. Therefore set it down, *that an habit of secrecy is both politic and moral.* And in this part, it is good that a man's face give his tongue leave to speak. For the discovery of a man's self by the tracts[11] of his countenance is a great weakness and betraying, by how much it is many times more marked and believed than a man's words.

For the second, which is Dissimulation, it followeth many times upon secrecy by a necessity, so that he that will be secret must be a dissembler in some degree. For men are too cunning to suffer a man to keep an indifferent[12] carriage between both, and to be secret without swaying the balance on either side. They will so beset a man with questions, and draw him on, and pick it out of him, that, without an absurd silence, he must show an inclination one way, or if he do not, they will gather as much by his silence as by his speech. As for equivocations or oraculous[13]

---

[7] purposely.
[8] disclosure, confidences.
[9] manner, way.
[10] talkative.

[11] traits, features.
[12] neutral, impartial.
[13] i.e., oracular: obscure, enigmatical.

speeches, they cannot hold out long. So that no man can be secret, except he give himself a little scope of dissimulation, which is, as it were, but the skirts or train of secrecy.

But for the third degree, which is Simulation and false profession, that I hold more culpable, and less politic, except it be in great and rare matters. And therefore a general custom of simulation (which is this last degree) is a vice, rising either of a natural falseness or fearfulness, or of a mind that hath some main faults, which because a man must needs disguise, it maketh him practise simulation in other things, lest his hand should be out of ure.[14]

The great advantages of simulation and dissimulation are three. First, to lay asleep opposition, and to surprise. For where a man's intentions are published, it is an alarum to call up all that are against them. The second is, to reserve to a man's self a fair retreat. For if a man engage himself by a manifest declaration, he must go through or take a fall. The third is, the better to discover the mind of another. For to him that opens himself men will hardly show themselves adverse, but will (fair)[15] let him go on, and turn their freedom of speech to freedom of thought. And therefore it is a good shrewd proverb of the Spaniard, *Tell a lie and find a troth*. As if there were no way of discovery but by simulation. There be also three disadvantages to set it even. The first, that simulation and dissimulation commonly carry with them a show of fearfulness, which in any business doth spoil the feathers of round[16] flying up to the mark. The second, that it puzzleth and perplexeth the conceits[17] of many that perhaps would otherwise co-operate with him, and makes a man walk almost alone to his own ends. The third and greatest is, that it depriveth a man of one of the most principal instruments for action, which is trust and belief. The best composition and temperature[18] is to have openness in fame and opinion, secrecy in habit, dissimulation in seasonable use, and a power to feign, if there be no remedy.

---

[14] use.
[15] simply.
[16] direct.

[17] thoughts, ideas, concepts.
[18] nature and temperament (i.e., combination and blending of humours).

VII. OF PARENTS AND CHILDREN

THE joys of parents are secret: and so are their griefs and fears. They cannot utter the one, nor they will not utter the other. Children sweeten labours, but they make misfortunes more bitter. They increase the cares of life, but they mitigate the remembrance of death. The perpetuity by generation is common to beasts, but memory, merit, and noble works are proper[1] to men. And surely a man shall see the noblest works and foundations have proceeded from childless men, which have sought to express the images of their minds, where those of their bodies have failed. So the care of posterity is most in them that have no posterity. They that are the first raisers of their houses are most indulgent towards their children, beholding them as the continuance not only of their kind but of their work; and so both children and creatures.

The difference in affection of parents towards their several children is many times unequal and sometimes unworthy, especially in the mother; as Salomon saith, *A wise son rejoiceth the father, but an ungracious son shames the mother.*[2] A man shall see, where there is a house full of children, one or two of the eldest respected, and the youngest made wantons, but in the midst some that are as it were forgotten, who many times nevertheless prove the best. The illiberality of parents in allowance towards their children is an harmful error; makes them base; acquaints them with shifts; makes them sort[3] with mean company; and makes them surfeit more when they come to plenty. And therefore the proof is best, when men keep their authority towards their children, but not their purse. Men have a foolish manner (both parents and schoolmasters and servants) in creating and breeding an emulation between brothers during childhood, which many times sorteth to[4] discord when they are men, and disturbeth families. The Italians make little difference between children and nephews or near kinsfolks; but so they be of the lump, they care not though they pass not through their own

---

[1] belonging to or peculiar to the species.
[2] Prov. 10:1.
[3] consort, go out (with).
[4] results in.

body. And to say truth, in nature it is much a like matter, insomuch that we see a nephew sometimes resembleth an uncle or a kinsman more than his own parent, as the blood happens. Let parents choose betimes the vocations and courses they mean their children should take, for then they are most flexible, and let them not too much apply themselves to the disposition of their children, as thinking they will take best to that which they have most mind to. It is true that if the affection* or aptness of the children be extraordinary, then it is good not to cross it; but generally the precept is good, *Optimum elige, suave et facile illud faciet consuetudo.*[5] Younger brothers are commonly fortunate, but seldom or never where the elder are disinherited.

VIII. OF MARRIAGE AND SINGLE LIFE

He that hath wife and children hath given hostages to fortune, for they are impediments to great enterprises, either of virtue or mischief. Certainly the best works and of greatest merit for the public have proceeded from the unmarried or childless men, which both in affection and means have married and endowed the public. Yet it were great reason that those that have children should have greatest care of future times, unto which they know they must transmit their dearest pledges. Some there are who, though they lead a single life, yet their thoughts do end with themselves, and account future times impertinences.[1] Nay, there are some other that account wife and children but as bills of charges. Nay more, there are some foolish, rich, covetous men that take a pride in having no children, because they may be thought so much the richer. For perhaps they have heard some talk, *Such an one is a great rich man,* and another except to it, *Yea, but he hath a great charge of children,* as if it were an abatement to his riches. But the most ordinary cause of a single life is liberty, especially in certain self-pleasing and humorous[2] minds, which are so sensible of every restraint as they will go near to

[5] "Choose the best; custom will make it agreeable and easy." Pythagoras. See Plutarch, *On Exile,* VIII.

[1] matters of no importance.
[2] eccentric, odd.

think their girdles and garters to be bonds and shackles. Unmarried men are best friends, best masters, best servants, but not always best subjects, for they are light to run away; and almost all fugitives are of that condition. A single life doth well with churchmen, for charity will hardly water the ground where it must first fill a pool. It is indifferent for judges and magistrates, for if they be facile[3] and corrupt, you shall have a servant five times worse than a wife. For soldiers, I find the generals commonly in their hortatives put men in mind of their wives and children; and I think the despising of marriage amongst the Turks maketh the vulgar soldier more base. Certainly wife and children are a kind of discipline of humanity; and single men, though they may be many times more charitable, because their means are less exhaust,[4] yet, on the other side, they are more cruel and hardhearted (good to make severe inquisitors) because their tenderness is not so oft called upon. Grave natures, led by custom and therefore constant, are commonly loving husbands, as was said of Ulysses: *Vetulam suam prætulit immortalitati.*[5] Chaste women are often proud and froward, as presuming upon the merit of their chastity. It is one of the best bonds both of chastity and obedience in the wife, if she think her husband wise, which she will never do if she find him jealous. Wives are young men's mistresses, companions for middle age, and old men's nurses. So as a man may have a quarrel[6] to marry when he will. But yet he was reputed one of the wise men, that made answer to the question, when a man should marry? – *A young man not yet, an elder man not at all.*[7] It is often seen that bad husbands have very good wives, whether it be that it raiseth the price of their husband's kindness when it comes, or that the wives take a pride in their patience. But this never fails if the bad husbands were of their own choosing, against their friends' consent, for then they will be sure to make good their own folly.

---

[3] complaisant, hence easily worked upon.

[4] exhausted.

[5] "He preferred his old wife to immortality." See Homer, *Odyssey,* V.218; Cicero, *On the Orator,* I.44. Ulysses' old wife was Penelope, whom he preferred to the immortality Calypso offered him.

[6] reason.

[7] attributed to Thales and Diogenes the Cynic. See Diogenes Laertius, I.26 and VI.54; also Plutarch, *Symposiacs,* III.vi.3.

IX. OF ENVY

THERE be none of the affections which have been noted to fascinate or bewitch, but love and envy. They both have vehement wishes; they frame themselves readily into imaginations and suggestions; and they come easily into the eye, especially upon the presence of the objects, which are the points that conduce to fascination, if any such thing there be. We see likewise the scripture calleth envy an *evil eye*, and the astrologers call the evil influences of the stars *evil aspects*, so that still there seemeth to be acknowledged, in the act of envy, an ejaculation[1] or irradiation of the eye. Nay some have been so curious[2] as to note that the times when the stroke or percussion of an envious eye doth most hurt are when the party envied is beheld in glory or triumph, for that sets an edge upon envy; and besides, at such times the spirits of the person envied do come forth most into the outward parts, and so meet the blow.

But leaving these curiosities[3] (though not unworthy to be thought on in fit place), we will handle, what persons are apt to envy others; what persons are most subject to be envied themselves; and what is the difference between public and private envy.

A man that hath no virtue in himself ever envieth virtue in others. For men's minds will either feed upon their own good or upon others' evil; and who wanteth the one will prey upon the other; and whoso is out of hope to attain to another's virtue will seek to come at even hand[4] by depressing another's fortune.

A man that is busy and inquisitive is commonly envious. For to know much of other men's matters cannot be because all that ado may concern his own estate;[5] therefore it must needs be that he taketh a kind of play-pleasure[6] in looking upon the fortunes of others. Neither can he that mindeth but his own business find much matter for envy. For envy is a gadding

---

[1] emission; literally, a darting out. For the scriptural reference see Mark 7:22.

[2] observant.

[3] subtleties (matters noticed by the "curious").

[4] equal to, even with.

[5] condition.

[6] i.e., pleasure like that of watching a play.

passion, and walketh the streets, and doth not keep home: *Non est curiosus, quin idem sit malevolus.*[7]

Men of noble birth are noted to be envious towards new men when they rise. For the distance is altered, and it is like a deceit of the eye that when others come on, they think themselves go back.

Deformed persons, and eunuchs, and old men, and bastards are envious. For he that cannot possibly mend his own case will do what he can to impair another's; except these defects light upon a very brave and heroical nature, which thinketh to make his natural wants part of his honour, in that it should be said that an eunuch or a lame man did such great matters, affecting* the honour of a miracle, as it was in Narses the eunuch, and Agesilaus and Tamberlanes, that were lame men.[8]

The same is the case of men that rise after calamities and misfortunes. For they are as men fallen out with the times, and think other men's harms a redemption of their own sufferings.

They that desire to excel in too many matters, out of levity and vainglory, are ever envious. For they cannot want work,[9] it being impossible but many in some one of those things should surpass them. Which was the character of Adrian the Emperor, that mortally envied poets and painters and artificers, in works wherein he had a vein* to excel.

Lastly, near kinsfolks and fellows in office and those that have been bred together are more apt to envy their equals when they are raised. For it doth upbraid unto them their own fortunes, and pointeth at them, and cometh oftener into their remembrance, and incurreth[10] likewise more into the note of others; and envy ever redoubleth from speech and fame. Cain's envy was the more vile and malignant towards his brother Abel, because when his sacrifice was better accepted, there was nobody to look on. Thus much for those that are apt to envy.

Concerning those that are more or less subject to envy: first,

[7] "All inquisitive persons are malevolent." Plautus, *Stichus*, I.iii.55.

[8] Narses: Byzantine general of Justinian the Great (483-565). Agesilaus: King of Sparta (444?-360 B.C.).

Tamberlane or Tamerlane: Mongol conqueror (1336?-1405).

[9] i.e., lack (occasion for) employment (of envy).

[10] runs.

persons of eminent virtue, when they are advanced, are less
envied. For their fortune seemeth but due unto them, and no
man envieth the payment of a debt, but rewards and liberality
rather. Again, envy is ever joined with the comparing of a man's
self, and where there is no comparison, no envy; and therefore
kings are not envied but by kings. Nevertheless it is to be noted
that unworthy persons are most envied at their first coming in,
and afterwards overcome it better; whereas, contrariwise, persons
of worth and merit are most envied when their fortune continueth long. For by that time, though their virtue be the same, yet
it hath not the same lustre, for fresh men grow up that darken it.

Persons of noble blood are less envied in their rising. For it
seemeth but right done to their birth. Besides, there seemeth
not much added to their fortune; and envy is as the sunbeams,
that beat hotter upon a bank or steep rising ground than upon
a flat. And for the same reason those that are advanced by
degrees are less envied than those that are advanced suddenly
and *per saltum*.[11]

Those that have joined with their honour great travels,[12]
cares, or perils are less subject to envy. For men think that they
earn their honours hardly, and pity them sometimes; and pity
ever healeth envy. Wherefore you shall observe that the more
deep and sober sort of politic persons, in their greatness, are
ever bemoaning themselves, what a life they lead, chanting a
quanta patimur.[13] Not that they feel it so, but only to abate the
edge of envy. But this is to be understood of business that is laid
upon men, and not such as they call unto themselves. For nothing increaseth envy more than an unnecessary and ambitious
engrossing of business. And nothing doth extinguish envy more
than for a great person to preserve all other inferior officers in
their full rights and pre-eminences of their places. For by that
means there be so many screens between him and envy.

Above all, those are most subject to envy which carry the
greatness of their fortunes in an insolent and proud manner,
being never well but while they are showing how great they are,

---

11 "by a jump".
12 labours.

13 "how much we suffer". politic
persons: politicians.

either by outward pomp or by triumphing over all opposition or competition; whereas wise men will rather do sacrifice to envy, in suffering themselves sometimes of purpose to be crossed and overborne in things that do not much concern them. Notwithstanding so much is true, that the carriage of greatness in a plain and open manner (so it be without arrogancy and vainglory) doth draw less envy than if it be in a more crafty and cunning fashion. For in that course a man doth but disavow fortune, and seemeth to be conscious of his own want in worth, and doth but teach others to envy him.

Lastly, to conclude this part, as we said in the beginning that the act of envy had somewhat in it of witchcraft, so there is no other cure of envy but the cure of witchcraft, and that is, to remove the *lot* (as they call it) and to lay it upon another. For which purpose, the wiser sort of great persons bring in ever upon the stage somebody upon whom to derive[14] the envy that would come upon themselves, sometimes upon ministers and servants, sometimes upon colleagues and associates, and the like; and for that turn there are never wanting some persons of violent and undertaking[15] natures, who, so they may have power and business, will take it at any cost.

Now, to speak of public envy. There is yet some good in public envy, whereas in private there is none. For public envy is as an ostracism, that eclipseth men when they grow too great. And therefore it is a bridle also to great ones, to keep them within bounds.

This envy, being in the Latin word *invidia*, goeth in the modern languages by the name of *discontentment*, of which we shall speak in handling Sedition. It is a disease in a state like to infection. For as infection spreadeth upon that which is sound and tainteth it, so when envy is gotten once into a state, it traduceth even the best actions thereof, and turneth them into an ill odour. And therefore there is little won by intermingling of plausible[16] actions. For that doth argue but a weakness and

---

[14] turn aside.
[15] opportunistically enterprising.

[16] deserving of applause, laudable.

fear of envy, which hurteth so much the more as it is likewise usual in infections, which if you fear them you call them upon you.

This public envy seemeth to beat chiefly upon principal officers or ministers rather than upon kings and estates themselves. But this is a sure rule, that if the envy upon the minister be great, when the cause of it in him is small, or if the envy be general in a manner upon all the ministers of an estate, then the envy (though hidden) is truly upon the state itself. And so much of public envy or discontentment, and the difference thereof from private envy, which was handled in the first place.

We will add this in general, touching the affection of envy, that of all other affections it is the most importune and continual. For of other affections there is occasion given but now and then; and therefore it was well said, *Invidia festos dies non agit*,[17] for it is ever working upon some or other. And it is also noted that love and envy do make a man pine, which other affections do not, because they are not so continual. It is also the vilest affection and the most depraved, for which cause it is the proper attribute of the devil, who is called *The envious man, that soweth tares amongst the wheat by night*;[18] as it always cometh to pass that envy worketh subtilly and in the dark, and to the prejudice of good things, such as is the wheat.

X. OF LOVE

THE stage is more beholding[1] to Love than the life of man. For as to the stage, love is ever matter of comedies, and now and then of tragedies, but in life it doth much mischief, sometimes like a syren, sometimes like a fury. You may observe that amongst all the great and worthy persons (whereof the memory remaineth, either ancient or recent) there is not one that hath

---

[17] "Envy takes no holidays."
[18] See Matt. 13:25.

[1] beholden.

been transported to the mad degree of love, which shows that great spirits and great business do keep out this weak passion. You must except nevertheless Marcus Antonius, the half partner of the empire of Rome, and Appius Claudius,[2] the decemvir and lawgiver; whereof the former was indeed a voluptuous man, and inordinate, but the latter was an austere and wise man; and therefore it seems (though rarely) that love can find entrance not only into an open heart, but also into a heart well fortified, if watch be not well kept. It is a poor saying of Epicurus, *Satis magnum alter alteri theatrum sumus,*[3] as if man, made for the contemplation of heaven and all noble objects, should do nothing but kneel before a little idol, and make himself a subject, though not of the mouth (as beasts are), yet of the eye, which was given him for higher purposes. It is a strange thing to note the excess of this passion, and how it braves[4] the nature and value of things, by this: that the speaking in a perpetual hyperbole is comely in nothing but in love. Neither is it merely in the phrase, for whereas it hath been well said that the arch-flatterer, with whom all the petty flatterers have intelligence,[5] is a man's self, certainly the lover is more. For there was never proud man thought so absurdly well of himself as the lover doth of the person loved; and therefore it was well said, *That it is impossible to love and to be wise.*[6] Neither doth this weakness appear to others only, and not to the party loved, but to the loved most of all, except the love be reciproque.[7] For it is a true rule that love is ever rewarded either with the reciproque or with an inward and secret contempt. By how much the more men ought to beware of this passion, which loseth not only other things but itself. As for the other losses, the poet's relation doth well figure them: that

---

[2] Appius Claudius (a decemvir, whom Bacon confuses with another Appius Claudius, a lawgiver) lusted after Virginia, who was saved from enslavement to him only by being killed by her father, Virginius (449 B.C.). See Livy, III.33.

[3] "We are a sufficiently large theatre to one another." Ascribed to Epicurus by Seneca, *Epistles,* VII.11. [Wright]

[4] outfaces, insults.

[5] are in league with. See Plutarch, *How a Flatterer may be Distinguished from a Friend,* 1.

[6] perhaps an adaptation of Publius Syrus, *Sentences,* 15.

[7] reciprocal, mutual.

he[8] that preferred Helena quitted[9] the gifts of Juno and Pallas. For whosoever esteemeth too much of amorous affection quitteth both riches and wisdom. This passion hath his floods in the very times of weakness, which are great prosperity and great adversity, though this latter hath been less observed, both which times kindle love, and make it more fervent, and therefore show it to be the child of folly. They do best who, if they cannot but admit love, yet make it keep quarter[10] and sever it wholly from their serious affairs and actions of life, for if it check[11] once with business, it troubleth men's fortunes, and maketh men that they can no ways be true to their own ends. I know not how, but martial men are given to love; I think it is but as they are given to wine, for perils commonly ask to be paid in pleasures. There is in man's nature a secret inclination and motion towards love of others, which if it be not spent upon some one or a few, doth naturally spread itself towards many, and maketh men become humane and charitable, as it is seen sometime in friars. Nuptial love maketh mankind; friendly love perfecteth it; but wanton love corrupteth and embaseth it.

XI. OF GREAT PLACE

MEN in great place are thrice servants: servants of the sovereign or state, servants of fame, and servants of business. So as they have no freedom, neither in their persons, nor in their actions, nor in their times. It is a strange desire to seek power and to lose liberty, or to seek power over others and to lose power over a man's self. The rising unto place is laborious, and by pains men come to greater pains; and it is sometimes base, and by indignities men come to dignities. The standing is slippery, and the regress is either a downfall or at least an eclipse, which is a melancholy thing. *Cum non sis qui fueris, non esse cur velis*

[8] i.e., Paris. Chosen to decide who was fairest amongst Juno, Minerva, and Venus, Paris rejected the bribes of power and wisdom offered by the first two but accepted that of Venus, the love of a beautiful woman. Having decided in her favour, he was awarded Helen. See Ovid, *Heroides*, XVI.133; Homer, *Iliad*, XXIV.25, 29 and III.46.

[9] renounced.

[10] proper place.

[11] interfere, block.

vivere.[1] Nay, retire men cannot when they would, neither will they when it were reason,[2] but are impatient of privateness, even in age and sickness, which require the shadow;[3] like old townsmen, that will be still sitting at their street door, though thereby they offer age to scorn. Certainly great persons had need to borrow other men's opinions, to think themselves happy; for if they judge by their own feeling, they cannot find it, but if they think with themselves what other men think of them, and that other men would fain be as they are, then they are happy as it were by report, when perhaps they find the contrary within. For they are the first that find their own griefs, though they be the last that find their own faults. Certainly men in great fortunes are strangers to themselves, and while they are in the puzzle of business, they have no time to tend their health either of body or mind. *Illi mors gravis incubat, qui notus nimis omnibus, ignotus moritur sibi.*[4] In place there is licence to do good and evil; whereof the latter is a curse, for in evil the best condition is not to will, the second not to can.[5] But power to do good is the true and lawful end of aspiring. For good thoughts (though God accept them) yet towards men are little better than good dreams, except they be put in act; and that cannot be without power and place as the vantage and commanding* ground. Merit and good works is the end of man's motion, and conscience[6] of the same is the accomplishment of man's rest. For if a man can be partaker of God's theatre, he shall likewise be partaker of God's rest. *Et conversus Deus, ut aspiceret opera quæ fecerunt manus suæ, vidit quod omnia essent bona nimis,*[7] and then the Sabbath. In the discharge of thy place set before thee the best examples, for imitation is a globe[8] of precepts. And after a time set before thee thine own example, and examine thyself strictly whether

---

[1] "When you are no longer what you were, there is no reason for wishing to live." Cicero, *Letters to his Friends*, VII.3.

[2] right, reasonable.

[3] retirement.

[4] "Death falls heavily upon him who, well known to others, dies ignorant of himself." Seneca, *Thyestes*, 401.

[5] i.e., be able.

[6] consciousness.

[7] "And God turned to behold the works which His hands had made, and saw that they were all very good." Cf. Genesis 1:31.

[8] collection.

thou didst not best at first. Neglect not also the examples of those that have carried themselves ill in the same place, not to set off thyself by taxing[9] their memory, but to direct thyself what to avoid. Reform, therefore, without bravery[10] or scandal of former times and persons, but yet set it down to thyself as well to create good precedents as to follow them. Reduce[11] things to the first institution, and observe wherein and how they have degenerate; but yet ask counsel of both times, of the ancient time, what is best, and of the latter time, what is fittest. Seek to make thy course regular that men may know beforehand what they may expect, but be not too positive and peremptory; and express thyself well when thou digressest from thy rule. Preserve the right of thy place, but stir not questions of jurisdiction, and rather assume thy right in silence and *de facto*, than voice it with claims and challenges. Preserve likewise the rights of inferior places, and think it more honour to direct in chief than to be busy in all. Embrace and invite helps and advices touching the execution of thy place, and do not drive away such as bring thee information, as meddlers, but accept of them in good part. The vices of authority are chiefly four: delays, corruption, roughness, and facility.* For[12] delays, give easy access; keep times appointed; go through with that which is in hand; and interlace[13] not business but of necessity. For corruption, do not only bind thine own hands or thy servants' hands from taking, but bind the hands of suitors also from offering. For integrity used doth the one, but integrity professed, and with a manifest detestation of bribery, doth the other. And avoid not only the fault, but the suspicion. Whosoever is found variable, and changeth manifestly without manifest cause giveth suspicion of corruption. Therefore always when thou changest thine opinion or course, profess it plainly, and declare it, together with the reasons that move thee to change, and do not think to steal it.[14] A servant or a favourite,

---

[9] censuring.
[10] ostentation.
[11] lead or take back again.

[12] as regards.
[13] intermix.
[14] do it by stealth.

if he be inward,[15] and no other apparent cause of esteem, is commonly thought but a by-way to close[16] corruption. For roughness, it is a needless cause of discontent; severity breedeth fear, but roughness breedeth hate. Even reproofs from authority ought to be grave, and not taunting. As for facility,* it is worse than bribery. For bribes come but now and then, but if importunity or idle respects[17] lead a man, he shall never be without. As Salomon saith, *To respect persons is not good; for such a man will transgress for a piece of bread.*[18] It is most true that was anciently spoken, *A place showeth the man.*[19] And it showeth some to the better, and some to the worse. *Omnium consensu capax imperii, nisi imperasset*[20] saith Tacitus of Galba, but of Vespasian he saith *Solus imperantium, Vespasianus mutatus in melius,*[21] though the one was meant of sufficiency,[22] the other of manners and affection.* It is an assured sign of a worthy and generous spirit, whom honour amends. For honour is, or should be, the place of virtue; and as in nature things move violently to their place and calmly in their place, so virtue in ambition is violent, in authority settled and calm. All rising to great place is by a winding stair, and if there be factions, it is good to side a man's self whilst he is in the rising, and to balance himself when he is placed. Use the memory of thy predecessor fairly and tenderly, for if thou dost not, it is a debt will sure be paid when thou art gone. If thou have colleagues, respect them, and rather call them when they look not for it, than exclude them when they have reason to look to be called. Be not too sensible or too remembering[23] of thy place in conversation and private answers to suitors, but let it rather be said, *When he sits in place he is another man.*

---

[15] intimate.

[16] secret, hidden.

[17] considerations, preferences.

[18] Proverbs 28:21.

[19] variously attributed to Solon, Bias, and Epaminondas.

[20] "Even had he not been emperor, all would have pronounced him fit to rule." *Hist.*, I.49.

[21] "Vespasian alone amongst the emperors changed for the better." *Hist.*, I.50.

[22] ability, capacity.

[23] mindful.

XII. OF BOLDNESS

It is a trivial[1] grammar-school text, but yet worthy a wise man's consideration. Question was asked of Demosthenes, *what was the chief part of an orator?* he answered, *action*; what next? *action*; what next again? *action*.[2] He said it that knew it best, and had by nature himself no advantage in that he commended. A strange thing that that part of an orator which is but superficial and rather the virtue of a player should be placed so high above those other noble parts of invention, elocution, and the rest; nay almost alone, as if it were all in all. But the reason is plain. There is in human nature generally more of the fool than of the wise; and therefore those faculties by which the foolish part of men's minds is taken are most potent. Wonderful like is the case of Boldness in civil business; what first? Boldness; what second and third? Boldness. And yet boldness is a child of ignorance and baseness, far inferior to other parts. But nevertheless it doth fascinate and bind hand and foot those that are either shallow in judgment or weak in courage, which are the greatest part; yea and prevaileth with wise men at weak times. Therefore we see it hath done wonders in popular[3] states, but with senates and princes less; and more ever upon the first entrance of bold persons into action than soon after, for boldness is an ill keeper of promise. Surely as there are mountebanks for the natural body, so are there mountebanks for the politic body, men that undertake great cures, and perhaps have been lucky in two or three experiments, but want the grounds of science, and therefore cannot hold out. Nay you shall see a bold fellow many times do Mahomet's miracle. Mahomet made the people believe that he would call an hill to him, and from the top of it offer up his prayers for the observers of his law. The people assembled; Mahomet called the hill to come to him, again and again; and when the hill stood still, he was never a whit abashed, but said,

---

[1] trite.

[2] See Cicero, *On the Orator*, III.lvi. 213. *Action* here means "speaking, orating".

[3] democratic.

If the hill will not come to Mahomet, Mahomet will go to the hill. So these men, when they have promised great matters and failed most shamefully, yet (if they have the perfection of boldness) they will but slight it over, and make a turn, and no more ado. Certainly to men of great judgment, bold persons are a sport to behold; nay and to the vulgar also, boldness has somewhat of the ridiculous. For if absurdity be the subject of laughter, doubt you not but great boldness is seldom without some absurdity. Especially it is a sport to see, when a bold fellow is out of countenance, for that puts his face into a most shrunken and wooden posture, as needs it must, for in bashfulness the spirits do a little go and come; but with bold men, upon like occasion they stand at a stay, like a stale⁴ at chess, where it is no mate, but yet the game cannot stir. But this last were fitter for a satire than for a serious observation. This is well to be weighed, that boldness is ever blind, for it seeth not dangers and inconveniences. Therefore it is ill in counsel, good in execution; so that the right use of bold persons is that they never command in chief, but be seconds and under the direction of others. For in counsel it is good to see dangers, and in execution not to see them, except they be very great.

XIII. OF GOODNESS AND GOODNESS OF NATURE

I TAKE Goodness in this sense, the affecting* of the weal of men, which is that the Grecians call *Philanthropia*; and the word *humanity* (as it is used) is a little too light to express it. Goodness I call the habit, and Goodness of Nature the inclination. This of all virtues and dignities of the mind is the greatest, being the character of the Deity, and without it man is a busy, mischievous, wretched thing, no better than a kind of vermin. Goodness answers to the theological virtue Charity, and admits no excess but error. The desire of power in excess caused the angels to fall; the desire of knowledge in excess caused man to fall: but in

⁴ stalemate.

charity there is no excess; neither can angel or man come in danger by it. The inclination to goodness is imprinted deeply in the nature of man, insomuch that if it issue not towards men, it will take unto other living creatures, as it is seen in the Turks, a cruel people, who nevertheless are kind to beasts, and give alms to dogs and birds; insomuch as Busbechius[1] reporteth, a Christian boy in Constantinople had like to have been stoned for gagging in a waggishness a long-billed fowl. Errors indeed in this virtue of goodness or charity may be committed. The Italians have an ungracious proverb, *Tanto buon che val niente: So good, that he is good for nothing.* And one of the doctors* of Italy, Nicholas Machiavel, had the confidence to put in writing, almost in plain terms, *That the Christian faith had given up good men in prey to those that are tyrannical and unjust.*[2] Which he spake, because indeed there was never law or sect or opinion did so much magnify goodness as the Christian religion doth. Therefore, to avoid the scandal and the danger both, it is good to take knowledge of the errors of an habit so excellent. Seek the good of other men, but be not in bondage to their faces or fancies, for that is but facility* or softness, which taketh an honest mind prisoner. Neither give thou Aesop's cock a gem, who would be better pleased and happier if he had a barleycorn.[3] The example of God teacheth the lesson truly: *He sendeth his rain, and maketh his sun to shine upon the just and unjust;*[4] but he doth not rain wealth nor shine honour and virtues upon men equally. Common benefits are to be communicate with all, but peculiar benefits with choice. And beware how in making the portraiture thou breakest the pattern. For divinity maketh the love of ourselves the pattern, the love of our neighbours but the portraiture. *Sell all thou hast, and give it to the poor, and follow me,*[5] but sell not all thou hast, except thou come and follow me; that is, except thou have a vocation wherein thou mayest do as much

---

[1] Augier Ghislein de Busbecq (1522-92): Flemish traveller and diplomat; see his *Letters from a Turkish Legation*, III.

[2] See Machiavelli, *Discourses on Livy*, II.2.

[3] See Phaedrus, III.12.

[4] Matt. 5:45.

[5] Mark 10:21.

good with little means as with great, for otherwise in feeding the streams thou driest the fountain. Neither is there only a habit of goodness, directed by right reason, but there is in some men, even in nature, a disposition towards it, as on the other side there is a natural malignity. For there be that in their nature do not affect* the good of others. The lighter sort of malignity turneth but to a crossness or frowardness or aptness to oppose or difficilness⁶ or the like, but the deeper sort to envy and mere mischief. Such men in other men's calamities are, as it were, in season, and are ever on the loading part;⁷ not so good as the dogs that licked Lazarus' sores, but like flies that are still buzzing upon any thing that is raw, *misanthropi*, that make it their practice to bring men to the bough, and yet have never a tree for the purpose in their gardens, as Timon had.⁸ Such dispositions are the very errors of human nature, and yet they are the fittest timber to make great politiques⁹ of; like to knee timber,¹⁰ that is good for ships, that are ordained to be tossed, but not for building houses, that shall stand firm. The parts and signs of goodness are many. If a man be gracious and courteous to strangers, it shows he is a citizen of the world, and that his heart is no island cut off from other lands, but a continent that joins to them. If he be compassionate towards the afflictions of others, it shows that his heart is like the noble tree that is wounded itself when it gives the balm.¹¹ If he easily pardons and remits offences, it shows that his mind is planted above injuries, so that he cannot be shot. If he be thankful for small benefits, it shows that he weighs men's minds, and not their trash. But above all, if he have St. Paul's perfection, that he would wish to be an *anathema* from Christ for the salvation of his brethren,¹² it shows much of a divine nature and a kind of conformity with Christ himself.

---

⁶ obstinacy.

⁷ flourish, and aggravate calamities. For the following reference to Lazarus, see Luke 16:21.

⁸ According to Plutarch (*Antony*, 70), Timon of Athens (fifth century B.C.), the type of the misanthrope, announced publicly that he intended to cut down a fig tree in his garden, and that anyone wish-ing to hang himself from it should hurry to do so. Cf. Shakespeare, *Timon of Athens*, V.i.208ff.

⁹ politicians.

¹⁰ timber with natural knees or angles in it.

¹¹ the frankincense tree; see Pliny, *Natural History*, XII.14.

¹² Cf. Romans 9:3.

XIV. OF NOBILITY

WE will speak of Nobility first as a portion of an estate,[1] then as a condition of particular persons. A monarchy where there is no nobility at all is ever a pure and absolute tyranny, as that of the Turks. For nobility attempers sovereignty, and draws the eyes of the people somewhat aside from the line royal. But for* democracies, they need it not; and they are commonly more quiet and less subject to sedition than where there are stirps of nobles. For men's eyes are upon the business and not upon the persons; or if upon the persons, it is for the business' sake, as fittest, and not for flags and pedigree. We see the Switzers last well, notwithstanding their diversity of religion and of cantons. For utility is their bond, and not respects.[2] The united provinces of the Low Countries in their government excel, for where there is an equality, the consultations are more indifferent,* and the payments and tributes more cheerful. A great and potent nobility addeth majesty to a monarch, but diminisheth power; and putteth life and spirit into the people, but presseth their fortune. It is well when nobles are not too great for sovereignty nor for justice, and yet maintained in that height, as the insolency of inferiors may be broken upon them before it come on too fast upon the majesty of kings. A numerous nobility causeth poverty and inconvenience in a state, for it is a surcharge of expense; and besides, it being of necessity that many of the nobility fall in time to be weak in fortune, it maketh a kind of disproportion between honour and means.

As for nobility in particular persons, it is a reverend thing to see an ancient castle or building not in decay, or to see a fair timber tree sound and perfect. How much more to behold an ancient noble family, which hath stood against the waves and weathers of time. For new nobility is but the act of power, but ancient nobility is the act of time. Those that are first raised to nobility are commonly more virtuous but less innocent than their descendants, for there is rarely any rising but by a com-

---

[1] state.   [2] regard for rank.

mixture of good and evil arts. But it is reason* the memory of their virtues remain to their posterity, and their faults die with themselves. Nobility of birth commonly abateth industry, and he that is not industrious, envieth him that is. Besides, noble persons cannot go much higher, and he that standeth at a stay³ when others rise can hardly avoid motions of envy. On the other side, nobility extinguisheth the passive⁴ envy from others towards them, because they are in possession of honour. Certainly, kings that have able men of their nobility shall find ease in employing them, and a better slide into their business, for people naturally bend to them, as born in some sort to command.

XV. OF SEDITIONS AND TROUBLES

SHEPHERDS of people had need know the calendars of tempests in state, which are commonly greatest when things grow to equality, as natural tempests are greatest about the *Equinoctia*. And as there are certain hollow blasts of wind and secret swellings of seas before a tempest, so are there in states:

> ——*Ille etiam cæcos instare tumultus*
> *Sæpe monet, fraudesque et operta tumescere bella.*¹

Libels and licentious discourses against the state, when they are frequent and open, and in like sort, false news often running up and down to the disadvantage of the state, and hastily embraced are amongst the signs of troubles. Virgil, giving the pedigree of Fame,² saith *she was sister to the Giants*:

> *Illam Terra parens, ira irritata Deorum,*
> *Extremam (ut perhibent) Cæo Enceladoque sororem*
> *Progenuit.*³

As if fames were the relics of seditions past, but they are no less

---

³ standstill.

⁴ i.e., subjection or liability to envy.

¹ "He [the sun] often gives warning that dark troubles are imminent and that treachery and secret wars are brewing." Virgil, *Georgics*,

I.464-5.

² Rumour.

³ "Enraged against the gods, earth gave birth to her, her last child (so they say), sister to Caeus and Enceladus." *Aeneid*, IV.178-80.

indeed the preludes of seditions to come. Howsoever he noteth it right, that seditious tumults and seditious fames differ no more but as brother and sister, masculine and feminine; especially if it come to that, that the best actions of a state, and the most plausible,* and which ought to give greatest contentment, are taken in ill sense and traduced; for that shows the envy great, as Tacitus saith: *Conflata magna invidia, seu bene seu male gesta premunt.*[4] Neither doth it follow that because these fames are a sign of troubles, that the suppressing of them with too much severity should be a remedy of troubles. For the despising of them many times checks them best, and the going about to stop them doth but make a wonder long-lived. Also that kind of obedience which Tacitus speaketh of is to be held suspected: *Erant in officio, sed tamen qui mallent mandata imperantium interpretari quam exequi;*[5] disputing, excusing, cavilling upon mandates and directions is a kind of shaking off the yoke and assay of disobedience, especially if in those disputings they which are for the direction speak fearfully and tenderly, and those that are against it audaciously.

Also, as Machiavel noteth well,[6] when princes, that ought to be common parents, make themselves as a party, and lean to a side, it is as a boat that is overthrown by uneven weight on the one side; as was well seen in the time of Henry the Third of France, for first himself entered league for the extirpation of the Protestants, and presently after the same league was turned upon himself.[7] For when the authority of princes is made but an accessory to a cause, and that there be other bands that tie faster than the band of sovereignty, kings begin to be put almost out of possession.

Also, when discords and quarrels and factions are carried openly and audaciously, it is a sign the reverence of[8] government is lost. For the motions of the greatest persons in a government

[4] "Once bad feelings are aroused [by a ruler], good and bad acts alike offend." *Hist.*, I.7.

[5] "They were on duty, but still they preferred to discuss rather than to obey the orders of their leaders." *Hist.*, II.39.

[6] perhaps in his *Discourses on Livy,* III.27.

[7] The Holy League was organized in 1576 by the Duc de Guise to ensure Catholic succession to the French throne.

[8] for.

ought to be as the motions of the planets under *primum mobile* (according to the old opinion), which is, that every of them is carried swiftly by the highest motion and softly in their own motion. And therefore, when great ones in their own particular motion move violently, and, as Tacitus expresseth it well, *liberius quam ut imperantium meminissent,*[9] it is a sign the orbs are out of frame. For reverence is that wherewith princes are girt from God, who threateneth the dissolving thereof: *Solvam cingula regum.*[10]

So when any of the four pillars of government are mainly[11] shaken or weakened (which are Religion, Justice, Counsel, and Treasure), men had need to pray for fair weather. But let us pass from this part of predictions (concerning which, nevertheless, more light may be taken from that which followeth); and let us speak first of the Materials of seditions; then of the Motives of them; and thirdly of the Remedies.

Concerning the Materials of seditions. It is a thing well to be considered, for the surest way to prevent seditions (if the times do bear it) is to take away the matter of them. For if there be fuel prepared, it is hard to tell whence the spark shall come that shall set it on fire. The matter of seditions is of two kinds, much poverty and much discontentment. It is certain, so many overthrown estates, so many votes for troubles. Lucan noteth well the state of Rome before the civil war,

> *Hinc usura vorax, rapidumque in tempore fœnus,*
> *Hinc concussa fides, et multis utile bellum.*[12]

This same *multis utile bellum* is an assured and infallible sign of a state disposed to seditions and troubles. And if this poverty and broken estate in the better sort be joined with a want and necessity in the mean people, the danger is imminent and great. For the rebellions of the belly are the worst. As for discontentments, they are in the politic body like to humours in the natural, which are apt to gather a preternatural heat and to

---

[9] "more freely than is consistent with obedience to authority". Cf. *Ann.*, III.4.

[10] "I will loose the girdles of kings." Cf. Job 12:18 and Isaiah 45:1.

[11] strongly, greatly.

[12] "Devouring usury, greedy for the reckoning day, shaken credit, war a gain to many." *Pharsalia*, I.181.

inflame. And let no prince measure the danger of them by this, whether they be just or unjust, for that were to imagine people to be too reasonable, who do often spurn at their own good; nor yet by this, whether the griefs[13] whereupon they rise be in fact great or small, for they are the most dangerous discontentments where the fear is greater than the feeling: *Dolendi modus, timendi non item*.[14] Besides, in great oppressions the same things that provoke the patience do withal mate the courage, but in fears it is not so. Neither let any prince or state be secure concerning discontentments, because they have been often, or have been long, and yet no peril hath ensued; for as it is true that every vapour or fume doth not turn into a storm, so it is nevertheless true that storms, though they blow over divers times, yet may fall at last; and, as the Spanish proverb noteth well, *The cord breaketh at the last by the weakest pull*.

The Causes and Motives of seditions are: innovation in religion, taxes, alteration of laws and customs, breaking of privileges, general oppression, advancement of unworthy persons, strangers, dearths, disbanded soldiers, factions grown desperate, and whatsoever in offending people joineth and knitteth them in a common cause.

For the Remedies, there may be some general preservatives, whereof we will speak; as for the just cure, it must answer to the particular disease, and so be left to counsel rather than rule.

The first remedy or prevention is to remove by all means possible that material cause of sedition whereof we spake, which is want and poverty in the estate. To which purpose serveth the opening and well-balancing of trade, the cherishing of manufactures, the banishing of idleness, the repressing of waste and excess by sumptuary laws, the improvement and husbanding of the soil, the regulating of prices of things vendible, the moderating of taxes and tributes and the like. Generally, it is to be foreseen[15] that the population of a kingdom (especially if it be not mown down by wars) do not exceed the stock of the kingdom

---

[13] grievances.

[14] "There is a limit to suffering, but not to fear." Pliny the Younger, *Epistles*, VIII.17.

[15] provided.

which should maintain them. Neither is the population to be reckoned only by number, for a smaller number that spend more and earn less do wear out an estate sooner than a greater number that live lower and gather more. Therefore the multiplying of nobility and other degrees of quality in an over proportion to the common people doth speedily bring a state to necessity; and so doth likewise an overgrown clergy, for they bring nothing to the stock; and in like manner, when more are bred scholars than preferments can take off.

It is likewise to be remembered that forasmuch as the increase of any estate must be upon the foreigner (for whatsoever is somewhere gotten is somewhere lost), there be but three things which one nation selleth unto another: the commodity as nature yieldeth it; the manufacture; and the vecture, or carriage. So that if these three wheels go, wealth will flow as in a spring tide. And it cometh many times to pass that *materiam superabit opus*,[16] that the work and carriage is more worth than the material, and enricheth a state more, as is notably seen in the Low Countrymen, who have the best mines above ground in the world.

Above all things, good policy is to be used that the treasure and monies in a state be not gathered into few hands. For otherwise a state may have a great stock and yet starve. And money is like muck, not good except it be spread. This is done chiefly by suppressing, or at the least keeping a strait hand upon the devouring trades of usury, ingrossing,[17] great pasturages, and the like.

For removing discontentments, or at least the danger of them, there is in every state (as we know) two portions of subjects: the noblesse and the commonalty. When one of these is discontent, the danger is not great, for common people are of slow motion, if they be not excited by the greater sort; and the greater sort are of small strength, except the multitude be apt and ready to move of themselves. Then is the danger, when the greater sort do but wait for the troubling of the waters amongst the meaner,

[16] See Ovid, *Metamorphoses*, II.5.
[17] engrossing. Great pasturages refers to the practice of turning arable land into sheep runs or pastures.

that then they may declare themselves. The poets feign that the rest of the gods would have bound Jupiter, which he hearing of, by the counsel of Pallas, sent for Briareus, with his hundred hands, to come in to his aid.[18] An emblem, no doubt, to show how safe it is for monarchs to make sure of the good will of common people.

To give moderate liberty for griefs and discontentments to evaporate (so it be without too great insolency or bravery) is a safe way. For he that turneth the humours back, and maketh the wound bleed inwards endangereth malign ulcers and pernicious imposthumations.[19]

The part of Epimetheus mought[20] well become Prometheus in the case of discontentments, for there is not a better provision against them. Epimetheus, when griefs and evils flew abroad, at last shut the lid, and kept hope in the bottom of the vessel.[21] Certainly the politic and artificial[22] nourishing and entertaining of hopes and carrying men from hopes to hopes is one of the best antidotes against the poison of discontentments. And it is a certain sign of a wise government and proceeding, when it can hold men's hearts by hopes, when it cannot by satisfaction; and when it can handle things in such manner as no evil shall appear so peremptory but that it hath some outlet of hope, which is the less hard to do, because both particular persons and factions are apt enough to flatter themselves, or at least to brave that[23] they believe not.

Also the foresight and prevention, that there be no likely or fit head whereunto discontented persons may resort, and under whom they may join, is a known but an excellent point of caution. I understand a fit head to be one that hath greatness

18 Briareus: son of Uranus (Heaven) by Gaea (Earth), a huge monster with a hundred hands and fifty heads. Cf. Homer, *Iliad*, I.396-406.

19 i.e., runs the risk of malignant ulcers and pernicious abscesses.

20 might.

21 In order to take revenge on Prometheus (Forethought) for stealing fire from heaven to give to man-

kind, and to punish mankind at the same time, Zeus gave Pandora to Epimetheus (Afterthought), the brother of Prometheus. Pandora brought with her a box which Epimetheus rashly opened, with the result that Bacon describes.

22 skilful, with artifice.

23 that which; what.

and reputation, that hath confidence with the discontented party, and upon whom they turn their eyes, and that is thought discontented in his own particular:[24] which kind of persons are either to be won and reconciled to the state, and that in a fast and true manner, or to be fronted with some other of the same party, that may oppose them, and so divide the reputation. Generally the dividing and breaking of all factions and combinations that are adverse to the state, and setting them at distance, or at least distrust, amongst themselves is not one of the worst remedies. For it is a desperate case, if those that hold with the proceeding of the state be full of discord and faction, and those that are against it be entire and united.

I have noted that some witty and sharp speeches which have fallen from princes have given fire to seditions. Cæsar did himself infinite hurt in that speech, *Sylla nescivit literas, non potuit dictare*,[25] for it did utterly cut off that hope which men had entertained, that he would at one time or other give over his dictatorship. Galba undid himself by that speech, *Legi a se militem, non emi*,[26] for it put the soldiers out of hope of the donative. Probus likewise, by that speech, *Si vixero, non opus erit amplius Romano imperio militibus*,[27] a speech of great despair for the soldiers. And many the like. Surely princes had need in tender matters and ticklish times to beware what they say, especially in these short speeches, which fly abroad like darts, and are thought to be shot out of their secret intentions. For as for large discourses, they are flat things, and not so much noted.

Lastly, let princes, against all events, not be without some great person, one or rather more, of military valour, near unto them for the repressing of seditions in their beginnings. For without that there useth[28] to be more trepidation in court upon the first breaking out of troubles than were fit. And the state

[24] private affairs.

[25] "Sulla did not know his letters: he could not dictate." Suetonius, *Julius Caesar*, 77.

[26] "I do not buy soldiers but enlist them." See Tacitus, *Hist.*, I.5.

[27] "If I live, the Roman Empire will no longer need soldiers." Flavius Vopiscus, *Probus*, XX. Marcus Aurelius Probus was Roman emperor A.D. 276-82.

[28] generally (is).

runneth the danger of that which Tacitus saith: *Atque is habitus animorum fuit, ut pessimum facinus auderent pauci, plures vellent, omnes paterentur.*[29] But let such military persons be assured[30] and well reputed of, rather than factious and popular,[31] holding also good correspondence[32] with the other great men in the state, or else the remedy is worse than the disease.

XVI. OF ATHEISM

I HAD rather believe all the fables in the Legend,[1] and the Talmud, and the Alcoran than that this universal frame is without a mind. And therefore God never wrought miracle to convince[2] atheism, because his ordinary works convince it. It is true that a little philosophy inclineth man's mind to atheism, but depth in philosophy bringeth men's minds about to religion. For while the mind of man looketh upon second causes scattered, it may sometimes rest in them, and go no further; but when it beholdeth the chain of them, confederate and linked together, it must needs fly to Providence and Deity. Nay, even that school which is most accused of atheism doth most demonstrate religion; that is, the school of Leucippus and Democritus and Epicurus.[3] For it is a thousand times more credible that four mutable elements and one immutable fifth essence, duly and eternally placed, need no God, than that an army of infinite small portions or seeds unplaced should have produced this order and beauty without a divine marshal. The scripture saith, *The fool hath said in his*

---

[29] "Such was the general state of mind that, while only a few dared the worst crime, many wished it done, and all acquiesced in it." *Hist.,* I.28.

[30] trustworthy.

[31] courting favour with the people.

[32] equally matched with.

[1] i.e., the *Golden Legend.*

[2] refute.

[3] Leucippus founded the Atomic philosophy about the fifth century B.C., Democritus (460?-361 B.C.) developed it, and Epicurus (342-270 B.C.) adopted it. It taught, amongst other things, that the physical universe is composed of indivisible, unchanging particles or atoms moving without direction or purpose in a void. In the next sentence Bacon contrasts it to the Aristotelian view.

heart, there is no God;[4] it is not said, *The fool hath thought in his heart;* so as he rather saith it by rote to himself, as that* he would have, than that he can thoroughly believe it, or be persuaded of it. For none deny there is a God, but those for whom it maketh[5] that there were no God. It appeareth in nothing more, that atheism is rather in the lip than in the heart of man, than by this: that atheists will ever be talking of that their opinion, as if they fainted in it within themselves, and would be glad to be strengthened by the consent of others. Nay more, you shall have atheists strive to get disciples, as it fareth with other sects. And, which is most of all, you shall have of[6] them that will suffer for atheism, and not recant; whereas if they did truly think that there were no such thing as God, why should they trouble themselves? Epicurus is charged that he did but dissemble for his credit's sake, when he affirmed there were blessed natures, but such as enjoyed themselves without having respect* to the government of the world. Wherein they say he did temporize, though in secret he thought there was no God. But certainly he is traduced, for his words are noble and divine: *Non Deos vulgi negare profanum; sed vulgi opiniones Diis applicare profanum.*[7] Plato could have said no more. And although he had the confidence to deny the administration, he had not the power to deny the nature.[8] The Indians of the west have names for their particular gods, though they have no name for God, as if the heathens should have had the names Jupiter, Apollo, Mars, &c. but not the word *Deus*, which shows that even those barbarous people have the notion, though they have not the latitude and extent of it. So that against atheists the very savages take part with the very subtlest philosophers. The contemplative atheist is rare: a Diagoras, a Bion, a Lucian[9] perhaps, and some others;

---

[4] Psalms 14:1 and 53:1.

[5] to whose advantage it is.

[6] amongst.

[7] "Profanity does not consist in denying the gods of the common people, but rather in applying to the gods the conceptions of the common people." Diogenes Laertius, X.123. Cf. Cicero, *On the Nature of the*

Gods, I.44.

[8] i.e., although he denied the rule of God in the world, he did not deny the existence of God.

[9] Diagoras of Melos lived in the fifth century B.C., Bion of Scythia in the third century B.C., and Lucian of Samosata in the second century A.D.

and yet they seem to be more than they are, for that all that impugn a received religion or superstition are by the adverse part branded with the name of atheists. But the great atheists indeed are hypocrites, which are ever handling holy things, but without feeling; so as they must needs be cauterized in the end. The causes of atheism are divisions in religion, if they be many; for any one main division addeth zeal to both sides, but many divisions introduce atheism. Another is scandal of priests, when it is come to that which St. Bernard saith, *Non est jam dicere, ut populus sic sacerdos; quia nec sic populus ut sacerdos.*[10] A third is custom of profane scoffing in holy matters, which doth by little and little deface the reverence of religion. And lastly, learned times, specially with peace and prosperity, for troubles and adversities do more bow men's minds to religion. They that deny a God destroy man's nobility, for certainly man is of kin to the beasts by his body, and if he be not of kin to God by his spirit, he is a base and ignoble creature. It destroys likewise magnanimity and the raising of human nature; for take an example of a dog, and mark what a generosity[11] and courage he will put on when he finds himself maintained by a man, who to him is instead of a God, or *melior natura,*[12] which courage is manifestly such as that creature, without that confidence of a better nature than his own, could never attain. So man, when he resteth and assureth himself upon divine protection and favour, gathereth a force and faith which human nature in itself could not obtain. Therefore, as atheism is in all respects hateful, so in this, that it depriveth human nature of the means to exalt itself above human frailty. As it is in particular persons, so it is in nations. Never was there such a state for magnanimity as Rome. Of this state hear what Cicero saith: *Quam volumus licet, patres conscripti, nos amemus, tamen nec numero Hispanos, nec robore Gallos, nec calliditate Pœnos, nec artibus Græcos, nec denique hoc ipso hujus gentis et terræ domestico nativoque sensu Italos*

---

10 "One cannot now say, as the people so the priest, for it no longer holds, as the priest so the people" [i.e., they are better]. *A Sermon to the Clergy.*

11 nobility.

12 "better nature". Ovid, *Met.*, I.21.

ipsos et Latinos; sed pietate, ac religione, atque hac una sapientia, quod Deorum immortalium numine omnia regi gubernarique perspeximus, omnes gentes nationesque superavimus.[13]

XVII. OF SUPERSTITION

IT were better to have no opinion of God at all than such an opinion as is unworthy of him. For the one is unbelief, the other is contumely, and certainly superstition is the reproach of the Deity. Plutarch saith well to that purpose: *Surely* (saith he) *I had rather a great deal men should say there was no such man at all as Plutarch, than that they should say that there was one Plutarch that would eat his children as soon as they were born;* as the poets speak of Saturn.[1] And as the contumely is greater towards God, so the danger is greater towards men. Atheism leaves a man to sense, to philosophy, to natural piety, to laws, to reputation, all which may be guides to an outward moral virtue, though religion were not, but superstition dismounts all these, and erecteth an absolute monarchy in the minds of men. Therefore atheism did never perturb states, for it makes men wary of themselves, as looking no further, and we see the times inclined to atheism (as the time of Augustus Cæsar) were civil times. But superstition hath been the confusion of many states, and bringeth in a new *primum mobile*, that ravisheth all the spheres of government. The master of superstition is the people, and in all superstition wise men follow fools, and arguments are fitted to practice in a reversed order. It was gravely said by some of the prelates in the Council of Trent, where the doctrine of the

---

[13] "No matter how highly we regard ourselves, we do not surpass the Spaniards in numbers, nor the Gauls in strength, nor the Carthaginians in cunning, nor the Greeks in art, nor finally the Italians and Latins themselves in their native feelings for race and country; but in piety and religion, in the belief – and in this is our only wisdom – that all things are guided and governed by the power of the immortal gods, we surpass all nations and peoples." Cicero, *On the Responses of the Soothsayers*, IX.19.

---

[1] *On Superstition*, X. Saturn here is Chronos (Cronus, Kronos), who devoured his children as soon as they were born.

schoolmen bare great sway, *that the schoolmen were like astrono-mers, which did feign eccentrics*[2] *and epicycles and such engines of orbs*[3] *to save the phænomena, though they knew there were no such things;* and in like manner, that the schoolmen had framed a number of subtle and intricate axioms and theorems to save the practice of the church. The causes of superstition are: pleasing and sensual[4] rites and ceremonies; excess of outward and phari-saical holiness; over-great reverence of traditions, which cannot but load the church; the stratagems of prelates for their own ambition and lucre; the favouring too much of good intentions, which openeth the gate to conceits* and novelties; the taking an aim at divine matters by human, which cannot but breed mix-ture of imaginations; and, lastly, barbarous times, especially joined with calamities and disasters. Superstition without a veil is a deformed thing, for as it addeth deformity to an ape to be so like a man, so the similitude of superstition to religion makes it the more deformed. And as wholesome meat corrupteth to little worms, so good forms and orders corrupt into a number of petty observances. There is a superstition in avoiding superstition, when men think to do best if they go furthest from the supersti-tion formerly received; therefore care would be had that (as it fareth in ill purgings) the good be not taken away with the bad, which commonly is done when the people is the reformer.

XVIII. OF TRAVEL

TRAVEL in the younger sort is a part of education, in the elder, a part of experience. He that travelleth into a country before he hath some entrance into the language goeth to school, and not to travel. That young men travel under some tutor or grave servant, I allow[1] well, so* that he be such a one that hath the language, and hath been in the country before, whereby he may be able to

[2] a modification of the Ptolemaic astronomy which (to account for seeming irregularities) postulated that the centre of the orbits of the planets was some distance from the earth.

[3] i.e., manufacturing of orbits.

[4] sensuous.

[1] approve.

tell them what things are worthy to be seen in the country where
they go, what acquaintances they are to seek, what exercises or
discipline the place yieldeth. For else young men shall go hooded,
and look abroad little. It is a strange thing that in sea voyages,
where there is nothing to be seen but sky and sea, men should
make diaries, but in land travel, wherein so much is to be observed, for the most part they omit it, as if chance were fitter to
be registered than observation. Let diaries therefore be brought
in use. The things to be seen and observed are: the courts of
princes, specially when they give audience to ambassadors; the
courts of justice, while they sit and hear causes, and so of consis-
tories ecclesiastic; the churches and monasteries, with the monuments which are therein extant; the walls and fortifications of
cities and towns, and so the havens and harbours; antiquities
and ruins; libraries; colleges, disputations, and lectures, where
any are; shipping and navies; houses and gardens of state and
pleasure near great cities; armories; arsenals; magazines; exchanges; burses; warehouses; exercises of horsemanship, fencing,
training of soldiers, and the like; comedies, such whereunto the
better sort of persons do resort; treasuries of jewels and robes;
cabinets and rarities; and, to conclude, whatsoever is memorable
in the places where they go. After all which the tutors or servants
ought to make diligent inquiry. As for triumphs, masks, feasts,
weddings, funerals, capital executions, and such shows, men need
not to be put in mind of them, yet are they not to be neglected.
If you will have a young man to put his travel into a little room,
and in short time to gather much, this you must do. First as was
said, he must have some entrance into the language before he
goeth. Then he must have such a servant or tutor as knoweth the
country, as was likewise said. Let him carry with him also some
card[2] or book describing the country where he travelleth, which
will be a good key to his inquiry. Let him keep also a diary. Let
him not stay long in one city or town; more or less as the place
deserveth, but not long; nay, when he stayeth in one city or
town, let him change his lodging from one end and part of the

[2] chart.

town to another, which is a great adamant[3] of acquaintance. Let him sequester himself from the company of his countrymen, and diet in such places where there is good company of the nation where he travelleth. Let him upon his removes from one place to another procure recommendation to some person of quality residing in the place whither he removeth, that he may use his favour in those things he desireth to see or know. Thus he may abridge his travel with much profit. As for the acquaintance which is to be sought in travel, that which is most of all profitable is acquaintance with the secretaries and employed men of ambassadors, for so in travelling in one country he shall suck the experience of many. Let him also see and visit eminent persons in all kinds, which are of great name abroad, that he may be able to tell how the life agreeth with the fame.* For* quarrels, they are with care and discretion to be avoided. They are commonly for mistresses, healths, place, and words. And let a man beware how he keepeth company with choleric and quarrelsome persons, for they will engage him into their own quarrels. When a traveller returneth home, let him not leave the countries where he hath travelled altogether behind him, but maintain a correspondence by letters with those of his acquaintance which are of most worth. And let his travel appear rather in his discourse than in his apparel or gesture, and in his discourse let him be rather advised in his answers than forward to tell stories, and let it appear that he doth not change his country manners[4] for those of foreign parts, but only prick in[5] some flowers of that he hath learned abroad into the customs of his own country.

XIX. OF EMPIRE

IT is a miserable state of mind to have few things to desire and many things to fear; and yet that commonly is the case of kings, who, being at the highest, want matter of desire, which makes their minds more languishing, and have many representations of

---

[3] magnet.   [5] plant.
[4] i.e., manners of his own country.

perils and shadows, which makes their minds the less clear. And this is one reason also of that effect which the Scripture speaketh of, *That the king's heart is inscrutable.*[1] For multitude of jealousies and lack of some predominant desire that should marshal and put in order all the rest maketh any man's heart hard to find or sound. Hence it comes likewise, that princes many times make themselves desires, and set their hearts upon toys: sometimes upon a building; sometimes upon erecting of an order; sometimes upon the advancing of a person; sometimes upon obtaining excellency in some art or feat of the hand, as Nero for playing on the harp, Domitian for certainty of the hand with the arrow, Commodus for playing at fence, Caracalla for driving chariots, and the like. This seemeth incredible unto those that know not the principle *that the mind of man is more cheered and refreshed by profiting in small things than by standing at a stay in great.* We see also that kings that have been fortunate conquerors in their first years, it being not possible for them to go forward infinitely, but that they must have some check or arrest in their fortunes, turn in their latter years to be superstitious and melancholy, as did Alexander the Great, Diocletian, and in our memory, Charles the Fifth, and others; for he that is used to go forward and findeth a stop, falleth out of his own favour, and is not the thing he was.

To speak now of the true temper of empire, it is a thing rare and hard to keep, for both temper and distemper[2] consist of contraries. But it is one thing to mingle contraries, another to interchange them. The answer of Apollonius to Vespasian is full of excellent instruction. Vespasian asked him, *what was Nero's overthrow?* He answered, *Nero could touch and tune the harp well; but in government sometimes he used to wind the pins too high, sometimes to let them down too low.*[3] And certain it is that nothing destroyeth authority so much as the unequal and

---

[1] Proverbs 25:3.

[2] temper: mixing, i.e., the proper mixing or blending of temperament (severity with indulgence); distemper is not a mixing but a capricious transition from one temperament to another.

[3] See Philostratus's life of Apollonius, V.28. Apollonius Tyanensis (born *c.* 4 B.C.) was a Neo-Pythagorean philosopher who pretended to magical powers.

untimely interchange of power pressed too far and relaxed too much.

This is true, that the wisdom of all these latter times in princes' affairs is rather fine deliveries[4] and shiftings of dangers and mischiefs when they are near, than solid and grounded courses to keep them aloof. But this is but to try masteries with fortune. And let men beware how they neglect and suffer matter of trouble to be prepared, for no man can forbid the spark, nor tell whence it may come. The difficulties in princes' business are many and great, but the greatest difficulty is often in their own mind. For it is common with princes (saith Tacitus) to will contradictories: *Sunt plerumque regum voluntates vehementes, et inter se contrariæ.*[5] For it is the solecism of power to think to command the end, and yet not to endure the mean.[6]

Kings have to deal with their neighbours, their wives, their children, their prelates or clergy, their nobles, their second-nobles or gentlemen, their merchants, their commons, and their men of war, and from all these arise dangers, if care and circumspection be not used.

First for* their neighbours: there can no general rule be given (the occasions are so variable), save one, which ever holdeth, which is, that princes do keep due sentinel that none of their neighbours do overgrow so (by increase of territory, by embracing of trade, by approaches, or the like) as they become more able to annoy them than they were. And this is generally the work of standing counsels to foresee and to hinder it. During that triumvirate of kings, King Henry the Eighth of England, Francis the First King of France, and Charles the Fifth Emperor, there was such a watch kept that none of the three could win a palm of ground, but the other two would straightways balance it, either by confederation or, if need were, by a war, and would not in any wise take up peace at interest.[7] And the like was done by that league (which Guicciardine[8] saith was the security of Italy) made

---

[4] i.e., skilful escapes.

[5] "As a rule the desires of kings are violent and inconsistent." Not Tacitus but Sallust, *The History of the War with Jugurtha*, CXIII. [Wright]

[6] means.

[7] i.e., purchase a peace now that will cost much later.

[8] Francesco Guicciardini (Florentine historian, 1483-1540), *Hist.*, I.i.

between Ferdinando, King of Naples, Lorenzius Medices, and Ludovicus Sforza, potentates, the one of Florence, the other of Milan. Neither is the opinion of some of the schoolmen to be received, *that a war cannot justly be made but upon a precedent injury or provocation.*[9] For there is no question but a just fear of an imminent danger, though there be no blow given, is a lawful cause of a war.

For their wives: there are cruel examples of them. Livia is infamed[10] for the poisoning of her husband; Roxalana, Solyman's wife, was the destruction of that renowned prince Sultan Mustapha, and otherwise troubled his house and succession; Edward the Second of England his queen had the principal hand in the deposing and murther of her husband.[11] This kind of danger is then to be feared chiefly, when the wives have plots for the raising of their own children, or else that they be advoutresses.[12]

For their children: the tragedies likewise of dangers from them have been many. And generally, the entering of fathers into suspicion of their children hath been ever unfortunate. The destruction of Mustapha (that we named before) was so fatal to Solyman's line, as the succession of the Turks from Solyman until this day is suspected to be untrue and of strange blood, for that Selymus the Second was thought to be supposititious.[13] The destruction of Crispus, a young prince of rare towardness,[14] by Constantinus the Great, his father, was in like manner fatal to his house, for both Constantinus and Constance, his sons, died violent deaths, and Constantius, his other son, did little better, who died indeed of sickness, but after that Julianus had taken arms against him. The destruction of Demetrius, son to Philip the Second of Macedon, turned upon the father, who died of re-

---

[9] perhaps St. Thomas Aquinas, *Summa Theologica*, II².Q.XL. [Wright]

[10] branded with infamy, infamous.

[11] Livia, wife of Emperor Drusus Caesar (sometimes confused with Augustus Caesar, as in the Latin translation of the *Essays*), was seduced by Sejanus, who (perhaps) persuaded her to poison her husband (A.D. 23). Roxalana, wife to Sultan Suleiman the Magnificent (*fl.* 1520-66), procured the assassination of her stepson, Mustapha, so that her own son would succeed. The wife of Edward the Second was Isabella (1292?-1358), the "she-wolf of France".

[12] adulteresses.

[13] i.e., supposititious, spurious.

[14] docility.

pentance.[15] And many like examples there are, but few or none where the fathers had good by such distrust, except it were where the sons were up in open arms against them, as was Selymus the First[16] against Bajazet, and the three sons of Henry the Second, King of England.

For their prelates: when they are proud and great, there is also danger from them, as it was in the times of Anselmus and Thomas Becket, Archbishops of Canterbury, who with their crosiers did almost try it with the king's sword, and yet they had to deal with stout and haughty kings, William Rufus, Henry the First, and Henry the Second. The danger is not from that state,[17] but where it hath a dependence of foreign authority, or where the churchmen come in and are elected, not by the collation of the king or particular patrons, but by the people.

For their nobles: to keep them at a distance, it is not amiss; but to depress them may make a king more absolute, but less safe and less able to perform any thing that he desires. I have noted it in my History of King Henry the Seventh of England, who depressed his nobility; whereupon it came to pass that his times were full of difficulties and troubles; for the nobility, though they continued loyal unto him, yet did they not co-operate with him in his business. So that in effect he was fain[18] to do all things himself.

For their second-nobles: there is not much danger from them, being a body dispersed. They may sometimes discourse high, but that doth little hurt; besides, they are a counterpoise to the higher nobility, that they grow not too potent; and, lastly, being the most immediate in authority with the common people, they do best temper popular commotions.

For their merchants: they are *vena porta*;[19] and if they flourish not, a kingdom may have good limbs, but will have empty veins, and nourish little. Taxes and imposts upon them do seldom good to the king's revenue, for that that he wins in the hundred he

---

[15] Demetrius was executed in 181 B.C. on the false accusation of his brother Perseus. Philip reigned from 220 to 179 B.C.

[16] i.e., Suleiman the Magnificent.

[17] i.e., the first estate, the clergy.

[18] obliged, forced.

[19] the "gate vein", which, it was believed, carried the blood to the liver.

leeseth[20] in the shire, the particular rates being increased, but the total bulk of trading rather decreased.

For their commons: there is little danger from them, except it be where they have great and potent heads, or where you meddle with the point of religion or their customs or means of life.

For their men of war: it is a dangerous state where they live and remain in a body, and are used to donatives; whereof we see examples in the janizaries and pretorian bands of Rome; but trainings of men and arming them in several places and under several commanders and without donatives are things of defence, and no danger.

Princes are like to heavenly bodies, which cause good or evil times, and which have much veneration but no rest. All precepts concerning kings are in effect comprehended in those two remembrances: *Memento quod es homo;* and *Memento quod es Deus, or vice Dei;*[21] the one bridleth their power, and the other their will.

XX. OF COUNSEL

THE greatest trust between man and man is the trust of giving counsel. For in other confidences men commit the parts of life, their lands, their goods, their child, their credit, some particular affair; but to such as they make their counsellors they commit the whole: by how much the more they are obliged[1] to all faith and integrity. The wisest princes need not think it any diminution to their greatness or derogation to their sufficiency to rely upon counsel. God himself is not without, but hath made it one of the great names of his blessed Son: *The Counsellor.*[2] Salomon hath pronounced that *in counsel is stability.* Things will have their first or second agitation:[3] if they be not tossed upon the arguments of counsel, they will be tossed upon the waves of fortune,

[20] loses.

[21] " 'Remember that you are a man'; and 'Remember that you are a God, or deputy of God'."

[1] bound.

[2] Isaiah 9:6. For Solomon's pronouncement, see Prov. 20:18.

[3] pun on Latin meanings of *agitare*: to toss and to discuss. [Selby]

and be full of inconstancy, doing and undoing, like the reeling of a drunken man. Salomon's son found the force of counsel, as his father saw the necessity of it.[4] For the beloved kingdom of God was first rent and broken by ill counsel, upon which counsel there are set for our instruction the two marks whereby bad counsel is for ever best discerned: that it was young counsel, for the persons, and violent counsel, for the matter.

The ancient times do set forth in figure both the incorporation and inseparable conjunction of counsel with kings and the wise and politic use of counsel by kings; the one, in that they say Jupiter did marry Metis, which signifieth counsel, whereby they intend that Sovereignty is married to Counsel; the other, in that which followeth, which was thus: They say, after Jupiter was married to Metis, she conceived by him and was with child, but Jupiter suffered her not to stay till she brought forth, but eat her up; whereby he became himself with child, and was delivered of Pallas armed, out of his head.[5] Which monstrous fable containeth a secret of empire, how kings are to make use of their council of state. That first they ought to refer matters unto them, which is the first begetting or impregnation, but when they are elaborate,[6] moulded, and shaped in the womb of their council, and grow ripe and ready to be brought forth, that then they suffer not their council to go through with the resolution and direction, as if it depended on them, but take the matter back into their own hands, and make it appear to the world that the decrees and final directions (which, because they come forth with prudence and power, are resembled to Pallas armed) proceeded from themselves; and not only from their authority, but (the more to add reputation to themselves) from their head and device.

Let us now speak of the inconveniences of counsel, and of the remedies. The inconveniences that have been noted in calling and using counsel are three. First, the revealing of affairs, whereby they become less secret. Secondly, the weakening of the authority of princes, as if they were less of themselves. Thirdly,

---

[4] I Kings 12:8.
[5] See Hesiod, *Theogony*, 886.

[6] elaborated.

the danger of being unfaithfully counselled, and more for the good of them that counsel than of him that is counselled. For which inconveniences, the doctrine of Italy and practice of France, in some kings' times, hath introduced *cabinet* councils,[7] a remedy worse than the disease.

As to secrecy, princes are not bound to communicate all matters with all counsellors, but may extract and select. Neither is it necessary that he that consulteth what he should do should declare what he will do. But let princes beware that the unsecreting of their affairs comes not from themselves. And as for cabinet councils, it may be their motto, *Plenus rimarum sum;*[8] one futile person that maketh it his glory to tell will do more hurt than many that know it their duty to conceal. It is true there be some affairs which require extreme secrecy, which will hardly go beyond one or two persons besides the king; neither are those councils unprosperous, for, besides the secrecy, they commonly go on constantly in one spirit of direction without distraction. But then it must be a prudent king, such as is able to grind with a hand mill,[9] and those inward* counsellors had need also be wise men, and especially true and trusty to the king's ends, as it was with King Henry the Seventh of England, who in his greatest business imparted himself to none, except it were to Morton and Fox.[10]

For weakening of authority, the fable showeth the remedy. Nay, the majesty of kings is rather exalted than diminished when they are in the chair of council; neither was there ever prince bereaved of his dependences by his council, except where there hath been either an over-greatness in one counsellor or an overstrict combination in divers, which are things soon found and holpen.[11]

For the last inconvenience, that men will counsel with an eye to themselves, certainly, *non inveniet fidem super terram*[12] is meant of the nature of times and not of all particular persons.

---

[7] secret councils.

[8] "I am full of cracks." Terence, *Eunuch*, I.105.

[9] do his own grinding, i.e., his own dirty work.

[10] the bishops of Ely and Exeter.

[11] remedied.

[12] "He shall not find faith upon the earth." Cf. Luke 18:8.

There be that* are in nature faithful and sincere and plain and direct, not crafty and involved; let princes, above all, draw to themselves such natures. Besides, counsellors are not commonly so united but that one counsellor keepeth sentinel over another, so that if any do counsel out of faction or private ends, it commonly comes to the king's ear. But the best remedy is, if princes know their counsellors, as well as their counsellors know them:

Principis est virtus maxima nosse suos.[13]

And on the other side, counsellors should not be too speculative[14] into their sovereign's person. The true composition of a counsellor is rather to be skilful in their master's business than in his nature, for then he is like to advise him, and not feed his humour. It is of singular use to princes if they take the opinions of their council both separately and together. For private opinion is more free, but opinion before others is more reverent. In private, men are more bold in their own humours; and in consort, men are more obnoxious[15] to others' humours; therefore it is good to take both; and of the inferior sort rather in private, to preserve freedom; of the greater rather in consort, to preserve respect. It is in vain for princes to take counsel concerning matters, if they take no counsel likewise concerning persons, for all matters are as dead images, and the life of the execution of affairs resteth in the good choice of persons. Neither is it enough to consult concerning persons *secundum genera*,[16] as in an idea or mathematical description, what the kind and character of the person should be, for the greatest errors are committed, and the most judgment is shown, in the choice of individuals. It was truly said, *Optimi consiliarii mortui;*[17] books will speak plain when counsellors blanch.[18] Therefore it is good to be conversant in them, specially the books of such as themselves have been actors upon the stage.

The councils at this day in most places are but familiar meet-

---

[13] "The chief virtue of a prince is to know his followers." Martial, *Epigrams*, VIII.xv.8.

[14] prying.

[15] subject to, exposed to, influenced by.

[16] "according to classes".

[17] "The best counsellors are the dead." Attributed elsewhere by Bacon to Alphonso of Aragon.

[18] shrink back, are evasive.

ings, where matters are rather talked on than debated. And they run too swift to the order or act of counsel. It were better that in causes of weight, the matter were propounded one day and not spoken to till the next day; *in nocte consilium*.[19] So was it done in the Commission of Union between England and Scotland, which was a grave and orderly assembly. I commend set days for petitions, for both it gives the suitors more certainty for their attendance, and it frees the meetings for matters of estate,* that they may *hoc agere*.[20] In choice of committees for ripening business for the council, it is better to choose indifferent* persons than to make an indifferency by putting in those that are strong on both sides. I commend also standing commissions, as for trade, for treasure, for war, for suits, for some provinces; for where there be divers particular councils and but one council of estate (as it is in Spain), they are, in effect, no more than standing commissions, save that they have greater authority. Let such as are to inform councils out of their particular professions (as lawyers, seamen, mintmen, and the like) be first heard before committees, and then, as occasion serves, before the council. And let them not come in multitudes or in a tribunitious[21] manner, for that is to clamour[22] councils, not to inform them. A long table and a square table, or seats about the walls, seem things of form, but are things of substance, for at a long table a few at the upper end, in effect, sway[23] all the business, but in the other form there is more use of the counsellors' opinions that sit lower. A king, when he presides in council, let him beware how he opens his own inclination too much in that which he propoundeth, for else counsellors will but take the wind of him,[24] and instead of giving free counsel, sing him a song of *placebo*.[25]

---

[19] "In the night is counsel." Erasmus, *Adages*, II.ii.43 (462B).

[20] "Keep to the business in hand."

[21] overbearing; i.e., like the Roman tribunes, who represented (and lorded it over) the common people.

[22] shout down.

[23] direct.

[24] i.e., follow his lead.

[25] "I will please" [the Lord in the land of the living]. The opening of the Vesper hymn for the dead. Cf. Psalms 116:9 (Vulgate).

XXI. OF DELAYS

FORTUNE is like the market, where many times, if you can stay a little, the price will fall. And again, it is sometimes like Sibylla's offer, which at first offereth the commodity at full, then consumeth part and part, and still holdeth up the price.[1] For occasion (as it is in the common verse) *turneth a bald noddle, after she hath presented her locks in front, and no hold taken;* or at least turneth the handle of the bottle first to be received, and after the belly, which is hard to clasp. There is surely no greater wisdom than well to time the beginnings and onsets of things. Dangers are no more light, if they once seem light, and more dangers have deceived men than forced them. Nay, it were better to meet some dangers half way, though they come nothing near, than to keep too long a watch upon their approaches, for if a man watch too long, it is odds he will fall asleep. On the other side, to be deceived with too long shadows (as some have been when the moon was low and shone on their enemies' back), and so to shoot off before the time, or to teach dangers to come on, by over early buckling[2] towards them, is another extreme. The ripeness or unripeness of the occasion (as we said) must ever be well weighed; and generally it is good to commit the beginnings of all great actions to Argus with his hundred eyes, and the ends to Briareus[3] with his hundred hands, first to watch and then to speed. For the helmet of Pluto,[4] which maketh the politic man* go invisible, is secrecy in the counsel and celerity in the execution. For when things are once come to the execution, there is no secrecy comparable to celerity, like the motion of a bullet in the air, which flieth so swift as it outruns the eye.

---

[1] The Sybil of Cumae offered Tarquin the Proud nine books for three hundred pieces of gold. When he refused, she destroyed three and then offered the rest to him at the same price. Again he refused and again she destroyed three and asked the same price for the rest. These, on the advice of his augur, he finally bought and preserved carefully for consultation as oracles. See Aulus Gellius, *Attic Nights,* I.19.

[2] preparing (for).

[3] son of Uranus (Heaven) by Gaea (Earth); a huge monster with a hundred hands and fifty heads. See Homer, *Iliad,* I.403.

[4] a helmet that made its wearer invisible. See *Iliad,* V.845.

XXII. OF CUNNING

WE take Cunning for a sinister or crooked wisdom. And certainly there is a great difference between a cunning man and a wise man, not only in point of honesty, but in point of ability. There be that* can pack[1] the cards, and yet cannot play well; so there are some that are good in canvasses and factions, that are otherwise weak men. Again, it is one thing to understand persons, and another thing to understand matters, for many are perfect in men's humours, that are not greatly capable of the real[2] part of business, which is the constitution of one that hath studied men more than books. Such men are fitter for practice than for counsel, and they are good but in their own alley:[3] turn them to new men, and they have lost their aim; so as the old rule to know a fool from a wise man, *Mitte ambos nudos ad ignotos, et videbis,*[4] doth scarce hold for them. And because these cunning men are like haberdashers of small wares, it is not amiss to set forth their shop.

It is a point of cunning to wait upon him with whom you speak with your eye,[5] as the Jesuits give it in precept, for there be many wise men that have secret hearts and transparent countenances. Yet this would be done with a demure abasing of your eye sometimes, as the Jesuits also do use.

Another is, that when you have anything to obtain of present[6] despatch, you entertain and amuse the party with whom you deal with some other discourse, that he be not too much awake to make objections. I knew a counsellor and secretary that never came to Queen Elizabeth of England with bills to sign, but he would always first put her into some discourse of estate,* that she mought* the less mind the bills.

The like surprise may be made by moving things when the party is in haste, and cannot stay to consider advisedly of that* is moved.

---

[1] stack (cards).
[2] material, impersonal.
[3] bowling alley.
[4] "Send them both naked to strangers, and you will see." Attributed to Aristippus; see Diogenes Laertius, II.73.
[5] to watch carefully him with whom you speak.
[6] immediate.

If a man would cross a business that he doubts[7] some other would handsomely[8] and effectually move, let him pretend to wish it well, and move it himself in such sort as may foil it.

The breaking off in the midst of that one was about to say, as if he took himself up, breeds a greater appetite in him with whom you confer to know more.

And because it works better when any thing seemeth to be gotten from you by question, than if you offer it of yourself, you may lay a bait for a question by showing another visage and countenance than you are wont, to the end to give occasion for the party to ask what the matter is of the change? As Nehemias did: *And I had not before that time been sad before the king.*[9]

In things that are tender and unpleasing, it is good to break the ice by some whose words are of less weight, and to reserve the more weighty voice to come in as by chance, so that he may be asked the question upon the other's speech, as Narcissus did, in relating to Claudius the marriage of Messalina and Silius.[10]

In things that a man would not be seen in himself, it is a point of cunning to borrow the name of the world; as to say, *The world says,* or *There is a speech abroad.*

I knew one that when he wrote a letter, he would put that which was most material in the postscript, as if it had been a bye-matter.

I knew another that, when he came to have speech, he would pass over that that he intended most, and go forth, and come back again, and speak of it as of a thing that he had almost forgot.

Some procure themselves to be surprised at such times as it is like the party that they work upon will suddenly come upon them, and to be found with a letter in their hand, or doing somewhat which they are not accustomed, to the end they may be

[7] fears.

[8] dexterously, skilfully.

[9] Nehemiah 2:1.

[10] Narcissus, secretary to Claudius, hesitated to tell the Emperor that his wife, the notorious Messalina, had forced a youth named Silius to marry her during Claudius's absence at Ostia, A.D. 48. Narcissus therefore got two women to mention the fact to the Emperor, who accordingly asked Narcissus about it. See Tacitus, *Ann.,* XI.30.

apposed[11] of those things which of themselves they are desirous to utter.

It is a point of cunning to let fall those words in a man's own name which he would have another man learn and use, and thereupon take advantage. I knew two that were competitors for the secretary's place in Queen Elizabeth's time, and yet kept good quarter[12] between themselves, and would confer one with another upon the business; and the one of them said, that to be a secretary *in the declination of a monarchy* was a ticklish thing, and that he did not affect* it; the other straight caught up those words, and discoursed with divers of his friends, that he had no reason to desire to be secretary in the declination of a monarchy. The first man took hold of it, and found means it was told the Queen, who hearing of *a declination of a monarchy*, took it so ill as she would never after hear of the other's suit.

There is a cunning, which we in England call *The turning of the cat*[13] *in the pan,* which is, when that which a man says to another, he lays[14] it as if another had said it to him. And to say truth, it is not easy, when such a matter passed between two, to make it appear from which of them it first moved and began.

It is a way that some men have, to glance and dart at others by justifying themselves by negatives, as to say *This I do not,* as Tigellinus did towards Burrhus, *Se non diversas spes, sed incolumitatem imperatoris simpliciter spectare.*[15]

Some have in readiness so many tales and stories, as there is nothing they would insinuate, but they can wrap it into a tale, which serveth both to keep themselves more in guard, and to make others carry it[16] with more pleasure.

It is a good point of cunning for a man to shape the answer he

[11] questioned.

[12] were on friendly terms.

[13] probably originally *cate* or *cake.*

[14] imputes.

[15] "That he did not pursue various personal goals, but was simply concerned with the well-being of the emperor." Tacitus, *Ann.,* XIV.57. Tigellinus, one of Nero's favourites, ministered to the worst of his master's desires and was most disliked by the Romans. Burrhus was his tutor, a respectable man.

[16] spread it abroad.

would have in his own words and propositions, for it makes the other party stick[17] the less.

It is strange how long some men will lie in wait to speak somewhat they desire to say, and how far about they will fetch,[18] and how many other matters they will beat over to come near it. It is a thing of great patience, but yet of much use.

A sudden, bold, and unexpected question doth many times surprise a man, and lay him open. Like to him that, having changed his name and walking in Paul's, another suddenly came behind him and called him by his true name, whereat straightways he looked back.

But these small wares and petty points of cunning are infinite, and it were a good deed to make a list of them, for that nothing doth more hurt in a state than that cunning men pass for wise.

But certainly some there are that know the resorts[19] and falls of business, that cannot sink into the main of it, like a house that hath convenient stairs and entries, but never a fair room. Therefore you shall see them find out pretty looses[20] in the conclusion, but are no ways able to examine or debate matters. And yet commonly they take advantage of their inability, and would be thought wits of direction. Some build rather upon the abusing of others, and (as we now say) *putting tricks upon them*, than upon soundness of their own proceedings. But Salomon saith, *Prudens advertit ad gressus suos: stultus divertit ad dolos.*[21]

XXIII. OF WISDOM FOR A MAN'S SELF

AN ant is a wise creature for itself, but it is a shrewd[1] thing in an orchard or garden. And certainly men that are great lovers of themselves waste the public. Divide with reason between self-love and society; and be so true to thyself as thou be not false to

[17] hesitate.
[18] go (round)about.
[19] springs, sources, risings.
[20] withdrawals, escapes; perhaps "lucky hits", taking *loose* to be a term of archery.
[21] "The wise man taketh heed to his steps; the fool turneth aside to deceit." Cf. Proverbs 14:8.
[1] mischievous.

others, specially to thy king and country. It is a poor centre of a man's actions, *himself*. It is right earth.[2] For that only stands fast upon his own centre, whereas all things that have affinity with the heavens move upon the centre of another, which they benefit. The referring of all to a man's self is more tolerable in a sovereign prince, because themselves are not only themselves, but their good and evil is at the peril of the public fortune. But it is a desperate evil in a servant to a prince, or a citizen in a republic. For whatsoever affairs pass such a man's hands, he crooketh them to his own ends, which must needs be often eccentric to the ends of his master or state. Therefore let princes or states choose such servants as have not this mark, except they mean their service should be made but the accessary. That which maketh the effect more pernicious is that all proportion is lost. It were disproportion enough for the servant's good to be preferred before the master's, but yet it is a greater extreme, when a little good of the servant shall carry things[3] against a great good of the master's. And yet that is the case of bad officers, treasurers, ambassadors, generals, and other false and corrupt servants, which set a bias upon their bowl, of their own petty ends and envies, to the overthrow of their master's great and important affairs. And for the most part, the good such servants receive is after the model of their own fortune, but the hurt they sell for that good is after the model of their master's fortune. And certainly it is the nature of extreme self-lovers, as they will set an house on fire, and it were but to roast their eggs; and yet these men many times hold credit with their masters, because their study is but to please them and profit themselves; and for either respect they will abandon the good of their affairs.

Wisdom for a man's self is, in many branches thereof, a depraved thing. It is the wisdom of rats, that will be sure to leave a house somewhat before it fall. It is the wisdom of the fox, that thrusts out the badger, who digged and made room for him. It is the wisdom of crocodiles, that shed tears when they would devour. But that which is specially to be noted is,

[2] exactly like the earth.   [3] prevail, be preferred.

that those which (as Cicero says of Pompey) are *sui amantes, sine rivali*,[4] are many times unfortunate. And whereas they have all their times sacrificed to themselves, they become in the end themselves sacrifices to the inconstancy of fortune, whose wings they thought by their self-wisdom to have pinioned.

XXIV. OF INNOVATIONS

As the births of living creatures at first are ill-shapen, so are all Innovations, which are the births of time. Yet notwithstanding, as those that first bring honour into their family are commonly more worthy than most that succeed, so the first precedent (if it be good) is seldom attained by imitation. For Ill, to man's nature as it stands perverted, hath a natural motion, strongest in continuance, but Good, as a forced motion, strongest at first. Surely every medicine is an innovation; and he that will not apply new remedies must expect new evils, for time is the greatest innovator, and if time of course alter things to the worse, and wisdom and counsel shall not alter them to the better, what shall be the end? It is true that what is settled by custom, though it be not good, yet at least it is fit; and those things which have long gone together are as it were confederate within themselves; whereas new things piece not so well, but though they help by their utility, yet they trouble by their inconformity. Besides, they are like strangers, more admired and less favoured. All this is true, if time stood still, which contrariwise moveth so round[1] that a froward retention of custom is as turbulent a thing as an innovation; and they that reverence too much old times are but a scorn to the new. It were good therefore that men in their innovations would follow the example of time itself, which indeed innovateth greatly, but quietly and by degrees scarce to be perceived. For otherwise, whatsoever is new is unlooked for, and ever it mends some, and pairs[2] other; and he that is holpen*

---

[4] "lovers of themselves without a rival". *To his Brother Quintus,* III.8.

[1] swiftly.
[2] impairs.

takes it for a fortune, and thanks the time; and he that is hurt, for a wrong, and imputeth it to the author. It is good also not to try experiments in states, except the necessity be urgent, or the utility evident, and well to beware that it be the reformation that draweth on the change, and not the desire of change that pretendeth the reformation. And lastly, that the novelty, though it be not rejected, yet be held for a suspect, and, as the Scripture saith, *that we make a stand upon the ancient way, and then look about us, and discover what is the straight and right way, and so to walk in it.*[8]

XXV. OF DISPATCH

AFFECTED* dispatch is one of the most dangerous things to business that can be. It is like that which the physicians call *predigestion,* or hasty digestion, which is sure to fill the body full of crudities[1] and secret seeds of diseases. Therefore measure not dispatch by the times of sitting but by the advancement of the business. And as in races it is not the large stride or high lift that makes the speed, so in business the keeping close to the matter and not taking of it too much at once procureth dispatch. It is the care of some only to come off speedily for the time or to contrive some false periods[2] of business, because they may seem men of dispatch. But it is one thing to abbreviate by contracting, another by cutting off. And business so handled at several sittings or meetings goeth commonly backward and forward in an unsteady manner. I knew a wise man that had it for a byword, when he saw men hasten to a conclusion, *Stay a little, that we may make an end the sooner.*[3]

On the other side, true dispatch is a rich thing. For time is the measure of business, as money is of wares, and business is bought at a dear hand where there is small dispatch. The Spartans and Spaniards have been noted to be of small dispatch; *Mi venga la*

---

[8] Cf. Jeremiah 6:16.

[1] indigestible matter.

[2] conclusions.

[3] Bacon elsewhere attributes the observation to Sir Amias Paulet, the ambassador with whom Bacon went to France in 1576-77.

muerte de Spagna; Let my death come from Spain, for then it will be sure to be long in coming.

Give good hearing to those that give the first information in business, and rather direct them in the beginning than interrupt them in the continuance of their speeches, for he that is put out of his own order will go forward and backward, and be more tedious while he waits upon his memory, than he could have been if he had gone on in his own course. But sometimes it is seen that the moderator is more troublesome than the actor.

Iterations are commonly loss of time. But there is no such gain of time as to iterate often the state of the question, for it chaseth away many a frivolous speech as it is coming forth. Long and curious* speeches are as fit for dispatch as a robe or mantle with a long train is for race. Prefaces and passages[4] and excusations[5] and other speeches of reference to the person are great wastes of time; and though they seem to proceed of modesty, they are bravery.* Yet beware of being too material[6] when there is any impediment or obstruction in men's wills, for preoccupation of mind ever requireth preface of speech, like a fomentation to make the unguent enter.

Above all things, order and distribution and singling out of parts is the life of dispatch; so* as the distribution be not too subtle, for he that doth not divide will never enter well into business, and he that divideth too much will never come out of it clearly. To choose time is to save time, and an unseasonable motion is but beating the air. There be three parts of business: the preparation, the debate or examination, and the perfection. Whereof, if you look for dispatch, let the middle only be the work of many, and the first and last the work of few. The proceeding upon somewhat conceived in writing doth for the most part facilitate dispatch, for though it should be wholly rejected, yet that negative is more pregnant of direction[7] than an indefinite, as ashes are more generative than dust.

---

4 transitions.
5 excuses.

6 matter of fact, to the point.
7 i.e., more useful for guidance.

XXVI. OF SEEMING WISE

It hath been an opinion that the French are wiser than they seem, and the Spaniards seem wiser than they are. But howsoever it be between nations, certainly it is so between man and man. For as the Apostle[1] saith of godliness, *Having a show of godliness, but denying the power thereof*, so certainly there are in point of wisdom and sufficiency, that do nothing or little very solemnly: *Magno conatu nugas*.[2] It is a ridiculous thing and fit for a satire to persons of judgment, to see what shifts these formalists[3] have, and what prospectives[4] to make *superficies* to seem body that hath depth and bulk. Some are so close and reserved, as they will not show their wares but by a dark light, and seem always to keep back somewhat; and when they know within themselves they speak of that they do not well know, would nevertheless seem to others to know of that which they may not well speak. Some help themselves with countenance and gesture, and are wise by signs, as Cicero saith of Piso, that when he answered him, he fetched one of his brows up to his forehead, and bent the other down to his chin: *Respondes, altero ad frontem sublato, altero ad mentum depresso supercilio, crudelitatem tibi non placere*.[5] Some think to bear it by speaking a great word and being peremptory, and go on, and take by admittance that which they cannot make good. Some, whatsoever is beyond their reach, will seem to despise or make light of it as impertinent or curious,* and so would have their ignorance seem judgment. Some are never without a difference, and commonly by amusing men with a subtilty blanch* the matter, of whom A. Gellius saith, *Hominem delirum, qui verborum minutiis rerum frangit pondera*.[6] Of which kind also, Plato in his Protagoras[7] bringeth

[1] i.e., St. Paul. See II Timothy 3:5.

[2] "Trifles gained by great effort." Terence, *The Self-Tormentor*, III. v.8.

[3] pretenders to wisdom.

[4] perspectives, i.e., optical instruments, here probably stereoscopic lenses.

[5] Bacon does not translate the beginning and end: "You reply . . . that cruelty gives you no pleasure." *Against Piso*, 6.

[6] "A raving man who breaks up the weighty matter by verbal subtleties." Not Gellius but Quintilian (misquoted), X.I. [Wright]

[7] one of Plato's Dialogues in which he satirizes Prodicus, a Sophist or public teacher.

in Prodicus in scorn, and maketh him make a speech that consisteth of distinctions from the beginning to the end. Generally such men in all deliberations find ease to be of the negative side, and affect a credit[8] to object and foretell difficulties, for when propositions are denied, there is an end of them, but if they be allowed,* it requireth a new work, which false point of wisdom is the bane of business. To conclude, there is no decaying merchant or inward beggar[9] hath so many tricks to uphold the credit of their wealth as these empty persons have to maintain the credit of their sufficiency. Seeming wise men may make shift to get opinion, but let no man choose them for employment, for certainly you were better take for business a man somewhat absurd than over-formal.

XXVII. OF FRIENDSHIP

IT had been hard for him that spake it to have put more truth and untruth together in few words than in that speech, *Whosoever is delighted in solitude is either a wild beast or a god.*[1] For it is most true that a natural and secret hatred and aversation[2] towards society in any man hath somewhat of the savage beast, but it is most untrue that it should have any character at all of the divine nature, except it proceed, not out of a pleasure in solitude, but out of a love and desire to sequester a man's self for a higher conversation,[3] such as is found to have been falsely and feignedly in some of the heathen, as Epimenides the Candian, Numa the Roman, Empedocles the Sicilian, and Apollonius of Tyana;[4] and truly and really in divers of the ancient hermits

[8] try to obtain a reputation.

[9] i.e., one secretly bankrupt but who puts up a show of wealth.

[1] Aristotle, *Politics*, I.2 (1253ᵃ).

[2] aversion.

[3] way of life, society.

[4] Epimenides, poet and prophet of Crete in the seventh century B.C., is supposed to have slept for fifty-seven years in a cave without waking; Pompilius Numa is said to have been the second king of Rome (after Romulus) and author of the Roman religion; Empedocles (*fl. c.* 444 B.C.), a poet and philosopher, is said to have thrown himself into the flames of Mt. Etna, so that by his sudden disappearance he might be believed to be a god; Apollonius Tyanensis (born *c.* 4 B.C.) was a Neo-Pythagorean philosopher who pretended to magical powers.

and holy fathers of the church. But little do men perceive what solitude is, and how far it extendeth. For a crowd is not company; and faces are but a gallery of pictures, and talk but a tinkling cymbal, where there is no love. The Latin adage meeteth with it a little: *Magna civitas, magna solitudo*,[5] because in a great town friends are scattered, so that there is not that fellowship, for the most part, which is in less neighbourhoods. But we may go further, and affirm most truly that it is a mere* and miserable solitude to want true friends, without which the world is but a wilderness; and even in this sense also of solitude, whosoever in the frame of his nature and affections is unfit for friendship, he taketh it of the beast and not from humanity.

A principal fruit of friendship is the ease and discharge of the fulness and swellings of the heart, which passions of all kinds do cause and induce. We know diseases of stoppings and suffocations are the most dangerous in the body, and it is not much otherwise in the mind; you may take sarza to open the liver, steel to open the spleen, flower of sulphur for the lungs, castoreum for the brain,[6] but no receipt openeth the heart but a true friend, to whom you may impart griefs, joys, fears, hopes, suspicions, counsels, and whatsoever lieth upon the heart to oppress it, in a kind of civil shrift or confession.

It is a strange thing to observe how high a rate great kings and monarchs do set upon this fruit of friendship whereof we speak; so great, as they purchase it many times at the hazard of their own safety and greatness. For princes, in regard of[7] the distance of their fortune from that of their subjects and servants, cannot gather this fruit, except (to make themselves capable thereof) they raise some persons to be as it were companions and almost equals to themselves, which many times sorteth to* inconvenience. The modern languages give unto such persons the name of favourites, or privadoes, as if it were matter of grace[8] or conversation.* But the Roman name attaineth the true use and cause

---

[5] "A great city is a great solitude." Cf. Erasmus, *Adages*, II.iv.54 (539F), where Strabo is cited as the source.

[6] sarza: sarsaparilla. castoreum: castor.

[7] because of.

[8] complaisance, obligingness.

thereof, naming them *participes curarum*,[9] for it is that which tieth the knot. And we see plainly that this hath been done, not by weak and passionate princes only, but by the wisest and most politic that ever reigned, who have oftentimes joined to themselves some of their servants, whom both themselves have called friends, and allowed others likewise to call them in the same manner, using the word which is received between private men.

L. Sylla,[10] when he commanded Rome, raised Pompey (after surnamed the Great) to that height that Pompey vaunted himself for Sylla's overmatch. For when he had carried the consulship for a friend of his against the pursuit of Sylla, and that Sylla did a little resent thereat, and began to speak great, Pompey turned upon him again, and in effect bade him be quiet; *for that more men adored the sun rising than the sun setting.* With Julius Cæsar, Decimus Brutus had obtained that interest, as he set him down in his testament for heir in remainder after his nephew. And this was the man that had power with him to draw him forth to his death. For when Cæsar would have discharged the senate in regard of some ill presages, and specially a dream of Calpurnia, this man lifted him gently by the arm out of his chair, telling him he hoped he would not dismiss the senate till his wife had dreamt a better dream. And it seemeth his favour was so great, as Antonius, in a letter which is recited *verbatim* in one of Cicero's Philippics, calleth him *venefica, witch*, as if he had enchanted Cæsar.[11] Augustus raised Agrippa (though of mean birth) to that height, as when he consulted with Mæcenas about the marriage of his daughter Julia, Mæcenas took the liberty to tell him *that he must either marry his daughter to Agrippa, or take away his life; there was no third way, he had made him so great.*[12] With Tiberius Cæsar, Sejanus had ascended to that height, as they two were termed and reckoned as a pair of friends. Tiberius in a letter to him saith, *Hæc pro amicitia nostra non occultavi;*[13]

---

[9] "partners in care" (a title given by Tiberius to Sejanus). See Tacitus, *Ann.*, IV.2; Dion Cassius, LVIII.4.

[10] i.e., Sulla. See Plutarch, *Pompey*, 14.

[11] See Plutarch, *Julius Caesar*, 64, and

Cicero, *Philippics*, XIII.11.

[12] Dion Cassius, LIV.6.

[13] "In consideration of our friendship, I have not hidden these things from you." Tacitus, *Ann.*, IV.40.

and the whole senate dedicated an altar to Friendship, as to a goddess, in respect of the great dearness of friendship between them two. The like or more was between Septimius Severus and Plautianus. For he forced his eldest son to marry the daughter of Plautianus, and would often maintain Plautianus in doing affronts to his son, and did write also in a letter to the senate, by these words: *I love the man so well, as I wish he may overlive me.*[14] Now if these princes had been as a Trajan or a Marcus Aurelius, a man might have thought that this had proceeded of an abundant goodness of nature, but being men so wise, of such strength and severity of mind, and so extreme lovers of themselves, as all these were, it proveth most plainly that they found their own felicity (though as great as ever happened to mortal men) but as an half piece,[15] except they mought* have a friend to make it entire; and yet, which is more, they were princes that had wives, sons, nephews; and yet all these could not supply the comfort of friendship.

It is not to be forgotten what Comineus[16] observeth of his first master, Duke Charles the Hardy; namely, that he would communicate his secrets with none, and least of all, those secrets which troubled him most. Whereupon he goeth on and saith that towards his latter time *that closeness did impair and a little perish his understanding.* Surely Comineus mought have made the same judgment also, if it had pleased him, of his second master, Louis the Eleventh, whose closeness was indeed his tormentor. The parable[17] of Pythagoras is dark but true: *Cor ne edito: Eat not the heart.* Certainly, if a man would give it a hard phrase, those that want friends to open themselves unto are cannibals of their own hearts. But one thing is most admirable (wherewith I will conclude this first fruit of friendship), which is that this communicating of a man's self to his friend works two contrary effects, for it redoubleth joys, and cutteth griefs in halfs. For there is no man that imparteth his joys to his friend

---

[14] Tacitus, *Ann.*, IV.74. Plautianus was Praetorian Prefect (d. A.D. 203).

[15] i.e., incomplete.

[16] Philippe de Comines: a French historian (1447?-1511?). Charles the Hardy (or the Bold) was Duke of Burgundy (1433-77).

[17] figurative observation. See Plutarch, *On the Education of Children*, VII.

but he joyeth the more, and no man that imparteth his griefs to his friend but he grieveth the less. So that it is in truth of operation upon a man's mind of like virtue as the alchemists use to attribute to their stone for man's body, that it worketh all contrary effects, but still* to the good and benefit of nature. But yet without praying in aid[18] of alchemists, there is a manifest image of this in the ordinary course of nature. For in bodies, union strengtheneth and cherisheth any natural action, and on the other side weakeneth and dulleth any violent impression, and even so it is of minds.

The second fruit of friendship is healthful and sovereign for the understanding, as the first is for the affections. For friendship maketh indeed a fair day in the affections from storm and tempests, but it maketh daylight in the understanding out of darkness and confusion of thoughts. Neither is this to be understood only of faithful counsel, which a man receiveth from his friend; but before you come to that, certain it is that whosoever hath his mind fraught with many thoughts, his wits and understanding do clarify and break up in the communicating and discoursing with another; he tosseth his thoughts more easily; he marshalleth them more orderly; he seeth how they look when they are turned into words; finally, he waxeth wiser than himself; and that more by an hour's discourse than by a day's meditation. It was well said by Themistocles to the king of Persia, *That speech was like cloth of Arras, opened and put abroad; whereby the imagery doth appear in figure; whereas in thoughts they lie but as in packs.*[19] Neither is this second fruit of friendship, in opening the understanding, restrained only to such friends as are able to give a man counsel (they indeed are best), but even without that a man learneth of himself, and bringeth his own thoughts to light, and whetteth his wits as against a stone, which itself cuts not. In a word, a man were better relate himself to a statua or picture than to suffer his thoughts to pass in smother.

Add now, to make this second fruit of friendship complete,

---

[18] (law) claiming or calling in aid.   [19] Plutarch, *Themistocles*, 29. put abroad: unfolded.

that other point which lieth more open and falleth within vulgar observation, which is faithful counsel from a friend. Heraclitus saith well in one of his enigmas, *Dry light is ever the best.* And certain it is that the light that a man receiveth by counsel from another is drier and purer than that which cometh from his own understanding and judgment, which is ever infused and drenched in his affections and customs. So as there is as much difference between the counsel that a friend giveth, and that a man giveth himself, as there is between the counsel of a friend and of a flatterer. For there is no such flatterer as is a man's self, and there is no such remedy against flattery of a man's self as the liberty of a friend. Counsel is of two sorts, the one concerning manners,* the other concerning business. For* the first, the best preservative to keep the mind in health is the faithful admonition of a friend. The calling of a man's self to a strict account is a medicine, sometime too piercing and corrosive. Reading good books of morality is a little flat and dead. Observing our faults in others is sometimes improper for our case. But the best receipt (best, I say, to work, and best to take) is the admonition of a friend. It is a strange thing to behold what gross errors and extreme absurdities many (especially of the greater sort) do commit, for want of a friend to tell them of them, to the great damage both of their fame and fortune; for, as St. James saith, they are as men *that look sometimes into a glass, and presently* forget their own shape and favour.*[20] As for business, a man may think, if he will, that two eyes see no more than one; or that a gamester seeth always more than a looker-on; or that a man in anger is as wise as he that hath said over the four and twenty letters; or that a musket may be shot off as well upon the arm as upon a rest; and such other fond and high* imaginations, to think himself all in all. But when all is done, the help of good counsel is that which setteth business straight. And if any man think that he will take counsel, but it shall be by pieces, asking counsel in one business of one man, and in another business of another man; it is well (that is to say, better perhaps than if he asked none at all), but he runneth two dangers: one, that he shall not be faithfully

[20] James 1:24. favour: face.

counselled, for it is a rare thing, except it be from a perfect and entire[21] friend, to have counsel given, but such as shall be bowed and crooked to some ends which he hath that giveth it. The other, that he shall have counsel given, hurtful and unsafe (though with good meaning), and mixed partly of mischief and partly of remedy; even as if you would call a physician that is thought good for the cure of the disease you complain of, but is unacquainted with your body, and therefore may put you in way for a present cure, but overthroweth your health in some other kind, and so cure the disease and kill the patient. But a friend that is wholly acquainted with a man's estate* will beware, by furthering any present business, how he dasheth upon other inconvenience. And therefore rest not upon[22] scattered counsels; they will rather distract and mislead than settle and direct.

After these two noble fruits of friendship (peace in the affections, and support of the judgment), followeth the last fruit, which is like the pomegranate, full of many kernels; I mean aid and bearing a part in all actions and occasions. Here the best way to represent to life the manifold use of friendship is to cast and see how many things there are which a man cannot do himself, and then it will appear that it was a sparing[23] speech of the ancients, to say *that a friend is another himself*, for that a friend is far more than himself. Men have their time, and die many times in desire of[24] some things which they principally take to heart, the bestowing of a child, the finishing of a work, or the like. If a man have a true friend, he may rest almost secure that the care of those things will continue after him. So that a man hath, as it were, two lives in his desires. A man hath a body, and that body is confined to a place, but where friendship is, all offices of life are as it were granted to him and his deputy. For he may exercise them by his friend. How many things are there which a man cannot, with any face or comeliness, say or do himself? A man can scarce allege his own merits with modesty, much less extol them; a man cannot sometimes brook to suppli-

---

[21] sincere, honest.
[22] depend not upon.
[23] short of the truth, understated. See Diogenes Laertius, VII.23; Aris-

totle, *The Great Ethics*, II.xv.5.
[24] i.e., still desiring (not having attained).

cate or beg; and a number of the like. But all these things are graceful in a friend's mouth, which are blushing in a man's own. So again, a man's person hath many proper[25] relations which he cannot put off. A man cannot speak to his son but as a father, to his wife but as a husband, to his enemy but upon terms; whereas a friend may speak as the case requires, and not as it sorteth with* the person. But to enumerate these things were endless; I have given the rule, where a man cannot fitly play his own part; if he have not a friend, he may quit the stage.

XXVIII. OF EXPENSE

RICHES are for spending, and spending for honour and good actions. Therefore extraordinary expense must be limited by the worth of the occasion, for voluntary undoing may be as well for a man's country as for the kingdom of heaven. But ordinary expense ought to be limited by a man's estate, and governed with such regard as it be within his compass, and not subject to deceit and abuse of servants, and ordered to the best show, that the bills may be less than the estimation abroad. Certainly if a man will keep but of even hand, his ordinary expenses ought to be but to the half of his receipts, and if he think to wax rich, but to the third part. It is no baseness for the greatest to descend and look into their own estate. Some forbear it, not upon negligence alone, but doubting* to bring themselves into melancholy, in respect[1] they shall find it broken. But wounds cannot be cured without searching. He that cannot look into his own estate at all had need both choose well those whom he employeth, and change them often, for new are more timorous and less subtle. He that can look into his estate but seldom, it behoveth him to turn all to certainties.[2] A man had need, if he be plentiful in some kind of expense, to be as saving again in some other. As if he be plentiful in diet, to be saving in apparel; if he be plentiful in

---

[25] personal, pertaining to himself.

[1] in case.

[2] i.e., fixed income and expenses.

the hall, to be saving in the stable; and the like. For he that is plentiful in expenses of all kinds will hardly be preserved from decay. In clearing[3] of a man's estate, he may as well hurt himself in being too sudden, as in letting it run on too long. For hasty selling is commonly as disadvantageable[4] as interest. Besides, he that clears at once will relapse, for finding himself out of straits, he will revert to his customs, but he that cleareth by degrees induceth a habit of frugality, and gaineth as well upon his mind as upon his estate. Certainly who hath a state to repair may not despise small things, and commonly it is less dishonourable to abridge petty charges than to stoop to petty gettings. A man ought warily to begin charges which once begun will continue, but in matters that return not he may be more magnificent.

XXIX. OF THE TRUE GREATNESS OF KINGDOMS AND ESTATES

THE speech of Themistocles the Athenian, which was haughty and arrogant in taking so much to himself, had been a grave and wise observation and censure, applied at large to others. Desired at a feast to touch a lute, he said, *He could not fiddle, but yet he could make a small town a great city*.[1] These words (holpen a little with a metaphor) may express two differing abilities in those that deal in business of estate. For if a true survey be taken of counsellors and statesmen, there may be found (though rarely) those which can make a small state great, and yet cannot fiddle, as on the other side, there will be found a great many that can fiddle very cunningly, but yet are so far from being able to make a small state great, as their gift lieth the other way, to bring a great and flourishing estate to ruin and decay. And certainly those degenerate arts and shifts, whereby many counsellors and governors gain both favour with their masters and estimation with the vulgar, deserve no better name than fiddling, being

[3] freeing from debt.
[4] disadvantageous.

[1] See Plutarch, *Themistocles*, 2.

things rather pleasing for the time and graceful to themselves only than tending to the weal and advancement of the state which they serve. There are also (no doubt) counsellors and governors which may be held sufficient (*negotiis pares*[2]), able to manage affairs, and to keep them from precipices and manifest inconveniences, which nevertheless are far from the ability to raise and amplify an estate in power, means, and fortune. But be the workmen what they may be, let us speak of the work; that is, the true Greatness of Kingdoms and Estates, and the means thereof. An argument fit for great and mighty princes to have in their hand, to the end that neither by over-measuring their forces they leese* themselves in vain enterprises, nor on the other side, by undervaluing them they descend to fearful and pusilla-nimous counsels.

The greatness of an estate in bulk and territory doth fall under measure, and the greatness of finances and revenue doth fall under[3] computation. The population may appear by musters, and the number and greatness of cities and towns by cards and maps. But yet there is not any thing amongst civil affairs more subject to error than the right valuation and true judgment concerning the power and forces of an estate. The kingdom of heaven is compared, not to any great kernel or nut, but to a grain of mustard seed, which is one of the least grains, but hath in it a property and spirit hastily to get up and spread.[4] So are there states great in territory, and yet not apt to enlarge or command; and some that have but a small dimension of stem, and yet apt to be the foundations of great monarchies.

Walled towns, stored arsenals and armouries, goodly races of horse, chariots of war, elephants, ordnance, artillery, and the like – all this is but a sheep in a lion's skin, except the breed and disposition of the people be stout and warlike. Nay, number (itself) in armies importeth not much, where the people is of weak courage, for (as Virgil saith) *It never troubles a wolf how many the sheep be.*[5] The army of the Persians in the plains of

---

[2] "equal to business". Tacitus, *Ann.*, VI.39; XVI.18.

[3] admits of (i.e., may be computed).

[4] See Matt. 13:31, 32.

[5] *Eclogues*, VII.52.

Arbela was such a vast sea of people, as it did somewhat astonish the commanders in Alexander's army, who came to him therefore, and wished him to set upon them by night, but he answered, *He would not pilfer the victory.*[6] And the defeat was easy. When Tigranes the Armenian, being encamped upon a hill with four hundred thousand men, discovered the army of the Romans, being not above fourteen thousand, marching towards him, he made himself merry with it, and said, *Yonder men are too many for an ambassage, and too few for a fight.*[7] But before the sun set, he found them enow to give him the chase with infinite slaughter. Many are the examples of the great odds between number and courage, so that a man may truly make a judgment that the principal point of greatness in any state is to have a race of military men. Neither is money the sinews of war (as it is trivially* said), where the sinews of men's arms, in base and effeminate people, are failing. For Solon said well to Crœsus (when in ostentation he showed him his gold), *Sir, if any other come that hath better iron than you, he will be master of all this gold.*[8] Therefore let any prince or state think soberly[9] of his forces, except his militia of natives be of good and valiant soldiers. And let princes, on the other side, that have subjects of martial disposition know their own strength, unless they be otherwise wanting unto themselves. As for mercenary forces (which is the help in this case), all examples show that whatsoever estate or prince doth rest upon them, *he may spread his feathers for a time, but he will mew them soon after.*[10]

The blessing of Judah and Issachar will never meet: *that the same people or nation should be both the lion's whelp and the ass between burthens;*[11] neither will it be, that a people overlaid with taxes should ever become valiant and martial. It is true that taxes levied by consent of the estate do abate men's courage less,

---

[6] See Plutarch, *Alexander*, 31.

[7] Plutarch, *Lucullus*, 27. ambassage: embassy. Tigranes: King of Armenia, defeated by the Roman Lucullus at Tigranocerta in 69 B.C.

[8] Bacon elsewhere attributes this observation to Mucianus, Roman consul of the first century and general of Vespasian. See also Machiavelli, *Discourses on Livy*, II.10. [Wright]

[9] have but a small opinion.

[10] See Machiavelli, *Disc. on Livy*, II.20, and *The Prince*, XII.

[11] See Genesis 49:9, 14.

as it hath been seen notably in the excises of the Low Countries, and, in some degree, in the subsidies of England. For you must note that we speak now of the heart and not of the purse. So that although the same tribute and tax, laid by consent or by imposing, be all one to the purse, yet it works diversely upon the courage. So that you may conclude, *that no people over-charged with tribute is fit for empire.*

Let states that aim at greatness take heed how their nobility and gentlemen do multiply too fast. For that maketh the common subject grow to be a peasant and base swain, driven out of heart, and in effect but the gentleman's labourer. Even as you may see in coppice woods, if you leave your staddles[12] too thick, you shall never have clean underwood, but shrubs and bushes. So in countries, if the gentlemen be too many, the commons will be base, and you will bring it to that, that not the hundred[13] poll will be fit for an helmet, especially as to the infantry, which is the nerve of an army; and so there will be great population and little strength. This which I speak of hath been nowhere better seen than by comparing of England and France; whereof England, though far less in territory and population, hath been (nevertheless) an overmatch; in regard* the middle people of England make good soldiers, which the peasants of France do not. And herein the device of King Henry the Seventh (whereof I have spoken largely in the history of his life) was profound and admirable, in making farms and houses of husbandry of a standard; that is, maintained with such a proportion of land unto them, as may breed a subject to live in convenient plenty and no servile condition, and to keep the plough in the hands of the owners, and not mere hirelings. And thus indeed you shall attain to Virgil's character which he gives to ancient Italy:

Terra potens armis atque ubere glebæ.[14]

Neither is that state (which, for any thing I know, is almost peculiar to England, and hardly to be found anywhere else,

---

[12] young trees left standing after the underbrush has been cleared away.
[13] hundredth (i.e., one head in a hundred). See Machiavelli, *Disc.*

on Livy, II.18.
[14] "A land powerful in arms and in the fertility of its soil." *Aeneid,* I.531.

except it be perhaps in Poland) to be passed over; I mean the state of free servants and attendants upon noblemen and gentlemen, which are no ways inferior unto the yeomanry for arms. And therefore out of all question, the splendour and magnificence and great retinues and hospitality of noblemen and gentlemen, received into custom, doth much conduce unto martial greatness. Whereas, contrariwise, the close and reserved living of noblemen and gentlemen causeth a penury of military forces.

By all means it is to be procured that the trunk of Nebuchadnezzar's tree[15] of monarchy be great enough to bear the branches and the boughs; that is, that the natural subjects of the crown or state bear a sufficient proportion to the stranger subjects that they govern. Therefore all states that are liberal of naturalization towards strangers are fit for empire. For to think that an handful of people can, with the greatest courage and policy in the world, embrace too large extent of dominion, it may hold for a time, but it will fail suddenly. The Spartans were a nice* people in point of naturalization, whereby, while they kept their compass, they stood firm; but when they did spread, and their boughs were becomen too great for their stem, they became a windfall upon the sudden. Never any state was in this point so open to receive strangers into their body as were the Romans. Therefore it sorted* with them accordingly, for they grew to the greatest monarchy. Their manner was to grant naturalization (which they called *jus civitatis*), and to grant it in the highest degree; that is, not only *jus commercii*, *jus connubii*, *jus hæreditatis*, but also *jus suffragii* and *jus honorum*.[16] And this not to singular persons alone but likewise to whole families; yea to cities, and sometimes to nations. Add to this their custom of plantation of colonies, whereby the Roman plant was removed into the soil of other nations. And putting both constitutions together, you will say that it was not the Romans that spread upon the world, but it was the world that spread upon the Romans, and that was the sure way of greatness. I have marvelled sometimes at Spain,

---

15 See Daniel 4:10. Cf. Machiavelli, *Disc. on Livy*, II.3.

16 "rights of citizenship", "right of trade", "right of marriage", "right of inheritance", "right of suffrage", "right of holding office".

how they clasp and contain so large dominions with so few natural Spaniards, but sure the whole compass of Spain is a very great body of a tree, far above Rome and Sparta at the first. And besides, though they have not had that usage to naturalize liberally, yet they have that which is next to it; that is, to employ almost indifferently* all nations in their militia of ordinary soldiers; yea and sometimes in their highest commands. Nay it seemeth at this instant they are sensible of this want of natives, as by the Pragmatical Sanction,[17] now published, appeareth.

It is certain that sedentary and within-door arts and delicate manufactures (that require rather the finger than the arm) have in their nature a contrariety to a military disposition. And generally all warlike people are a little idle, and love danger better than travail. Neither must they be too much broken of it, if they shall be preserved in vigour. Therefore it was great advantage in the ancient states of Sparta, Athens, Rome, and others, that they had the use of slaves, which commonly did rid[18] those manufactures. But that is abolished in greatest part by the Christian law. That which cometh nearest to it is to leave those arts chiefly to strangers (which for that purpose are the more easily to be received), and to contain the principal bulk of the vulgar natives within those three kinds – tillers of the ground; free servants; and handicraftsmen of strong and manly arts, as smiths, masons, carpenters, etc., not reckoning professed soldiers.

But above all, for empire and greatness, it importeth most, that a nation do profess arms as their principal honour, study, and occupation. For the things which we formerly have spoken of are but habilitations towards arms; and what is habilitation without intention and act? Romulus, after his death (as they report or feign), sent a present[19] to the Romans, that above all they should intend[20] arms, and then they should prove the greatest empire of the world. The fabric of the state of Sparta was wholly (though not wisely) framed and composed to that

---

[17] royal decree. The one published under Philip IV gave certain privileges to people who married and to those who had six or more children.

[18] dispose of.

[19] a writ. See Plutarch, *Romulus*, 28; Livy, I.16.

[20] devote their attention to.

scope and end. The Persians and Macedonians had it for a flash. The Gauls, Germans, Goths, Saxons, Normans, and others had it for a time. The Turks have it at this day, though in great declination. Of Christian Europe, they that have it are, in effect, only the Spaniards. But it is so plain *that every man profiteth in that* he most intendeth, that it needeth not to be stood upon. It is enough to point at it, that no nation which doth not directly profess arms may look to have greatness fall into their mouths. And on the other side, it is a most certain oracle of time that those states that continue long in that profession (as the Romans and Turks principally have done) do wonders. And those that have professed arms but for an age, have notwithstanding commonly attained that greatness in that age which maintained them long after, when their profession and exercise of arms hath grown to decay.

Incident to this point is, for a state to have those laws or customs which may reach forth unto them just occasions (as may be pretended) of war. For there is that justice imprinted in the nature of men that they enter not upon wars (whereof so many calamities do ensue) but upon some, at the least specious, grounds and quarrels.* The Turk hath at hand, for cause of war, the propagation of his law or sect, a quarrel that he may always command. The Romans, though they esteemed the extending the limits of their empire to be great honour to their generals when it was done, yet they never rested upon that alone to begin a war. First, therefore, let nations that pretend to greatness have this: that they be sensible of wrongs, either upon borderers, merchants, or politic ministers, and that they sit not too long upon a provocation. Secondly, let them be prest[21] and ready to give aids and succours to their confederates, as it ever was with the Romans; insomuch as if the confederates had leagues defensive with divers other states, and, upon invasion offered, did implore their aids severally, yet the Romans would ever be the foremost, and leave it to none other to have the honour. As for the wars which were anciently made on the

[21] ready, eager.

behalf of a kind of party or tacit conformity of estate,[22] I do not see how they may be well justified: as when the Romans made a war for the liberty of Græcia; or when the Lacedæmonians and Athenians made wars to set up or pull down democracies and oligarchies; or when wars were made by foreigners, under the pretence of justice or protection, to deliver the subjects of others from tyranny and oppression; and the like. Let it suffice that no estate expect to be great that is not awake upon any just occasion of arming.

No body can be healthful without exercise, neither natural body nor politic, and certainly to a kingdom or estate, a just and honourable war is the true exercise. A civil war indeed is like the heat of a fever, but a foreign war is like the heat of exercise, and serveth to keep the body in health; for in a slothful peace both courages[23] will effeminate and manners* corrupt. But howsoever it be for happiness, without all question, for greatness it maketh, to be still* for the most part in arms; and the strength of a veteran army (though it be a chargeable business) always on foot is that which commonly giveth the law or at least the reputation amongst all neighbour states, as may well be seen in Spain, which hath had, in one part or other, a veteran army almost continually now by the space of six score years.

To be master of the sea is an abridgement of a monarchy. Cicero, writing to Atticus of Pompey his preparation against Cæsar, saith, *Consilium Pompeii plane Themistocleum est; putat enim, qui mari potitur, eum rerum potiri.*[24]And without doubt Pompey had tired out Cæsar, if upon vain confidence he had not left that way. We see the great effects of battles by sea. The battle of Actium decided the empire of the world. The battle of Lepanto arrested the greatness of the Turk. There be many examples where sea fights have been final to the war, but this is when princes or states have set up their rest upon[25] the battles. But thus much is certain, that he that commands the sea is at

---

[22] similarity of political institutions.

[23] spirits.

[24] "The policy of Pompey is clearly that of Themistocles, for he thinks that he who rules the sea rules all." Cicero, *To Atticus*, X.8.

[25] have risked everything on.

great liberty, and may take as much and as little of the war as he will. Whereas those that be strongest by land are many times nevertheless in great straits. Surely at this day with us of Europe, the vantage of strength at sea (which is one of the principal dowries of this kingdom of Great Britain) is great, both because most of the kingdoms of Europe are not merely* inland but girt with the sea most part of their compass, and because the wealth of both Indies seems in great part but an accessory to the command of the seas.

The wars of latter ages seem to be made in the dark in respect of[26] the glory and honour which reflected upon men from the wars in ancient time. There be now for martial encouragement some degrees and orders of chivalry, which nevertheless are conferred promiscuously upon soldiers and no soldiers; and some remembrance perhaps upon the scutcheon; and some hospitals for maimed soldiers; and such like things. But in ancient times the trophies erected upon the place of the victory, the funeral laudatives and monuments for those that died in the wars, the crowns and garlands personal, the style of Emperor, which the great kings of the world after borrowed, the triumphs of the generals upon their return, the great donatives and largesses upon the disbanding of the armies were things able to inflame all men's courages. But above all, that of the Triumph amongst the Romans was not pageants or gaudery, but one of the wisest and noblest institutions that ever was. For it contained three things: honour to the general; riches to the treasury out of the spoils; and donatives to the army. But that honour perhaps were not fit for monarchies, except it be in the person of the monarch himself or his sons, as it came to pass in the times of the Roman emperors, who did impropriate[27] the actual triumphs to themselves and their sons for such wars as they did achieve in person, and left only, for wars achieved by subjects, some triumphal garments and ensigns to the general.

To conclude, no man can *by care taking* (as the Scripture[28]

---

[26] in comparison with. [28] Matt. 6:27; Luke 12:25.
[27] appropriate.

saith) *add a cubit to his stature* in this little model of a man's body, but in the great frame of kingdoms and commonwealths it is in the power of princes or estates to add amplitude and greatness to their kingdoms, for by introducing such ordinances, constitutions, and customs, as we have now touched, they may sow greatness to their posterity and succession. But these things are commonly not observed, but left to take their chance.

XXX. OF REGIMENT OF HEALTH

THERE is a wisdom in this beyond the rules of physic: a man's own observation, what he finds good of, and what he finds hurt of, is the best physic to preserve health. But it is a safer conclusion to say, *This agreeth not well with me, therefore I will not continue it*, than this, *I find no offence[1] of this, therefore I may use it.* For strength of nature in youth passeth over many excesses, which are owing a man till his age.[2] Discern of the coming on of years, and think not to do the same things still, for age will not be defied. Beware of sudden change in any great point of diet, and if necessity enforce it, fit the rest to it. For it is a secret both in nature and state, that it is safer to change many things than one. Examine thy customs of diet, sleep, exercise, apparel, and the like, and try in any thing thou shalt judge hurtful to discontinue it by little and little, but so, as if thou dost find any inconvenience by the change, thou come back to it again, for it is hard to distinguish that which is generally held good and wholesome from that which is good particularly and fit for thine own body. To be free minded and cheerfully disposed at hours of meat and of sleep and of exercise is one of the best precepts of long lasting. As for the passions and studies of the mind, avoid envy, anxious fears, anger fretting inwards, subtle and knotty inquisitions, joys and exhilarations in excess, sadness not communicated. Entertain hopes, mirth rather than joy, variety of delights rather than surfeit of them, wonder and admiration,

[1] harm in. "Regiment" in the title means "management".   [2] exacted as a debt in old age.

and therefore novelties, studies that fill the mind with splendid and illustrious objects, as histories, fables, and contemplations of nature. If you fly physic in health altogether, it will be too strange for your body when you shall need it. If you make it too familiar, it will work no extraordinary effect when sickness cometh. I commend rather some diet for certain seasons than frequent use of physic, except it be grown into a custom. For those diets alter the body more, and trouble it less. Despise no new accident in your body, but ask opinion of it. In sickness, respect* health principally; and in health, action. For those that put their bodies to endure in health may in most sicknesses, which are not very sharp, be cured only with diet and tendering.[8] Celsus could never have spoken it as a physician, had he not been a wise man withal, when he giveth it for one of the great precepts of health and lasting, that a man do vary and interchange contraries, but with an inclination to the more benign extreme: use fasting and full eating, but rather full eating; watching and sleep, but rather sleep; sitting and exercise, but rather exercise; and the like.[4] So shall nature be cherished, and yet taught masteries.[5] Physicians are some of them so pleasing and conformable[6] to the humour of the patient, as they press not the true cure of the disease; and some other are so regular in proceeding according to art for the disease, as they respect not sufficiently the condition of the patient. Take one of a middle temper,* or if it may not be found in one man, combine two of either sort, and forget not to call as well the best acquainted with your body, as the best reputed of for his faculty.

XXXI. OF SUSPICION

SUSPICIONS amongst thoughts are like bats amongst birds, they ever fly by twilight. Certainly they are to be repressed, or at the least well guarded, for they cloud the mind; they leese* friends;

[8] care.
[4] See Aulus Cornelius Celsus, *On Medicine*, I.l.
[5] i.e., mastery over disease.
[6] indulgent.

and they check* with business, whereby business cannot go on currently[1] and constantly. They dispose kings to tyranny, husbands to jealousy, wise men to irresolution and melancholy. They are defects, not in the heart but in the brain, for they take place in the stoutest natures, as in the example of Henry the Seventh of England. There was not a more suspicious man nor a more stout. And in such a composition* they do small hurt. For commonly they are not admitted but with examination, whether they be likely or no. But in fearful natures they gain ground too fast. There is nothing makes a man suspect much, more than to know little; and therefore men should remedy suspicion by procuring to know more, and not to keep their suspicions in smother. What would men have? Do they think those they employ and deal with are saints? Do they not think they will have their own ends, and be truer to themselves than to them? Therefore there is no better way to moderate suspicions than to account upon[2] such suspicions as true and yet to bridle them as false. For so far a man ought to make use of suspicions as to provide as if that should be true that he suspects, yet it may do him no hurt. Suspicions that the mind of itself gathers are but buzzes; but suspicions that are artificially nourished, and put into men's heads by the tales and whisperings of others have stings. Certainly the best mean* to clear the way in this same wood of suspicions is frankly to communicate them with the party that he suspects, for thereby he shall be sure to know more of the truth of them than he did before, and withal shall make that party more circumspect not to give further cause of suspicion. But this would[3] not be done to men of base natures, for they, if they find themselves once suspected, will never be true. The Italian says, *Sospetto licentia fede*, as if suspicion did give a passport[4] to faith; but it ought rather to kindle it to discharge itself.[5]

---

[1] smoothly.
[2] act as if.
[3] should.

[4] licence; i.e., suspicion frees men from the obligation to be loyal.
[5] to free itself (from suspicion); prove itself innocent.

XXXII. OF DISCOURSE

SOME in their discourse desire rather commendation of wit,[1] in being able to hold[2] all arguments, than of judgment, in discerning what is true, as if it were a praise to know what might be said, and not what should be thought. Some have certain commonplaces[3] and themes wherein they are good, and want variety, which kind of poverty is for the most part tedious, and when it is once perceived, ridiculous. The honourablest part of talk is to give the occasion,[4] and again to moderate[5] and pass to somewhat else, for then a man leads the dance. It is good in discourse and speech of conversation to vary and intermingle speech of the present occasion with arguments, tales with reasons, asking of questions with telling of opinions, and jest with earnest, for it is a dull thing to tire, and, as we say now, to jade[6] any thing too far. As for jest, there be certain things which ought to be privileged from it; namely, religion, matters of state, great persons, any man's present business of importance, and any case that deserveth pity. Yet there be some that think their wits have been asleep, except they dart out somewhat that is piquant, and to the quick. That is a vein which would be bridled:

Parce, puer, stimulis, et fortius utere loris.[7]

And generally, men ought to find the difference between saltness and bitterness. Certainly, he that hath a satirical vein, as he maketh others afraid of his wit, so he had need be afraid of others' memory. He that questioneth much, shall learn much and content[8] much, but especially if he apply[9] his questions to the skill of the persons whom he asketh; for he shall give them occasion to please themselves in speaking, and himself shall continually gather knowledge. But let his questions not be troublesome, for that is fit for a poser.[10] And let him be sure to

---

[1] for their ingenuity, play of mind.
[2] uphold, support any argument.
[3] subjects.
[4] suggest the subject.
[5] control, limit.
[6] ride.

[7] "Spare the whip, my son, and pull harder on the reins." Ovid, *Met.*, II.127.
[8] give pleasure.
[9] suit.
[10] examiner.

leave other men their turns to speak. Nay, if there be any that would reign and take up all the time, let him find means to take them off, and to bring others on, as musicians use to do with those that dance too long galliards. If you dissemble sometimes your knowledge of that you are thought to know, you shall be thought another time to know that you know not. Speech of a man's self ought to be seldom, and well chosen. I knew one was wont to say in scorn, *He must needs be a wise man, he speaks so much of himself*; and there is but one case wherein a man may commend himself with good grace, and that is in commending virtue in another, especially if it be such a virtue whereunto himself pretendeth. Speech of touch[11] towards others should be sparingly used; for discourse ought to be as a field,[12] without coming home to any man. I knew two noblemen, of the west part of England, whereof the one was given to scoff, but kept ever royal cheer in his house; the other would ask of those that had been at the other's table, *Tell truly, was there never a flout or dry blow[13] given?* To which the guest would answer, *Such and such a thing passed.* The lord would say, *I thought he would mar a good dinner.* Discretion of speech is more than eloquence; and to speak agreeably[14] to him with whom we deal, is more than to speak in good words or in good order. A good continued speech, without a good speech of interlocution, shows slowness; and a good reply or second speech, without a good settled speech, showeth shallowness and weakness. As we see in beasts, that those that are weakest in the course, are yet nimblest in the turn, as it is betwixt the greyhound and the hare. To use too many circumstances[15] ere one come to the matter, is wearisome; to use none at all, is blunt.

---

[11] malicious speech.
[12] i.e., ranging widely.
[13] malicious jest.

[14] suitably.
[15] to dwell too long on incidental considerations.

XXXIII. OF PLANTATIONS

PLANTATIONS[1] are amongst ancient, primitive, and heroical works. When the world was young it begat more children; but now it is old it begets fewer, for I may justly account new plantations to be the children of former kingdoms. I like a plantation in a pure soil; that is, where people are not displanted to the end to plant in others. For else it is rather an extirpation than a plantation. Planting of countries is like planting of woods, for you must make account to leese* almost twenty years profit, and expect your recompense in the end. For the principal thing that hath been the destruction of most plantations hath been the base and hasty drawing of profit in the first years. It is true, speedy profit is not to be neglected, as far as may stand[2] with the good of the plantation but no further. It is a shameful and unblessed thing to take the scum of people and wicked condemned men to be the people with whom you plant; and not only so, but it spoileth the plantation, for they will ever live like rogues, and not fall to work, but be lazy, and do mischief, and spend victuals, and be quickly weary, and then certify[3] over to their country to the discredit of the plantation. The people wherewith you plant ought to be gardeners, ploughmen, labourers, smiths, carpenters, joiners, fishermen, fowlers, with some few apothecaries, surgeons, cooks, and bakers. In a country of plantation, first look about what kind of victual the country yields of itself to hand, as chestnuts, walnuts, pineapples, olives, dates, plums, cherries, wild honey, and the like, and make use of them. Then consider what victual or esculent things there are, which grow speedily and within the year, as parsnips, carrots, turnips, onions, radish, artichokes of Hierusalem,[4] maize, and the like. For* wheat, barley, and oats, they ask too much labour, but with pease and beans you may begin, both because they ask less labour, and because they serve for meat as well as for bread. And of rice likewise cometh a great increase, and it is a kind of meat. Above all, there ought to be brought store of biscuit, oatmeal, flour, meal, and the like in the beginning, till bread may be had. For beasts or birds,

---

[1] colonies.
[2] be consistent.
[3] report.
[4] i.e., the Jerusalem artichoke.

take chiefly such as are least subject to diseases, and multiply fastest, as swine, goats, cocks, hens, turkeys, geese, house doves, and the like. The victual in plantations ought to be expended almost as in a besieged town; that is, with certain[5] allowance. And let the main part of the ground employed to gardens or corn be to[6] a common stock; and to be laid in and stored up and then delivered out in proportion; besides some spots of ground that any particular person will manure for his own private.[7] Consider likewise what commodities the soil where the plantation is doth naturally yield, that they may some way help to defray the charge of the plantation (so it be not, as was said, to the untimely prejudice of the main business), as it hath fared with tobacco in Virginia. Wood commonly aboundeth but too much, and therefore timber is fit to be one. If there be iron ore and streams whereupon to set the mills, iron is a brave[8] commodity where wood aboundeth. Making of bay salt, if the climate be proper for it, would be put in experience.[9] Growing silk[10] likewise, if any be, is a likely commodity. Pitch and tar, where store of firs and pines are, will not fail. So drugs and sweet woods, where they are, cannot but yield great profit. Soap ashes[11] likewise and other things that may be thought of. But moil not too much under ground, for the hope of mines is very uncertain, and useth to* make the planters lazy in other things. For government, let it be in the hands of one, assisted with some counsel; and let them have commission to exercise martial laws, with some limitation. And above all, let men make that profit of being in the wilderness, as they have God always and his service before their eyes. Let not the government of the plantation depend upon too many counsellors and undertakers[12] in the country that planteth, but upon a temperate number, and let those be rather noblemen and gentlemen than merchants, for they look ever to the present gain. Let there be freedoms from custom[13] till the plantation be of strength, and not only freedom

[5] fixed, measured.
[6] for.
[7] for himself.
[8] fine, excellent.
[9] should be tried. Bay salt is a coarse salt derived from sea water.
[10] vegetable silk.
[11] wood ashes (used for making soap).
[12] contractors, projectors.
[13] i.e., taxes.

from custom, but freedom to carry their commodities where they may make their best of them, except there be some special cause of caution. Cram not in people by sending too fast company after company, but rather harken how they waste, and send supplies proportionably, but so as the number may live well in the plantation, and not by surcharge be in penury. It hath been a great endangering to the health of some plantations, that they have built along the sea and rivers, in marish[14] and unwholesome grounds. Therefore, though you begin there to avoid carriage and other like discommodities,* yet build still* rather upwards from the streams than along. It concerneth likewise the health of the plantation that they have good store of salt with them, that they may use it in their victuals when it shall be necessary. If you plant where savages are, do not only entertain them with trifles and gingles,[15] but use them justly and graciously, with sufficient guard nevertheless; and do not win their favour by helping them to invade their enemies, but for their defence it is not amiss; and send oft of them over to the country that plants, that they may see a better condition than their own, and commend it when they return. When the plantation grows to strength, then it is time to plant with women as well as with men, that the plantation may spread into generations, and not be ever pieced from without. It is the sinfullest thing in the world to forsake or destitute[16] a plantation once in forwardness, for besides the dishonour it is the guiltiness of blood of many commiserable[17] persons.

XXXIV. OF RICHES

I CANNOT call Riches better than the baggage of virtue. The Roman word is better, *impedimenta*.[1] For as the baggage is to an army, so is riches to virtue. It cannot be spared nor left behind, but it hindereth the march; yea and the care of it sometimes loseth or disturbeth the victory. Of great riches there

---

[14] marshy, swampy.
[15] rattles.
[16] desert.

[17] worthy of pity.

[1] baggage (literally, a hindrance).

is no real use, except it be in the distribution; the rest is but conceit.* So saith Salomon, *Where much is, there are many to consume it; and what hath the owner but the sight of it with his eyes?*[2] The personal fruition in any man cannot reach to feel great riches; there is a custody of them, or a power of dole and donative of them, or a fame of them, but no solid use to the owner. Do you not see what feigned prices are set upon little stones and rarities, and what works of ostentation are undertaken, because there might seem to be some use of great riches? But then you will say, they may be of use to buy men out of dangers or troubles. As Salomon saith, *Riches are as a strong hold, in the imagination of the rich man.*[3] But this is excellently expressed, that it is in imagination and not always in fact. For certainly great riches have sold more men than they have bought out. Seek not proud riches, but such as thou mayest get justly, use soberly, distribute cheerfully, and leave contentedly. Yet have no abstract[4] nor friarly contempt of them. But distinguish, as Cicero saith well of Rabirius Posthumus, *In studio rei amplificandæ apparebat, non avaritiæ prædam, sed instrumentum bonitati quæri.*[5] Hearken also to Salomon, and beware of hasty gathering of riches: *Qui festinat ad divitias, non erit insons.*[6] The poets feign that when Plutus (which is Riches) is sent from Jupiter, he limps and goes slowly, but when he is sent from Pluto, he runs and is swift of foot.[7] Meaning that riches gotten by good means and just labour pace slowly, but when they come by the death of others (as by the course of inheritance, testaments, and the like), they come tumbling upon a man. But it mought* be applied likewise to Pluto, taking him for the devil. For when riches come from the devil (as by fraud and oppression and unjust means), they come upon speed. The ways to enrich are many, and most of them foul. Parsimony is one of the best, and yet is not innocent, for it withholdeth men from works of

[2] Eccles. 5:11.

[3] Proverbs 18:11.

[4] pertaining to one withdrawn from the world; hermitic.

[5] "In his zeal for increasing his estate, it was apparent that he was seeking not a prey for avarice but an instrument for good." Cicero, *Speech on Behalf of C. Rabirius Postumus*, 2.

[6] "He who hastens toward riches will not be innocent." Proverbs 28:20.

[7] See, for example, Lucian, *Timon or the Misanthrope*, 20-1.

liberality and charity. The improvement of the ground is the most natural obtaining of riches, for it is our great mother's blessing, the earth's, but it is slow. And yet where men of great wealth do stoop to husbandry, it multiplieth riches exceedingly. I knew a nobleman in England that had the greatest audits[8] of any man in my time; a great grazier, a great sheep-master, a great timber man, a great collier, a great corn-master, a great lead-man, and so of iron, and a number of the like points of husbandry. So as the earth seemed a sea to him in respect of the perpetual importation. It was truly observed by one,[9] that himself came very hardly to a little riches and very easily to great riches. For when a man's stock is come to that, that he can expect[10] the prime of markets, and overcome[11] those bargains which for their greatness are few men's money, and be partner in the industries of younger men, he cannot but increase mainly.* The gains of ordinary trades and vocations are honest and furthered by two things chiefly, by diligence and by a good name for good and fair dealing. But the gains of bargains are of a more doubtful nature, when men shall wait upon others' necessity, broke[12] by servants and instruments to draw them on, put off others cunningly that would be better chapmen, and the like practices, which are crafty and naught.[13] As for the chopping of bargains, when a man buys not to hold but to sell over again, that commonly grindeth double, both upon the seller and upon the buyer. Sharings do greatly enrich, if the hands be well chosen that are trusted. Usury is the certainest means of gain, though one of the worst, as that whereby a man doth eat his bread: *In sudore vultus alieni*,[14] and besides, doth plough upon Sundays. But yet certain though it be, it hath flaws, for that the scriveners and brokers do value[15] unsound men to serve their own turn. The fortune in being the first in an invention or in a privilege doth cause sometimes a wonderful overgrowth in riches, as it was

---

[8] revenue, income.

[9] Lampon, a rich merchant in Plutarch, *Whether an Aged Man Ought to Meddle in State Affairs*, 6.

[10] wait for.

[11] win, complete.

[12] deal, do business with.

[13] bad, worthless.

[14] "in the sweat of another's face". Cf. Genesis 3:19.

[15] represent as solvent. scriveners: money brokers.

with the first sugar man in the Canaries. Therefore if a man can play the true logician, to have as well judgment as invention, he may do great matters, especially if the times be fit. He that resteth upon gains certain shall hardly grow to great riches, and he that puts all upon adventures doth oftentimes break and come to poverty; it is good therefore to guard adventures with certainties, that may uphold losses. Monopolies and coemption[16] of wares for resale, where they are not restrained, are great means to enrich, especially if the party have intelligence what things are like to come into request, and so store himself beforehand. Riches gotten by service, though it be of the best rise,[17] yet when they are gotten by flattery, feeding humours, and other servile conditions, they may be placed amongst the worst. As for fishing for testaments and executorships (as Tacitus saith of Seneca, *testamenta et orbos tamquam indagine capi*[18]) it is yet worse, by how much men submit themselves to meaner persons than in service. Believe not much them that seem to despise riches, for they despise them that despair of them, and none worse when they come to them. Be not pennywise; riches have wings, and sometimes they fly away of themselves, sometimes they must be set flying to bring in more. Men leave their riches either to their kindred or to the public, and moderate portions prosper best in both. A great state left to an heir is as a lure to all the birds of prey round about to seize on him, if he be not the better stablished in years and judgment. Likewise glorious[19] gifts and foundations are like *sacrifices without salt*,[20] and but the painted sepulchres of alms, which soon will putrefy and corrupt inwardly. Therefore measure not thine advancements by quantity, but frame them by measure,[21] and defer not charities till death, for certainly, if a man weigh it rightly, he that doth so is rather liberal of another man's than of his own.

[16] cornering.

[17] source.

[18] "Wills and wardships were caught, so to speak, in his net." *Ann.,* XIII.42.

[19] ostentatious.

[20] In a letter to King James, Bacon observed that according to Jewish law there should be no sacrifice without salt, that is, the seasoning of a good intention with lasting spiritual wisdom. Cf. Leviticus 2:13.

[21] i.e., do not measure your gifts (advancements) by quantity, but let them be to you in proportion to the object.

XXXV. OF PROPHECIES

I MEAN not to speak of divine prophecies, nor of heathen oracles, nor of natural predictions, but only of prophecies that have been of certain memory and from hidden causes. Saith the Pythonissa[1] to Saul, *Tomorrow thou and thy son shall be with me.* Homer hath these verses:

> *At domus Æneæ cunctis dominabitur oris,*
> *Et nati natorum, et qui nascentur ab illis.*[2]

A prophecy, as it seems, of the Roman empire. Seneca the tragedian hath these verses:

> *Venient annis*
> *Sæcula seris, quibus Oceanus*
> *Vincula rerum laxet, et ingens*
> *Pateat Tellus, Tiphysque novos*
> *Detegat orbes; nec sit terris*
> *Ultima Thule:*[3]

a prophecy of the discovery of America. The daughter of Polycrates dreamed that Jupiter bathed her father, and Apollo anointed him, and it came to pass that he was crucified in an open place, where the sun made his body run with sweat, and the rain washed it.[4] Philip of Macedon dreamed he sealed up his wife's belly, whereby he did expound it, that his wife should be barren, but Aristander the soothsayer told him his wife was with child, because men do not use to seal vessels that are empty.[5] A phantasm that appeared to M. Brutus in his tent said to him, *Philippis iterum me videbis.*[6] Tiberius said to Galba, *Tu quoque, Galba, degustabis imperium.*[7] In Vespasian's time there went a prophecy in the East, that those that should come forth of Judea

---

[1] Pythonessa: here identified with the witch of Endor. See I Sam. 28:19.

[2] "The house of Aeneas will reign in every land, and his children's children, and those to be born of them." Actually quoted from Virgil, *Aeneid*, III.97-8, altered from Homer, *Iliad*, XX.307-8. [Wright]

[3] "In years to come Oceanus will loosen the bonds of things, revealing a vast land, and Tiphys will discover new lands; nor will Thule be the end of the earth." *Medea*, II.374-8.

[4] See Herodotus, III.39ff. and 124-5.

[5] See Plutarch, *Alexander*, 2.

[6] "Thou shalt see me again at Philippi." See Plutarch, *Marcus Brutus* (36) and *Julius Caesar* (69).

[7] "Thou too, Galba, shalt taste of empire." See Tacitus, *Ann.*, VI.20 and Suetonius, *Galba*, 4.

should reign over the world, which though it may be was meant
of our Saviour, yet Tacitus expounds it of Vespasian.[8] Domitian
dreamed, the night before he was slain, that a golden head was
growing out of the nape of his neck, and indeed the succession
that followed him for many years made golden times.[9] Henry
the Sixth of England said of Henry the Seventh, when he was a
lad, and gave him water, *This is the lad that shall enjoy the
crown for which we strive*.[10] When I was in France, I heard from
one Dr. Pena that the Queen Mother, who was given to curious
arts, caused the King[11] her husband's nativity to be calculated
under a false name; and the astrologer gave a judgment, that he
should be killed in a duel, at which the Queen laughed, thinking
her husband to be above challenges and duels, but he was slain
upon a course at tilt, the splinters of the staff of Montgomery
going in at his beaver. The trivial[12] prophecy which I heard
when I was a child and Queen Elizabeth was in the flower of her
years, was,

> When hempe is sponne
> England's done:

whereby it was generally conceived that after the princes had
reigned which had the principial[13] letters of that word *hempe*
(which were Henry, Edward, Mary, Philip, and Elizabeth),
England should come to utter confusion, which, thanks be to
God, is verified only in the change of the name, for that the
King's style is now no more of England but of Britain. There
was also another prophecy before the year of eighty-eight, which
I do not well understand:

> There shall be seen upon a day,
> Between the Baugh and the May,
> The black fleet of Norway.
> When that that is come and gone,
> England build houses of lime and stone,
> For after wars shall you have none.

[8] Tacitus, *Hist.*, V.13.

[9] See Suetonius, *Domitian*, 23.

[10] Cf. Shakespeare, *3 Henry VI*, IV.
vi.68, which is probably derived
from a similar passage in Holin-
shed's *Chronicles*.

[11] Henry II of France, accidentally
killed in a tournament in 1559.

[12] common.

[13] initial.

It was generally conceived to be meant of the Spanish fleet that came in eighty-eight, for that the king of Spain's surname, as they say, is Norway. The prediction of Regiomontanus,

Octogesimus octavus mirabilis annus,[14]

was thought likewise accomplished in the sending of that great fleet, being the greatest in strength, though not in number, of all that ever swam upon the sea. As for Cleon's dream, I think is was a jest. It was that he was devoured of a long dragon; and it was expounded of[15] a maker of sausages, that troubled him exceedingly. There are numbers of the like kind, especially if you include dreams and predictions of astrology. But I have set down these few only of certain credit for example. My judgment is that they ought all to be despised, and ought to serve but for winter talk by the fireside. Though when I say *despised,* I mean it as for belief, for otherwise, the spreading or publishing of them is in no sort to be despised. For they have done much mischief, and I see many severe laws made to suppress them. That that hath given them grace* and some credit consisteth in three things. First, that men mark when they hit, and never mark when they miss, as they do generally also of dreams. The second is that probable conjectures or obscure traditions many times turn themselves into prophecies, while the nature of man, which coveteth divination, thinks it no peril to foretell that which indeed they do but collect. As that of Seneca's verse. For so much was then subject to demonstration that the globe of the earth had great parts beyond the Atlantic, which mought* be probably conceived not to be all sea, and adding thereto the tradition in Plato's Timæus and his Atlanticus,[16] it mought encourage one to turn it to a prediction. The third and last (which is the great one) is that almost all of them, being infinite in number, have been impostures, and by idle and crafty brains merely contrived and feigned after the event past.

---

[14] "Eighty-eight will be a marvellous year." Regiomontanus was Johannes Müller (1436-76), a German astrologer and mathematician.

[15] by. For the story see Aristophanes, *The Knights,* V.195ff.

[16] the dialogue usually called the *Critias.*

XXXVI. OF AMBITION

AMBITION is like choler, which is an humour that maketh men active, earnest, full of alacrity, and stirring, if it be not stopped. But if it be stopped, and cannot have his way, it becometh adust, and thereby malign and venomous. So ambitious men, if they find the way open for their rising, and still get forward, they are rather busy than dangerous, but if they be checked in their desires, they become secretly discontent, and look upon men and matters with an evil eye, and are best pleased when things go backward, which is the worst property* in a servant of a prince or state. Therefore it is good for princes, if they use ambitious men, to handle it so as they be still progressive and not retrograde, which because it cannot be without inconvenience, it is good not to use such natures at all. For if they rise not with their service, they will take order[1] to make their service fall with them. But since we have said it were good not to use men of ambitious natures, except it be upon necessity, it is fit we speak in what cases they are of necessity.[2] Good commanders in the wars must be taken, be they never so ambitious, for the use of their service dispenseth with[3] the rest, and to take a soldier without ambition is to pull off his spurs. There is also great use of ambitious men in being screens to princes in matters of danger and envy, for no man will take that part, except he be like a seeled dove that mounts and mounts because he cannot see about him. There is use also of ambitious men in pulling down the greatness of any subject that overtops, as Tiberius used Macro in the pulling down of Sejanus.[4] Since therefore they must be used in such cases, there resteth[5] to speak how they are to be bridled, that they may be less dangerous. There is less danger of them if they be of mean birth than if they be noble; and if they be rather harsh of nature than gracious and popular; and if they be rather new raised than grown cunning and fortified in their greatness. It is counted by some a weakness in princes to have favourites,

[1] measures.
[2] i.e., necessary.
[3] excuses, makes up for.
[4] See Dion Cassius, LVIII.9. Tiberius gave Macro Sejanus's place as commander of the praetorian guard.
[5] remains.

but it is of all others the best remedy against ambitious great ones. For when the way of pleasuring and displeasuring lieth by the favourite, it is impossible any other should be over-great. Another means to curb them is to balance them by others as proud as they. But then there must be some middle counsellors to keep things steady, for without that ballast the ship will roll too much. At the least, a prince may animate and inure some meaner persons to be as it were scourges to ambitious men. As for the having of them obnoxious* to ruin, if they be of fearful natures, it may do well; but if they be stout and daring, it may precipitate their designs, and prove dangerous. As for the pulling of them down, if the affairs require it, and that it may not be done with safety suddenly, the only way is the interchange continually of favours and disgraces, whereby they may not know what to expect, and be as it were in a wood. Of ambitions, it is less harmful, the ambition to prevail in great things, than that other to appear in every thing, for that breeds confusion, and mars business. But yet it is less danger to have an ambitious man stirring in business than great in dependences.[6] He that seeketh to be eminent amongst able men hath a great task, but that is ever good for the public. But he that plots to be the only figure amongst ciphers is the decay of a whole age. Honour hath three things in it: the vantage ground to do good; the approach to kings and principal persons; and the raising of a man's own fortunes. He that hath the best of these intentions, when he aspireth, is an honest man; and that prince that can discern of these intentions in another that aspireth is a wise prince. Generally, let princes and states choose such ministers as are more sensible of duty than of rising, and such as love business rather upon conscience than upon bravery,* and let them discern a busy nature from a willing mind.

---

6 retainers, followers.

XXXVII. OF MASQUES AND TRIUMPHS[1]

THESE things are but toys to come amongst such serious observations. But yet, since princes will have such things, it is better they should be graced with elegancy than daubed with cost. Dancing to song is a thing of great state and pleasure. I understand it, that the song be in choir, placed aloft, and accompanied with some broken music,[2] and the ditty fitted to the device. Acting in song, especially in dialogues, hath an extreme good grace; I say acting, not dancing (for that is a mean and vulgar thing); and the voices of the dialogue would* be strong and manly (a base and a tenor, no treble), and the ditty high and tragical, not nice* or dainty. Several choirs placed one over against another, and taking the voice by catches, anthemwise, give great pleasure. Turning dances into figure is a childish curiosity. And generally let it be noted that those things which I here set down are such as do naturally take the sense, and not respect petty wonderments.[3] It is true, the alterations of scenes, so it be quietly and without noise, are things of great beauty and pleasure, for they feed and relieve the eye, before it be full of the same object. Let the scenes abound with light, specially coloured and varied, and let the masquers, or any other that are to come down from the scene have some motions upon the scene itself before their coming down, for it draws the eye strangely, and makes it with great pleasure to desire to see that it cannot perfectly discern. Let the songs be loud and cheerful, and not chirpings or pulings. Let the music likewise be sharp and loud and well placed. The colours that show best by candlelight are white, carnation, and a kind of sea-water-green, and oes, or spangs,[4] as they are of no great cost, so they are of most glory. As for rich embroidery, it is lost and not discerned. Let the suits of the masquers be graceful, and such as become the person when the vizards are off, not after examples of known attires: Turks, soldiers, mariners, and the like. Let anti-masques not be long; they have been commonly of fools, satyrs, baboons, wild men,

---

[1] shows or celebrations.

[2] music by different families of instruments sounding together.

[3] surprises, marvels.

[4] spangles. oes: round spangles.

antics, beasts, sprites, witches, Ethiops, pigmies, turquets,[5] nymphs, rustics, Cupids, statuas moving, and the like. As for angels, it is not comical enough to put them in anti-masques; and any thing that is hideous, as devils, giants, is on the other side as unfit. But chiefly let the music of them be recreative, and with some strange changes. Some sweet odours suddenly coming forth, without any drops falling, are, in such a company as there is steam and heat, things of great pleasure and refreshment. Double masques, one of men, another of ladies, addeth state and variety. But all is nothing except the room be kept clear and neat.

For jousts and tourneys and barriers, the glories of them are chiefly in the chariots, wherein the challengers make their entry; especially if they be drawn with strange beasts, as lions, bears, camels, and the like; or in the devices of their entrance; or in the bravery* of their liveries; or in the goodly furniture of their horses and armour. But enough of these toys.

XXXVIII. OF NATURE IN MEN

NATURE is often hidden, sometimes overcome, seldom extinguished. Force maketh nature more violent in the return;[1] doctrine and discourse maketh nature less importune;* but custom only doth alter and subdue nature. He that seeketh victory over his nature, let him not set himself too great nor too small tasks, for the first will make him dejected by often failings, and the second will make him a small proceeder, though by often prevailings. And at the first let him practise with helps, as swimmers do with bladders or rushes, but after a time let him practise with disadvantages, as dancers do with thick shoes. For it breeds great perfection, if the practice be harder than the use. Where nature is mighty, and therefore the victory hard, the degrees had need be, first to stay and arrest nature in time, like to him that would say over the four and twenty letters when he was angry; then to

---

[5] players in Turkish attire.   [1] i.e., when the force is withdrawn.

go less in quantity, as if one should, in forbearing wine, come from drinking healths to a draught at a meal; and lastly, to discontinue altogether. But if a man have the fortitude and resolution to enfranchise himself at once, that is the best:

> *Optimus ille animi vindex lædentia pectus*
> *Vincula qui rupit, dedoluitque semel.*[2]

Neither is the ancient rule amiss, to bend nature as a wand to a contrary extreme, whereby to set it right, understanding it, where the contrary extreme is no vice. Let not a man force a habit upon himself with a perpetual continuance, but with some intermission. For both the pause reinforceth the new onset, and if a man that is not perfect be ever in practice, he shall as well practise his errors as his abilities, and induce one habit of both, and there is no means to help this but by seasonable intermissions. But let not a man trust his victory over his nature too far, for nature will lay buried a great time, and yet revive upon the occasion or temptation. Like as it was with Æsop's damsel, turned from a cat to a woman, who sat very demurely at the board's end, till a mouse ran before her. Therefore let a man either avoid the occasion altogether, or put himself often to it, that he may be little moved with it. A man's nature is best perceived in privateness, for there is no affectation; in passion, for that putteth a man out of his precepts; and in a new case or experiment, for there custom leaveth him. They are happy men whose natures sort with their vocations; otherwise they may say, *multum incola fuit anima mea,*[3] when they converse in[4] those things they do not affect.* In studies, whatsoever a man commandeth upon himself, let him set hours for it; but whatsoever is agreeable to his nature, let him take no care for any set times, for his thoughts will fly to it of themselves, so as the spaces of other business or studies will suffice. A man's nature runs either to herbs or weeds; therefore let him seasonably water the one, and destroy the other.

---

[2] "He is the best master of his soul who bursts the chains that gall his breast and is once for all free from grief." Ovid, *Remedy of Love,* 293-4.

[3] "my soul has long been a sojourner", i.e., dwelt long in uncongenial circumstances. See Psalms 120:6.

[4] are engaged in.

XXXIX. OF CUSTOM AND EDUCATION

MEN's thoughts are much according to their inclination, their discourse and speeches according to their learning and infused opinions, but their deeds are after[1] as they have been accustomed. And therefore as Machiavel well noteth (though in an evil-favoured instance), there is no trusting to the force of nature nor to the bravery* of words, except it be corroborate by custom. His instance is, that for the achieving of a desperate conspiracy, a man should not rest upon the fierceness of any man's nature or his resolute undertakings, but take such an one as hath had his hands formerly in blood.[2] But Machiavel knew not of a Friar Clement, nor a Ravillac, nor a Jaureguy, nor a Baltazar Gerard;[3] yet his rule holdeth still, that nature nor the engagement of words are not so forcible as custom. Only superstition is now so well advanced that men of the first blood[4] are as firm as butchers by occupation, and votary resolution is made equipollent to custom even in matter of blood. In other things the predominancy of custom is everywhere visible; insomuch as a man would wonder to hear men profess, protest, engage, give great words, and then do just as they have done before, as if they were dead images and engines moved only by the wheels of custom. We see also the reign or tyranny of custom, what it is. The Indians (I mean the sect[5] of their wise men) lay themselves quietly upon a stack of wood, and so sacrifice themselves by fire. Nay the wives strive to be burned with the corpses of their husbands. The lads of Sparta of ancient time were wont to be scourged upon the altar of Diana without so much as queching.[6] I remember, in the beginning of Queen Elizabeth's time of England, an Irish rebel condemned, put up a petition to the Deputy that he might be hanged in a with[7] and not in an halter, because it had

[1] according.
[2] *Disc. on Livy*, III.6.
[3] Clement assassinated Henry III of France in 1589. Ravaillac killed Henry IV of France in 1610. Jaureguy tried to kill William the Silent in 1582; and Guérard succeeded in doing so in 1584.
[4] i.e., who have shed their first blood.
[5] i.e., the Gymnosophists. See Plutarch, *Alexander*, 64, 65.
[6] flinching or stirring. See Montaigne, *Essays*, II.32.
[7] withy.

been so used with former rebels. There be monks in Russia, for penance, that will sit a whole night in a vessel of water, till they be engaged[8] with hard ice. Many examples may be put of the force of custom both upon mind and body. Therefore, since custom is the principal magistrate of man's life, let men by all means endeavour to obtain good customs. Certainly custom is most perfect when it beginneth in young years; this we call education, which is, in effect, but an early custom. So we see, in languages the tongue is more pliant to all expressions and sounds, the joints are more supple to all feats of activity and motions in youth than afterwards. For it is true that late learners cannot so well take the ply,[9] except it be in some minds that have not suffered themselves to fix, but have kept themselves open and prepared to receive continual amendment, which is exceeding rare. But if the force of custom simple and separate be great, the force of custom copulate and conjoined and collegiate [10] is far greater. For there example teacheth, company comforteth,[11] emulation quickeneth, glory raiseth, so as in such places the force of custom is in his exaltation.[12] Certainly the great multiplication of virtues upon human nature resteth upon societies well ordained and disciplined. For commonwealths and good governments do nourish virtue grown, but do not much mend the seeds. But the misery is that the most effectual means are now applied to the ends least to be desired.

XL. OF FORTUNE

IT cannot be denied, but outward accidents conduce much to fortune: favour, opportunity, death of others, occasion fitting virtue. But chiefly the mould of a man's fortune is in his own hands. *Faber quisque fortunæ suæ,* saith the poet.[1] And the most

---

[8] bound, fixed.

[9] be bent in any direction.

[10] corporate.

[11] strengthens.

[12] (astrology) at its point of greatest influence.

[1] "Every man the architect of his own fortune." As the Latin translation of the *Essays* seems to show, the "poet" (*comicus*) Bacon probably had in mind was Plautus (*Trinummus,* II.ii.34), but the phrase was in popular use long before Plautus's time.

frequent of external causes is that the folly of one man is the fortune of another. For no man prospers so suddenly as by others' errors. *Serpens nisi serpentem comederit non fit draco.*[2] Overt and apparent[3] virtues bring forth praise, but there be secret and hidden virtues that bring forth fortune: certain deliveries* of a man's self, which have no name. The Spanish name, *desenvoltura*,[4] partly expresseth them, when there be not stonds[5] nor restiveness in a man's nature, but that the wheels of his mind keep way with the wheels of his fortune. For so Livy (after he had described Cato Major in these words, *In illo viro tantum robur corporis et animi fuit, ut quocunque loco natus esset, fortunam sibi facturus videretur*)[6] falleth upon that,[7] that he had *versatile ingenium.*[8] Therefore if a man look sharply and attentively, he shall see Fortune, for though she be blind, yet she is not invisible. The way of fortune is like the milken way in the sky, which is a meeting or knot of a number of small stars, not seen asunder but giving light together. So are there a number of little and scarce discerned virtues, or rather faculties and customs, that make men fortunate. The Italians note some of them, such as a man would little think. When they speak of one that cannot do amiss, they will throw in into his other conditions that he hath *Poco di matto.*[9] And certainly there be not two more fortunate properties* than to have a little of the fool and not too much of the honest. Therefore extreme lovers of their country or masters were never fortunate, neither can they be. For when a man placeth his thoughts without himself, he goeth not his own way. An hasty fortune maketh an enterpriser and remover[10] (the French hath it better, *entreprenant*, or *remuant*), but the exercised[11] fortune maketh the able man. Fortune is to be honoured and respected, and it be but for her daughters, Confidence and Reputation. For those two felicity breedeth, the first within a

---

[2] "A serpent does not become a dragon except by eating another serpent." Greek proverb.

[3] evident, conspicuous.

[4] graceful and easy expression.

[5] hindrances.

[6] "Such was the strength of his body and mind that he could have made himself a fortune regardless of his birthplace." Livy, XXXIX.40.

[7] notes the fact.

[8] versatile mind.

[9] "a little of the fool".

[10] a restless man.

[11] achieved with difficulty.

man's self, the latter in others towards him. All wise men, to decline[12] the envy of their own virtues, use to ascribe them to Providence and Fortune, for so they may the better assume them; and, besides, it is greatness in a man to be the care of the higher powers. So Cæsar said to the pilot in the tempest, *Cæsarem portas, et fortunam ejus.*[13] So Sylla chose the name of *Felix* and not of *Magnus.*[14] And it hath been noted that those who ascribe openly too much to their own wisdom and policy end infortunate.* It is written that Timotheus the Athenian, after he had, in the account he gave to the state of his government, often interlaced this speech, *and in this Fortune had no part*, never prospered in any thing he undertook afterwards.[15] Certainly there be, whose fortunes are like Homer's verses, that have a slide and easiness more than the verses of other poets, as Plutarch saith of Timoleon's fortune in respect of* that of Agesilaus or Epaminondas.[16] And that this should be, no doubt it is much in a man's self.

XLI. OF USURY

MANY have made witty invectives against Usury.[1] They say that it is a pity the devil should have God's part, which is the tithe.[2] That the usurer is the greatest sabbath-breaker, because his plough goeth every Sunday. That the usurer is the drone that Virgil speaketh of:

Ignavum fucos pecus a præsepibus arcent.[3]

That the usurer breaketh the first law that was made for mankind after the fall, which was, *in sudore vultus tui comedes panem tuum;* not, *in sudore vultus alieni;*[4] that usurers should

---

[12] avoid, turn aside.

[13] "You carry Caesar and his fortune." Plutarch, *Caesar*, 38.

[14] "Fortunate" and not "Great". Plutarch, *Sylla*, 34.

[15] Timotheus: an Athenian general of the fourth century B.C. See Plutarch, *Sylla*, 6.

[16] Timoleon: a Corinthian general of the fourth century B.C. See Plutarch, *Timoleon*, 36.

[1] simply interest paid on a loan, not necessarily exorbitant.

[2] See Leviticus 27:30.

[3] "They drove the lazy herd of drones from the hive." *Georgics*, IV.168.

[4] "in the sweat of thy face shalt thou eat bread" [cf. Gen. 3:19]; not "in the sweat of another's face".

have orange-tawny bonnets[5] because they do judaize; that it is against nature for money to beget money; and the like. I say this only, that usury is a *concessum propter duritiem cordis,*[6] for since there must be borrowing and lending, and men are so hard of heart as they will not lend freely, usury must be permitted. Some others have made suspicious and cunning propositions of banks, discovery* of men's estates, and other inventions. But few have spoken of usury usefully. It is good to set before us the incommodities and commodities[7] of usury, that the good may be either weighed out or culled out, and warily to provide that, while we make forth to that which is better, we meet not with that which is worse.

The discommodities of usury are, first, that it makes fewer merchants. For were it not for this lazy trade of usury, money would not lie still, but would in great part be employed upon merchandising, which is the *vena porta*[8] of wealth in a state. The second, that it makes poor merchants. For as a farmer cannot husband his ground so well if he sit[9] at a great rent, so the merchant cannot drive his trade so well if he sit at great usury. The third is incident to the other two, and that is the decay of customs of kings or states, which ebb or flow with merchandising. The fourth, that it bringeth the treasure of a realm or state into a few hands. For the usurer being at certainties, and others at uncertainties, at the end of the game most of the money will be in the box; and ever a state flourisheth when wealth is more equally spread. The fifth, that it beats down the price of land, for the employment of money is chiefly either merchandising or purchasing, and usury waylays both. The sixth, that it doth dull and damp all industries, improvements, and new inventions, wherein money would be stirring, if it were not for this slug.[10] The last, that it is the canker and ruin of many men's estates,

---

[5] The Jews were required to wear yellow head-dresses in medieval Europe.

[6] "a thing allowed because of the hardness of men's hearts". Cf. Matt. 19:8.

[7] disadvantages and advantages.

[8] the "gate vein", which, it was believed, carried the blood to the liver.

[9] is settled.

[10] hindrance.

which in process of time breeds a public poverty.

On the other side, the commodities of usury are, first, that howsoever usury in some respect hindereth merchandising, yet in some other it advanceth it; for it is certain that the greatest part of trade is driven by young merchants upon borrowing at interest; so as if the usurer either call in or keep back his money, there will ensue presently a great stand of trade. The second is, that were it not for this easy borrowing upon interest, men's necessities would draw upon them a most sudden undoing, in that they would be forced to sell their means (be it lands or goods) far under foot;[11] and so, whereas usury doth but gnaw upon them, bad markets would swallow them quite up. As for mortgaging or pawning, it will little mend the matter; for either men will not take pawns without use,[12] or if they do, they will look precisely for[13] the forfeiture. I remember a cruel monied man in the country that would say, The devil take this usury; it keeps us from forfeitures of mortgages and bonds. The third and last is that it is a vanity to conceive that there would be ordinary borrowing without profit; and it is impossible to conceive the number of inconveniences that will ensue if borrowing be cramped. Therefore to speak of the abolishing of usury is idle. All states have ever had it, in one kind or rate or other. So as that opinion must be sent to Utopia.

To speak now of the reformation and reiglement[14] of usury; how the discommodities of it may be best avoided, and the commodities retained. It appears by the balance of commodities and discommodities of usury, two things are to be reconciled. The one, that the tooth of usury be grinded, that it bite not too much; the other, that there be left open a means to invite monied men to lend to the merchants for the continuing and quickening of trade. This cannot be done except you introduce two several sorts of usury, a less and a greater. For if you reduce usury to one low rate, it will ease the common borrower, but the merchant will be to seek for[15] money. And it is to be noted that the trade

---

[11] too low.
[12] i.e., will not lend on mortgages without interest.
[13] be strict regarding.
[14] regulation.
[15] at a loss for.

of merchandise, being the most lucrative, may bear usury at a good rate; other contracts not so.

To serve both intentions, the way would be briefly thus. That there be two rates of usury: the one free and general for all, the other under licence only to certain persons and in certain places of merchandising. First therefore, let usury in general be reduced to five in the hundred; and let that rate be proclaimed to be free and current; and let the state shut itself out to take[16] any penalty for the same. This will preserve borrowing from any general stop or dryness. This will ease infinite borrowers in the country. This will in good part raise the price of land, because land purchased at sixteen years' purchase will yield six in the hundred and somewhat more; whereas this rate of interest yields but five. This by like reason will encourage and edge[17] industrious and profitable improvements, because many will rather venture in that kind* than take five in the hundred, especially having been used to greater profit. Secondly, let there be certain persons licensed to lend to known merchants upon usury at a higher rate, and let it be with the cautions following. Let the rate be, even with the merchant himself, somewhat more easy than that he used formerly to pay, for by that means all borrowers shall have some ease by this reformation, be he merchant or whosoever. Let it be no bank or common stock, but every man be master of his own money. Not that I altogether mislike banks, but they will hardly be brooked in regard of* certain suspicions. Let the state be answered some small matter for the licence, and the rest left to the lender, for if the abatement be but small, it will no whit discourage the lender. For he, for example, that took before ten or nine in the hundred will sooner descend to eight in the hundred, than give over his trade of usury, and go from certain gains to gains of hazard. Let these licensed lenders be in number indefinite, but restrained to certain principal cities and towns of merchandising, for then they will be hardly able to colour[18] other men's monies in the country: so as the licence of nine will

---

[16] i.e., undertake not to exact.
[17] stimulate.
[18] i.e., treat as their own. to colour: to make a thing appear what it is not; to misrepresent.

not suck away the current rate of five, for no man will lend his monies far off, nor put them into unknown hands.

If it be objected that this doth in a sort authorize usury, which before was in some places but permissive, the answer is that it is better to mitigate usury by declaration than to suffer it to rage by connivance.

XLII. OF YOUTH AND AGE

A MAN that is young in years may be old in hours, if he have lost no time. But that happeneth rarely. Generally youth is like the first cogitations, not so wise as the second. For there is a youth in thoughts, as well as in ages. And yet the invention of young men is more lively than that of old, and imaginations stream into their minds better, and as it were more divinely. Natures that have much heat and great and violent desires and perturbations are not ripe for action till they have passed the meridian of their years, as it was with Julius Cæsar and Septimius Severus. Of the latter of whom it is said, *Juventutem egit erroribus, imo furoribus, plenam.*[1] And yet he was the ablest emperor, almost, of all the list. But reposed[2] natures may do well in youth. As it is seen in Augustus Cæsar, Cosmus, Duke of Florence, Gaston de Fois,[3] and others. On the other side, heat and vivacity in age is an excellent composition* for business. Young men are fitter to invent than to judge, fitter for execution than for counsel, and fitter for new projects than for settled business. For the experience of age, in things that fall within the compass of it, directeth them, but in new things abuseth[4] them. The errors of young men are the ruin of business; but the errors of aged men amount but to this, that more might have been done, or sooner. Young men in the conduct and manage of actions embrace more than they

---

[1] "He spent his youth in folly, nay, in madness." Spartianus, *Severus,* II.

[2] calm.

[3] Cosimo de' Medici, the Great (1519-74), became Duke of Florence in 1537. Gaston de Foix, Duc de Nemours (1489-1512), a French commander killed at Ravenna.

[4] deceives, misleads.

can hold; stir more than they can quiet; fly to the end, without consideration of the means and degrees; pursue some few principles which they have chanced upon absurdly; care not to innovate,[5] which draws unknown inconveniences; use extreme remedies at first; and that which doubleth all errors, will not acknowledge or retract them, like an unready horse that will neither stop nor turn. Men of age object too much, consult too long, adventure too little, repent too soon, and seldom drive business home to the full period,* but content themselves with a mediocrity of success. Certainly it is good to compound employments of both: for that will be good for the present, because the virtues of either age may correct the defects of both; and good for succession, that young men may be learners, while men in age are actors; and, lastly, good for extern[6] accidents, because authority followeth old men, and favour and popularity youth. But for the moral part, perhaps youth will have the pre-eminence, as age hath for the politic. A certain rabbin, upon the text, *Your young men shall see visions, and your old men shall dream dreams,*[7] inferreth that young men are admitted nearer to God than old, because vision is a clearer revelation than a dream. And certainly the more a man drinketh of the world, the more it intoxicateth, and age doth profit rather in the powers of understanding than in the virtues of the will and affections. There be some have[8] an over-early ripeness in their years, which fadeth betimes. These are, first, such as have brittle wits,* the edge whereof is soon turned, such as was Hermogenes the rhetorician, whose books are exceeding subtle, who afterwards waxed stupid.[9] A second sort is of those that have some natural dispositions which have better grace in youth than in age, such as is a fluent and luxuriant speech, which becomes youth well, but not age; so Tully saith of Hortensius, *Idem manebat, neque idem decebat.*[10]

---

[5] are hasty or careless in their innovations.

[6] external.

[7] See Joel 2:28. The rabbin is Abrabanel.

[8] who have.

[9] Hermogenes (*fl.* A.D. 170): a Greek rhetorician who fell into a mental debility at the age of twenty-five.

[10] "He remained the same, though it did not become him." Cicero, *Brutus*, 25. Tully was a popular name for Marcus Tullius Cicero; Hortensius (114-50 B.C.): a Roman orator, rival to Cicero.

The third is of such as take too high a strain at the first, and are magnanimous more than tract of years can uphold. As was Scipio Africanus, of whom Livy saith in effect, *Ultima primis cedebant.*[11]

XLIII. OF BEAUTY

VIRTUE is like a rich stone, best plain set; and surely virtue is best in a body that is comely, though not of delicate features, and that hath rather dignity of presence than beauty of aspect. Neither is it almost[1] seen that very beautiful persons are otherwise of great virtue, as if nature were rather busy not to err than in labour to produce excellency. And therefore they prove accomplished, but not of great spirit, and study rather behaviour than virtue. But this holds not always, for Augustus Cæsar, Titus Vespasianus, Philip le Bel of France, Edward the Fourth of England, Alcibiades of Athens, Ismael the Sophy of Persia were all high and great spirits,[2] and yet the most beautiful men of their times. In beauty, that of favour* is more than that of colour, and that of decent and gracious[3] motion more than that of favour. That is the best part of beauty which a picture cannot express, no nor the first sight of life. There is no excellent beauty that hath not some strangeness in the proportion. A man cannot tell whether Apelles or Albert Durer[4] were the more trifler; whereof the one would make a personage by geometrical proportions, the other, by taking the best parts out of divers faces, to make one excellent. Such personages, I think, would please nobody but the painter that made them. Not but I think a painter may make a better face than ever was, but he must do it by a kind of felicity (as a musician that maketh an excellent air in music), and not by rule. A man shall see faces that, if you

---

[11] "The close of his life fell short of its beginning." Ovid, *Heroides,* IX.23; cf. Livy, XXXVIII.53.

[1] generally, for the most part.

[2] Ismail (*c.* 1480-1524) was the first Shah of Persia.

[3] becoming and graceful.

[4] Apelles is perhaps a mistake for Zeuxis who, when painting a picture of Helen, selected five of the most beautiful virgins in the country, so that his painting might present the best features of each. Albrecht Dürer wrote a treatise *On the Symmetry of the Parts of the Human Body* (1528).

examine them part by part, you shall find never a good, and yet altogether do well. If it be true that the principal part of beauty is in decent motion, certainly it is no marvel though persons in years seem many times more amiable: *Pulchrorum autumnus pulcher;*[5] for no youth can be comely but by pardon,[6] and considering the youth as to make up the comeliness. Beauty is as summer fruits, which are easy to corrupt, and cannot last; and for the most part it makes a dissolute youth and an age a little out of countenance; but yet certainly again, if it light well,[7] it maketh virtue shine and vices blush.

XLIV. OF DEFORMITY

DEFORMED persons are commonly even with nature, for as nature hath done ill by them, so do they by nature, being for the most part (as the Scripture saith) *void of natural affection;*[1] and so they have their revenge of nature. Certainly there is a consent[2] between the body and the mind, and where nature erreth in the one, she ventureth in the other. *Ubi peccat in uno, periclitatur in altero.* But because there is in man an election touching the frame of his mind and a necessity in the frame of his body, the stars of natural inclination are sometimes obscured by the sun of discipline and virtue. Therefore it is good to consider of deformity, not as a sign, which is more deceivable,[3] but as a cause, which seldom faileth of the effect. Whosoever hath anything fixed in his person that doth induce contempt hath also a perpetual spur in himself to rescue and deliver himself from scorn. Therefore all deformed persons are extreme bold. First, as in their own defence, as being exposed to scorn, but in process of time by a general habit. Also it stirreth in them industry, and especially of this kind, to watch and observe the weakness of others, that they may have somewhat to repay. Again, in their

---

[5] "The autumn of the beautiful is beautiful." Quoted by Plutarch, *Alcibiades*, I, from Euripides. [Northup]

[6] only if allowances are made.

[7] i.e., if beauty fall on a worthy person.

[1] Romans 1:31; II Tim. 3:3.

[2] agreement.

[3] deceptive.

superiors it quencheth jealousy towards them, as persons that they think they may at pleasure despise; and it layeth their competitors and emulators asleep, as never believing they should be in possibility of advancement, till they see them in possession. So that upon the matter,[4] in a great wit[*] deformity is an advantage to rising. Kings in ancient times (and at this present in some countries) were wont to put great trust in eunuchs, because they that are envious towards all are more obnoxious and officious[5] towards one. But yet their trust towards them hath rather been as to good spials[6] and good whisperers than good magistrates and officers. And much like is the reason of deformed persons. Still the ground is, they will, if they be of spirit, seek to free themselves from scorn, which must be either by virtue or malice; and therefore let it not be marvelled if sometimes they prove excellent persons, as was Agesilaus, Zanger the son of Soyman, Æsop, Gasca, President of Peru; and Socrates may go likewise amongst them, with others.[7]

XLV. OF BUILDING

HOUSES are built to live in, and not to look on; therefore let use be preferred before uniformity, except where both may be had. Leave the goodly fabrics of houses, for beauty only, to the enchanted palaces of the poets, who build them with small cost. He that builds a fair house upon an ill seat committeth himself to prison. Neither do I reckon it an ill seat only where the air is unwholesome, but likewise where the air is unequal, as you shall see many fine seats set upon a knap of ground, environed with higher hills round about it, whereby the heat of the sun is pent in, and the wind gathereth as in troughs; so as you shall have, and that suddenly, as great diversity of heat and cold as if you

[4] on the whole.
[5] submissive and dutiful.
[6] spies.
[7] Agesilaus was lame. Zanger, son of Suleiman the Magnificent, was known as "the crooked". Aesop has been represented as a perfect monster of ugliness and deformity. Pedro de la Gasca, who defeated Pizarro in Peru in 1547, had extremely long legs. The ugliness of Socrates was proverbial. [Selby]

dwelt in several places. Neither is it ill air only that maketh an ill seat, but ill ways, ill markets, and, if you will consult with Momus,[1] ill neighbours. I speak not of many more: want of water; want of wood, shade, and shelter; want of fruitfulness, and mixture of grounds of several natures; want of prospect; want of level grounds; want of places at some near distance for sports of hunting, hawking, and races; too near the sea, too remote; having the commodity* of navigable rivers or the discommodity of their overflowing; too far off from great cities, which may hinder business, or too near them, which lurcheth[2] all provisions, and maketh everything dear; where a man hath a great living laid together, and where he is scanted – all which, as it is impossible perhaps to find together, so it is good to know them, and think of them, that a man may take as many as he can; and if he have several dwellings, that he sort[3] them so, that what he wanteth in the one he may find in the other. Lucullus answered Pompey well, who, when he saw his stately galleries and rooms so large and lightsome in one of his houses, said, *Surely an excellent place for summer, but how do you in winter?* Lucullus answered, *Why, do you not think me as wise as some fowl are, that ever change their abode towards the winter?*[4]

To pass from the seat to the house itself, we will do as Cicero doth in the orator's art, who writes books *De Oratore*, and a book he entitles *Orator*, whereof the former delivers the precepts of the art, and the latter the perfection. We will therefore describe a princely palace, making a brief model thereof. For it is strange to see now in Europe such huge buildings as the Vatican and Escurial and some others be, and yet scarce a very fair room in them.

First therefore, I say you cannot have a perfect palace except you have two several[5] sides, a side for the banquet, as is spoken of in the book of Hester,[6] and a side for the household, the one for feasts and triumphs,* and the other for dwelling. I under-

---

[1] See Aesop, *Fables*, 275, where Momus criticizes a house built by Athena on the grounds that it lacked wheels and so could not be removed, if necessary, from bad neighbours.

[2] swallows up, absorbs.

[3] arranges.

[4] Cf. Plutarch, *Lucullus*, 39.

[5] separate, different.

[6] Esther.

stand both these sides to be not only returns[7] but parts of the front; and to be uniform without, though severally partitioned within; and to be on both sides of a great and stately tower in the midst of the front, that, as it were, joineth them together on either hand. I would have on the side of the banquet, in front, one only goodly room above stairs, of some forty foot high, and under it a room for a dressing or preparing place at times of triumphs. On the other side, which is the household side, I wish it divided at the first into a hall and a chapel (with a partition between), both of good state and bigness; and those not to go all the length, but to have at the further end a winter and a summer parlour, both fair. And under these rooms a fair and large cellar sunk under ground, and likewise some privy kitchens, with butteries and pantries and the like. As for the tower, I would have it two stories, of eighteen foot high apiece, above the two wings; and a goodly leads[8] upon the top, railed with statuas interposed; and the same tower to be divided into rooms, as shall be thought fit. The stairs likewise to the upper rooms, let them be upon a fair open newel, and finely railed in with images of wood cast into a brass colour, and a very fair landing-place at the top. But this to be, if you do not point[9] any of the lower rooms for a dining place of servants. For otherwise you shall have the servants' dinner after your own, for the steam of it will come up as in a tunnel. And so much for the front. Only I understand the height of the first stairs to be sixteen foot, which is the height of the lower room.

Beyond this front is there to be a fair court, but three sides of it, of a far lower building than the front. And in all the four corners of that court fair staircases, cast into turrets, on the outside, and not within the row of buildings themselves. But those towers are not to be of the height of the front, but rather proportionable to the lower building. Let the court not be paved, for that striketh up a great heat in summer and much cold in winter. But only some side alleys, with a cross, and the quarters to

---

[7] sides of the house built back from the front (usually on a right-angle continuation) and forming a court.

[8] leaded roof.

[9] appoint.

graze,[10] being kept shorn, but not too near shorn. The row of return[11] on the banquet side, let it be all stately galleries, in which galleries let there be three or five fine cupolas in the length of it, placed at equal distance, and fine coloured windows of several works. On the household side, chambers of presence and ordinary entertainments, with some bedchambers; and let all three sides be a double house, without thorough lights on the sides, that you may have rooms from the sun, both for forenoon and afternoon. Cast[12] it also that you may have rooms both for summer and winter, shady for summer, and warm for winter. You shall have sometimes fair houses so full of glass that one cannot tell where to become[13] to be out of the sun or cold. For inbowed[14] windows, I hold them of good use (in cities, indeed, upright do better, in respect of* the uniformity towards the street), for they be pretty retiring places for conference; and besides, they keep both the wind and sun off, for that which would strike almost thorough the room doth scarce pass the window. But let them be but few, four in the court, on the sides only.

Beyond this court let there be an inward court of the same square and height, which is to be environed with the garden on all sides; and in the inside, cloistered on all sides, upon decent and beautiful arches, as high as the first story. On the under story towards the garden, let it be turned to a grotta, or place of shade, or estivation.[15] And only have opening and windows towards the garden, and be level upon the floor, no whit sunken under ground, to avoid all dampishness. And let there be a fountain or some fair work of statuas in the midst of this court, and to be paved as the other court was. These buildings to be for privy lodgings on both sides, and the end for privy galleries. Whereof you must foresee that one of them be for an infirmary, if the prince or any special person should be sick, with chambers, bed-chamber, antecamera, and recamera[16] joining to it. This upon the second story. Upon the ground story, a fair gallery, open,

[10] to be turfed.
[11] the whole side of the court.
[12] plan.
[13] to betake oneself.

[14] embowed, bay.
[15] summering.
[16] antechamber and the room behind.

upon pillars; and upon the third story likewise, an open gallery, upon pillars, to take the prospect and freshness of the garden. At both corners of the further side, by way of return, let there be two delicate or rich cabinets, daintily[17] paved, richly hanged, glazed with crystalline glass, and a rich cupola in the midst, and all other elegancy that may be thought upon. In the upper gallery too, I wish that there may be, if the place will yield it, some fountains running in divers places from the wall, with some fine avoidances.[18] And thus much for the model of the palace, save that you must have, before you come to the front, three courts. A green court plain, with a wall about it; a second court of the same, but more garnished, with little turrets, or rather embellishments, upon the wall; and a third court, to make a square with the front, but not to be built, nor yet enclosed with a naked wall, but enclosed with tarrasses,[19] leaded aloft, and fairly garnished, on the three sides; and cloistered on the inside, with pillars and not with arches below. As for offices, let them stand at distance, with some low galleries, to pass from them to the palace itself.

XLVI. OF GARDENS

GOD Almighty first planted a Garden. And indeed it is the purest of human pleasures. It is the greatest refreshment to the spirits of man, without which buildings and palaces are but gross handiworks, and a man shall ever see that when ages grow to civility[1] and elegancy, men come to build stately sooner than to garden finely, as if gardening were the greater perfection. I do hold it, in the royal ordering of gardens, there ought to be gardens for all the months in the year, in which severally* things of beauty may be then in season. For December and January and the latter part of November, you must take such things as are green all winter: holly, ivy, bays, juniper, cypress trees, yew, pine-apple trees,[2] fir trees, rosemary, lavender, periwinkle, the white, the purple, and the blue, germander, flags, orange trees, lemon trees, and myr-

[17] elegantly.
[18] outlets for water.
[19] terraces.

[1] civilization.
[2] pine trees (whose cones were called apples).

tles, if they be stoved,[3] and sweet marjoram, warm set. There followeth, for the latter part of January and February, the mezereon tree, which then blossoms, crocus vernus, both the yellow and the grey, primroses, anemones, the early tulippa, hyacinthus orientalis, chamaïris,[4] fritellaria. For March, there come violets, specially the single blue, which are the earliest, the yellow daffodil, the daisy, the almond tree in blossom, the peach tree in blossom, the cornelian tree in blossom, sweetbriar. In April follow the double white violet, the wallflower, the stock-gilliflower, the cowslip, flower-de-lices, and lilies of all natures, rosemary flowers, the tulippa, the double piony, the pale daffodil, the French honeysuckle, the cherry tree in blossom, the damma-sin and plum trees in blossom, the white thorn in leaf, the lilac tree. In May and June come pinks of all sorts, specially the blush-pink, roses of all kinds, except the musk, which comes later, honeysuckles, strawberries, bugloss, columbine, the French mari-gold, flos Africanus, cherry tree in fruit, ribes,[5] figs in fruit, rasps, vine flowers, lavender in flowers, the sweet satyrian with the white flower, herba muscaria, lilium convallium, the apple tree in blossom. In July come gilliflowers of all varieties, musk roses, the lime tree in blossom, early pears and plums in fruit, genitings,[6] quadlins.[7] In August come plums of all sorts in fruit, pears, apricocks, barberries, filberds, musk-melons, monk's-hoods, of all colours. In September come grapes, apples, poppies of all colours, peaches, melocotones,[8] nectarines, cornelians, wardens, quinces. In October and the beginning of November come services, medlars, bullaces,[9] roses cut or removed to come late, holly oaks, and such like. These particulars are for the climate of London, but my meaning is perceived, that you may have *ver perpetuum*,[10] as the place affords.

And because the breath of flowers is far sweeter in the air (where it comes and goes like the warbling of music) than in the hand, therefore nothing is more fit for that delight than to know

---

[3] kept warm (in a hot-house).
[4] a kind of iris.
[5] currants.
[6] jennetings, early apples.
[7] codlings.

[8] a peach grafted on a quince.
[9] small wild plum.
[10] "perpetual spring". Virgil, *Georgics*, II.149.

what be the flowers and plants that do best perfume the air. Roses, damask and red, are fast[11] flowers of their smells, so that you may walk by a whole row of them, and find nothing of their sweetness; yea though it be in a morning's dew. Bays likewise yield no smell as they grow. Rosemary little, nor sweet marjoram. That which above all others yields the sweetest smell in the air is the violet, specially the white double violet, which comes twice a year, about the middle of April and about Bartholomew-tide. Next to that is the musk rose. Then the strawberry leaves dying, which [yield] a most excellent cordial smell. Then the flower of the vines; it is a little dust, like the dust of a bent, which grows upon the cluster in the first coming forth. Then sweetbriar. Then wallflowers, which are very delightful to be set under a parlour or lower chamber window. Then pinks and gilliflowers, specially the matted pink and clove gilliflower. Then the flowers of the lime tree. Then the honeysuckles, so they be somewhat afar off. Of bean flowers I speak not, because they are field flowers. But those which perfume the air most delightfully, not passed by as the rest, but being trodden upon and crushed, are three; that is, burnet, wild thyme, and water-mints. Therefore you are to set whole alleys of them, to have the pleasure when you walk or tread.

For gardens (speaking of those which are indeed prince-like, as we have done of buildings), the contents ought not well to be under thirty acres of ground, and to be divided into three parts: a green in the entrance; a heath[12] or desert in the going forth; and the main garden in the midst, besides alleys on both sides. And I like well that four acres of ground be assigned to the green, six to the heath, four and four to either side, and twelve to the main garden. The green hath two pleasures: the one, because nothing is more pleasant to the eye than green grass kept finely shorn; the other, because it will give you a fair alley in the midst, by which you may go in front upon[13] a stately hedge, which is to enclose the garden. But because the alley will be long and, in

---

[11] tenacious (i.e., do not yield their odour).

[12] i.e., garden left wild.

[13] advance towards.

great heat of the year or day, you ought not to buy the shade in the garden by going in the sun through the green, therefore you are, of either side the green, to plant a covert[14] alley, upon carpenter's work, about twelve foot in height, by which you may go in shade into the garden. As for the making of knots[15] or figures with divers coloured earths, that they may lie under the windows of the house on that side which the garden stands, they be but toys; you may see as good sights many times in tarts. The garden is best to be square, encompassed on all the four sides with a stately arched hedge. The arches to be upon pillars of carpenter's work, of some ten foot high and six foot broad, and the spaces between of the same dimension with the breadth of the arch. Over the arches let there be an entire[16] hedge of some four foot high, framed also upon carpenter's work, and upon the upper hedge, over every arch, a little turret with a belly, enough to receive a cage of birds; and over every space between the arches some other little figure, with broad plates of round coloured glass gilt for the sun to play upon. But this hedge I intend to be raised upon a bank, not steep but gently slope,[17] of some six foot, set all with flowers. Also I understand that this square of the garden should not be the whole breadth of the ground, but to leave on either side ground enough for diversity of side alleys, unto which the two covert alleys of the green may deliver you. But there must be no alleys with hedges at either end of this great enclosure: not at the hither end, for letting[18] your prospect upon this fair hedge from the green, nor at the further end, for letting your prospect from the hedge through the arches upon the heath.

For the ordering of the ground within the great hedge, I leave it to variety of device, advising nevertheless that whatsoever form you cast it into, first, it be not too busy[19] or full of work. Wherein I, for my part, do not like images cut out in juniper or other garden stuff; they be for children. Little low hedges, round like welts,[20] with some pretty pyramids, I like well, and in some places fair columns upon frames of carpenter's work. I would

[14] i.e., covered, sheltered.
[15] beds.
[16] continuous, unbroken.
[17] sloping.

[18] hindering, blocking.
[19] elaborate.
[20] edges, borders.

also have the alleys spacious and fair. You may have closer alleys upon the side grounds, but none in the main garden. I wish also in the very middle a fair mount with three ascents and alleys, enough for four to walk abreast, which I would have to be perfect circles, without any bulwarks or embossments; and the whole mount to be thirty foot high; and some fine banqueting-house, with some chimneys neatly cast, and without too much glass.

For fountains, they are a great beauty and refreshment, but pools mar all, and make the garden unwholesome and full of flies and frogs. Fountains I intend to be of two natures: the one that sprinkleth or spouteth water; the other a fair receipt[21] of water, of some thirty or forty foot square, but without fish or slime or mud. For the first, the ornaments of images gilt or of marble, which are in use, do well, but the main matter is so to convey the water as it never stay, either in the bowls or in the cistern, that the water be never by rest discoloured, green or red or the like, or gather any mossiness or putrefaction. Besides that, it is to be cleansed every day by the hand. Also some steps up to it and some fine pavement about it doth well. As for the other kind of fountain, which we may call a bathing pool, it may admit much curiosity* and beauty, wherewith we will not trouble ourselves; as that the bottom be finely paved, and with images; the sides likewise; and withal embellished with coloured glass, and such things of lustre; encompassed also with fine rails of low statuas. But the main point is the same which we mentioned in the former kind of fountain, which is that the water be in perpetual motion, fed by a water higher than the pool, and delivered into it by fair spouts, and then discharged away under ground by some equality of bores,[22] that it stay little. And for fine devices, of arching water without spilling and making it rise in several forms (of feathers, drinking glasses, canopies, and the like), they be pretty things to look on, but nothing to health and sweetness.

For the heath, which was the third part of our plot, I wish it to be framed, as much as may be, to a natural wildness. Trees I would have none in it, but some thickets made only of sweetbriar

---

[21] receptacle.   [22] pipes of equal dimensions.

and honeysuckle and some wild vine amongst; and the ground set with violets, strawberries, and primroses. For these are sweet, and prosper in the shade. And these to be in the heath, here and there, not in any order. I like also little heaps, in the nature of molehills (such as are in wild heaths), to be set, some with wild thyme; some with pinks; some with germander, that gives a good flower to the eye; some with periwinkle; some with violets; some with strawberries; some with cowslips; some with daisies; some with red roses; some with lilium convallium; some with sweet williams red; some with bear's-foot, and the like low flowers, being withal sweet and sightly. Part of which heaps are to be with standards of little bushes pricked* upon their top, and part without. The standards to be roses, juniper, holly, barberries (but here and there, because of the smell of their blossom), red currants, gooseberry, rosemary, bays, sweetbriar, and such like. But these standards to be kept with cutting, that they grow not out of course.[23]

For the side grounds, you are to fill them with variety of alleys, private, to give a full shade, some of them wheresoever the sun be. You are to frame some of them likewise for shelter, that when the wind blows sharp, you may walk as in a gallery. And those alleys must be likewise hedged at both ends to keep out the wind; and these closer alleys must be ever finely gravelled, and no grass, because of going wet.[24] In many of these alleys likewise, you are to set fruit trees of all sorts, as well upon the walls as in ranges. And this would* be generally observed, that the borders wherein you plant your fruit trees be fair and large and low and not steep, and set with fine flowers, but thin and sparingly lest they deceive[25] the trees. At the end of both the side grounds I would have a mount of some pretty height, leaving the wall of the enclosure breast high, to look abroad into the fields.

For the main garden, I do not deny but there should be some fair alleys ranged on both sides with fruit trees; and some pretty tufts of fruit trees and arbours with seats, set in some decent

---

[23] bounds, line.
[24] because then you would have to go in the wet.
[25] rob (of nourishment).

order; but these to be by no means set too thick, but to leave the main garden so as it be not close, but the air open and free. For as for shade, I would have you rest upon the alleys of the side grounds, there to walk, if you be disposed, in the heat of the year or day, but to make account that the main garden is for the more temperate parts of the year, and in the heat of summer, for the morning and the evening, or overcast days.

For aviaries, I like them not, except they be of that largeness as they may be turfed, and have living plants and bushes set in them; that the birds may have more scope and natural nestling, and that no foulness appear in the floor of the aviary. So I have made a platform[26] of a princely garden, partly by precept, partly by drawing, not a model, but some general lines of it, and in this I have spared for no cost. But it is nothing for great princes, that for the most part taking advice with workmen, with no less cost set their things together; and sometimes add statuas and such things for state and magnificence, but nothing to the true pleasure of a garden.

XLVII. OF NEGOTIATING

IT is generally better to deal by speech than by letter, and by the mediation of a third than by a man's self. Letters are good when a man would draw an answer by letter back again, or when it may serve for a man's justification afterwards to produce his own letter, or where it may be danger to be interrupted or heard by pieces.[1] To deal in person is good when a man's face breedeth regard, as commonly with inferiors, or in tender* cases, where a man's eye upon the countenance of him with whom he speaketh may give him a direction how far to go, and generally, where a man will reserve to himself liberty either to disavow or to expound. In choice of instruments it is better to choose men of a plainer sort, that are like to do that that is committed to them,

---

[26] pattern.

[1] i.e., danger of being interrupted and only partially heard.

and to report back again faithfully the success,[2] than those that are cunning* to contrive out of other men's business somewhat to grace themselves, and will help the matter in report[3] for satisfaction sake. Use also such persons as affect* the business wherein they are employed, for that quickeneth much, and such as are fit for the matter, as bold men for expostulation, fair-spoken men for persuasion, crafty men for inquiry and observation, froward and absurd* men for business that doth not well bear out itself. Use also such as have been lucky, and prevailed before in things wherein you have employed them, for that breeds confidence, and they will strive to maintain their prescription.[4] It is better to sound a person with whom one deals afar off than to fall upon the point at first, except you mean to surprise him by some short question. It is better dealing with men in appetite[5] than with those that are where they would be. If a man deal with another upon conditions, the start or first performance is all, which a man cannot reasonably demand, except either the nature of the thing be such, which must go before, or else a man can persuade the other party that he shall still need him in some other thing, or else that he be counted the honester man. All practice[6] is to discover* or to work.[7] Men discover themselves in trust, in passion, at unawares, and of necessity, when they would have somewhat done and cannot find an apt pretext. If you would work any man, you must either know his nature and fashions,[8] and so lead him; or his ends, and so persuade him; or his weakness and disadvantages, and so awe him; or those that have interest in[9] him, and so govern him. In dealing with cunning persons we must ever consider their ends to interpret their speeches; and it is good to say little to them, and that which they least look for. In all negotiations of difficulty, a man may not look to sow and reap at once, but must prepare business, and so ripen it by degrees.

[2] result.
[3] i.e., will give too favourable a report.
[4] reputation, right to the title (of lucky).
[5] desiring something, with ambition.
[6] negotiation.
[7] manipulate.
[8] habits.
[9] influence over.

XLVIII. OF FOLLOWERS AND FRIENDS

COSTLY followers are not to be liked, lest while a man maketh his train longer, he make his wings shorter. I reckon to be costly not them alone which charge[1] the purse, but which are wearisome and importune* in suits. Ordinary followers ought to challenge[2] no higher conditions than countenance, recommendation, and protection from wrongs. Factious followers are worse to be liked, which follow not upon affection to him with whom they range themselves, but upon discontentment conceived against some other; whereupon commonly ensueth that ill intelligence[3] that we many times see between great personages. Likewise glorious* followers, who make themselves as trumpets of the commendation of those they follow, are full of inconvenience, for they taint business through want of secrecy, and they export honour from a man, and make him a return in envy. There is a kind of followers likewise which are dangerous, being indeed espials,* which inquire the secrets of the house, and bear tales of them to others. Yet such men many times are in great favour, for they are officious,* and commonly exchange tales. The following by certain estates* of men, answerable to that which a great person himself professeth (as of soldiers to him that hath been employed in the wars, and the like), hath ever been a thing civil,* and well taken even in monarchies, so* it be without too much pomp or popularity.* But the most honourable kind of following is to be followed as one that apprehendeth[4] to advance virtue and desert in all sorts of persons. And yet, where there is no eminent odds in sufficiency,[5] it is better to take with the more passable[6] than with the more able. And besides, to speak truth, in base times active men are of more use than virtuous. It is true that in government it is good to use men of one rank equally, for to countenance some extraordinarily is to make them insolent and the rest discontent, because they may claim a due. But contrariwise, in favour,[7] to use men with much difference and

---

[1] put a burden on.
[2] claim.
[3] misunderstanding.
[4] knows how, inclines himself.

[5] ability.
[6] commonplace, ordinary.
[7] i.e., in favouring or indulging men.

election is good, for it maketh the persons preferred more thankful, and the rest more officious,* because all is of favour. It is good discretion not to make too much of any man at the first, because one cannot hold out that proportion. To be governed (as we call it) by one is not safe, for it shows softness, and gives a freedom to scandal and disreputation;[8] for those that would not censure or speak ill of a man immediately will talk more boldly of those that are so great with them, and thereby wound their honour. Yet to be distracted with many is worse, for it makes men to be of the last impression and full of change. To take advice of some few friends is ever honourable, *for lookers-on many times see more than gamesters; and the vale best discovereth* the hill.*[9] There is little friendship in the world, and least of all between equals, which was wont to be magnified. That that is, is between superior and inferior, whose fortunes may comprehend the one the other.

XLIX. OF SUITORS

MANY ill matters and projects are undertaken, and private suits do putrefy the public good. Many good matters are undertaken with bad minds; I mean not only corrupt minds, but crafty minds, that intend not performance. Some embrace suits, which never mean to deal effectually in them, but if they see there may be life in the matter by some other mean,* they will be content to win a thank, or take a second[1] reward, or at least to make use in the meantime of the suitor's hopes. Some take hold of suits only for an occasion to cross some other, or to make an information whereof they could not otherwise have apt pretext; without care what become of the suit when that turn is served; or generally to make other men's business a kind of entertainment[2] to bring in their own. Nay some undertake suits with a full purpose to let them fall, to the end to gratify the adverse party or competitor. Surely there is in some sort a right in every suit,

8 disrepute.
9 Machiavelli, *The Prince*, Dedication.

1 inferior, secondary.
2 curtain raiser, preliminary, introduction.

either a right in equity, if it be a suit of controversy, or a right of
desert, if it be a suit of petition. If affection lead a man to favour
the wrong side in justice, let him rather use his countenance[3] to
compound the matter than to carry it. If affection lead a man to
favour the less worthy in desert, let him do it without depraving
or disabling[4] the better deserver. In suits which a man doth not
well understand, it is good to refer them to some friend of trust
and judgment, that may report whether he may deal in them
with honour, but let him choose well his referendaries,[5] for else
he may be led by the nose.[6] Suitors are so distasted[7] with delays
and abuses* that plain dealing in denying to deal in suits at first,
and reporting the success barely, and in challenging no more
thanks than one hath deserved is grown not only honourable but
also gracious.[8] In suits of favour the first coming ought to take
little place,[9] so far forth[10] consideration may be had of his trust,
that if intelligence of the matter could not otherwise have been
had but by him, advantage be not taken of the note, but the
party left to his other means, and in some sort recompensed for
his discovery. To be ignorant of the value of a suit is simplicity,
as well as to be ignorant of the right thereof is want of conscience. Secrecy in suits is a great mean* of obtaining, for voicing[11] them to be in forwardness may discourage some kind of
suitors, but doth quicken and awake others. But timing of the
suit is the principal. Timing, I say, not only in respect of the
person that should grant it, but in respect of those which are like
to cross it. Let a man in the choice of his mean rather choose the
fittest mean than the greatest mean, and rather them that deal
in certain things than those that are general. The reparation
of a denial is sometimes equal to the first grant, if a man show
himself neither dejected nor discontented. *Iniquum petas ut
æquum feras,*[12] is a good rule where a man hath strength of

---

[3] influence (to get the parties to agree, rather than to force it through).

[4] defaming or disparaging.

[5] referees.

[6] deceived.

[7] disgusted.

[8] something to be thankful for, a positive favour.

[9] be of little weight.

[10] so far.

[11] reporting, proclaiming (that they are going well).

[12] "Ask for more than is just, that you may get as much as is just." Quintilian, IV.v.16.

favour;[13] but otherwise a man were better rise in his suit, for he that would have ventured at first to have lost the suitor, will not in the conclusion lose both the suitor and his own former favour.[14] Nothing is thought so easy a request to a great person as his letter; and yet, if it be not in a good cause, it is so much out of his reputation. There are no worse instruments than these general contrivers of suits, for they are but a kind of poison and infection to public proceedings.

L. OF STUDIES

STUDIES serve for delight, for ornament, and for ability. Their chief use for delight is in privateness and retiring;[1] for ornament, is in discourse; and for ability, is in the judgment and disposition of business. For expert men[2] can execute and perhaps judge of particulars, one by one, but the general counsels and the plots and marshalling of affairs come best from those that are learned. To spend too much time in studies is sloth; to use them too much for ornament is affectation; to make judgment wholly by their rules is the humour of a scholar. They perfect nature, and are perfected by experience, for natural abilities are like natural plants, that need proyning[3] by study; and studies themselves do give forth directions too much at large, except they be bounded in by experience. Crafty men contemn studies; simple men admire them; and wise men use them, for they teach not their own use, but that is a wisdom without them and above them, won by observation. Read not to contradict and confute, nor to believe and take for granted, nor to find talk and discourse, but to weigh and consider. Some books are to be tasted,

---

[13] i.e., is strongly favoured by the person to whom he addresses his petition.

[14] i.e., a man (the intermediary or "fittest mean") would be well advised to work up to what he wants, for he who follows the first principle (of asking for more than is just) risks losing (perhaps "ruining the chances of") his employer the

suitor, but he who follows the second principle will lose neither the suitor nor whatever favour or influence he has with the person being petitioned.

[1] privacy and retirement.

[2] men of experience (contrasted to learned men).

[3] pruning.

others to be swallowed, and some few to be chewed and digested; that is, some books are to be read only in parts; others to be read, but not curiously;* and some few to be read wholly and with diligence and attention. Some books also may be read by deputy, and extracts made of them by others, but that would* be only in the less important arguments and the meaner sort of books; else distilled books are like common distilled waters, flashy⁴ things. Reading maketh a full man, conference a ready man, and writing an exact man. And therefore, if a man write little, he had need have a great memory; if he confer little, he had need have a present wit: and if he read little, he had need have much cunning, to seem to know that he doth not. Histories make men wise, poets witty, the mathematics subtile, natural philosophy deep, moral grave, logic and rhetoric able to contend. *Abeunt studia in mores.*⁵ Nay there is no stond* or impediment in the wit but may be wrought out by fit studies, like as diseases of the body may have appropriate exercises. Bowling is good for the stone and reins; shooting for the lungs and breast; gentle walking for the stomach; riding for the head; and the like. So if a man's wit be wandering, let him study the mathematics, for in demonstrations, if his wit be called away never so little, he must begin again. If his wit be not apt to distinguish or find differences, let him study the schoolmen, for they are *cymini sectores.*⁶ If he be not apt to beat over⁷ matters, and to call up one thing to prove and illustrate another, let him study the lawyers' cases. So every defect of the mind may have a special receipt.

LI. OF FACTION

MANY have an opinion not wise, that for a prince to govern his estate,* or for a great person to govern his proceedings, according to the respect of factions is a principal part of policy; whereas

---

⁴ insipid, flat.

⁵ "Studies go to form character." Ovid, *Heroides*, XV.83.

⁶ "hair splitters" (literally, "carvers of cummin seed"). Dion Cassius,

LXX.3. Cf. Theocritus, *Idylls*, X.55.

⁷ synthesize, find resemblances and relationships in.

contrariwise, the chiefest wisdom is either in ordering those things which are general, and wherein men of several* factions do nevertheless agree, or in dealing with correspondence to[1] particular persons, one by one. But I say not that the consideration of factions is to be neglected. Mean men in their rising must adhere, but great men, that have strength in themselves, were better to maintain themselves indifferent* and neutral. Yet even in beginners, to adhere so moderately, as he be a man of the one faction which is most passable with[2] the other, commonly giveth best way. The lower and weaker faction is the firmer in conjunction; and it is often seen that a few that are stiff do tire out a greater number that are more moderate. When one of the factions is extinguished, the remaining subdivideth, as the faction between Lucullus and the rest of the nobles of the senate (which they called *Optimates*) held out awhile against the faction of Pompey and Cæsar, but when the senate's authority was pulled down, Cæsar and Pompey soon after brake. The faction or party of Antonius and Octavianus Cæsar against Brutus and Cassius held out likewise for a time, but when Brutus and Cassius were overthrown, then soon after Antonius and Octavianus brake and subdivided. These examples are of wars, but the same holdeth in private factions. And therefore those that are seconds in factions do many times, when the faction subdivideth, prove principals; but many times also they prove ciphers and cashiered, for many a man's strength is in opposition, and when that faileth he groweth out of use. It is commonly seen that men once placed take in with the contrary faction to that by which they enter, thinking belike that they have the first sure, and now are ready for a new purchase. The traitor in faction lightly[3] goeth away with it, for when matters have stuck long in balancing, the winning of some one man casteth[4] them, and he getteth all the thanks. The even carriage between two factions proceedeth not always of moderation but of a trueness to a man's self, with end to make use of both. Certainly in Italy they hold it a little suspect in popes when they have often in their mouth *Padre*

---

[1] in a manner suitable to.

[2] acceptable to.

[3] easily.

[4] decides (makes the balance sink).

commune,[5] and take it to be a sign of one that meaneth to refer all to the greatness of his own house. Kings had need beware how they side themselves, and make themselves as of a faction or party; for leagues within the state are ever pernicious to monarchies, for they raise an obligation paramount to obligation of sovereignty, and make the king *tanquam unus ex nobis*,[6] as was to be seen in the League of France.[7] When factions are carried too high and too violently, it is a sign of weakness in princes; and much to the prejudice both of their authority and business. The motions of factions under kings ought to be like the motions (as the astronomers speak) of the inferior orbs, which may have their proper* motions, but yet still are quietly carried by the higher motion of *primum mobile*.

LII. OF CEREMONIES AND RESPECTS

HE that is only real had need have exceeding great parts of virtue, as the stone had need to be rich that is set without foil. But if a man mark it well, it is in praise and commendation of men as it is in gettings and gains; for the proverb is true, *That light gains make heavy purses*, for light gains come thick, whereas great come but now and then. So it is true that small matters win great commendation, because they are continually in use and in note; whereas the occasion of any great virtue cometh but on festivals. Therefore it doth much add to a man's reputation, and is (as Queen Isabella said) *like perpetual letters commendatory*, to have good forms. To attain them it almost sufficeth not to despise them; for so shall a man observe them in others, and let him trust himself with the rest. For if he labour too much to express them, he shall lose their grace, which is to be natural and unaffected. Some men's behaviour is like a verse, wherein every syllable is measured; how can a man comprehend great matters,

[5] Common Father.
[6] "like one of us". See Gen. 3:22.
[7] the Holy League, organized in 1576 by the Duc de Guise to ensure Catholic succession to the French throne.

that breaketh[1] his mind too much to small observations? Not to use ceremonies at all is to teach others not to use them again, and so diminisheth respect to himself; especially they be not to be omitted to strangers and formal natures; but the dwelling upon them and exalting them above the moon is not only tedious, but doth diminish the faith and credit of him that speaks. And certainly there is a kind of conveying of effectual and imprinting[2] passages amongst compliments, which is of singular use, if a man can hit upon it. Amongst a man's peers a man shall be sure of familiarity, and therefore it is good a little to keep state. Amongst a man's inferiors one shall be sure of reverence, and therefore it is good a little to be familiar. He that is too much in anything, so that he giveth another occasion of satiety, maketh himself cheap. To apply[3] one's self to others is good, so it be with demonstration that a man doth it upon regard, and not upon facility.[4] It is a good precept generally in seconding another, yet to add somewhat of one's own, as: if you will grant his opinion, let it be with some distinction; if you will follow his motion, let it be with condition; if you allow* his counsel, let it be with alleging further reason. Men had need beware how they be too perfect in compliments, for be they never so sufficient* otherwise, their enviers will be sure to give them that attribute, to the disadvantage of their greater virtues. It is loss also in business to be too full of respects, or to be curious* in observing times and opportunities. Salomon saith, *He that considereth the wind shall not sow, and he that looketh to the clouds shall not reap.*[5] A wise man will make more opportunities than he finds. Men's behaviour should be like their apparel, not too strait or point-device, but free for exercise or motion.

---

[1] subdues, disciplines.
[2] impressive.
[3] accommodate.

[4] i.e., because of personal regard and not because of good nature.
[5] Eccles. 11:4.

LIII. OF PRAISE

PRAISE is the reflexion of virtue. But it is as the glass or body which giveth the reflexion. If it be from the common people, it is commonly false and naught, and rather followeth vain persons than virtuous. For the common people understand not many excellent virtues. The lowest virtues draw praise from them; the middle virtues work in them astonishment or admiration; but of the highest virtues they have no sense or perceiving at all. But shows and *species virtutibus similes*[1] serve best with them. Certainly fame is like a river, that beareth up things light and swoln, and drowns things weighty and solid. But if persons of quality and judgment concur, then it is (as the Scripture saith) *Nomen bonum instar unguenti fragrantis.*[2] It filleth all round about, and will not easily away. For the odours of ointments are more durable than those of flowers. There be so many false points of praise, that a man may justly hold it a suspect. Some praises proceed merely of flattery; and if he be an ordinary flatterer, he will have certain common attributes,[3] which may serve every man; if he be a cunning flatterer, he will follow the arch-flatterer, which is a man's self: and wherein a man thinketh best of himself, therein the flatterer will uphold him most; but if he be an impudent flatterer, look wherein a man is conscious to himself that he is most defective, and is most out of countenance in himself: that will the flatterer entitle him to perforce, *spreta conscientia.*[4] Some praises come of good wishes and respects, which is a form due in civility to kings and great persons, *laudando præcipere,*[5] when by telling men what they are, they represent to them what they should be. Some men are praised maliciously to their hurt, thereby to stir envy and jealousy towards them: *Pessimum genus inimicorum laudantium;*[6] insomuch as it was a proverb amongst the Grecians that *he that was praised to his hurt,*

---

[1] "appearances resembling virtues". Tacitus, *Ann.*, XV.48.

[2] "A good name is like a fragrant ointment." Cf. Eccles. 7:1.

[3] i.e., stock complimentary expressions.

[4] "scorning the other's awareness" (of the flattery).

[5] "to teach by praising". Perhaps from Pliny, *Epist.*, III.18.

[6] "The worst kind of enemies are they that praise." Tacitus, *Agricola*, 41.

should have a push[7] rise upon his nose; as we say, *that a blister will rise upon one's tongue that tells a lie.* Certainly moderate praise, used with opportunity and not vulgar, is that which doth the good. Salomon saith, *He that praiseth his friend aloud, rising early, it shall be to him no better than a curse.*[8] Too much magnifying of man or matter doth irritate contradiction, and procure envy and scorn. To praise a man's self cannot be decent, except it be in rare cases, but to praise a man's office or profession, he may do it with good grace, and with a kind of magnanimity. The Cardinals of Rome, which are theologues and friars and schoolmen, have a phrase of notable contempt and scorn towards civil business, for they call all temporal business of wars, embassages,* judicature, and other employments, *sbirrerie,* which is *under-sheriffries,* as if they were but matters for under-sheriffs and catchpoles, though many times those under-sheriffries do more good than their high speculations. St. Paul, when he boasts of himself, he doth oft interlace, *I speak like a fool,*[9] but speaking of his calling, he saith, *Magnificabo apostolatum meum.*[10]

LIV. OF VAINGLORY

IT was prettily devised of* Æsop: *The fly sat upon the axle-tree of the chariot wheel, and said, What a dust do I raise!* So are there some vain persons, that whatsoever goeth alone or moveth upon greater means, if they have never so little hand in it, they think it is they that carry it. They that are glorious* must needs be factious, for all bravery* stands upon comparisons. They must needs be violent to make good their own vaunts. Neither can they be secret, and therefore not effectual, but according to the French proverb, *Beaucoup de bruit, peu de fruit: Much bruit, little fruit.* Yet certainly there is use of this quality in civil affairs. Where there is an opinion and fame to be created either of virtue or greatness, these men are good trumpeters. Again, as Titus Livius noteth in the case of Antiochus and the Ætolians, *There*

---

7 pimple. See, for example, Theocritus, *Idylls,* IX.24; XII.23.

8 Prov. 27:14.

9 II Cor. 11:23.

10 "I will magnify my office." Cf. Rom. 11:13.

are sometimes great effects of cross lies;[1] as if a man that negoti-
ates between two princes, to draw them to join in a war against
the third, doth extol the forces of either of them above measure,
the one to the other; and sometimes he that deals between man
and man raiseth his own credit with both by pretending greater
interest than he hath in either. And in these and the like kinds,
it often falls out that somewhat is produced of nothing, for lies
are sufficient to breed opinion, and opinion brings on substance.
In militar[2] commanders and soldiers vainglory is an essential
point, for as iron sharpens iron, so by glory* one courage sharp-
eneth another. In cases of great enterprise upon charge and adventure,[3] a composition of glorious natures doth put life into
business, and those that are of solid and sober natures have more
of the ballast than of the sail. In fame of learning the flight will
be slow without some feathers of ostentation. *Qui de contem-
nenda gloria libros scribunt, nomen suum inscribunt.*[4] Socrates,
Aristotle, Galen were men full of ostentation. Certainly vainglory helpeth to perpetuate a man's memory, and virtue was
never so beholding to human nature, as it received his due at the
second hand. Neither had the fame of Cicero, Seneca, Plinius
Secundus borne her age so well, if it had not been joined with
some vanity in themselves, like unto varnish, that makes ceilings
not only shine but last. But all this while, when I speak of vainglory, I mean not of that property that Tacitus doth attribute to
Mucianus, *Omnium, quæ dixerat feceratque, arte quadam osten-
tator,*[5] for that proceeds not of vanity but of natural magnanimity and discretion, and in some persons is not only comely
but gracious. For excusations, cessions,[6] modesty itself well governed are but arts of ostentation. And amongst those arts there is
none better than that which Plinius Secundus speaketh of, which
is to be liberal of praise and commendation to others, in that

[1] Livy, XXXVII. 48.

[2] military.

[3] expense and risk.

[4] "Those who write books about
despising fame write their own
names on the title page." Cicero,
Tusculan Disputations, I.15.

[5] "One who had the art of displaying everything he said or did to
the best advantage." Tacitus,
Hist., II.80. Mucianus: Governor
of Syria and Roman consul of the
first century.

[6] concessions, yieldings to others.

wherein a man's self hath any perfection. For saith Pliny very wittily, *In commending another you do yourself right; for he that you commend is either superior to you in that you commend, or inferior. If he be inferior, if he be to be commended, you much more; if he be superior, if he be not to be commended, you much less.*[7] Glorious men are the scorn of wise men, the admiration of fools, the idols of parasites, and the slaves of their own vaunts.

LV. OF HONOUR AND REPUTATION

THE winning of Honour is but the revealing of a man's virtue and worth without disadvantage. For some in their actions do woo and affect* honour and reputation, which sort of men are commonly much talked of, but inwardly little admired. And some, contrariwise, darken their virtue in the show of it, so as they be undervalued in opinion. If a man perform that which hath not been attempted before, or attempted and given over, or hath been achieved, but not with so good circumstance, he shall purchase more honour than by effecting a matter of greater difficulty or virtue, wherein he is but a follower. If a man so temper his actions as in some one of them he doth content every faction or combination of people, the music will be the fuller. A man is an ill husband of his honour that entereth into any action, the failing wherein may disgrace him more than the carrying of it through can honour him. Honour that is gained and broken upon another[1] hath the quickest reflexion, like diamonds cut with facets. And therefore let a man contend to excel any competitors of his in honour, in outshooting them, if he can, in their own bow. Discreet followers and servants help much to reputation. *Omnis fama a domesticis emanat.*[2] Envy, which is the canker of honour, is best extinguished by declaring[3] a man's self

---

[7] quoted loosely from Pliny, *Epist.*, VI.17.

[1] gained at the expense of another.

[2] "All fame emanates from those of our household." Cicero, *On the Petition of the Consulate*, V.17.

[3] by making it known that he intends, etc.

in his ends rather to seek merit than fame, and by attributing a man's successes rather to divine Providence and felicity than to his own virtue or policy. The true marshalling of the degrees of sovereign honour are these. In the first place are *conditores imperiorum*, founders of states and commonwealths, such as were Romulus, Cyrus, Cæsar, Ottoman, Ismael.[4] In the second place are *legislatores*, lawgivers, which are also called *second founders* or *perpetui principes*,[5] because they govern by their ordinances after they are gone; such were Lycurgus, Solon, Justinian, Eadgar, Alphonsus of Castile, the Wise, that made the *Siete Partidas*.[6] In the third place are *liberatores* or *salvatores*,[7] such as compound[8] the long miseries of civil wars, or deliver their countries from servitude of strangers or tyrants, as Augustus Cæsar, Vespasianus, Aurelianus, Theodoricus, King Henry the Seventh of England, King Henry the Fourth of France. In the fourth place are *propagatores* or *propugnatores imperii*,[9] such as in honourable wars enlarge their territories, or make noble defence against invaders. And in the last place are *patres patriæ*,[10] which reign justly, and make the times good wherein they live. Both which last kinds need no examples, they are in such number. Degrees of honour in subjects are, first, *participes curarum*:[11] those upon whom princes do discharge the greatest weight of their affairs, their *right hands*, as we call them. The next are *duces belli*, great leaders: such as are princes' lieutenants, and do them notable services in the wars. The third are *gratiosi*, favourites: such as exceed not this scantling,[12] to be solace to the sovereign and harmless to the people. And the fourth, *negotiis pares*:[13] such as have great places under princes, and execute their places with sufficiency.* There is an honour, likewise, which may be ranked

---

[4] Ottoman: Osman I. Ismael: Ismail (*c.* 1480-1524), first Shah of Persia.

[5] "perpetual princes".

[6] Eadgar: Edgar, an Anglo-Saxon king of the tenth century. Alphonsus: Alfonso X, King of Castile (1221-84), the Wise, drew up the *Siete Partidas* [*Seven Parts*], a digest of the laws of Spain.

[7] "liberators" or "saviours".

[8] settle.

[9] "extenders" or "defenders of empire".

[10] "fathers of their country". See Suetonius, *Tiberius*, 67.

[11] "partners of their cares".

[12] limit, measure.

[13] "men capable of negotiating, doing business".

amongst the greatest, which happeneth rarely; that is, of such as sacrifice themselves to death or danger for the good of their country, as was M. Regulus, and the two Decii.[14]

LVI. OF JUDICATURE

JUDGES ought to remember that their office is *jus dicere*, and not *jus dare*, to interpret law, and not to make law, or give law. Else will it be like the authority claimed by the church of Rome, which under pretext of exposition of Scripture doth not stick to add and alter, and to pronounce that which they do not find, and by show of antiquity to introduce novelty. Judges ought to be more learned than witty, more reverend than plausible,* and more advised than confident. Above all things, integrity is their portion and proper virtue. *Cursed* (saith the law) *is he that removeth the landmark.*[1] The mislayer of a mere-stone[2] is to blame. But it is the unjust judge that is the capital remover of landmarks, when he defineth amiss of lands and property. One foul sentence doth more hurt than many foul examples. For these do but corrupt the stream, the other corrupteth the fountain. So saith Salomon, *Fons turbatus, et vena corrupta, est justus cadens in causa sua coram adversario.*[3] The office of judges may have reference unto the parties that sue, unto the advocates that plead, unto the clerks and ministers of justice underneath them, and to the sovereign or state above them.

First, for the causes or parties that sue. *There be* (saith the Scripture) *that turn judgment into wormwood;*[4] and surely there be also that turn it into vinegar, for injustice maketh it bitter,

---

[14] Marcus Atilius Regulus, a Roman commander taken prisoner by the Carthaginians, was sent by them to Rome to negotiate peace or at least an exchange of prisoners. Upon his urging, the Senate rejected all proposals, and he then returned, as he had promised, to Carthage, where he was put to death (250 B.C.). The Decii, father and son (Romans of the Decius family), sacrificed themselves in battle for the preservation of their country.

[1] Deut. 19:14 and 27:17; Prov. 22:28 and 23:10.

[2] boundary stone, landmark.

[3] "A righteous man falling down before the wicked is as a troubled fountain and a corrupt spring." Prov. 25:26.

[4] Amos 5:7.

and delays make it sour. The principal duty of a judge is to suppress force and fraud, whereof force is the more pernicious when
it is open, and fraud when it is close and disguised. Add thereto
contentious suits, which ought to be spewed out as the surfeit of
courts. A judge ought to prepare his way to a just sentence, as
God useth to prepare his way, by *raising valleys* and *taking down
hills:*[5] so when there appeareth on either side an high hand,
violent prosecution, cunning advantages taken, combination,
power, great counsel, then is the virtue of a judge seen, to make
inequality equal, that he may plant his judgment as upon an
even ground. *Qui fortiter emungit, elicit sanguinem,*[6] and where
the winepress is hard wrought, it yields a harsh wine, that tastes
of the grape-stone. Judges must beware of hard constructions
and strained inferences, for there is no worse torture than the
torture of laws. Specially in case of laws penal, they ought to have
care that that which was meant for terror be not turned into
rigour, and that they bring not upon the people that shower
whereof the Scripture speaketh, *Pluet super eos laqueos,*[7] for
penal laws pressed are a *shower of snares* upon the people.
Therefore let penal laws, if they have been sleepers of long, or if
they be grown unfit for the present time, be by wise judges
confined in the execution: *Judicis officium est, ut res, ita tempora
rerum, etc.*[8] In causes of life and death, judges ought (as far as
the law permitteth) in justice to remember mercy, and to cast a
severe eye upon the example, but a merciful eye upon the person.

Secondly, for the advocates and counsel that plead. Patience
and gravity of hearing is an essential part of justice, and an
overspeaking judge is no well-tuned cymbal. It is no grace to a
judge first to find that which he might have heard in due time
from the bar; or to show quickness of conceit* in cutting off
evidence or counsel too short; or to prevent[9] information by
questions, though pertinent. The parts of a judge in hearing are
four: to direct the evidence; to moderate length, repetition, or

---

[5] Isaiah 40:4.

[6] "He who blows his nose violently
makes it bleed." Cf. Prov. 30:33.

[7] "He shall rain snares upon them."
Psalms 11:6.

[8] "It is the duty of the judge to
consider the times as well as the
facts." Ovid, *Sorrows,* I.i.37.

[9] anticipate.

impertinency* of speech; to recapitulate, select, and collate the material points of that which hath been said; and to give the rule or sentence. Whatsoever is above these is too much, and proceedeth either of glory* and willingness to speak, or of impatience to hear, or of shortness of memory, or of want of a staid and equal attention. It is a strange thing to see that the boldness of advocates should prevail with judges; whereas they should imitate God, in whose seat they sit, who *respresseth the presumptuous, and giveth grace to the modest*.[10] But it is more strange that judges should have noted favourites, which cannot but cause multiplication of fees and suspicion of by-ways.[11] There is due from the judge to the advocate some commendation and gracing,* where causes are well handled and fair pleaded, especially towards the side which obtaineth not, for that upholds in the client the reputation of his counsel, and beats down in him the conceit* of his cause. There is likewise due to the public a civil reprehension of advocates, where there appeareth cunning counsel, gross neglect, slight information, indiscreet pressing, or an over-bold defence. And let not the counsel at the bar chop[12] with the judge, nor wind himself into the handling of the cause anew after the judge hath declared his sentence; but on the other side, let not the judge meet the cause half way, nor give occasion for the party to say his counsel or proofs were not heard.

Thirdly, for that that concerns clerks and ministers. The place of justice is an hallowed place, and therefore not only the bench but the foot-pace and precincts and purprise[13] thereof ought to be preserved without scandal and corruption. For certainly *Grapes* (as the Scripture saith) *will not be gathered of thorns or thistles;*[14] neither can justice yield her fruit with sweetness amongst the briars and brambles of catching and polling[15] clerks and ministers. The attendance of courts is subject to four bad instruments. First, certain persons that are sowers of suits, which make the court swell, and the country pine. The second sort is of those that engage courts in quarrels of jurisdiction, and are not

---

[10] James 4:6. Cf. Prov. 3:34.
[11] i.e., indirect ways of influencing the judge.
[12] bargain, argue.

[13] enclosure.
[14] Matt. 7:16.
[15] greedy and avaricious, predatory.

truly *amici curiæ* but *parasiti curiæ*,[16] in puffing a court up beyond her bounds for their own scraps and advantage. The third sort is of those that may be accounted the left hands of courts, persons that are full of nimble and sinister tricks and shifts, whereby they pervert the plain and direct courses of courts, and bring justice into oblique lines and labyrinths. And the fourth is the poller and exacter of fees, which justifies the common resemblance of the courts of justice to the bush whereunto while the sheep flies for defence in weather, he is sure to lose part of his fleece. On the other side, an ancient clerk, skilful in precedents, wary in proceeding and understanding in the business of the court, is an excellent finger of a court, and doth many times point the way to the judge himself.

Fourthly, for that which may concern the sovereign and estate. Judges ought above all to remember the conclusion of the Roman Twelve Tables, *Salus populi suprema lex;*[17] and to know that laws, except they be in order to that end, are but things captious and oracles not well inspired. Therefore it is an happy thing in a state when kings and states do often consult with judges, and again when judges do often consult with the king and state, the one, when there is matter of law intervenient in business of state, the other, when there is some consideration of state intervenient in matter of law. For many times the things deduced to judgment may be *meum* and *tuum*, when the reason and consequence thereof may trench to[18] point of estate: I call matter of estate not only the parts of sovereignty but whatsoever introduceth any great alteration or dangerous precedent, or concerneth manifestly any great portion of people. And let no man weakly conceive that just laws and true policy have any antipathy, for they are like the spirits and sinews, that one moves with the other. Let judges also remember that Salomon's throne was supported by lions on both sides:[19] let them be lions, but yet lions under the throne, being circumspect that they do not check or oppose

---

[16] not truly "friends of the court" but "parasites of the court".

[17] "The welfare of the people is the highest law." The Twelve Tables were a code of Roman law drawn up in the fifth century B.C., but the quotation is not from them but from Cicero, *On the Laws*, III.iii.8. [Wright]

[18] encroach upon.

[19] I Kings 10:20.

any points of sovereignty. Let not judges also be so ignorant of their own right as to think there is not left to them, as a principal part of their office, a wise use and application of laws. For they may remember what the apostle saith of a greater law than theirs: *Nos scimus quia lex bona est, modo quis ea utatur legitime.*[20]

LVII. OF ANGER

To seek to extinguish Anger utterly is but a bravery* of the Stoics. We have better oracles: *Be angry, but sin not. Let not the sun go down upon your anger.*[1] Anger must be limited and confined both in race[2] and in time. We will first speak how the natural inclination and habit to be angry may be attempered[3] and calmed. Secondly, how the particular motions of anger may be repressed, or at least refrained from doing mischief. Thirdly, how to raise anger or appease anger in another.

For the first, there is no other way but to meditate and ruminate well upon the effects of anger, how it troubles man's life. And the best time to do this is to look back upon anger when the fit is thoroughly over. Seneca saith well, *That anger is like ruin, which breaks itself upon that it falls.*[4] The Scripture exhorteth us *To possess our souls in patience.*[5] Whosoever is out of patience is out of possession of his soul. Men must not turn bees,

> ... *animasque in vulnere ponunt.*[6]

Anger is certainly a kind of baseness, as it appears well in the weakness of those subjects in whom it reigns: children, women, old folks, sick folks. Only men must beware that they carry their anger rather with scorn than with fear, so that they may seem rather to be above the injury than below it, which is a thing easily done, if a man will give law to himself in it.

For the second point, the causes and motives of anger are

---

[20] "We know that the law is good, provided that a man use it lawfully." I Tim. 1:8.

[1] Ephesians 4:26.

[2] extent.

[3] moderated, softened.

[4] Seneca, *On Anger*, I.1.

[5] Luke 21:19.

[6] "and leave their lives behind them in the wound". Virgil, *Georgics*, IV.238.

chiefly three. First, to be too sensible of hurt, for no man is angry that feels not himself hurt; and therefore tender and delicate persons must needs be oft angry: they have so many things to trouble them, which more robust natures have little sense of. The next is the apprehension and construction[7] of the injury offered to be, in the circumstances thereof, full of contempt, for contempt is that which putteth an edge upon anger as much or more than the hurt itself. And therefore when men are ingenious in picking out circumstances of contempt, they do kindle their anger much. Lastly, opinion of the touch of a man's reputation doth multiply and sharpen anger. Wherein the remedy is that a man should have, as Gonsalvo was wont to say, *telam honoris crassiorem*.[8] But in all refrainings of anger, it is the best remedy to win time, and to make a man's self believe that the opportunity of his revenge is not yet come, but that he foresees a time for it, and so to still himself in the meantime, and reserve it.

To contain anger from mischief, though it take hold of a man, there be two things whereof you must have special caution. The one, of extreme bitterness of words, especially if they be aculeate and proper, for *communia maledicta*[9] are nothing so much; and again, that in anger a man reveal no secrets, for that makes him not fit for society. The other, that you do not peremptorily break off, in any business, in a fit of anger, but howsoever you show bitterness, do not act anything that is not revocable.

For raising and appeasing anger in another, it is done chiefly by choosing of times, when men are frowardest and worst disposed, to incense them. Again, by gathering (as was touched before) all that you can find out to aggravate the contempt. And the two remedies are by the contraries. The former [is] to take good times, when first to relate to a man an angry business, for the first impression is much; and the other is to sever, as much as may be, the construction of the injury from the point of contempt,[10] imputing it to misunderstanding, fear, passion, or what you will.

[7] interpretation.

[8] "honour of a stouter web". Gonsalvo: Hernandez Gonsalvo de Cordoba (1453-1515), The Great Captain, a Spanish warrior.

[9] common insults.

[10] i.e., to prevent . . . the interpretation of the injury as a sign of contempt.

LVIII. OF VICISSITUDE OF THINGS

SALOMON saith, *There is no new thing upon the earth*.[1] So that as Plato had an imagination *That all knowledge was but remembrance*, so Salomon giveth his sentence *That all novelty is but oblivion*.[2] Whereby you may see that the river of Lethe runneth as well above ground as below. There is an abstruse astrologer that saith, *if it were not for two things that are constant (the one is, that the fixed stars ever stand at like distance one from another, and never come nearer together, nor go further asunder; the other, that the diurnal motion[3] perpetually keepeth time), no individual would last one moment.* Certain it is that the matter is in a perpetual flux, and never at a stay. The great winding sheets that bury all things in oblivion are two: deluges and earthquakes. As for conflagrations and great droughts, they do not merely* dispeople and destroy. Phaëton's car went but a day. And the three years' drought in the time of Elias[4] was but particular,[5] and left people alive. As for the great burnings by lightnings, which are often in the West Indies, they are but narrow. But in the other two destructions, by deluge and earthquake, it is further to be noted that the remnant of people which hap to be reserved are commonly ignorant and mountainous people, that can give no account of the time past, so that the oblivion is all one as if none had been left. If you consider well of the people of the West Indies, it is very probable that they are a newer or a younger people than the people of the old world. And it is much more likely that the destruction that hath heretofore been there was not by earthquakes (as the Egyptian priest told Solon concerning the island of Atlantis, *that it was swallowed by an earthquake*),[6] but rather that it was desolated by a particular deluge. For earthquakes are seldom in those parts. But on the other side, they have such pouring rivers as the rivers of Asia and Africk and Europe are but brooks to them. Their Andes likewise, or mountains, are far higher than those with us;

---

[1] Eccles. 1:9.

[2] Plato, *Phaedo*, 72E; Eccles. 1:11.

[3] i.e., of the heavens round the earth.

[4] Cf. I Kings 17 and 18.

[5] partial, restricted to one place.

[6] See Plato, *Timaeus*, 25D.

whereby it seems that the remnants of generation of men were in such a particular deluge saved. As for the observation that Machiavel[7] hath, that the jealousy of sects doth much extinguish the memory of things, traducing Gregory the Great, that he did what in him lay to extinguish all heathen antiquities, I do not find that those zeals do any great effects, nor last long, as it appeared in the succession of Sabinian,[8] who did revive the former antiquities.

The vicissitude or mutations in the Superior Globe[9] are no fit matter for this present argument. It may be Plato's great year,[10] if the world should last so long, would have some effect, not in renewing the state of like individuals (for that is the fume* of those that conceive the celestial bodies have more accurate influences upon these things below than indeed they have) but in gross. Comets, out of question, have likewise power and effect over the gross and mass of things, but they are rather gazed upon and waited upon* in their journey than wisely observed in their effects, specially in their respective effects; that is, what kind of comet, for magnitude, colour, version[11] of the beams, placing in the region of heaven, or lasting, produceth what kind of effects.

There is a toy which I have heard, and I would not have it given over,[12] but waited upon* a little. They say it is observed in the Low Countries (I know not in what part) that every five and thirty years the same kind and suit[13] of years and weathers comes about again, as great frosts, great wet, great droughts, warm winters, summers with little heat, and the like; and they call it the *Prime*. It is a thing I do the rather mention, because computing backwards I have found some concurrence.

But to leave these points of nature, and to come to men. The greatest vicissitude of things amongst men is the vicissitude of sects and religions. For those orbs rule in men's minds most. The true religion is *built upon the rock*;[14] the rest are tossed upon

---

[7] *Discourses on Livy*, II.5.
[8] Pope, 604-606, immediate successor to Gregory.
[9] i.e., the heavens.
[10] See *Timaeus*, 39D.

[11] direction.
[12] passed by.
[13] succession, order.
[14] Cf. Matt. 16:18.

the waves of time. To speak therefore of the causes of new sects, and to give some counsel concerning them, as far as the weakness of human judgment can give stay to so great revolutions.

When the religion formerly received is rent by discords, and when the holiness of the professors of religion is decayed and full of scandal, and withal the times be stupid, ignorant, and barbarous, you may doubt* the springing up of a new sect, if then also there should arise any extravagant and strange spirit to make himself author thereof. All which points held when Mahomet published his law. If a new sect have not two properties, fear it not, for it will not spread. The one is the supplanting or the opposing of authority established, for nothing is more popular than that. The other is the giving licence to pleasures and a voluptuous life. For as for speculative heresies (such as were in ancient times the Arians, and now the Arminians), though they work mightily upon men's wits,* yet they do not produce any great alterations in states, except it be by the help of civil occasions. There be three manner of plantations of new sects. By the power of signs and miracles; by the eloquence and wisdom of speech and persuasion; and by the sword. For martyrdoms, I reckon them amongst miracles, because they seem to exceed the strength of human nature, and I may do the like of superlative and admirable holiness of life. Surely there is no better way to stop the rising of new sects and schisms than to reform abuses; to compound the smaller differences; to proceed mildly, and not with sanguinary persecutions; and rather to take off the principal authors by winning and advancing them than to enrage them by violence and bitterness.

The changes and vicissitude in wars are many, but chiefly in three things: in the seats or stages of the war; in the weapons; and in the manner of the conduct. Wars in ancient time seemed more to move from east to west, for the Persians, Assyrians, Arabians, Tartars (which were the invaders) were all eastern people. It is true, the Gauls were western, but we read but of two incursions of theirs: the one to Gallo-Græcia,¹⁵ the other to

¹⁵ Galatia.

Rome. But East and West have no certain points of heaven,[16] and no more have the wars, either from the east or west, any certainty of observation. But North and South are fixed; and it hath seldom or never been seen that the far southern people have invaded the northern, but contrariwise. Whereby it is manifest that the northern tract of the world is in nature the more martial region, be it in respect of* the stars of that hemisphere, or of the great continents that are upon the north, whereas the south part, for aught that is known, is almost all sea; or (which is most apparent) of the cold of the northern parts, which is that which, without aid of discipline, doth make the bodies hardest and the courages warmest.

Upon the breaking and shivering of a great state and empire you may be sure to have wars. For great empires, while they stand, do enervate and destroy the forces of the natives which they have subdued, resting upon their own protecting forces; and then when they fail also, all goes to ruin, and they become a prey. So was it in the decay of the Roman empire, and likewise in the empire of Almaigne[17] after Charles the Great,[18] every bird taking a feather; and were not unlike to befall to Spain, if it should break. The great accessions and unions of kingdoms do likewise stir up wars; for when a state grows to an over-power, it is like a great flood, that will be sure to overflow. As it hath been seen in the states of Rome, Turkey, Spain, and others. Look when the world hath fewest barbarous peoples, but such as commonly will not marry or generate, except they know means to live (as it is almost everywhere at this day, except Tartary), there is no danger of inundations of people; but when there be great shoals of people, which go on to populate without foreseeing means of life and sustentation, it is of necessity that once in an age or two they discharge a portion of their people upon other nations; which the ancient northern people were wont to do by lot, casting lots what part should stay at home, and what should seek their fortunes. When a warlike state grows soft and effeminate, they may be sure of a war. For commonly such states

---

[16] i.e., no fixed dividing-point (they are relative terms).

[17] Germany.

[18] Charlemagne.

are grown rich in the time of their degenerating; and so the prey inviteth, and their decay in valour encourageth a war.

As for the weapons, it hardly falleth under rule and observation, yet we see even they have returns and vicissitudes. For certain it is that ordnance was known in the city of the Oxidrakes in India,[19] and was that which the Macedonians called thunder and lightning and magic. And it is well known that the use of ordnance hath been in China above two thousand years. The conditions of weapons and their improvement are, first, the fetching afar off,[20] for that outruns the danger, as it is seen in ordnance and muskets. Secondly, the strength of the percussion, wherein likewise ordnance do exceed all arietations[21] and ancient inventions. The third is the commodious use of them, as that they may serve in all weathers, that the carriage may be light and manageable, and the like.

For the conduct of the war: at the first, men rested extremely upon number; they did put the wars likewise upon main force and valour, pointing* days for pitched fields, and so trying it out upon an even match; and they were more ignorant in ranging and arraying their battles.[22] After they grew to rest upon number rather competent than vast, they grew to advantages of place, cunning diversions, and the like; and they grew more skilful in the ordering of their battles.

In the youth of a state arms do flourish; in the middle age of a state, learning; and then both of them together for a time; in the declining age of a state, mechanical arts and merchandise. Learning hath his infancy, when it is but beginning and almost childish; then his youth, when it is luxuriant and juvenile; then his strength of years, when it is solid and reduced;[23] and lastly, his old age, when it waxeth dry and exhaust.* But it is not good to look too long upon these turning wheels of vicissitude, lest we become giddy. As for the philology of them, that is but a circle of tales, and therefore not fit for this writing.

---

[19] reference unknown.
[20] striking from a distance.
[21] assaults with battering-rams.

[22] bodies of troops, forces.
[23] kept within bounds.

LIX. OF FAME, A FRAGMENT

THE poets make Fame* a monster. They describe her in part finely and elegantly; and in part gravely and sententiously. They say, look how many feathers she hath, so many eyes she hath underneath; so many tongues; so many voices; she pricks up so many ears.

This is a flourish. There follow excellent parables: as that she gathereth strength in going; that she goeth upon the ground, and yet hideth her head in the clouds; that in the day-time she sitteth in a watch-tower, and flieth most by night; that she mingleth things done with things not done; and that she is a terror to great cities. But that which passeth all the rest is: they do recount that the earth, mother of the Giants that made war against Jupiter and were by him destroyed, thereupon in an anger brought forth Fame;[1] for certain it is that rebels, figured by the Giants, and seditious fames and libels, are but brothers and sisters, masculine and feminine. But now, if a man can tame this monster, and bring her to feed at the hand, and govern her, and with her fly[2] other ravening fowl and kill them, it is somewhat worth. But we are infected with the style of the poets. To speak now in a sad and serious manner. There is not in all the politics a place less handled, and more worthy to be handled, than this of fame. We will therefore speak of these points. What are false fames; and what are true fames; and how they may be best discerned; how fames may be sown and raised; how they may be spread and multiplied; and how they may be checked and laid dead. And other things concerning the nature of fame. Fame is of that force, as there is scarcely any great action wherein it hath not a great part; especially in the war. Mucianus undid Vitellius, by a fame that he scattered, that Vitellius had in purpose to remove the legions of Syria into Germany, and the legions of Germany into Syria; whereupon the legions of Syria were infinitely inflamed.[3] Julius Cæsar took Pompey unpro-

---

[1] Cf. Virgil, *Aeneid*, IV.175-90.

[2] attack.

[3] Tacitus, *Hist.*, II.80. Mucianus: Governor of Syria and Roman consul of the first century. Aulus Vitellius (*c.* A.D. 15-69): extravagant Roman consul and Emperor for one year.

vided, and laid asleep his industry and preparations, by a fame that he cunningly gave out, how Cæsar's own soldiers loved him not, and being wearied with wars, and laden with the spoils of Gaul, would forsake him as soon as he came into Italy.[4] Livia settled all things for the succession of her son Tiberius, by continual giving out that her husband Augustus was upon recovery and amendment.[5] And it is an usual thing with the bashaws, to conceal the death of the great Turk from the Janizaries and men of war, to save the sacking of Constantinople and other towns, as their manner is. Themistocles made Xerxes King of Persia post apace out of Græcia, by giving out that the Grecians had a purpose to break his bridge of ships which he had made athwart Hellespont.[6] There be a thousand such like examples, and the more they are, the less they need to be repeated, because a man meeteth with them everywhere. Therefore let all wise governors have as great a watch and care over fames, as they have of the actions and designs themselves.

THE REST WAS NOT FINISHED.

---

[4] Caesar, The Civil Wars, I.6.
[5] Tacitus, Ann., I.5. Livia Drusilla (c. 55 B.C. to A.D. 29): beautiful and influential wife of Augustus;
Tiberius was her son by a former marriage.
[6] Herodotus, VIII.108, 109.

The Proficience and

Advancement of Learning

Divine and Humane

1605

The First Book

TO THE KING

THERE were under the Law (excellent King) both daily sacrifices and freewill offerings, the one proceeding upon[1] ordinary observance, the other upon a devout cheerfulness.[2] In like manner there belongeth to kings from their servants both tribute of duty and presents of affection. In the former of these I hope I shall not live to be wanting, according to my most humble duty, and the good pleasure of your Majesty's employments; for the latter, I thought it more respective to make choice of some oblation which might rather refer to the propriety* and excellency of your individual person than to the business of your crown and state.

Wherefore representing your Majesty many times unto my mind, and beholding you not with the inquisitive eye of presumption to discover that which the Scripture telleth me is inscrutable,[3] but with the observant eye of duty and admiration, leaving aside the other parts of your virtue and fortune, I have been touched, yea and possessed with an extreme wonder at those your virtues and faculties which the philosophers call intellectual: the largeness of your capacity, the faithfulness of your memory, the swiftness of your apprehension, the penetration of your judgment, and the facility and order of your elocution; and I have often thought that of all the persons living that I have known, your Majesty were the best instance to make a man of Plato's opinion[4] that all knowledge is but remembrance, and that the mind of man by nature knoweth all things, and hath but her own native and original notions (which by the strangeness and darkness of this tabernacle of the body are

---

[1] arising, resulting from.
[2] Cf. Lev. 22:18; Num. 29:39; Deut. 12:6; Psalms 119:108; etc.
[3] Cf. Prov. 25:3.
[4] in the *Meno*, 86AB, and *Phaedo*, 72E-77A.

sequestered) again revived and restored; such a light of nature I have observed in your Majesty, and such a readiness to take flame and blaze from the least occasion presented, or the least spark of another's knowledge delivered. And as the Scripture saith of the wisest king, *That his heart was as the sands of the sea*,[5] which though it be one of the largest bodies, yet it consisteth of the smallest and finest portions, so hath God given your Majesty a composition of understanding admirable, being able to compass and comprehend the greatest matters, and nevertheless to touch and apprehend the least; whereas it should seem an impossibility in nature for the same instrument to make itself fit for great and small works. And for your gift of speech, I call to mind what Cornelius Tacitus saith of Augustus Cæsar: *Augusto profluens, et quæ principem deceret, eloquentia fuit*,[6] for if we note it well, speech that is uttered with labour and difficulty, or speech that savoureth of the affectation of art and precepts, or speech that is framed after the imitation of some pattern of eloquence, though never so excellent – all this has somewhat servile and holding of the subject.[7] But your Majesty's manner of speech is indeed prince-like, flowing as from a fountain and yet streaming and branching itself into nature's order, full of facility and felicity, imitating none, and inimitable by any. And as in your civil estate* there appeareth to be an emulation and contention of your Majesty's virtue with your fortune; a virtuous disposition with a fortunate regiment;* a virtuous expectation (when time was) of your greater fortune, with a prosperous possession thereof in the due time; a virtuous observation of the laws of marriage, with most blessed and happy fruit of marriage; a virtuous and most Christian desire of peace, with a fortunate inclination in your neighbour princes thereunto; so likewise in these intellectual matters there seemeth to be no less contention between the excellency of your Majesty's gifts of nature and the universality and perfection of your learning. For I am well assured that this which I shall say is no amplification[8] at all, but a positive and measured truth, which

[5] Cf. I Kings 4:29.

[6] "Augustus had an easy and fluent way of speaking, such as became a

sovereign." *Ann.*, XIII.3.

[7] lacking in originality.

[8] rhetorical flourish, exaggeration.

is that there hath not been since Christ's time any king or temporal monarch which hath been so learned in all literature and erudition, divine and human. For let a man seriously and diligently revolve and peruse the succession of the emperors of Rome, of which Cæsar the dictator, who lived some years before Christ, and Marcus Antoninus were the best learned, and so descend to the emperors of Græcia or of the West, and then to the lines of France, Spain, England, Scotland, and the rest; and he shall find this judgment is truly made. For it seemeth much in a king, if by the compendious extractions of other men's wits and labours he can take hold of any superficial ornaments and shows of learning, or if he countenance and prefer[9] learning and learned men, but to drink indeed of the true fountains of learning, nay to have such a fountain of learning in himself, in a king, and in a king born, is almost a miracle. And the more, because there is met in your Majesty a rare conjunction as well of divine and sacred literature as of profane and human, so as your Majesty standeth invested of that triplicity which in great veneration was ascribed to the ancient Hermes: the power and fortune of a King, the knowledge and illumination of a Priest, and the learning and universality of a Philosopher. This propriety inherent[10] and individual attribute in your Majesty deserveth to be expressed not only in the fame and admiration of the present time, nor in the history or tradition of the ages succeeding, but also in some solid work, fixed memorial, and immortal monument, bearing a character or signature both of the power of a king and the difference[11] and perfection of such a king.

Therefore I did conclude with myself that I could not make unto your Majesty a better oblation than of some treatise tending to that end, whereof the sum will consist of these two parts: the former concerning the excellency of learning and knowledge, and the excellency of the merit and true glory in the augmentation and propagation thereof; the latter, what the particular acts and works are which have been embraced and

[9] advance, promote.

[10] i.e., inherent property (logic): an essential quality common to all members of a species and peculiar to them.

[11] distinguishing mark.

undertaken for the advancement of learning, and again what defects and undervalues[12] I find in such particular acts; to the end that though I cannot positively or affirmatively advise your Majesty, or propound unto you framed particulars, yet I may excite your princely cogitations to visit the excellent treasure of your own mind, and thence to extract particulars for this purpose agreeable to your magnanimity and wisdom.

In the entrance to the former of these – to clear the way, and as it were to make silence to have the true testimonies concerning the dignity of learning to be better heard without the interruption of tacit objections – I think good to deliver it from the discredits and disgraces which it hath received, all from ignorance, but ignorance severally* disguised, appearing sometimes in the zeal and jealousy of divines, sometimes in the severity and arrogancy of politiques,* and sometimes in the errors and imperfections of learned men themselves.

I hear the former sort say that knowledge is of those things which are to be accepted of with great limitation and caution; that the aspiring to over-much knowledge was the original temptation and sin, whereupon ensued the fall of man; that knowledge hath in it somewhat of the serpent, and therefore where it entereth into a man it makes him swell – *Scientia inflat*[13] – that Salomon gives a censure, *that there is no end of making books, and that much reading is weariness of the flesh*; and again in another place, *that in spacious knowledge there is much contristation, and that he that increaseth knowledge increaseth anxiety*; that St. Paul gives a caveat, *that we be not spoiled through vain philosophy*;[14] that experience demonstrates how learned men have been arch-heretics, how learned times have been inclined to atheism, and how the contemplation of second causes doth derogate from our dependence upon God, who is the first cause.

To discover* then the ignorance and error of this opinion and the misunderstanding in the grounds thereof, it may well

[12] shortcomings.
[13] "Knowledge puffeth up." I Cor. 8:1.
[14] Cf. Eccles. 12:12; 1:18; Col. 2:8.

appear these men do not observe or consider that it was not the pure knowledge of nature and universality, a knowledge by the light whereof man did give names unto other creatures in Paradise, as they were brought before him, according unto their proprieties,* which gave the occasion to the fall, but it was the proud knowledge of good and evil, with an intent in man to give law unto himself and to depend no more upon God's commandments, which was the form of the temptation.[15] Neither is it any quantity of knowledge how great soever that can make the mind of man to swell, for nothing can fill, much less extend, the soul of man but God and the contemplation of God; and therefore Salomon speaking of the two principal senses of inquisition, the eye and the ear, affirmeth that the eye is never satisfied with seeing, nor the ear with hearing, and if there be no fulness, then is the continent[16] greater than the content; so of knowledge itself and the mind of man, whereto the senses are but reporters, he defineth likewise in these words, placed after that calendar or ephemerides which he maketh of the diversities of times and seasons for all actions and purposes, and concludeth thus: *God hath made all things beautiful, or decent,*[17] *in the true return of their seasons.*[18] *Also he hath placed the world in man's heart, yet cannot man find out the work which God worketh from the beginning to the end*, declaring not obscurely that God hath framed the mind of man as a mirror or glass capable of[19] the image of the universal world, and joyful to receive the impression thereof, as the eye joyeth to receive light; and not only delighted in beholding the variety of things and vicissitude of times, but raised[20] also to find out and discern the ordinances and decrees which throughout all those changes are infallibly observed. And although he doth insinuate that the supreme or summary law of nature, which he calleth *the work which God worketh from the beginning to the end*, is not possible to be found out by man; yet that doth not derogate from the capacity of the mind, but may be referred to the impedi-

---

[15] See Gen. 2:19, 20; 3:1ff.

[16] container. See Eccles. 1:8.

[17] becoming, suitable.

[18] according to their proper seasons,

each at its proper time. See Eccles. 3:11.

[19] able to receive.

[20] desirous.

ments, as of shortness of life, ill conjunction[21] of labours, ill tradition of knowledge over from hand to hand, and many other inconveniences whereunto the condition of man is subject. For that nothing parcel[22] of the world is denied to man's inquiry and invention he doth in another place rule over, when he saith, *The spirit of man is as the lamp of God, wherewith he searcheth the inwardness of all secrets.*[23] If then such be the capacity and receit[24] of the mind of man, it is manifest that there is no danger at all in the proportion or quantity of knowledge, how large soever, lest it should make it swell or outcompass itself; no, but it is merely the quality of knowledge, which be it in quantity more or less, if it be taken without the true corrective thereof, hath in it some nature of venom or malignity, and some effects of that venom, which is ventosity[25] or swelling. This corrective spice, the mixture whereof maketh knowledge so sovereign, is Charity, which the apostle immediately addeth to the former clause, for so he saith, *knowledge bloweth up, but charity buildeth up*; not unlike unto that which he delivereth in another place: *If I spake* (saith he) *with the tongues of men and angels, and had not charity, it were but as a tinkling cymbal*;[26] not but that it is an excellent thing to speak with the tongues of men and angels, but because if it be severed from charity, and not referred to the good of men and mankind, it hath rather a sounding and unworthy glory than a meriting and substantial virtue. And as for that censure of Salomon concerning the excess of writing and reading books and the anxiety of spirit which redoundeth from knowledge, and that admonition of St. Paul, *That we be not seduced by vain philosophy*, let those places be rightly understood, and they do indeed excellently set forth the true bounds and limitations whereby human knowledge is confined and circumscribed, and yet without any such contracting or coarctation,[27] but that it may comprehend all the universal nature of things. For these limitations are three. The first, *that we do not so place our felicity in knowledge, as we forget our mortality.*

[21] imperfect co-operation or co-ordination.
[22] no part.
[23] Prov. 20:27.
[24] power of receiving.
[25] windiness.
[26] I Cor. 8:1 and 13:1.
[27] restriction.

The second, *that we make application of our knowledge to give ourselves repose and contentment, and not distaste or repining.* The third, *that we do not presume by the contemplation of nature to attain to the mysteries of God.* For as touching the first of these, Salomon doth excellently expound himself in another place of the same book, where he saith, *I saw well that knowledge recedeth as far from ignorance as light doth from darkness, and that the wise man's eyes keep watch in his head, whereas the fool roundeth about in darkness: but withal I learned that the same mortality involveth them both.*[28] And for the second, certain it is, there is no vexation or anxiety of mind which resulteth from knowledge otherwise than merely* by accident, for all knowledge and wonder (which is the seed of knowledge) is an impression of pleasure in itself; but when men fall to framing conclusions out of their knowledge, applying it to their particular,[29] and ministering to themselves thereby weak fears or vast desires, there groweth that carefulness[30] and trouble of mind which is spoken of, for then knowledge is no more *Lumen siccum,* whereof Heraclitus the profound said, *Lumen siccum optima anima,*[31] but it becometh *Lumen madidum* or *maceratum,*[32] being steeped and infused in the humours of the affections. And as for the third point, it deserveth to be a little stood[33] upon and not to be lightly passed over, for if any man shall think by view and inquiry into these sensible and material things to attain that light whereby he may reveal unto himself the nature or will of God, then indeed is he spoiled by vain philosophy, for the contemplation of God's creatures and works produceth (having regard to the works and creatures themselves) knowledge, but having regard to God, no perfect knowledge, but wonder, which is broken knowledge. And therefore it was most aptly said by one of Plato's school, *that the sense of man carrieth a resemblance with the sun, which (as we see) openeth and revealeth all the terrestrial globe; but then again it obscureth and concealeth the stars and celestial globe; so doth the sense discover natural*

---

[28] Eccles. 2:13, 14. roundeth: wanders.

[29] their own selves or persons.

[30] anxiety.

[31] "A dry light is the best soul."

[32] "a light saturated with moisture".

[33] dwelt.

things, but it darkeneth and shutteth up divine.[34] And hence
it is true that it hath proceeded that divers great learned men
have been heretical, whilst they have sought to fly up to the
secrets of the Deity by the waxen wings of the senses. And as for
the conceit* that too much knowledge should incline a man to
atheism, and that the ignorance of second causes should make a
more devout dependence upon God which is the first cause, first,
it is good to ask the question which Job asked of his friends, *Will
you lie for God, as one man will do for another, to gratify him?*[35]
For certain it is that God worketh nothing in nature but by
second causes; and if they would have it otherwise believed, it is
mere imposture, as it were in favour towards God, and nothing
else but to offer to the author of truth the unclean sacrifice of a
lie. But farther, it is an assured truth and a conclusion of experience that a little or superficial knowledge of philosophy may
incline the mind of man to atheism, but a farther proceeding
therein doth bring the mind back again to religion; for in the
entrance of philosophy, when the second causes, which are next
unto the senses, do offer themselves to the mind of man, if it
dwell and stay there, it may induce some oblivion of the highest
cause, but when a man passeth on farther, and seeth the dependence of causes and the works of Providence, then, according to
the allegory of the poets, he will easily believe that the highest
link of nature's chain must needs be tied to the foot of Jupiter's
chair.[36] To conclude therefore, let no man, upon a weak conceit
of sobriety or an ill-applied moderation, think or maintain that
a man can search too far or be too well studied in the book of
God's word or in the book of God's works, divinity or philosophy,
but rather let men endeavour an endless progress or proficience
in both; only let men beware that they apply both to charity
and not to swelling; to use, and not to ostentation; and again,
that they do not unwisely mingle or confound these learnings
together.

As for the disgraces which learning receiveth from politiques,
they be of this nature: that learning doth soften men's minds,

---

[34] Philo Judaeus, *On Dreams*, I.83-4.   [36] See Homer, *Iliad*, VIII.19; Plato,
[35] Job 13:7, 9.   *Theaetetus*, 153C.

and makes them more unapt for the honour and exercise of arms; that it doth mar and pervert men's dispositions for matter of government and policy in making them too curious* and irresolute by variety of reading, or too peremptory or positive by strictness of rules and axioms, or too immoderate and over-weening by reason of the greatness of examples, or too incompatible and differing from the times by reason of the dissimilitude of examples; or at least that it doth divert men's travails* from action and business, and bringeth them to a love of leisure and privateness; and that it doth bring into states a relaxation of discipline, whilst every man is more ready to argue than to obey and execute. Out of this conceit Cato surnamed the Censor, one of the wisest men indeed that ever lived, when Carneades the philosopher came in embassage* to Rome, and that the young men of Rome began to flock about him, being allured with the sweetness and majesty of his eloquence and learning, gave counsel in open senate that they should give him his dispatch with all speed, lest he should infect and inchant the minds and affections of the youth, and at unawares bring in an alteration of the manners and customs of the state.[37] Out of the same conceit or humour did Virgil, turning his pen to the advantage of his country and the disadvantage of his own profession, make a kind of separation between policy and government and between arts and sciences in the verses so much renowned, attributing and challenging* the one to the Romans, and leaving and yielding the other to the Grecians: *Tu regere imperio populos, Romane, memento, Hæ tibi erunt artes*, etc.[38] So likewise we see that Anytus, the accuser of Socrates, laid it as an article of charge and accusation against him that he did with the variety and power of his discourses and disputations withdraw young men from due reverence to the laws and customs of their country, and that he did profess a dangerous and pernicious science, which was to make the worse matter seem the better, and to suppress truth by force of eloquence and speech.[39]

---

[37] See Plutarch, *Cato*, 22.

[38] "Remember, Roman, thou shalt rule the nations as their master; these shall be thy arts," etc.

Aeneid, VI.851.

[39] See Plato, *Apology*, 23E; cf. 19AB; Xenophon, *Memorabilia*, I.i.1.

But these and the like imputations have rather a countenance of gravity than any ground of justice, for experience doth warrant that both in persons and in times there hath been a meeting and concurrence in learning and arms, flourishing and excelling in the same men and the same ages. For as for men, there cannot be a better nor the like instance as of that pair, Alexander the Great and Julius Cæsar the dictator, whereof the one was Aristotle's scholar in philosophy, and the other was Cicero's rival in eloquence; or if any man had rather call for scholars that were great generals than generals that were great scholars, let him take Epaminondas the Theban, or Xenophon the Athenian, whereof the one was the first that abated the power of Sparta, and the other was the first that made way to the overthrow of the monarchy of Persia. And this concurrence is yet more visible in times than in persons, by how much an age is greater object than a man. For both in Egypt, Assyria, Persia, Græcia, and Rome the same times that are most renowned for arms are likewise most admired for learning, so that the greatest authors and philosophers and the greatest captains and governors have lived in the same ages. Neither can it otherwise be, for as in man the ripeness of strength of the body and mind cometh much about an age,[40] save that the strength of the body cometh somewhat the more early, so in states, arms and learning, whereof the one correspondeth to the body, the other to the soul of man, have a concurrence or near sequence in times.

And for matter of policy and government, that learning should rather hurt than enable[41] thereunto is a thing very improbable. We see it is accounted an error to commit a natural body to empiric physicians, which commonly have a few pleasing receits[42] whereupon they are confident and adventurous, but know neither the causes of diseases nor the complexions[43] of patients nor peril of accidents[44] nor the true method of cures. We see it is a like error to rely upon advocates or lawyers which are only men of practice and not grounded in their books, who are many

[40] i.e., about the same age.
[41] disqualify rather than qualify.
[42] prescriptions, medicines.
[43] constitutions.
[44] symptoms.

times easily surprised when matter falleth out besides their experience, to the prejudice of the causes they handle. So by like reason it cannot be but a matter of doubtful consequence, if states be managed by empiric statesmen, not well mingled with men grounded in learning. But contrariwise, it is almost without instance contradictory that ever any government was disastrous that was in the hands of learned governors. For howsoever it hath been ordinary with politic men to extenuate and disable[45] learned men by the names of *Pedantes*, yet in the records of time it appeareth in many particulars that the governments of princes in minority (notwithstanding the infinite disadvantage of that kind of state) have nevertheless excelled the government of princes of mature age, even for that reason which they seek to traduce, which is that by that occasion the state hath been in the hands of *Pedantes*: for so was the state of Rome for the first five years, which are so much magnified, during the minority of Nero, in the hands of Seneca, a *Pedanti*;[46] so it was again for ten years space or more, during the minority of Gordianus the younger, with great applause and contentation* in the hands of Misitheus, a *Pedanti*;[47] so was it before that, in the minority of Alexander Severus, in like happiness, in hands not much unlike, by reason of the rule of the women, who were aided by the teachers and preceptors.[48] Nay, let a man look into the government of the bishops of Rome, as by name[49] into the government of Pius Quintus and Sextus Quintus[50] in our times, who were both at their entrance esteemed but as pedantical friars, and he shall find that such popes do greater things, and proceed upon truer principles of estate* than those which have ascended to the papacy from an education and breeding in affairs of estate and courts of princes; for although men bred in learning are perhaps to seek

---

[45] to belittle and disparage.

[46] Suetonius, *Nero*, 7; Tacitus, *Ann.*, XIII.2.

[47] Gordianus III (c. A.D. 226-44): Roman emperor (238-44). Misitheus: his father-in-law, praetorian prefect, learned and virtuous (d. 243). See Capitolinus, *Gordianus Tertius*, XXIII. contentation: satisfaction.

[48] Severus (A.D. 205-35): Roman emperor (222-35): guided by his grandmother and his mother, particularly the latter, who herself invoked the aid of a council of wise and virtuous senators.

[49] for example.

[50] both popes: Quintus V and Sextus V.

in points of convenience and accommodating for the present,[51] which the Italians call *ragioni di stato*,[52] whereof the same Pius Quintus could not hear spoken with patience, terming them inventions against religion and the moral virtues, yet on the other side, to recompense that, they are perfect in those same plain grounds of religion, justice, honour, and moral virtue, which if they be well and watchfully pursued, there will be seldom use[53] of those other, no more than of physic in a sound or well-dieted body. Neither can the experience of one man's life furnish examples and precedents for the events of one man's life, for as it happeneth sometimes that the grandchild or other descendant resembleth the ancestor more than the son, so many times occurrences of present times may sort* better with ancient examples than with those of the later or immediate times; and lastly, the wit of one man can no more countervail learning than one man's means can hold way with[54] a common purse.

And as for those particular seducements or indispositions of the mind for policy and government, which learning is pretended to insinuate, if it be granted that any such thing be, it must be remembered withal that learning ministereth in every of them greater strength of medicine or remedy than it offereth cause of indisposition or infirmity. For if by a secret operation it make men perplexed and irresolute, on the other side by plain precept it teacheth them when and upon what ground to resolve; yea, and how to carry things in suspense without prejudice till they resolve. If it make men positive and regular,[55] it teacheth them what things are in their nature demonstrative,[56] and what are conjectural, and as well the use of distinctions and exceptions as the latitude of principles and rules. If it mislead by disproportion or dissimilitude of examples, it teacheth men the force of circumstances, the errors of comparisons, and all the cautions of application, so that in all these it doth rectify more effectually than it can pervert. And these medicines it conveyeth into men's

---

[51] are perhaps deficient in matters of expediency and temporizing.

[52] "reasons of state, political considerations".

[53] need.

[54] can equal.

[55] opinionated and hidebound.

[56] i.e., demonstrable.

minds much more forcibly by the quickness[57] and penetration of examples. For let a man look into the errors of Clement the Seventh, so lively described by Guicciardine, who served under him, or into the errors of Cicero painted out by his own pencil in his epistles to Atticus, and he will fly apace from being irresolute. Let him look into the errors of Phocion, and he will beware how he be obstinate or inflexible. Let him but read the fable of Ixion, and it will hold him from being vaporous* or imaginative. Let him look into the errors of Cato the second, and he will never be one of the Antipodes, to tread opposite to the present world.[58]

And for the conceit* that learning should dispose men to leisure and privateness, and make men slothful, it were a strange thing if that which accustometh the mind to a perpetual motion and agitation should induce slothfulness; whereas contrariwise it may be truly affirmed that no kind of men love business for itself but those that are learned; for other persons love it for profit, as an hireling that loves the work for the wages; or for honour, as because it beareth them up in the eyes of men, and refresheth their reputation which otherwise would wear;[59] or because it putteth them in mind of their fortune, and giveth them occasion to pleasure and displeasure; or because it exerciseth some faculty wherein they take pride, and so entertaineth them in good humour and pleasing conceits toward themselves; or because it advanceth any other their ends. So that as it is said of untrue valours that some men's valours are in the eyes of them that look on, so such men's industries are in the eyes of others, or at least in regard* of their own designments;[60] only learned men love business as an action according to nature, as agreeable to health of mind as exercise is to health of body, taking pleasure in the action itself, and not in the purchase,[61] so that of all men they are the most indefatigable, if it be towards any business which can hold or detain their mind.

---

[57] vividness, liveliness.

[58] See Guicciardini, *Hist.*, XVI.5; Cicero, *To Atticus*, XVI.7; Plutarch, *Phocion*; Lucian, *Dialogues of the Gods*, (6), 217-20; Cicero, *To Atticus*, II.9. painted out: depicted. vaporous: boastful.

[59] i.e., wear out, decrease.

[60] designs, aims (i. e., their industry is assumed for a purpose).

[61] gain, advantage.

And if any man be laborious in reading and study and yet idle in business and action, it groweth from some weakness of body or softness of spirit, such as Seneca speaketh of: *Quidam tam sunt umbratiles, ut putent in turbido esse quicquid in luce est,*[62] and not of learning. Well may it be that such a point of a man's nature may make him give himself to learning, but it is not learning that breedeth any such point in his nature.

And that learning should take up too much time or leisure, I answer, the most active or busy man that hath been or can be hath (no question) many vacant times of leisure, while he expecteth* the tides and returns[63] of business (except he be either tedious and of no dispatch, or lightly and unworthily ambitious to meddle in things that may be better done by others), and then the question is but how those spaces and times of leisure shall be filled and spent: whether in pleasures or in studies, as was well answered by Demosthenes to his adversary Æschines, that was a man given to pleasure, and told him *that his orations did smell of the lamp: Indeed* (said Demosthenes) *there is a great difference between the things that you and I do by lamplight.*[64] So as no man need doubt* that learning will expulse[65] business, but rather it will keep and defend the possession of the mind against idleness and pleasure, which otherwise at unawares may enter to the prejudice of both.

Again, for that other conceit that learning should undermine the reverence of laws and government, it is assuredly a mere depravation* and calumny without all[66] shadow of truth. For to say that a blind custom of obedience should be a surer obligation than duty taught and understood, it is to affirm that a blind man may tread surer by a guide than a seeing man can by a light. And it is without all controversy that learning doth make the minds of men gentle, generous, maniable,[67] and pliant to government; whereas ignorance makes them churlish, thwart, and mutinous,

[62] "Some men are so much creatures of the shade that they deem everything in the light to be troublesome." *Epist.*, III.6.

[63] i.e., ebbs and flows.

[64] Cf. Plutarch, *Demosthenes*, 8, where the target is not Aeschines but another. [Wright]

[65] expel.

[66] any.

[67] manageable, tractable.

and the evidence of time doth clear[68] this assertion, considering that the most barbarous, rude, and unlearned times have been most subject to tumults, seditions, and changes.

And as to the judgment of Cato the Censor, he was well punished for his blasphemy against learning, in the same kind wherein he offended; for when he was past threescore years old, he was taken with an extreme desire to go to school again and to learn the Greek tongue, to the end to peruse the Greek authors,[69] which doth well demonstrate that his former censure of the Grecian learning was rather an affected gravity than according to the inward sense of his own opinion. And as for Virgil's verses, though it pleased him to brave* the world in taking to the Romans the art of empire, and leaving to others the arts of subjects, yet so much is manifest, that the Romans never ascended to that height of empire till the time they had ascended to the height of other arts; for in the time of the two first Cæsars, which had the art of government in greatest perfection, there lived the best poet, Virgilius Maro; the best historiographer, Titus Livius; the best antiquary, Marcus Varro; and the best, or second orator, Marcus Cicero; that to the memory of man are known. As for the accusation of Socrates, the time must be remembered when it was prosecuted, which was under the Thirty Tyrants,[70] the most base, bloody, and envious persons that have governed; which revolution of state was no sooner over but Socrates, whom they had made a person criminal, was made a person heroical, and his memory accumulate[71] with honours divine and human; and those discourses of his, which were then termed corrupting of manners, were after acknowledged for sovereign medicines of the mind and manners,* and so have been received ever since till this day. Let this therefore serve for answer to politiques, which in their humorous* severity or in their feigned gravity have presumed to throw imputations upon learning, which redargution[72] nevertheless (save that we know

[68] prove, justify.
[69] See, for example, Plutarch, *Cato*, 2,23.
[70] a committee that ruled Athens for eight months (404-403 B.C.). But

the trial and death of Socrates occurred after the restoration of the democracy. [Wright]
[71] loaded.
[72] refutation.

not whether our labours may extend to other ages) were not needful for the present, in regard of* the love and reverence towards learning which the example and countenance of two so learned princes, Queen Elizabeth and your Majesty, being as Castor and Pollux, *lucida sidera*,[73] stars of excellent light and most benign influence, hath wrought in all men of place and authority in our nation.

Now therefore we come to that third sort of discredit or diminution of credit, that groweth unto learning from learned men themselves, which commonly cleaveth fastest. It is either from their fortune or from their manners or from the nature of their studies. For the first, it is not in their power; and the second is accidental; the third only is proper to be handled. But because we are not in hand[74] with true measure but with popular estimation and conceit, it is not amiss to speak somewhat of the two former. The derogations therefore which grow to learning from the fortune or condition of learned men are either in respect of scarcity of means or in respect of privateness of life and meanness of employments.

Concerning want, and that it is the case of learned men usually to begin with little and not to grow rich so fast as other men, by reason they convert not their labours chiefly to lucre and increase, it were good to leave the commonplace* in commendation of poverty to some friar to handle, to whom much was attributed by Machiavel in this point, when he said, *That the kingdom of the clergy had been long before at an end, if the reputation and reverence towards the poverty of friars had not borne out the scandal of the superfluities and excesses of bishops and prelates.*[75] So a man might say that the felicity and delicacy of princes and great persons had long since turned to rudeness and barbarism, if the poverty of learning had not kept up civility* and honour of life. But without any such advantages, it is worthy the observation what a reverend and honoured thing poverty of fortune was for some ages in the Roman state, which nevertheless was a state without paradoxes. For we see what Titus Livius saith in his

---

[73] See Horace, I.iii.2.
[74] concerned, dealing with.

[75] *Disc. on Livy,* III.1. borne out: compensated for.

introduction: *Cæterum aut me amor negotii suscepti fallit, aut nulla unquam respublica nec major, nec sanctior, nec bonis exemplis ditior fuit; nec in quam tam seræ avaritia luxuriaque immigraverint; nec ubi tantus ac tam diu paupertati ac parsimoniæ honos fuerit.*[76] We see likewise, after that the state of Rome was not itself but did degenerate, how that person that took upon him to be counsellor to Julius Cæsar after his victory, where to begin his restoration of the state, maketh it of all points the most summary[77] to take away the estimation of wealth: *Verum hæc et omnia mala pariter cum honore pecuniæ desinent; si neque magistratus, neque alia vulgo cupienda, venalia erunt.*[78] To conclude this point, as it was truly said that *rubor est virtutis color,*[79] though sometime it come from vice, so it may be fitly said that *paupertas est virtutis fortuna,*[80] though sometime it may proceed from misgovernment and accident. Surely Salomon hath pronounced it both in censure, *Qui festinat ad divitias non erit insons,*[81] and in precept, *Buy the truth, and sell it not; and so of wisdom and knowledge,* judging that means were to be spent upon learning, and not learning to be applied to means. And as for the privateness or obscureness (as it may be in vulgar estimation accounted) of life of contemplative men, it is a theme so common to extol a private life, not taxed with sensuality and sloth, in comparison and to the disadvantage of a civil[82] life, for safety, liberty, pleasure, and dignity, or at least freedom from indignity, as no man handleth it but handleth it well, such a consonancy it hath to men's conceits* in the expressing and to men's consents in the allowing.* This only I will add, that learned men forgotten in states, and not living in the eyes of men, are like the

76 "Unless love of my subject deceives me, no republic was ever greater, more pious, or richer in good examples [than Rome]; nor any to which avarice and luxury arrived so late; nor any in which poverty and thrift were esteemed so long." Livy, Preface.

77 efficacious, important.

78 "Truly, these and all other evils will disappear as soon as wealth ceases to be honoured and the magistracies and other things popularly desired cease to be available for money." Sallust (attr. author), *First Letter to Caesar on the State*, VIII.

79 "A blush is virtue's colour." Attr. to Diogenes the Cynic. See Diogenes Laertius, VI.54.

80 "Poverty is virtue's fortune."

81 "He that hasteth to be rich will not be innocent." Cf. Prov. 28:22. For the next precept, see Prov. 23:23.

82 public.

images of Cassius and Brutus in the funeral of Junia, of which not being represented, as many others were, Tacitus saith, *Eo ipso præfulgebant, quod non visebantur.*[83]

And for meanness of employment, that which is most traduced[84] to contempt is that the government of youth is commonly allotted to them, which age, because it is the age of least authority, it is transferred to the disesteeming of those employments wherein youth is conversant,[85] and which are conversant about youth. But how unjust this traducement is (if you will reduce things from popularity of opinion to measure of reason) may appear in that we see men are more curious* what they put into a new vessel than into a vessel seasoned, and what mould they lay about a young plant than about a plant corroborate;[86] so as the weakest terms and times of all things use* to have the best applications and helps. And will you hearken to the Hebrew Rabbins? *Your young men shall see visions, and your old men shall dream dreams;*[87] say they youth is the worthier age, for that visions are nearer apparitions of God than dreams. And let it be noted that howsoever the conditions of life of *Pedantes* have been scorned upon theatres, as the ape of tyranny, and that the modern looseness or negligence hath taken no due regard to the choice of schoolmasters and tutors, yet the ancient wisdom of the best times did always make a just complaint that states were too busy with their laws and too negligent in point of education, which excellent part of ancient discipline hath been in some sort revived of late times by the colleges of the Jesuits, of whom, although in regard of their superstition I may say, *Quo meliores, eo deteriores,*[88] yet in regard of this and some other points concerning human learning and moral matters, I may say, as Agesilaus said to his enemy Pharnabazus, *Talis quum sis, utinam*

---

[83] "They outshone them all, from the very fact that they were not to be seen." *Ann.*, III.76. It was the custom at Roman funerals to carry in procession the images of the ancestors and relations of the deceased. However, at the funeral of Junia (A.D. 22), the wife of Cassius and the sister of Brutus, their images were not carried because they had been guilty of the murder of the first Caesar. [Selby]

[84] held up (to).

[85] concerned with.

[86] grown strong.

[87] Joel 2:28.

[88] "The better the worse." A saying of Diogenes. See Diogenes Laertius, VI.46. [Wright]

noster esses.[89] And thus much touching the discredits drawn from the fortunes of learned men.

As touching the manners of learned men, it is a thing personal and individual, and no doubt there be amongst them, as in other professions, of all temperatures,* but yet so as it is not without truth which is said, that *abeunt studia in mores,* studies have an influence and operation upon the manners of those that are conversant in them.[90]

But upon an attentive and indifferent* review, I for my part cannot find any disgrace to learning can proceed from the manners of learned men not inherent to[91] them as they are learned, except it be a fault (which was the supposed fault of Demosthenes, Cicero, Cato the second, Seneca, and many more) that because the times they read of are commonly better than the times they live in, and the duties taught better than the duties practised, they contend sometimes too far to bring things to perfection, and to reduce* the corruption of manners* to honesty of precepts or examples of too great height. And yet hereof they have caveats enough in their own walks. For Solon, when he was asked whether he had given his citizens the best laws, answered wisely, *Yea of such as they would receive,*[92] and Plato, finding that his own heart could not agree with the corrupt manners of his country, refused to bear place or office, saying *that a man's country was to be used as his parents were, that is, with humble persuasions, and not with contestations;*[93] and Cæsar's counsellor put in the same caveat, *Non ad vetera instituta revocans quæ jampridem corruptis moribus ludibrio sunt;*[94] and Cicero noteth this error directly in Cato the second, when he writes to his friend Atticus: *Cato optime sentit, sed nocet interdum reipublicæ; loquitur enim tanquam in republica Platonis, non tanquam in*

---

[89] "Thou art such that I would thou wert one of us." See Plutarch, *Agesilaus,* 12. Pharnabazus (*fl.* 395 B.C.): satrap of Persian provinces near the Hellespont.

[90] Ovid, *Her.,* XV.83.

[91] in.

[92] See Plutarch, *Solon,* 15.

[93] See Plato, *Epist.,* VII, 331C; *Crito,*

51C. Bacon probably got the passage from Cicero, *Letters to His Friends,* I.ix.18. [Ellis]

[94] "Not to restore things to their old institutions, which are held in contempt because of the long corruption of morals." Sallust (Caesar's counsellor, attr. author), *Second Letter to Caesar on the State,* V.

fæce Romuli;[95] and the same Cicero doth excuse and expound the philosophers for going too far and being too exact in their prescripts, when he saith, *Isti ipsi præceptores virtutis et magistri videntur fines officiorum paulo longius quam natura vellet pro-tulisse, ut cum ad ultimum animo contendissemus, ibi tamen, ubi oportet, consisteremus;*[96] and yet himself might have said, *Monitis sum minor ipse meis,*[97] for it was his own fault, though not in so extreme a degree.

Another fault likewise, much of this kind, hath been incident to learned men, which is that they have esteemed the preservation, good, and honour of their countries or masters before their own fortunes or safeties. For so saith Demosthenes unto the Athenians: *If it please you to note it, my counsels unto you are not such whereby I should grow great amongst you, and you become little amongst the Grecians, but they be of that nature, as they are sometimes not good for me to give, but are always good for you to follow.*[98] And so Seneca, after he had consecrated that *Quinquennium Neronis*[99] to the eternal glory of learned governors, held on his honest and loyal course of good and free counsel, after his master grew extremely corrupt in his government. Neither can this point otherwise be, for learning endueth men's minds with a true sense of the frailty of their persons, the casualty[100] of their fortunes, and the dignity of their soul and vocation, so that it is impossible for them to esteem that any greatness of their own fortune can be a true or worthy end of their being and ordainment;[101] and therefore are desirous to give their account to God, and so likewise to their masters under God (as kings and the states that they serve), in these words: *Ecce tibi*

---

[95] "Cato has fine intentions, but he occasionally does harm to the state; for he speaks as though we were living in the republic of Plato rather than in the excrement of Romulus." Cicero, *To Atticus,* II.i.3.

[96] "Those same teachers and masters of virtue seem to have set the standard of duty somewhat higher than nature can bear, in order that when we strive our utmost to attain it we might still reach the level we ought to." Cicero, *Speech on Behalf of Murena,* XXI.65.

[97] "I am myself unequal to my own precepts." Ovid, *The Art of Love,* II.548.

[98] Demosthenes, *On the Chersonese,* 187.

[99] "the first five years of Nero's reign". See Aurelius Victor, *Caesar,* V.2.

[100] instability, uncertainty.

[101] ordination, appointed condition.

lucrefeci, and not *Ecce mihi lucrefeci,*[102] whereas the corrupter sort of mere politiques,* that have not their thoughts established by learning in the love and apprehension of duty, nor never look abroad into universality, do refer all things to themselves, and thrust themselves into the centre of the world, as if all lines should meet in them and their fortunes, never caring in all tempests what becomes of the ship of estates,* so they may save themselves in the cockboat of their own fortune; whereas men that feel the weight of duty, and know the limits of self-love use to* make good[103] their places and duties, though with peril. And if they stand[104] in seditious and violent alterations, it is rather the reverence which many times both adverse parts do give to honesty than any versatile advantage of their own carriage. But for this point of tender[105] sense and fast obligation of duty, which learning doth endue the mind withal, howsoever fortune may tax it and many in the depth of their corrupt principles may despise it, yet it will receive an open allowance,* and therefore needs the less disproof or excusation.*

Another fault incident commonly to learned men, which may be more probably defended than truly denied, is that they fail sometimes in applying themselves to particular persons, which want of exact application ariseth from two causes: the one, because the largeness of their mind can hardly confine itself to dwell in the exquisite observation or examination of the nature and customs of one person, for it is a speech for a lover and not for a wise man, *Satis magnum alter alteri theatrum sumus.*[106] Nevertheless I shall yield that he that cannot contract the sight of his mind as well as disperse and dilate it wanteth a great faculty. But there is a second cause, which is no inability but a rejection upon choice and judgment. For the honest and just bounds of observation by one person upon another extend no farther but to understand him sufficiently, whereby not to give him offence, or whereby to be able to give him faithful counsel,

---

[102] " 'Lo, I have gained for you', and not 'Lo, I have gained for myself' ". Cf. Matt. 25:20.

[103] be true to.

[104] remain safe, survive.

[105] scrupulous.

[106] "We are a sufficiently large theatre to each other." Ascribed to Epicurus by Seneca, *Epist.*, VII.11.

or whereby to stand upon reasonable guard and caution in respect of a man's self, but to be speculative* into another man, to the end to know how to work him or wind him or govern him, proceedeth from a heart that is double and cloven and not entire* and ingenuous; which as in friendship it is want of integrity, so towards princes or superiors is want of duty. For the custom of the Levant, which is that subjects do forbear to gaze or fix their eyes upon princes, is in the outward ceremony barbarous, but the moral is good, for men ought not by cunning and bent[107] observations to pierce and penetrate into the hearts of kings, which the Scripture hath declared to be inscrutable.[108]

There is yet another fault (with which I will conclude this part) which is often noted in learned men, that they do many times fail to observe decency and discretion in their behaviour and carriage, and commit errors in small and ordinary points of action; so as the vulgar sort of capacities do make a judgment of them in greater matters by that which they find wanting in them in smaller. But this consequence[109] doth oft deceive men, for which I do refer them over to that which was said by Themistocles, arrogantly and uncivilly being applied to himself out of his own mouth, but being applied to the general state of this question pertinently and justly, when being invited to touch a lute, he said *he could not fiddle, but he could make a small town a great state.*[110] So no doubt many may be well seen[111] in the passages of government and policy, which are to seek* in little and punctual occasions. I refer them also to that which Plato said of his master Socrates, whom he compared to the gallipots of apothecaries, which on the outside had apes and owls and antiques, but contained within sovereign and precious liquors and confections,[112] acknowledging that to an external report[113] he was not without superficial levities and deformities, but was inwardly replenished with excellent virtues and powers. And so much touching the point of manners of learned men.

But in the meantime I have no purpose to give allowance* to

[107] crafty.
[108] See Prov. 25:3.
[109] inference.
[110] See Plutarch, *Themistocles*, 2.
[111] versed.
[112] *Symposium*, 215B.
[113] to a superficial view.

some conditions and courses base and unworthy, wherein divers professors of learning have wronged themselves and gone too far; such as were those trencher philosophers, which in the later age of the Roman state were usually in the houses of great persons, being little better than solemn parasites, of which kind, Lucian maketh a merry description of the philosopher that the great lady took to ride with her in her coach, and would needs have him carry her little dog, which he doing officiously and yet uncomely, the page scoffed and said *that he doubted* the philosopher of a Stoic would turn to be a Cynic*.[114] But above all the rest, the gross and palpable flattery whereunto many (not unlearned) have abased and abused their wits and pens, turning (as Du Bartas saith) Hecuba into Helena and Faustina into Lucretia,[115] hath most diminished the price and estimation of learning. Neither is the modern dedications of books and writings, as to patrons, to be commended, for that books (such as are worthy the name of books) ought to have no patrons but truth and reason; and the ancient custom was to dedicate them only to private and equal friends, or to intitle the books with their names; or if to kings and great persons, it was to some such as the argument of the book was fit and proper for. But these and the like courses may deserve rather reprehension than defence.

Not that I can tax or condemn the morigeration[116] or application of learned men to men in fortune. For the answer was good that Diogenes made to one that asked him in mockery, *How it came to pass that philosophers were the followers of rich men, and not rich men of philosophers?* He answered soberly and yet sharply, *Because the one sort knew what they had need of, and the other did not*.[117] And of the like nature was the answer which Aristippus made, when having a petition to Dionysius and no ear given to him, he fell down at his feet, whereupon Dionysius

---

[114] Lucian, *On Salaried Posts in Great Houses*, 33, 34. *Cynic* originally meant doglike.

[115] Du Bartas, *Divine Days and Weeks*, the Second Day. Faustina, (c. A.D. 120-75): profligate wife of Emperor Marcus Aurelius Antoninus. Lucretia: raped by Sextus Tarquinius, committed suicide (c. 511 B.C.) through shame.

[116] obsequiousness.

[117] not Diogenes but Aristippus. See Diogenes Laertius, *Aristippus*, II.69 and, for the next reference, II.79. [Wright]

stayed and gave him the hearing and granted it; and afterward some person tender* on the behalf of philosophy reproved Aristippus that he would offer the profession of philosophy such an indignity, as for a private suit to fall at a tyrant's feet, but he answered, *It was not his fault, but it was the fault of Dionysius, that had his ears in his feet.* Neither was it accounted weakness but discretion in him that would not dispute his best with Adrianus Cæsar, excusing himself, *that it was reason to yield to him that commanded thirty legions.*[118] These and the like applications and stooping to points of necessity and convenience cannot be disallowed,* for though they may have some outward baseness, yet in a judgment truly made they are to be accounted submissions to the occasion and not to the person.

Now I proceed to those errors and vanities which have intervened amongst the studies themselves of the learned, which is that which is principal and proper to the present argument, wherein my purpose is not to make a justification of the errors but by a censure and separation of the errors to make a justification of that which is good and sound, and to deliver that from the aspersion of the other. For we see that it is the manner of men to scandalize and deprave* that which retaineth the state and virtue by taking advantage upon that which is corrupt and degenerate, as the Heathens in the primitive church used to blemish and taint the Christians with the faults and corruptions of heretics. But nevertheless I have no meaning at this time to make any exact animadversion of the errors and impediments in matters of learning which are more secret and remote from vulgar opinion, but only to speak unto such as do fall under, or near unto, a popular observation.

There be therefore chiefly three vanities in studies, whereby learning hath been most traduced. For those things we do esteem vain which are either false or frivolous, those which either have no truth or no use, and those persons we esteem vain which are either credulous or curious;* and curiosity is either in matter or words, so that in reason as well as in experience there fall out to be these three distempers (as I may term them) of learning: the

[118] See Spartianus, *Hadrian*, XV.

first, fantastical learning; the second, contentious learning; and the last, delicate learning; vain imaginations, vain altercations, and vain affectations; and with the last I will begin. Martin Luther, conducted (no doubt) by an higher Providence, but in discourse of reason finding what a province he had undertaken against the Bishop of Rome and the degenerate traditions of the church, and finding his own solitude[119] being no ways aided by the opinions of his own time, was enforced to awake all antiquity and to call former times to his succours to make a party against the present time, so that the ancient authors, both in divinity and in humanity, which had long time slept in libraries, began generally to be read and revolved. This by consequence did draw on a necessity of a more exquisite[120] travail* in the languages original wherein those authors did write, for the better understanding of those authors and the better advantage of pressing and applying their words. And thereof grew again a delight in their manner of style and phrase, and an admiration of that kind of writing, which was much furthered and precipitated by the enmity and opposition that the propounders of those (primitive but seeming new) opinions had against the schoolmen, who were generally of the contrary part, and whose writings were altogether in a differing style and form, taking liberty to coin and frame new terms of art to express their own sense and to avoid circuit of speech without regard to the pureness, pleasantness, and (as I may call it) lawfulness of the phrase or word. And again, because the great labour then was with the people (of whom the Pharisees were wont to say, *Execrabilis ista turba, quæ non novit legem*[121]), for the winning and persuading of them, there grew of necessity in chief price and request eloquence and variety of discourse, as the fittest and forciblest access into the capacity of the vulgar sort. So that these four causes concurring, the admiration of ancient authors, the hate of the schoolmen, the exact study of languages, and the efficacy of preaching did bring in an affectionate* study of eloquence and copie[122] of speech, which

---

[119] his solitary position.
[120] careful, painstaking.
[121] "this accursed mob, that knoweth not the law". John 7:49.
[122] i.e., *copia*: copiousness, fluency.

then began to flourish. This grew speedily to an excess, for men began to hunt more after words than matter, and more after the choiceness of the phrase, and the round and clean[123] composition of the sentence, and the sweet falling of the clauses, and the varying and illustration of their works with tropes and figures than after the weight of matter, worth of subject, soundness of argument, life of invention, or depth of judgment. Then grew the flowing and watery vein of Osorius, the Portugal bishop, to be in price. Then did Sturmius spend such infinite and curious pains upon Cicero the Orator and Hermogenes the Rhetorician, besides his own books of periods and imitation and the like. Then did Car of Cambridge and Ascham, with their lectures and writings, almost deify Cicero and Demosthenes, and allure all young men that were studious unto that delicate and polished kind of learning.[124] Then did Erasmus take occasion to make the scoffing echo, *Decem annos consumpsi in legendo Cicerone*, and the echo answered in Greek, "Ονε, Asine.[125] Then grew the learning of the schoolmen to be utterly despised as barbarous. In sum, the whole inclination and bent of those times was rather towards copie than weight.

Here therefore is the first distemper of learning, when men study words and not matter, whereof though I have represented an example of late times, yet it hath been and will be *secundum majus et minus*[126] in all time. And how is it possible but this should have an operation to discredit learning, even with vulgar capacities, when they see learned men's works like the first letter of a patent or limned book, which though it hath large flourishes, yet it is but a letter? It seems to me that Pygmalion's frenzy is a good emblem or portraiture of this vanity, for words are but the images of matter, and except they have life of reason and inven-

[123] polished.

[124] Osorius (d. 1580): bishop of Sylves in Algarves, historian of Portuguese discoveries and conquests of the reign of Emmanuel the Great. Sturmius (1507-89): "the German Cicero", professor at Paris and Strasbourg. Hermogenes flourished in the second century. Nicholas Carr (1523-68): professor of Greek at the University of Cambridge.

[125] "I have spent ten years in reading Cicero." The echo's answer (the last three letters of the boast) is "Ass." *Colloquies*, "Juvenis and Echo".

[126] "more or less".

tion, to fall in love with them is all one as to fall in love with a picture.

But yet notwithstanding, it is a thing not hastily to be condemned, to clothe and adorn the obscurity even of philosophy itself with sensible[127] and plausible* elocution. For hereof we have great examples in Xenophon, Cicero, Seneca, Plutarch, and of Plato also in some degree; and hereof likewise there is great use, for surely to the severe inquisition* of truth and the deep progress into philosophy, it is some hindrance, because it is too early satisfactory to the mind of man, and quencheth the desire of further search, before we come to a just period;* but then if a man be to have any use[128] of such knowledge in civil* occasions, of conference, counsel, persuasion, discourse, or the like, then shall he find it prepared to his hands in those authors which write in that manner. But the excess of this is so justly contemptible that as Hercules, when he saw the image of Adonis, Venus' minion, in a temple, said in disdain, *Nil sacri es*,[129] so there is none of Hercules' followers in learning, that is, the more severe and laborious sort of inquirers into truth, but will despise those delicacies and affectations as indeed capable of no divineness. And thus much of the first disease or distemper of learning.

The second, which followeth, is in nature worse than the former, for as substance of matter is better than beauty of words, so contrariwise vain matter is worse than vain words; wherein it seemeth the reprehension of St. Paul was not only proper for those times, but prophetical for the times following, and not only respective* to divinity but extensive[130] to all knowledge: *Devita profanas vocum novitates, et oppositiones falsi nominis scientiæ*.[131] For he assigneth two marks and badges of suspected and falsified science: the one, the novelty and strangeness of terms; the other, the strictness of positions,[132] which of necessity doth induce oppositions, and so questions and altercations.

---

[127] appealing to the senses.

[128] i.e., is going to, is to, have any occasion to use.

[129] "Thou art no divinity." Scholiast on Theocritus, *Idylls*, V.2; Erasmus, *Adages*, I.viii.37 (311E).

[130] extendible.

[131] "Avoid profane novelties of terms and the oppositions of what is falsely called knowledge." I Tim. 6:20.

[132] principles, propositions, maxims.

Surely, like as many substances in nature which are solid do putrefy and corrupt into worms, so it is the property of good and sound knowledge to putrefy and dissolve into a number of subtile, idle, unwholesome, and (as I may term them) vermiculate questions, which have indeed a kind of quickness* and life of spirit, but no soundness of matter or goodness of quality. This kind of degenerate learning did chiefly reign amongst the schoolmen, who having sharp and strong wits and abundance of leisure and small variety of reading, but their wits being shut up in the cells of a few authors (chiefly Aristotle their dictator) as their persons were shut up in the cells of monasteries and colleges, and knowing little history, either of nature or time, did out of no great quantity of matter and infinite agitation of wit spin out unto us those laborious webs of learning which are extant in their books. For the wit and mind of man, if it work upon matter, which is the contemplation of the creatures of God, worketh according to the stuff, and is limited thereby, but if it work upon itself, as the spider worketh his web, then it is endless, and brings forth indeed cobwebs of learning, admirable for the fineness of thread and work but of no substance or profit.

This same unprofitable subtility or curiosity is of two sorts: either in the subject itself that they handle, when it is a fruitless speculation or controversy (whereof there are no small number both in divinity and philosophy), or in the manner or method of handling of a knowledge, which amongst them was this: upon every particular position or assertion to frame objections, and to those objections, solutions; which solutions were for the most part not confutations but distinctions; whereas indeed the strength of all sciences is, as the strength of the old man's faggot, in the bond.[133] For the harmony of a science, supporting each part the other, is and ought to be the true and brief confutation and suppression of all the smaller sort of objections, but on the other side, if you take out every axiom, as the sticks of the faggot, one by one, you may quarrel with them and bend them and break them at your pleasure; so that as was said of Seneca, *Ver-*

[133] See Aesop, *Fables,* 52.

borum minutiis rerum frangit pondera;[134] so a man may truly say of the schoolmen, *Quæstionum minutiis scientiarum frangunt soliditatem.*[135] For were it not better for a man in a fair room to set up one great light or branching candlestick of lights than to go about with a small watch candle[136] into every corner? And such is their method, that rests not so much upon evidence of truth proved by arguments, authorities, similitudes, examples, as upon particular confutations and solutions of every scruple, cavillation,[137] and objection, breeding for the most part one question as fast it solveth another, even as in the former resemblance,[138] when you carry the light into one corner, you darken the rest; so that the fable and fiction of Scylla seemeth to be a lively image of this kind of philosophy or knowledge, which was transformed into a comely virgin for the upper parts, but then *Candida succinctam latrantibus inguina monstris;*[139] so the generalities of the schoolmen are for a while good and proportionable,[140] but then when you descend into their distinctions and decisions, instead of a fruitful womb for the use and benefit of man's life, they end in monstrous altercations and barking questions. So as it is not possible but this quality of knowledge must fall under popular contempt, the people being apt to contemn truth upon occasion of controversies and altercations, and to think they are all out of their way which never meet,[141] and when they see such digladiation[142] about subtilities and matter of no use nor moment, they easily fall upon that judgment of Dionysius of Syracusa, *Verba ista sunt senum otiosorum.*[143]

Notwithstanding, certain it is that if those schoolmen to their great thirst of truth and unwearied travail of wit had joined

---

[134] "He breaks up the weight of the matter by verbal subtleties." Cf. Quintilian, X.1.

[135] "They break up the solidity of the sciences by hair-splitting questions."

[136] night-light.

[137] i.e., cavil.

[138] comparison.

[139] "her fair white loins begirt with barking monsters". Virgil, *Eclog.*, VI.75.

[140] adequate.

[141] i.e., they are all wrong who never agree.

[142] wrangling, disputing.

[143] "Those are the words of old men with nothing to do." See Diogenes Laertius, III.18.

variety and universality of reading and contemplation, they had proved excellent lights to the great advancement of all learning and knowledge. But as they are, they are great undertakers indeed, and fierce with dark keeping;[144] but as in the inquiry of the divine truth their pride inclined to leave the oracle of God's word and to vanish in the mixture of their own inventions, so in the inquisition of nature they ever left the oracle of God's works and adored the deceiving and deformed images which the unequal[145] mirror of their own minds or a few received authors or principles did represent unto them. And thus much for the second disease of learning.

For the third vice or disease of learning, which concerneth deceit or untruth, it is of all the rest the foulest, as that which doth destroy the essential form of knowledge, which is nothing but a representation of truth, for the truth of being and the truth of knowing are one, differing no more than the direct beam and the beam reflected. This vice therefore brancheth itself into two sorts: delight in deceiving and aptness to be deceived, imposture and credulity; which, although they appear to be of a diverse nature, the one seeming to proceed of cunning and the other of simplicity, yet certainly they do for the most part concur, for as the verse noteth,

Percontatorem fugito, nam garrulus idem est,[146]

an inquisitive man is a prattler; so upon the like reason a credulous man is a deceiver, as we see it in fame,* that he that will easily believe rumours will as easily augment rumours and add somewhat to them of his own, which Tacitus wisely noteth, when he saith, *Fingunt simul creduntque,*[147] so great an affinity hath fiction and belief.

This facility of credit and accepting or admitting things weakly authorized or warranted is of two kinds according to the subject: for it is either a belief of history (as the lawyers

---

[144] i.e., with being kept in the dark.
[145] uneven.
[146] "Shun the inquisitive man, for he is a babbler." Horace, *Epist.*, I.xviii.69.

[147] "They no sooner invent stories than they believe them." *Hist.*, I.51.

speak, matter of fact) or else of matter of art and opinion. As to the former, we see the experience and inconvenience of this error in ecclesiastical history, which hath too easily received and registered reports and narrations of miracles wrought by martyrs, hermits, or monks of the desert and other holy men, and their relics, shrines, chapels, and images, which though they had a passage[148] for a time, by the ignorance of the people, the superstitious simplicity of some, and the politic toleration of others, holding them but as divine poesies, yet after a period of time, when the mist began to clear up, they grew to be esteemed but as old wives' fables, impostures of the clergy, illusions of spirits, and badges of antichrist, to the great scandal and detriment of religion.

So in natural history we see there hath not been that choice and judgment used as ought to have been, as may appear in the writings of Plinius, Cardanus, Albertus, and divers of the Arabians,[149] being fraught with much fabulous matter, a great part not only untried but notoriously untrue, to the great derogation of the credit of natural philosophy with the grave and sober kind of wits. Wherein the wisdom and integrity of Aristotle is worthy to be observed, that having made so diligent and exquisite* a history of living creatures,[150] hath mingled it sparingly with any vain or feigned matter, and yet on the other side hath cast all prodigious narrations which he thought worthy the recording into one book, excellently discerning that matter of manifest truth, such whereupon observation and rule was to be built, was not to be mingled or weakened with matter of doubtful credit; and yet again that rarities and reports that seem uncredible are not to be suppressed or denied to the memory of men.

And as for the facility of credit which is yielded to arts and opinions, it is likewise of two kinds: either when too much belief is attributed to the arts themselves, or to certain authors

---

[148] acceptance.

[149] all writers on natural history — Pliny the Elder in the first century, Jeronimo Cardan in the sixteenth century, Albertus Magnus in the fourteenth century; the most noted of the Arabians was Averroës.

[150] This history of narrations of prodigies (*De Mirabilibus Auscultationibus*) is not Aristotle's. [Wright]

in any art. The sciences themselves which have had better intelligence and confederacy with the imagination of man than with his reason are three in number: Astrology, Natural Magic, and Alchemy, of which sciences nevertheless the ends or pretences are noble. For astrology pretendeth to discover that correspondence or concatenation which is between the superior globe and the inferior; natural magic pretendeth to call and reduce* natural philosophy from variety of speculations to the magnitude of works; and alchemy pretendeth to make separation of all the unlike parts of bodies which in mixtures of nature are incorporate.[151] But the derivations and prosecutions[152] to these ends, both in the theories and in the practices, are full of error and vanity, which the great professors themselves have sought to veil over and conceal by enigmatical writings, and referring themselves to auricular traditions, and such other devices to save the credit of impostures. And yet surely to alchemy this right is due, that it may be compared to the husbandman whereof Æsop makes the fable, that when he died told his sons that he had left unto them gold buried under ground in his vineyard, and they digged over all the ground, and gold they found none, but by reason of their stirring and digging the mould about the roots of their vines they had a great vintage the year following;[153] so assuredly the search and stir to make gold hath brought to light a great number of good and fruitful inventions and experiments, as well for the disclosing of nature as for the use of man's life.

And as for the overmuch credit that hath been given unto authors in sciences, in making them dictators, that their words should stand, and not consuls[154] to give advice, the damage is infinite that sciences have received thereby, as the principal cause that hath kept them low, at a stay without growth or advancement. For hence it hath comen that in arts mechanical the first deviser comes shortest, and time addeth and perfecteth; but in sciences the first author goeth furthest, and time

[151] i.e., which are incorporated in mixtures as they exist in nature.
[152] devices and methods.
[153] *Fables*, 33.

[154] The 1625 edition has *counsels*. Ellis guesses that Bacon wrote *counsell^rs*.

leeseth* and corrupteth. So we see, artillery, sailing, printing, and the like were grossly managed at the first, and by time accommodated and refined, but contrariwise the philosophies and sciences of Aristotle, Plato, Democritus, Hippocrates, Euclides, Archimedes, of most vigour at the first, and by time degenerate and imbased;[155] whereof the reason is no other but that in the former many wits and industries have contributed in one, and in the latter many wits and industries have been spent about the wit of some one, whom many times they have rather depraved than illustrated. For as water will not ascend higher than the level of the first spring-head from whence it descendeth, so knowledge derived from Aristotle and exempted from liberty of examination will not rise again higher than the knowledge of Aristotle. And therefore, although the position* be good, *Oportet discentem credere*,[156] yet it must be coupled with this, *Oportet edoctum judicare*;[157] for disciples do owe unto masters only a temporary belief and a suspension of their own judgment until they be fully instructed, and not an absolute resignation or perpetual captivity; and therefore to conclude this point, I will say no more but so let great authors have their due as time which is the author of authors be not deprived of his due, which is further and further to discover truth. Thus have I gone over these three diseases of learning, besides the which there are some other rather peccant humours than formed diseases, which nevertheless are not so secret and intrinsic[158] but that they fall under a popular observation and traducement,* and therefore are not to be passed over.

The first of these is the extreme affecting* of two extremities, the one Antiquity, the other Novelty, wherein it seemeth the children of time do take after the nature and malice of the father. For as he devoureth his children, so one of them seeketh to devour and suppress the other, while antiquity envieth there should be new additions, and novelty cannot be content to add but it must deface. Surely the advice of the prophet is

---

[155] embased, debased.

[156] "The learner should take things on trust." Aristotle, *On Sophistical Refutations*, 2(165b).

[157] "The learned man should exercise his judgment."

[158] hidden.

the true direction in this matter, *State super vias antiquas, et videte quænam sit via recta et bona, et ambulate in ea.*[159] Antiquity deserveth that reverence, that men should make a stand thereupon and discover what is the best way, but when the discovery is well taken, then to make progression. And to speak truly, *Antiquitas sæculi juventus mundi.*[160] These times are the ancient times, when the world is ancient, and not those which we account ancient *ordine retrogrado*, by a computation backward from ourselves.

Another error induced by the former, is a distrust that any thing should be now to be found out, which the world should have missed and passed over so long time, as if the same objection were to be made to time that Lucian[161] maketh to Jupiter and other the heathen gods, of which he wondereth that they begot so many children in old time and begot none in his time, and asketh whether they were become septuagenary, or whether the law *Pappia*,[162] made against old men's marriages, had restrained them. So it seemeth men doubt* lest time is become past children and generation, wherein contrariwise we see commonly the levity and unconstancy of men's judgments, which, till a matter be done, wonder that it can be done, and as soon as it is done, wonder again that it was no sooner done; as we see in the expedition of Alexander into Asia, which at first was prejudged as a vast and impossible enterprise, and yet afterwards it pleaseth Livy to make no more of it than this, *Nil aliud quam bene ausus vana contemnere.*[163] And the same happened to Columbus in the western navigation. But in intellectual matters it is much more common, as may be seen in most of the propositions of Euclid, which till they be demonstrate,[164] they seem strange to our assent,[165] but being demonstrate, our mind ac-

---

[159] "Stand in the ancient paths and see which is the straight and good road, and walk in it." Jeremiah 6:16.

[160] "Ancient time was the youth of the world." Perhaps borrowed from Giordano Bruno. [Wright] Cf. II Esdras 14:10.

[161] Seneca really made the remark. See Lactantius, *On False Religion*, I.16. [Wright]

[162] The *Lex Papia Poppaea*: actually a law (passed in the time of Augustus) designed to encourage men to marry before a certain age.

[163] "It was nothing but the daring to despise groundless fears." Livy, IX.17.

[164] demonstrated.

[165] i.e., we hesitate to assent to them.

cepteth of them by a kind of relation[166] (as the lawyers speak) as if we had known them before.

Another error, that hath also some affinity with the former, is a conceit* that of former opinions or sects, after variety and examination,[167] the best hath still* prevailed and suppressed the rest, so as if a man should begin the labour of a new search, he were but like to light upon somewhat formerly rejected and by rejection brought into oblivion, as if the multitude or the wisest for the multitude's sake, were not ready to give passage* rather to that which is popular and superficial than to that which is substantial and profound; for the truth is, that time seemeth to be of the nature of a river or stream, which carrieth down to us that which is light and blown up, and sinketh and drowneth that which is weighty and solid.

Another error, of a diverse nature from all the former, is the over-early and peremptory reduction of knowledge into arts and methods, from which time commonly sciences receive small or no augmentation. But as young men, when they knit and shape perfectly,[168] do seldom grow to a further stature, so knowledge, while it is in aphorisms and observations, it is in growth, but when it once is comprehended in exact methods,[169] it may perchance be further polished and illustrate, and accommodated for use and practice, but it increaseth no more in bulk and substance.

Another error, which doth succeed that which we last mentioned, is that after the distribution of particular arts and sciences men have abandoned universality, or *philosophia prima,* which cannot but cease and stop all progression. For no perfect discovery can be made upon a flat or a level; neither is it possible to discover the more remote and deeper parts of any science, if you stand but upon the level of the same science, and ascend not to a higher science.

Another error hath proceeded from too great a reverence and a kind of adoration of the mind and understanding of man, by

---

[166] (law) retroactive application.
[167] after a variety of opinions have been propounded and examined.

[168] once they are mature (set and formed) in limb and body.
[169] systems.

means whereof men have withdrawn themselves too much from the contemplation of nature and the observations of experience, and have tumbled up and down in their own reason and conceits. Upon these intellectualists, which are notwithstanding commonly taken for the most sublime and divine philosophers, Heraclitus gave a just censure, saying, *Men sought truth in their own little worlds, and not in the great and common world,*[170] for they disdain to spell and so by degrees to read in the volume of God's works; and contrariwise by continual meditation and agitation of wit do urge and as it were invocate[171] their own spirits to divine and give oracles unto them, whereby they are deservedly deluded.

Another error that hath some connexion with this latter is that men have used* to infect their meditations, opinions, and doctrines with some conceits which they have most admired, or some sciences which they have most applied,[172] and given all things else a tincture according to them, utterly untrue and unproper. So hath Plato intermingled his philosophy with theology, and Aristotle with logic, and the second school of Plato, Proclus and the rest with the mathematics. For these were the arts which had a kind of primogeniture with them severally. So have the alchemists made a philosophy out of a few experiments of the furnace, and Gilbertus,[173] our countryman, hath made a philosophy out of the observations of a loadstone. So Cicero, when, reciting the several opinions of the nature of the soul, he found a musician that held the soul was but a harmony, saith pleasantly, *Hic ab arte sua non recessit, etc.*[174] But of these conceits Aristotle speaketh seriously and wisely when he saith, *Qui respiciunt ad pauca de facili pronunciant.*[175]

Another error is an impatience of doubt and haste to assertion without due and mature suspension of judgment. For the two ways of contemplation are not unlike the two ways of action

---

[170] Sextus Empiricus, *Against the Logicians,* I.133.

[171] invoke.

[172] devoted themselves to, studied.

[173] William Gilbert.

[174] "This man has not gone outside the limits of his own art." *Tusculan Disputations,* I.x.20.

[175] "Those who take into account only a few considerations dogmatize easily." *On Generation and Corruption,* I.2 (316ª).

commonly spoken of by the ancients: the one plain and smooth in the beginning, and in the end impassable; the other rough and troublesome in the entrance, but after a while fair and even. So it is in contemplation: if a man will begin with certainties, he shall end in doubts, but if he will be content to begin with doubts, he shall end in certainties.

Another error is in the manner of the tradition[176] and delivery of knowledge, which is for the most part magistral and peremptory and not ingenuous and faithful, in a sort as may be soonest believed and not easiliest examined. It is true that in compendious treatises for practice that form is not to be disallowed. But in the true handling of knowledge men ought not to fall either on the one side into the vein of Velleius the Epicurean, *Nil tam metuens, quam ne dubitare aliqua de re videretur*,[177] nor on the other side into Socrates his ironical doubting of all things, but to propound things sincerely, with more or less asseveration, as they stand in a man's own judgment proved more or less.

Other errors there are in the scope[178] that men propound to themselves, whereunto they bend their endeavours, for whereas the more constant and devote kind of professors of any science ought to propound to themselves to make some additions to their science, they convert their labours to aspire to certain second prizes, as to be a profound interpreter or commenter, to be a sharp champion or defender, to be a methodical compounder or abridger; and so the patrimony of knowledge cometh to be sometimes improved but seldom augmented.

But the greatest error of all the rest is the mistaking or misplacing of the last or furthest end of knowledge. For men have entered into a desire of learning and knowledge, sometimes upon a natural curiosity and inquisitive appetite; sometimes to entertain their minds with variety and delight; sometimes for ornament and reputation; and sometimes to enable them to victory of wit and contradiction; and most times for lucre and

---

[176] delivery, passing on.
[177] "Fearing nothing so much as to appear doubtful about anything."

Cicero, *On the Nature of the Gods*, I.viii.18.
[178] end, goal.

profession;[179] and seldom sincerely to give a true account of their gift of reason to the benefit and use of men; as if there were sought in knowledge a couch, whereupon to rest a searching and restless spirit; or a terrace, for a wandering and variable mind to walk up and down with a fair prospect; or a tower of state, for a proud mind to raise itself upon; or a fort or commanding* ground, for strife and contention; or a shop, for profit or sale; and not a rich storehouse, for the glory of the Creator and the relief of man's estate.* But this is that which will indeed dignify and exalt knowledge: if contemplation and action may be more nearly and straitly conjoined and united together than they have been, a conjunction like unto that of the two highest planets, Saturn, the planet of rest and contemplation, and Jupiter, the planet of civil society and action. Howbeit, I do not mean, when I speak of use and action, that end before mentioned of the applying of knowledge to lucre and profession; for I am not ignorant how much that diverteth and interrupteth the prosecution and advancement of knowledge, like unto the golden ball thrown before Atalanta, which while she goeth aside and stoopeth to take up, the race is hindered,

Declinat cursus, aurumque volubile tollit.[180]

Neither is my meaning, as was spoken of Socrates,[181] to call philosophy down from heaven to converse upon the earth; that is, to leave natural philosophy aside, and to apply knowledge only to manners* and policy.* But as both heaven and earth do conspire and contribute to the use and benefit of man, so the end ought to be, from both philosophies to separate and reject vain speculations and whatsoever is empty and void, and to preserve and augment whatsoever is solid and fruitful, that knowledge may not be as a courtesan, for pleasure and vanity only, or as a

[179] livelihood.

[180] "She leaves the path and picks up the rolling gold." Ovid, *Met.*, X.667. Atalanta challenged every suitor for her hand to a race. If he won, she would marry him; if she won, he was to die. Hippomenes (Melanion) finally over-

came her with the help of Aphrodite. During the race he dropped, one after the other, three golden apples; these Atalanta could not resist, and as she went out of her way to pick them up, she lost the contest.

[181] See Cicero, *Tusc. Disp.*, V.iv.10.

bond-woman, to acquire and gain to her master's use, but as a spouse, for generation, fruit, and comfort.

Thus have I described and opened, as by a kind of dissection, those peccant humours (the principal of them) which have not only given impediment to the proficience[182] of learning, but have given also occasion to the traducement* thereof, wherein if I have been too plain, it must be remembered, *Fidelia vulnera amantis, sed dolosa oscula malignantis.*[183] This I think I have gained, that I ought to be the better believed in that which I shall say pertaining to commendation, because I have proceeded so freely in that which concerneth censure. And yet I have no purpose to enter into a laudative[184] of learning, or to make a hymn to the muses (though I am of opinion that it is long since their rites were duly celebrated), but my intent is, without varnish or amplification, justly to weigh the dignity of knowledge in the balance with other things, and to take the true value thereof by testimonies and arguments divine and human.

First therefore, let us seek the dignity of knowledge in the archetype or first platform,* which is in the attributes and acts of God, as far as they are revealed to man and may be observed with sobriety; wherein we may not seek it by the name of learning, for all learning is knowledge acquired, and all knowledge in God is original; and therefore we must look for it by another name, that of wisdom or sapience, as the Scriptures call it.[185]

It is so then, that in the work of the creation we see a double emanation of virtue from God: the one referring more properly to power, the other to wisdom; the one expressed in making the subsistence[186] of the matter, and the other in disposing the beauty of the form. This being supposed, it is to be observed that for any thing which appeareth[187] in the history of the creation, the confused mass and matter of heaven and earth was made in a moment, and the order and disposition of that chaos or mass was the work of six days; such a note[188] of difference it

---

183 "Faithful are the wounds of a friend; but the kisses of an enemy are deceitful." Prov. 27:6.
184 panegyric.

185 Cf. Prov. 8ff.
186 substance.
187 i.e., to the contrary.
188 mark, sign.

pleased God to put upon the works of power and the works of wisdom; wherewith concurreth that in the former it is not set down that God said, *Let there be heaven and earth,* as it is set down of the works following, but actually that God made heaven and earth, the one carrying the style of a manufacture, and the other of a law, decree, or counsel.

To proceed to that which is next in order, from God to spirits, we find, as far as credit is to be given to the celestial hierarchy of that supposed Dionysius the senator of Athens,[189] the first place or degree is given to the angels of love, which are termed Seraphim, the second to the angels of light, which are termed Cherubim, and the third and so following places to thrones, principalities, and the rest, which are all angels of power and ministry; so as the angels of knowledge and illumination are placed before the angels of office and domination.

To descend from spirits and intellectual forms to sensible and material forms, we read the first form that was created was light, which hath a relation and correspondence in nature and corporal things to knowledge in spirits and incorporal things.

So in the distribution of days, we see the day wherein God did rest and contemplate his own works was blessed above all the days wherein he did effect and accomplish them.

After the creation was finished, it is set down unto us that man was placed in the garden to work therein; which work so appointed to him could be no other than work of contemplation; that is, when the end of work is but for exercise and experiment, not for necessity; for there being then no reluctation[190] of the creature nor sweat of the brow, man's employment must of consequence have been matter of delight in the experiment and not matter of labour for the use. Again, the first acts which man performed in Paradise consisted of the two summary* parts of knowledge, the view of creatures and the imposition of names. As for the knowledge which induced the fall, it was, as was touched before, not the natural knowledge of creatures but the

---

[189] Dionysius the Areopagite was probably not (as Bacon suggests) the author of *The Celestial Hierarchy*, a work on the nature and faculties of angels which influenced many medieval thinkers, including Dante. [Ellis and Selby]

[190] struggle, effort.

moral knowledge of good and evil; wherein the supposition was that God's commandments or prohibitions were not the originals of good and evil, but that they had other beginnings, which man aspired to know, to the end to make a total defection from God, and to depend wholly upon himself.

To pass on: in the first event or occurrence after the fall of man, we see (as the Scriptures have infinite mysteries, not violating at all the truth of the story or letter) an image of the two estates, the contemplative state and the active state, figured in the two persons of Abel and Cain, and in the two simplest and most primitive trades of life, that of the shepherd (who, by reason of his leisure, rest in a place, and living in view of heaven, is a lively image of a contemplative life) and that of the husbandman, where we see again the favour and election of God went to the shepherd, and not to the tiller of the ground.

So in the age before the flood the holy records within those few memorials which are there entered and registered have vouchsafed to mention and honour the name of the inventors and authors of music and works in metal. In the age after the flood the first great judgment of God upon the ambition of man was the confusion of tongues, whereby the open trade and intercourse of learning and knowledge was chiefly imbarred.[191]

To descend to Moses the lawgiver, and God's first pen, he is adorned by the Scriptures with this addition and commendation, that he was *seen in all the learning of the Egyptians*;[192] which nation we know was one of the most ancient schools of the world, for so Plato brings in the Egyptian priest saying unto Solon, *You Grecians are ever children; you have no knowledge of antiquity, nor antiquity of knowledge.*[193] Take a view of the ceremonial law of Moses: you shall find, besides the prefiguration of Christ, the badge or difference* of the people of God, the exercise and impression of obedience, and other divine uses and fruits thereof, that some of the most learned Rabbins have travelled* profitably and profoundly to observe, some of them a natural, some of them a moral, sense or reduction[194] of many

---

[191] embarred, stopped.
[192] Acts 7:22.

[193] *Timaeus,* 22B.
[194] interpretation.

of the ceremonies and ordinances. As in the law of the leprosy, where it is said, *If the whiteness have overspread the flesh, the patient may pass abroad for clean; but if there be any whole flesh remaining, he is to be shut up for unclean;*[195] one of them noteth a principle of nature, that putrefaction is more contagious before maturity than after, and another noteth a position* of moral philosophy, that men abandoned to vice do not so much corrupt manners, as those that are half good and half evil. So in this and very many other places in that law there is to be found, besides the theological sense, much aspersion[196] of philosophy.

So likewise in that excellent book of Job, if it be revolved with diligence, it will be found pregnant and swelling with natural philosophy, as for example, cosmography and the roundness of the world, *Qui extendit aquilonem super vacuum, et appendit terram super nihilum,*[197] wherein the pensileness of the earth, the pole of the north, and the finiteness or convexity of heaven are manifestly touched. So again matter of astronomy, *Spiritus ejus ornavit cœlos, et obstetricante manu ejus eductus est Coluber tortuosus.*[198] And in another place, *Nunquid conjungere valebis micantes stellas Pleiadas, aut gyrum Arcturi poteris dissipare?*[199] where the fixing of the stars, ever standing at equal distance, is with great elegancy noted. And in another place, *Qui facit Arcturum, et Oriona, et Hyadas, et interiora Austri,* [200] where again he takes knowledge of the depression of the southern pole, calling it the secrets of the south, because the southern stars were in that climate unseen. Matter of generation: *Annon sicut lac mulsisti me, et sicut caseum coagulasti me?* etc.[201] Matter of minerals: *Habet argentum venarum suarum principia: et auro locus est in quo conflatur, ferrum de terra*

[195] Leviticus 13:12-14.

[196] intermixture.

[197] "[He] stretcheth out the north over the empty space, and hangeth the earth upon nothing." Job 26:7.

[198] "By his spirit he hath garnished the heavens; his hand hath formed the crooked serpent." Job 26:13.

[199] "Canst thou bind the glittering stars of the Pleiades, or scatter the array of Arcturus?" Job 38:31.

[200] "Which maketh Arcturus, Orion, and Pleiades, and the secrets of the south." Job 9:9.

[201] "Hast thou not poured me out as milk, and curdled me like cheese?" Job 10:10.

tollitur, et lapis solutus calore in æs vertitur;[202] and so forwards[203] in that chapter.

So likewise in the person of Salomon the king, we see the gift or endowment of wisdom and learning, both in Salomon's petition and in God's assent thereunto, preferred before all other terrene and temporal felicity.[204] By virtue of which grant or donative of God, Salomon became enabled not only to write those excellent parables or aphorisms concerning divine and moral philosophy, but also to compile a natural history of all verdure, from the cedar upon the mountain to the moss upon the wall (which is but a rudiment[205] between putrefaction and an herb) and also of all things that breathe or move. Nay, the same Salomon the king, although he excelled in the glory of treasure and magnificent buildings, of shipping and navigation, of service and attendance, of fame and renown, and the like, yet he maketh no claim to any of those glories, but only to the glory of inquisition of truth, for so he saith expressly, *The glory of God is to conceal a thing, but the glory of the king is to find it out;*[206] as if, according to the innocent play of children, the Divine Majesty took delight to hide his works, to the end to have them found out, and as if kings could not obtain a greater honour than to be God's playfellows in that game, considering the great commandment of wits and means, whereby nothing needeth to be hidden from them.

Neither did the dispensation of God vary in the times after our Saviour came into the world, for our Saviour himself did first show his power to subdue ignorance by his conference with the priests and doctors of the law, before he showed his power to subdue nature by his miracles.[207] And the coming of the Holy Spirit was chiefly figured and expressed in the similitude and gift of tongues, which are but *vehicula scientiæ.*[208]

So in the election of those instruments which it pleased God

202 "Surely there is a vein for the silver, and a place for gold where they fine it. Iron is taken out of the earth, and brass is molten out of the stone." Job 28:1, 2.

203 and so forth.

204 See I Kings 3:5ff. and 4:29f.

205 half-way form or stage between two species, "partakers of two kinds" (*Nov. Org.*, II.xxx).

206 Prov. 25:2.

207 Luke 2:46.

208 "carriers of knowledge". See Acts 2:1ff.

to use for the plantation of the faith, notwithstanding that at the first he did employ persons altogether unlearned otherwise than by inspiration, more evidently to declare his immediate working, and to abase all human wisdom or knowledge; yet nevertheless that counsel of his was no sooner performed, but in the next vicissitude and succession he did send his divine truth into the world waited on with other learnings as with servants or handmaids, for so we see St. Paul, who was only learned[209] amongst the apostles, had his pen most used in the scriptures of the New Testament.

So again we find that many of the ancient bishops and fathers of the Church were excellently read and studied in all the learning of the heathen, insomuch that the edict of the emperor Julianus (whereby it was interdicted unto Christians to be admitted into schools, lectures, or exercises of learning) was esteemed and accounted a more pernicious engine and machination against the Christian faith than were all the sanguinary prosecutions of his predecessors; neither could the emulation and jealousy of Gregory the first of that name, bishop of Rome, ever obtain the opinion[210] of piety or devotion, but contrariwise received the censure of humour,* malignity, and pusillanimity even amongst holy men, in that he designed to obliterate and extinguish the memory of heathen antiquity and authors. But contrariwise it was the Christian Church, which amidst the inundations of the Scythians on the one side from the north-west and the Saracens from the east, did preserve in the sacred lap and bosom thereof the precious relics even of heathen learning, which otherwise had been extinguished as if no such thing had ever been.

And we see before our eyes that in the age of ourselves and our fathers, when it pleased God to call the church of Rome to account for their degenerate manners and ceremonies and sundry doctrines obnoxious and framed to uphold the same abuses, at one and the same time it was ordained by the Divine Providence that there should attend withal a renovation and new spring of

[209] i.e., who was the only learned man.

[210] reputation.

all other knowledges. And on the other side we see the Jesuits, who, partly in themselves and partly by the emulation and provocation of their example, have much quickened and strengthened the state of learning – we see (I say) what notable service and reparation they have done to the Roman see.

Wherefore to conclude this part, let it be observed that there be two principal duties and services, besides ornament and illustration, which philosophy and human learning do perform to faith and religion. The one, because they are an effectual inducement to the exaltation of the glory of God. For as the Psalms and other Scriptures do often invite us to consider and magnify the great and wonderful works of God,[211] so if we should rest only in the contemplation of the exterior of them as they first offer themselves to our senses, we should do a like injury unto the majesty of God, as if we should judge or construe of the store of some excellent jeweller by that only which is set out toward the street in his shop. The other, because they minister a singular help and preservative against unbelief and error. For our Saviour saith, *You err, not knowing the Scriptures, nor the power of God*,[212] laying before us two books or volumes to study, if we will be secured from error: first the Scriptures, revealing the will of God; and then the creatures expressing his power; whereof the latter is a key unto the former, not only opening our understanding to conceive the true sense of the Scriptures by the general notions of reason and rules of speech, but chiefly opening our belief in drawing us into a due meditation of the omnipotency of God, which is chiefly signed and engraven upon his works. Thus much therefore for divine testimony and evidence concerning the true dignity and value of learning.

As for human proofs, it is so large a field, as in a discourse of this nature and brevity it is fit rather to use choice of those things which we shall produce than to embrace the variety of them. First therefore, in the degrees of human honour amongst the heathen, it was the highest to obtain to a veneration and adoration as a God. This unto the Christians is as the forbidden

[211] See, for example, Psalms 19, 66, 104.
[212] Matt. 22:29.

fruit. But we speak now separately of human testimony, according to which that which the Grecians call *apotheosis*, and the Latins *relatio inter divos*, was the supreme honour which man could attribute unto man, specially when it was given, not by a formal decree or act of state, as it was used* among the Roman emperors, but by an inward assent and belief, which honour being so high had also a degree or middle term, for there were reckoned above human honours, honours heroical and divine; in the attribution and distribution of which honours we see antiquity made this difference: that whereas founders and uniters of states and cities, lawgivers, extirpers[213] of tyrants, fathers of the people, and other eminent persons in civil merit were honoured but with the titles of worthies or demi-gods, such as were Hercules, Theseus, Minos, Romulus, and the like; on the other side, such as were inventors and authors of new arts, endowments, and commodities towards man's life were ever consecrated amongst the gods themselves, as was Ceres, Bacchus, Mercurius, Apollo, and others – and justly, for the merit of the former is confined within the circle of an age or a nation, and is like fruitful showers, which though they be profitable and good, yet serve but for that season and for a latitude[214] of ground where they fall, but the other is indeed like the benefits of heaven, which are permanent and universal. The former again is mixed with strife and perturbation, but the latter hath the true character of divine presence, coming in *aura leni*,[215] without noise or agitation.

Neither is certainly that other merit of learning, in repressing the inconveniencies which grow from man to man,[216] much inferior to the former, of relieving the necessities which arise from nature; which merit was lively set forth by the ancients in that feigned relation of Orpheus' theatre, where all beasts and birds assembled, and forgetting their several appetites, some of prey, some of game,[217] some of quarrel, stood all sociably together listening unto the airs and accords of the harp, the sound where-

---

[213] extirpators, destroyers.
[214] area.
[215] "a gentle wind": from the Vulgate. Cf. "a still small voice": I Kings 19:12.
[216] i.e., the conflicts arising from human intercourse.
[217] playfulness.

of no sooner ceased, or was drowned by some louder noise, but every beast returned to his own nature; wherein is aptly described the nature and condition of men, who are full of savage and unreclaimed desires, of profit, of lust, of revenge, which as long as they give ear to precepts, to laws, to religion, sweetly touched with eloquence and persuasion of books, of sermons, of harangues, so long is society and peace maintained, but if these instruments be silent, or that sedition and tumult make them not audible, all things dissolve into anarchy and confusion.

But this appeareth more manifestly, when kings themselves or persons of authority under them or other governors in commonwealths and popular estates are endued with learning. For although he might be thought partial to his own profession, that said, *Then should people and estates be happy, when either kings were philosophers, or philosophers kings*;[218] yet so much is verified by experience that under learned princes and governors there have been ever the best times; for howsoever kings may have their imperfections in their passions and customs, yet if they be illuminate by learning, they have those notions of religion, policy, and morality, which do preserve them and refrain them from all ruinous and peremptory[219] errors and excesses, whispering evermore in their ears, when counsellors and servants stand mute and silent. And senators or counsellors likewise which be learned do proceed upon more safe and substantial principles than counsellors which are only men of experience, the one sort keeping dangers afar off, whereas the other discover them not till they come near hand,[220] and then trust to the agility of their wit to ward or avoid them.

Which felicity of times under learned princes (to keep still the law of brevity, by using the most eminent and selected examples) doth best appear in the age which passed from the death of Domitianus the emperor until the reign of Commodus, comprehending a succession of six princes, all learned or singular favourers and advancers of learning; which age, for temporal respects, was the most happy and flourishing that ever the

218 Plato, *Republic*, V.473CD, etc.   220 i.e., near at hand.
219 destructive.

Roman empire (which then was a model of the world) enjoyed; a matter revealed and prefigured unto Domitian in a dream the night before he was slain;[221] for he thought there was grown behind upon his shoulders a neck and a head of gold, which came accordingly to pass in those golden times which succeeded: of which princes we will make some commemoration; wherein although the matter will be vulgar, and may be thought fitter for a declamation than agreeable to a treatise infolded[222] as this is, yet because it is pertinent to the point in hand, *neque semper arcum tendit Apollo*,[223] and to name them only were too naked and cursory, I will not omit it altogether.

The first was Nerva,[224] the excellent temper of whose government is by a glance in Cornelius Tacitus touched to the life: *Postquam divus Nerva res olim insociabiles miscuisset, imperium et libertatem.*[225] And in token of his learning, the last act of his short reign left to memory was a missive to his adopted son Trajan, proceeding upon some inward discontent at the ingratitude of the times, comprehended in a verse of Homer's:

Telis, Phœbe, tuis lacrymas ulciscere nostras.[226]

Trajan, who succeeded, was for his person not learned; but if we will hearken to the speech of our Saviour, that saith, *He that receiveth a prophet in the name of a prophet shall have a prophet's reward*,[227] he deserveth to be placed amongst the most learned princes; for there was not a greater admirer of learning or benefactor of learning: a founder of famous libraries, a perpetual advancer of learned men to office, and a familiar converser with learned professors and preceptors, who were noted to have then most credit in court. On the other side, how much Trajan's virtue and government was admired and renowned, surely no testimony of grave and faithful history doth more lively set forth, than that legend[228] tale of Gregorius Magnus,

---

[221] See Suetonius, *Domitian*, 23.
[222] compressed.
[223] "Nor does Apollo always bend his bow." Horace, *Odes*, II.x.19.
[224] Roman emperor, A.D. 96-98.
[225] "The divine Nerva blended things once irreconcilable, sovereignty and freedom." *Agricola*, 3.
[226] "O Phoebus, with thy shafts avenge our tears." *Iliad*, I.42.
[227] Matt. 10:21.
[228] legendary.

bishop of Rome, who was noted for the extreme envy he bare towards all heathen excellency: and yet he is reported, out of the love and estimation of Trajan's moral virtues, to have made unto God passionate and fervent prayers for the delivery of his soul out of hell, and to have obtained it, with a caveat that he should make no more such petitions.[229] In this prince's time also the persecutions against the Christians received intermission, upon the certificate of Plinius Secundus, a man of excellent learning and by Trajan advanced.[230]

Adrian, his successor, was the most curious* man that lived, and the most universal inquirer, insomuch as it was noted for an error in his mind, that he desired to comprehend all things, and not to reserve himself for the worthiest things: falling into the like humour that was long before noted in Philip of Macedon; who, when he would needs overrule and put down an excellent musician in an argument touching music, was well answered by him again, *God forbid, sir* (saith he), *that your fortune should be so bad, as to know these things better than I*.[231] It pleased God likewise to use the curiosity of this emperor as an inducement to the peace of his Church in those days. For having Christ in veneration, not as a God or Saviour but as a wonder or novelty, and having his picture in his gallery, matched with Apollonius (with whom in his vain imagination he thought he had some conformity), yet it served the turn to allay the bitter hatred of those times against the Christian name, so as the Church had peace during his time. And for his government civil, although he did not attain to that of Trajan's in glory of arms or perfection of justice, yet in deserving of the weal of the subject he did exceed him. For Trajan erected many famous monuments and buildings; insomuch as Constantine the Great in emulation was wont to call him *Parietaria*, wallflower, because his name was upon so many walls: but his buildings and works were more of glory and triumph than use and necessity. But Adrian spent his whole reign, which was peaceable, in a perambulation or survey of the Roman empire, giving order and

---

[229] See Dante, *Purgatory*, X.73; *Paradise*, XX.106.

[230] See Pliny, *Epist.*, X.96.

[231] See Plutarch, *How a Flatterer May Be Distinguished from a Friend*, 27. Adrian: Hadrian.

making assignation where he went, for re-edifying[232] of cities, towns, and forts decayed, and for cutting of rivers and streams, and for making bridges and passages,[233] and for policing of cities and commonalties[234] with new ordinances and constitutions, and granting new franchises and incorporations; so that his whole time was a very restoration of all the lapses and decays of former times.

Antoninus Pius, who succeeded him, was a prince excellently learned, and had the patient and subtle wit of a schoolman; insomuch as in common speech (which leaves no virtue untaxed) he was called *Cymini Sector*, a carver or a divider of cummin seed, which is one of the least seeds;[235] such a patience he had and settled spirit to enter into the least and most exact differences of causes, a fruit no doubt of the exceeding tranquillity and serenity of his mind; which being no ways charged or incumbered, either with fears, remorses, or scruples, but having been noted for a man of the purest goodness, without all fiction or affectation, that hath reigned or lived, made his mind continually present and entire.[236] He likewise approached a degree nearer unto Christianity, and became, as Agrippa said unto St. Paul, *half a Christian*,[237] holding their religion and law in good opinion, and not only ceasing persecution, but giving way to the advancement of Christians.

There succeeded him the first *Divi fratres*,[238] the two adoptive brethren, Lucius Commodus Verus,[239] son to Ælius Verus, who delighted much in the softer kind of learning, and was wont to call the poet Martial his Virgil; and Marcus Aurelius Antoninus; whereof the latter, who obscured his colleague and survived him long, was named the Philosopher: who, as he excelled all the rest in learning, so he excelled them likewise in perfection of all royal virtues; insomuch as Julianus the emperor, in his book intituled *Cæsares*, being as a pasquil or satire to deride all his predecessors, feigned that they were all invited

---

[232] rebuilding.
[233] roads.
[234] corporations.
[235] See Dion Cassius, LXX.3.
[236] ready and undistracted.

[237] Cf. Acts 26:28.
[238] "divine brothers". In imperial times *divus* was the epithet of the deified emperors.
[239] i.e., L. Aurelius Verus.

to a banquet of the gods, and Silenus the jester sat at the nether end of the table, and bestowed a scoff on every one as they came in; but when Marcus Philosophus came in, Silenus was gravelled[240] and out of countenance, not knowing where to carp at him, save at the last he gave a glance[241] at his patience towards his wife. And the virtue of this prince, continued with that of his predecessor, made the name of Antoninus so sacred in the world that though it were extremely dishonoured in Commodus, Caracalla, and Heliogabalus, who all bare the name, yet when Alexander Severus refused the name because he was a stranger to the family, the senate with one acclamation said, *Quomodo Augustus, sic et Antoninus.*[242] In such renown and veneration was the name of these two princes in those days, that they would have had it as a perpetual addition in all the emperors' style. In this emperor's time also the Church for the most part was in peace; so as in this sequence of six princes we do see the blessed effects of learning in sovereignty, painted forth in the greatest table[243] of the world.

But for a tablet or picture of smaller volume (not presuming to speak of your Majesty that liveth), in my judgment the most excellent is that of Queen Elizabeth, your immediate predecessor in this part of Britain, a prince that, if Plutarch were now alive to write lives by parallels, would trouble him I think to find for her a parallel amongst women. This lady was endued with learning in her sex singular, and rare even amongst masculine princes; whether we speak of learning, of language, or of science, modern or ancient, divinity or humanity. And unto the very last year of her life she accustomed to appoint set hours for reading, scarcely any young student in an university more daily or more duly. As for her government, I assure myself I shall not exceed if I do affirm that this part of the island never had forty-five years of better times; and yet not through the calmness of the season, but through the wisdom of her regiment.[244] For if there be considered of the one side, the truth of

---

240 baffled.

241 glancing reference, hint.

242 "Let the name of Antoninus be as the name of Augustus." See Lam-

pridius, *Severus*, 5-10.

243 picture, tableau,

244 government.

religion established, the constant peace and security, the good administration of justice, the temperate use of the prerogative, not slackened, nor much strained, the flourishing state of learning, sortable[245] to so excellent a patroness, the convenient estate* of wealth and means, both of crown and subject, the habit of obedience, and the moderation of discontents; and there be considered on the other side the differences of religion, the troubles of neighbour countries, the ambition of Spain, and opposition of Rome; and then that she was solitary and of herself: these things I say considered, as I could not have chosen an instance so recent and so proper, so I suppose I could not have chosen one more remarkable or eminent to the purpose now in hand, which is concerning the conjunction of learning in the prince with felicity in the people.

Neither hath learning an influence and operation only upon civil merit and moral virtue, and the arts or temperature of peace and peaceable government; but likewise it hath no less power and efficacy in enablement[246] towards martial and military virtue and prowess; as may be notably represented in the examples of Alexander the Great and Cæsar the dictator, mentioned before, but now in fit place to be resumed: of whose virtues and acts in war there needs no note or recital, having been the wonders of time in that kind; but of their affections* towards learning, and perfections in learning, it is pertinent to say somewhat.

Alexander[247] was bred and taught under Aristotle the great philosopher, who dedicated divers of his books of philosophy unto him. He was attended with Callisthenes and divers other learned persons, that followed him in camp throughout his journeys and conquests. What price and estimation he had learning in doth notably appear in these three particulars: first, in the envy he used to express that he bare towards Achilles, in this, that he had so good a trumpet of his praises as Homer's verses; secondly, in the judgment or solution he gave touching that precious cabinet of Darius, which was found among his

---

[245] suitable.
[246] qualifying men for.

[247] For most of the following particulars on Alexander see Plutarch's life.

jewels, whereof question was made what thing was worthy to be put into it, and he gave his opinion for Homer's works; thirdly, in his letter to Aristotle, after he had set forth his books of nature, wherein he expostulateth with him for publishing the secrets or mysteries of philosophy, and gave him to understand that himself esteemed it more to excel other men in learning and knowledge than in power and empire. And what use he had of learning doth appear, or rather shine, in all his speeches and answers, being full of science and use of science, and that in all variety.

And herein again it may seem a thing scholastical, and somewhat idle, to recite things that every man knoweth; but yet, since the argument I handle leadeth me thereunto, I am glad that men shall perceive I am as willing to flatter (if they will so call it) an Alexander, or a Cæsar, or an Antoninus, that are dead many hundred years since, as any that now liveth: for it is the displaying of the glory of learning in sovereignty that I propound to myself, and not an humour* of declaiming in any man's praises. Observe then the speech he used of Diogenes, and see if it tend not to the true state of one of the greatest questions of moral philosophy: whether the enjoying of outward things, or the contemning of them, be the greatest happiness; for when he saw Diogenes so perfectly contented with so little, he said to those that mocked at his condition, *Were I not Alexander, I would wish to be Diogenes.* But Seneca inverteth it, and saith; *Plus erat, quod hic nollet accipere, quam quod ille posset dare.*[248] *There were more things which Diogenes would have refused, than there were which Alexander could have given or enjoyed.*

Observe again that speech which was usual with him, *That he felt his mortality chiefly in two things, sleep and lust*, and see if it were not a speech extracted out of the depth of natural philosophy, and liker to have comen out of the mouth of Aristotle or Democritus than from Alexander.

See again that speech of humanity and poesy: when upon the bleeding of his wounds, he called unto him one of his flatterers that was wont to ascribe to him divine honour, and said, *Look, this is very blood; this is not such a liquor as Homer speaketh of, which ran from Venus' hand when it was pierced by Diomedes.*[249]

See likewise his readiness in reprehension[250] of logic, in the speech he used to Cassander, upon a complaint that was made against his father Antipater: for when Alexander happed to say, *Do you think these men would have come from so far to complain, except they had just cause of grief?* and Cassander answered, *Yea, that was the matter, because they thought they should not be disproved;* said Alexander laughing: *See the subtilties of Aristotle, to take a matter both ways, pro et contra, etc.*

But note again how well he could use the same art which he reprehended, to serve his own humour, when bearing a secret grudge to Callisthenes because he was against the new ceremony of his adoration: feasting one night where the same Callisthenes was at the table, it was moved by some after supper, for entertainment sake, that Callisthenes, who was an eloquent man, might speak of some theme or purpose at[251] his own choice; which Callisthenes did, choosing the praise of the Macedonian nation for his discourse, and performing the same with so good manner as the hearers were much ravished; whereupon Alexander, nothing pleased, said *It was easy to be eloquent upon so good a subject:* but saith he, *Turn your style,*[252] *and let us hear what you can say against us:* which Callisthenes presently undertook, and did with that sting and life, that Alexander interrupted him and said, *The goodness of the cause made him eloquent before, and despite made him eloquent then again.*

Consider further, for tropes of rhetoric, that excellent use of a metaphor or translation wherewith he taxed Antipater, who was an imperious and tyrannous governor: for when one of Antipater's friends commended him to Alexander for his moderation, that he did not degenerate, as his other lieutenants did, into the Persian pride, in use of purple, but kept the ancient habit of Macedon, of black: *True* (saith Alexander), *but Antipater is all purple within.* Or that other, when Parmenio came to him in the plain of Arbela, and showed him the innumerable

---

[249] See *Iliad*, V. 340.
[250] demonstration of falsity; censure.

[251] proposal, proposition of.
[252] i.e., erase. style: stylus.

multitude of his enemies, specially as they appeared by the infinite number of lights, as it had been a new firmament of stars, and thereupon advised him to assail them by night: whereupon he answered *That he would not steal the victory.*

For matter of policy, weigh that significant distinction, so much in all ages embraced, that he made between his two friends Hephæstion and Craterus, when he said, *That the one loved Alexander, and the other loved the king*: describing the principal difference of princes' best servants, that some in affection love their person, and other in duty love their crown.

Weigh also that excellent taxation* of an error, ordinary with counsellors of princes, that they counsel their masters according to the model of their own mind and fortune, and not of their masters'; when upon Darius' great offers Parmenio had said, *Surely I would accept these offers, were I as Alexander;* saith Alexander, *So would I were I as Parmenio.*

Lastly, weigh that quick and acute reply which he made when he gave so large gifts to his friends and servants, and was asked what he did reserve for himself, and he answered, *Hope*; weigh, I say, whether he had not cast up his account aright, because *hope* must be the portion of all that resolve upon great enterprises. For this was Cæsar's portion when he went first into Gaul, his estate being then utterly overthrown with largesses. And this was likewise the portion of that noble prince, howsoever transported with ambition, Henry Duke of Guise, of whom it was usually said, that he was the greatest usurer in France, because he had turned all his estate into obligations.[253]

To conclude therefore: as certain critics are used to say hyperbolically *That if all sciences were lost they might be found in Virgil,* so certainly this may be said truly, there are the prints and footsteps of learning in those few speeches which are reported of this prince: the admiration of whom, when I consider him not as Alexander the Great, but as Aristotle's scholar, hath carried me too far.

As for Julius Cæsar,[254] the excellency of his learning needeth

[253] i.e., he had spent all his money in securing friends.

[254] For the facts on Caesar see the lives of Suetonius and Plutarch.

not to be argued from his education or his company or his speeches, but in a further degree doth declare itself in his writings and works, whereof some are extant and permanent, and some unfortunately perished. For first, we see there is left unto us that excellent history of his own wars, which he intituled only a Commentary, wherein all succeeding times have admired the solid weight of matter, and the real[255] passages and lively images of actions and persons, expressed in the greatest propriety of words and perspicuity of narration that ever was; which that it was not the effect of a natural gift, but of learning and precept, is well witnessed by that work of his intituled *De Analogia*, being a grammatical philosophy, wherein he did labour to make this same *Vox ad placitum* to become *Vox ad licitum*, and to reduce* custom of speech to congruity of speech; and took as it were the pictures of words from the life of reason.

So we receive from him, as a monument both of his power and learning, the then reformed computation of the year; well expressing[256] that he took it to be as great a glory to himself to observe and know the law of the heavens, as to give law to men upon the earth.

So likewise in that book of his, *Anti-Cato*, it may easily appear that he did aspire as well to victory of wit as victory of war: undertaking therein a conflict against the greatest champion with the pen that then lived, Cicero the orator.

So again in his book of Apophthegms which he collected, we see that he esteemed it more honour to make himself but a pair of tables,[257] to take the wise and pithy words of others, than to have every word of his own to be made an apophthegm or an oracle, as vain princes, by custom of flattery, pretend to do. And yet if I should enumerate divers of his speeches, as I did those of Alexander, they are truly such as Salomon noteth, when he saith, *Verba sapientum tanquam aculei, et tanquam clavi in*

---

[255] realistic.

[256] demonstrating. The "reformed computation of the year" was the Julian Calendar (usually indicated by O.S. – Old Style), in which the New Year began March 25; it was replaced by the Gregorian Calendar (N.S. – New Style), a revision introduced in 1582 but not adopted by Great Britain until 1752.

[257] tablets of wood covered with wax, on which the Romans wrote.

altum defixi:[258] whereof I will only recite three, not so delectable for elegancy, but admirable for vigour and efficacy.

As first, it is reason he be thought a master of words, that could with one word appease a mutiny in his army, which was thus. The Romans, when their generals did speak to their army, did use the word *Milites*,[259] but when the magistrates spake to the people, they did use the word *Quirites*.[260] The soldiers were in tumult, and seditiously prayed to be cashiered; not that they so meant, but by expostulation[261] thereof to draw Cæsar to other conditions; wherein he being resolute not to give way, after some silence, he began his speech, *Ego, Quirites*, which did admit them already cashiered; wherewith they were so surprised, crossed, and confused, as they would not suffer him to go on in his speech, but relinquished their demands, and made it their suit to be again called by the name of *Milites*.

The second speech was thus: Cæsar did extremely affect* the name of king; and some were set on as he passed by, in popular acclamation to salute him king. Whereupon, finding the cry weak and poor, he put it off thus in a kind of jest, as if they had mistaken his surname: *Non Rex sum, sed Cæsar;*[262] a speech, that if it be searched, the life and fulness of it can scarce be expressed. For, first, it was a refusal of the name, but yet not serious; again, it did signify an infinite confidence and magnanimity, as if he presumed Cæsar was the greater title, as by his worthiness it is come to pass till this day. But chiefly it was a speech of great allurement toward his own purpose; as if the state did strive with him but for a name, whereof mean families were vested, for *Rex* was a surname with the Romans, as well as *King* is with us.

The last speech which I will mention was used to Metellus: when Cæsar, after war declared, did possess himself of the city of Rome; at which time entering into the inner treasury to take the money there accumulate,* Metellus being tribune forbade him. Whereto Cæsar said *That if he did not desist, he would*

[258] "The words of the wise are as goads and as nails driven deep in." Cf. Eccles. 12:11.
[259] "soldiers".
[260] "citizens" (civilians).
[261] demand.
[262] "I am not king but Caesar."

lay him dead in the place. And presently taking himself up,[263] he added, *Young man, it is harder for me to speak it than to do it: Adolescens, durius est mihi hoc dicere quam facere.* A speech compounded of the greatest terror and greatest clemency that could proceed out of the mouth of man.

But to return and conclude with him; it is evident himself knew well his own perfection in learning, and took it upon him; as appeared when, upon occasion that some spake what a strange resolution it was in Lucius Sylla[264] to resign his dictature, he scoffing at him, to his own advantage answered *That Sylla could not skill[265] of letters, and therefore knew not how to dictate.*

And here it were fit to leave this point touching the concurrence of military virtue and learning (for what example should come with any grace after those two of Alexander and Cæsar?), were it not in regard of the rareness of circumstance, that I find in one other particular, as that which did so suddenly pass from extreme scorn to extreme wonder: and it is of Xenophon the philosopher, who went from Socrates' school into Asia, in the expedition of Cyrus the younger against King Artaxerxes.[266] This Xenophon at that time was very young, and never had seen the wars before; neither had any command in the army, but only followed the war as a voluntary, for the love and conversation* of Proxenus his friend. He was present when Falinus came in message[267] from the great king to the Grecians, after that Cyrus was slain in the field, and they a handful of men left to themselves in the midst of the king's territories, cut off from their country by many navigable rivers and many hundred miles. The message imported that they should deliver up their arms and submit themselves to the king's mercy. To which message before answer was made, divers of the army conferred familiarly with Falinus; and amongst the rest Xenophon happened to say, *Why, Falinus, we have now but these two things left, our arms and our virtue;[268] and if we yield up our arms, how shall we*

---

[263] at once, immediately, checking himself.

[264] Sulla.

[265] had no understanding.

[266] For Xenophon see his own *Anabasis,* II.

[267] i.e., bearing a message.

[268] courage.

make use of our virtue? Whereto Falinus smiling on him said,
*If I be not deceived, young gentleman, you are an Athenian:
and I believe you study philosophy, and it is pretty that* you say:
but you are much abused if you think your virtue can withstand
the king's power.* Here was the scorn; the wonder followed:
which was that this young scholar or philosopher, after all the
captains were murdered in parley by treason, conducted those
ten thousand foot through the heart of all the king's high
countries, from Babylon to Grecia in safety, in despite of all the
king's forces, to the astonishment of the world, and the encouragement of the Grecians in times succeeding to make invasion
upon the kings of Persia; as was after purposed by Jason the
Thessalian,[269] attempted by Agesilaus the Spartan, and achieved
by Alexander the Macedonian, all upon the ground of the act
of that young scholar.

To proceed now from imperial and military virtue to moral
and private virtue: first, it is an assured truth which is contained
in the verses,

> *Scilicet ingenuas didicisse fideliter artes
> Emollit mores, nec sinit esse feros.*[270]

It taketh away the wildness and barbarism and fierceness of
men's minds; but indeed the accent had need be upon *fideliter*:
for a little superficial learning doth rather work a contrary effect.
It taketh away all levity, temerity, and insolency, by copious
suggestion of all doubts and difficulties, and acquainting[271] the
mind to balance reasons on both sides, and to turn back the first
offers and conceits* of the mind, and to accept of nothing but
examined[272] and tried. It taketh away vain admiration of anything, which is the root of all weakness. For all things are
admired either because they are new, or because they are great.
For* novelty, no man that wadeth in learning or contemplation
thoroughly, but will find that printed in his heart, *Nil novi
super terram.*[273] Neither can any man marvel at the play of

---

269 Tyrant of Pherae and Tagus of
Thessaly (d. 370 B.C.).

270 "Certainly a faithful study of the
liberal arts refines manners and
decreases barbarism." Ovid, *Epistles from Pontus,* II.ix.47.

271 accustoming.

272 i.e., but what has been examined.

273 "There is nothing new on the
earth." Cf. Eccles. 1:9.

puppets, that goeth behind the curtain and adviseth[274] well of the motion. And for magnitude, as Alexander the Great, after that he was used to great armies and the great conquests of the spacious provinces in Asia, when he received letters out of Greece, of some fights and services[275] there, which were commonly for a passage,[276] or a fort, or some walled town at the most, he said *It seemed to him that he was advertised of the battles of the frogs and the mice, that the old tales went of.*[277] So certainly, if a man meditate much upon the universal frame of nature, the earth with men upon it (the divineness of souls except) will not seem much other than an ant-hill, whereas some ants carry corn, and some carry their young, and some go empty, and all to and fro a little heap of dust. It taketh away or mitigateth fear of death or adverse fortune, which is one of the greatest impediments of virtue, and imperfections of manners.* For if a man's mind be deeply seasoned with the consideration of the mortality and corruptible nature of things, he will easily concur with Epictetus, who went forth one day and saw a woman weeping for her pitcher of earth that was broken, and went forth the next day and saw a woman weeping for her son that was dead, and thereupon said, *Heri vidi fragilem frangi, hodie vidi mortalem mori.*[278] And therefore Virgil did excellently and profoundly couple the knowledge of causes and the conquest of all fears together, as *concomitantia:*[279]

> *Felix qui potuit rerum cognoscere causas,*
> *Quique metus omnes, et inexorabile fatum*
> *Subjecit pedibus, strepitumque Acherontis avari.*[280]

It were too long to go over the particular remedies which learning doth minister to all the diseases of the mind: sometimes

---

[274] informs himself.

[275] battles.

[276] crossing (of a river).

[277] Plutarch, *Agesilaus*, 15. advertised: informed, advised.

[278] "Yesterday I saw a fragile thing broken, today a mortal thing dead." Not in Epictetus but in the commentary on him by Simplicius. [Wright]

[279] "parallel matters".

[280] "Happy the man who doth the causes know
Of all that is: serene he stands, above
All fears; above the inexorable fate,
And that insatiate gulf that roars below."

– *Georgics*, II.490f.

purging the ill humours, sometimes opening the obstructions, sometimes helping digestion, sometimes increasing appetite, sometimes healing the wounds and exulcerations[281] thereof, and the like; and therefore I will conclude with that which hath *rationem totius*;[282] which is that it disposeth the constitution of the mind not to be fixed or settled in the defects thereof, but still to be capable and susceptible of growth and reformation. For the unlearned man knows not what it is to descend into himself, or to call himself to account, nor the pleasure of that *suavissima vita, indies sentire se fieri meliorem*.[283] The good parts he hath he will learn to show to the full, and use them dexterously, but not much to increase them. The faults he hath he will learn how to hide and colour them, but not much to amend them, like an ill mower, that mows on still and never whets his scythe. Whereas with the learned man it fares otherwise, that he doth ever intermix the correction and amendment of his mind with the use and employment thereof. Nay further, in general and in sum, certain it is that *Veritas* and *Bonitas* differ but as the seal and the print: for Truth prints Goodness, and they be the clouds of error which descend in the storms of passions and perturbations.

From moral virtue let us pass on to matter of power and commandment, and consider whether in right reason there be any comparable with that wherewith knowledge investeth and crowneth man's nature. We see the dignity of the commandment[284] is according to the dignity of the commanded: to have commandment over beasts, as herdmen have, is a thing contemptible: to have commandment over children, as schoolmasters have, is a matter of small honour: to have commandment over galley slaves is a disparagement rather than an honour. Neither is the commandment of tyrants much better, over people which have put off the generosity of their minds: and therefore it was ever holden that honours in free monarchies and commonwealths had a sweetness more than in tyrannies, because the

---

[281] ulcerations.
[282] "the essence of the whole". Cf. Eccles. 12:13.
[283] "most agreeable life, feeling itself grow better every day". Xenophon, *Mem.*, I.6.
[284] authority.

commandment extendeth more over the wills of men, and not only over their deeds and services. And therefore, when Virgil putteth himself forth[285] to attribute to Augustus Cæsar the best of human honours, he doth it in these words:

> *Victorque volentes*
> *Per populos dat jura, viamque affectat Olympo.*[286]

But yet the commandment of knowledge is yet higher than the commandment over the will; for it is a commandment over the reason, belief, and understanding of man, which is the highest part of the mind, and giveth law to the will itself. For there is no power on earth which setteth up a throne or chair of estate in the spirits and souls of men, and in their cogitations, imaginations, opinions, and beliefs, but knowledge and learning. And therefore we see the detestable and extreme pleasure that arch-heretics, and false prophets, and impostors are transported with, when they once find in themselves that they have a superiority in the faith and conscience of men; so great as if they have once tasted of it, it is seldom seen that any torture or persecution can make them relinquish or abandon it. But as this is that which the author of the Revelation calleth the depth or profoundness of Satan,[287] so by argument of contraries, the just and lawful sovereignty over men's understanding, by force of truth rightly interpreted, is that which approacheth nearest to the similitude of the divine rule.

As for fortune and advancement, the beneficence of learning is not so confined to give fortune only to states and commonwealths, as it doth not likewise give fortune to particular persons. For it was well noted long ago that Homer hath given more men their livings than either Sylla or Cæsar or Augustus ever did, notwithstanding their great largesses and donatives and distributions of lands to so many legions. And no doubt it is hard to say whether arms or learning have advanced greater numbers. And in case of sovereignty we see that if arms or descent have carried away the kingdom, yet learning hath

---

[285] strives his utmost.

[286] "The conqueror gives laws to willing peoples and takes the road

to heaven." *Georgics*, IV.561.

[287] Rev. 2:24.

carried the priesthood, which ever hath been in some competition with empire.

Again, for the pleasure and delight of knowledge and learning, it far surpasseth all other in nature; for shall the pleasures of the affections so exceed the pleasure of the sense, as much as the obtaining of desire or victory exceedeth a song or a dinner; and must not of consequence the pleasures of the intellect or understanding exceed the pleasures of the affections? We see in all other pleasures there is satiety, and after they be used, their verdure departeth; which showeth well they be but deceits of pleasure, and not pleasures, and that it was the novelty which pleased, and not the quality. And therefore we see that voluptuous men turn friars, and ambitious princes turn melancholy. But of knowledge there is no satiety, but satisfaction and appetite are perpetually interchangeable; and therefore appeareth to be good in itself simply, without fallacy or accident. Neither is that pleasure of small efficacy and contentment to the mind of man, which the poet Lucretius describeth elegantly,

Suave mari magno, turbantibus æquora ventis, etc.[288]

It is a view of delight (saith he) *to stand or walk upon the shore side, and to see a ship tossed with tempest upon the sea; or to be in a fortified tower, and to see two battles join upon a plain. But it is a pleasure incomparable, for the mind of man to be settled, landed, and fortified in the certainty of truth; and from thence to descry and behold the errors, perturbations, labours, and wanderings up and down of other men.*

Lastly, leaving the vulgar arguments, that by learning man excelleth man in that wherein man excelleth beasts, that by learning man ascendeth to the heavens and their motions, where in body he cannot come, and the like: let us conclude with the dignity and excellency of knowledge and learning in that whereunto man's nature doth most aspire, which is immortality or continuance; for to this tendeth generation and raising of houses and families; to this tend buildings, foundations, and monuments; to this tendeth the desire of memory, fame, and celebra-

[288] *On the Nature of Things*, II.1-10.

tion; and in effect the strength of all other human desires. We see then how far the monuments of wit and learning are more durable than the monuments of power or of the hands. For have not the verses of Homer continued twenty-five hundred years, or more, without the loss of a syllable or letter; during which time infinite palaces, temples, castles, cities, have been decayed and demolished? It is not possible to have the true pictures or statuas of Cyrus, Alexander, Cæsar, no, nor of the kings or great personages of much later years; for the originals cannot last, and the copies cannot but leese* of the life and truth. But the images of men's wits and knowledges remain in books, exempted from the wrong of time and capable of perpetual renovation. Neither are they fitly to be called images, because they generate still, and cast their seeds in the minds of others, provoking and causing infinite actions and opinions in succeeding ages. So that if the invention of the ship was thought so noble, which carrieth riches and commodities from place to place, and consociateth the most remote regions in participation of their fruits, how much more are letters to be magnified, which as ships pass through the vast seas of time, and make ages so distant to participate of the wisdom, illuminations, and inventions, the one of the other? Nay further, we see some of the philosophers which were least divine, and most immersed in the senses, and denied generally the immortality of the soul, yet came to this point, that whatsoever motions the spirit of man could act and perform without the organs of the body, they thought might remain after death; which were only those of the understanding, and not of the affection; so immortal and incorruptible a thing did knowledge seem unto them to be. But we, that know by divine revelation that not only the understanding but the affections purified, not only the spirit but the body changed, shall be advanced to immortality, do disclaim in[289] these rudiments of the senses. But it must be remembered, both in this last point, and so it may likewise be needful in other places, that in probation[290] of the dignity of knowledge

[289] renounce.
[290] proof.

or learning, I did in the beginning separate divine testimony from human, which method I have pursued, and so handled them both apart.

Nevertheless I do not pretend, and I know it will be impossible for me by any pleading of mine, to reverse the judgment, either of Æsop's cock, that preferred the barleycorn before the gem;[291] or of Midas, that being chosen judge between Apollo, president of the Muses, and Pan, god of the flocks, judged for plenty;[292] or of Paris, that judged for beauty and love against wisdom and power;[293] or of Agrippina (*Occidat matrem, modo imperet*)[294] that preferred empire with any condition never so detestable; or of Ulysses, *qui vetulam prætulit immortalitati*,[295] being a figure of those which prefer custom and habit before all excellency; or of a number of the like popular judgments. For these things must continue as they have been: but so will that also continue whereupon learning hath ever relied, and which faileth not: *Justificata est sapientia a filiis suis.*[296]

[291] Phaedrus, III. 12.

[292] See Ovid, *Met.*, XI.153ff.

[293] Chosen to decide the fairest amongst Juno, Minerva, and Venus, Paris rejected the bribes of the first two but accepted that of Venus – beauty and love – awarded to him in the form of Helen. See Homer, *Iliad*, XXIV. 25, 29.

[294] "Let him kill his mother, provided that he become emperor."

Tacitus, *Ann.*, XIV.9. Agrippina, mother of Nero, said this about herself.

[295] "who preferred an old woman to immortality". See Homer, *Odyssey*, V.218. Ulysses' old wife was Penelope, whom he preferred to the immortality Calypso offered him.

[296] "Wisdom is justified of [by] her children." Matt. 11:19.

The Second Book

TO THE KING

IT might seem to have more convenience,[1] though it come often otherwise to pass (excellent King), that those which are fruitful in their generations, and have in themselves the foresight of immortality in their descendants should likewise be more careful of the good estate* of future times, unto which they know they must transmit and commend over their dearest pledges. Queen Elizabeth was a sojourner[2] in the world in respect of her unmarried life, and was a blessing to her own times, and yet so as the impression of her good government, besides her happy memory, is not without some effect which doth survive her. But to your Majesty, whom God hath already blessed with so much royal issue worthy to continue and represent you for ever, and whose youthful and fruitful bed doth yet promise many the like renovations, it is proper and agreeable to be conversant not only in the transitory parts of good government but in those acts also which are in their nature permanent and perpetual. Amongst the which (if affection* do not transport me) there is not any more worthy than the further endowment of the world with sound and fruitful knowledge; for why should a few received authors stand up like Hercules' Columns,[3] beyond which there should be no sailing or discovering, since we have so bright and benign a star as your Majesty to conduct and prosper us? To return therefore where we left, it remaineth to consider of what kind those acts are, which have been undertaken and performed by kings and others for the increase and advancement of learning, wherein I purpose to speak actively without digressing or dilating.

[1] i.e., to be more fitting.
[2] transient, temporary resident.
[3] the Pillars of Hercules.

Let this ground therefore be laid, that all works are over-comen by amplitude of reward, by soundness of direction, and by the conjunction of labours. The first multiplieth endeavour, the second preventeth error, and the third supplieth[3] the frailty of man. But the principal of these is direction, for *Claudus in via antevertit cursorem extra viam;*[4] and Salomon excellently setteth it down, *If the iron be not sharp, it requireth more strength; but wisdom is that which prevaileth;*[5] signifying that the invention or election of the mean* is more effectual than any inforcement or accumulation of endeavours. This I am induced to speak, for that (not derogating from the noble intention of any that have been deservers towards the state of learning) I do observe nevertheless that their works and acts are rather matters of magnificence and memory than of progression and proficience,* and tend rather to augment the mass of learning in the multitude of learned men than to rectify or raise the sciences themselves.

The works or acts of merit towards learning are conversant* about three objects: the places of learning, the books of learning, and the persons of the learned. For as water, whether it be the dew of heaven or the springs of the earth, doth scatter and leese itself in the ground, except it be collected into some receptacle, where it may by union comfort* and sustain itself; and for that cause the industry of man hath made and framed spring-heads, conduits, cisterns, and pools, which men have accustomed likewise to beautify and adorn with accomplishments of magnificence and state, as well as of use and necessity; so this excellent liquor of knowledge, whether it descend from divine inspiration or spring from human sense, would soon perish and vanish to oblivion, if it were not preserved in books, traditions, conferences, and places appointed, as universities, colleges, and schools, for the receipt and comforting* of the same.

The works which concern the seats and places of learning are four: foundations and buildings, endowments with revenues, endowments with franchises and privileges, institutions and

---

[3] assists.
[4] "A cripple on his course arrives before the runner off his course."

St. Augustine, *Sermons,* CLXIX.
[5] Eccles. 10:10.

ordinances for government, all tending to quietness and privateness of life and discharge[6] of cares and troubles, much like the stations which Virgil prescribeth for the hiving of bees:

> *Principio sedes apibus statioque petenda,*
> *Quo neque sit ventis aditus, etc.*[7]

The works touching books are two: first, libraries, which are as the shrines where all the relics of the ancient saints, full of true virtue, and that without delusion or imposture, are preserved and reposed; secondly, new editions of authors, with more correct impressions, more faithful translations, more profitable glosses, more diligent annotations, and the like.

The works pertaining to the persons of learned men (besides the advancement and countenancing of them in general) are two: the reward and designation of readers in sciences already extant and invented; and the reward and designation of writers and inquirers concerning any parts of learning not sufficiently laboured and prosecuted.

These are summarily the works and acts, wherein the merits of many excellent princes and other worthy personages have been conversant. As for any particular commemorations, I call to mind what Cicero said, when he gave general thanks: *Difficile non aliquem, ingratum quenquam præterire.*[8] Let us rather, according to the Scriptures, look unto that part of the race which is before us than look back to that which is already attained.[9]

First, therefore, amongst so many great foundations of colleges in Europe I find it strange that they are all dedicated to professions, and none left free to arts and sciences at large. For if men judge that learning should be referred to action, they judge well, but in this they fall into the error described in the ancient fable,[10] in which the other parts of the body did suppose the stomach had been idle, because it neither performed the office

---

[6] lightening.

[7] "First find for your bees a settled sure abode, where neither winds can enter, etc." *Georgics*, IV.8.

[8] "It is difficult to remember all, yet ungracious to forget any." Cicero (attr. author), *Speech Delivered before the Senate after his Return from Exile*, XII.30.

[9] Cf. Philippians 3:13.

[10] Livy, II.32. See Shakespeare, *Coriolanus*, I.i.99ff.

of motion, as the limbs do, nor of sense, as the head doth, but yet notwithstanding it is the stomach that digesteth and distributeth to all the rest. So if any man think philosophy and universality[11] to be idle studies, he doth not consider that all professions are from thence served and supplied. And this I take to be a great cause that hath hindered the progression of learning, because these fundamental knowledges have been studied but in passage.[12] For if you will have a tree bear more fruit than it hath used to do, it is not any thing you can do to the boughs, but it is the stirring of the earth and putting new mould about the roots that must work it. Neither is it to be forgotten that this dedicating of foundations and dotations to professory[13] learning hath not only had a malign aspect and influence upon the growth of sciences, but hath also been prejudicial to states and governments. For hence it proceedeth that princes find a solitude[14] in regard* of able men to serve them in causes of estate, because there is no education collegiate which is free,[15] where such as were so disposed might give themselves to histories, modern languages, books of policy and civil discourse, and other the like enablements* unto service of estate.

And because founders of colleges do plant and founders of lectures do water, it followeth well in order to speak of the defect which is in public lectures; namely, in the smallness and meanness of the salary or reward which in most places is assigned unto them, whether they be lectures of arts or of professions. For it is necessary to the progression of sciences that readers[16] be of the most able and sufficient* men, as those which are ordained for generating and propagating of sciences and not for transitory use. This cannot be, except their condition and endowment be such as may content the ablest man to appropriate his whole labour and continue his whole age in that function and attendance, and therefore must have a proportion answerable to that mediocrity or competency of advancement[17] which

---

[11] the study of general principles.

[12] in passing, incidentally.

[13] professional, specialized.

[14] vacuum, deficiency.

[15] liberal.

[16] lecturers.

[17] i.e., as may content the ablest man to devote all his energy to and

may be expected from a profession or the practice of a profession. So as, if you will have sciences flourish, you must observe David's military law, which was, *that those which stayed with the carriage should have equal part with those which were in the action*;[18] else will the carriages be ill attended. So readers in sciences are indeed the guardians of the stores and provisions of sciences whence men in active courses are furnished, and therefore ought to have equal entertainment[19] with them; otherwise if the fathers in sciences be of the weakest sort or be ill maintained,

Et patrum invalidi referent jejunia nati.[20]

Another defect I note, wherein I shall need some alchemist to help me, who call upon men to sell their books and to build furnaces, quitting and forsaking Minerva and the Muses as barren virgins, and relying upon Vulcan. But certain it is that unto the deep, fruitful, and operative[21] study of many sciences, specially natural philosophy and physic, books be not only the instrumentals,[22] wherein also the beneficence of men hath not been altogether wanting; for we see spheres, globes, astrolabes, maps, and the like have been provided as appurtenances to astronomy and cosmography, as well as books; we see likewise that some places instituted for physic have annexed the commodity of gardens for simples of all sorts, and do likewise command the use of dead bodies for anatomies. But these do respect but a few things. In general, there will hardly be any main proficience in the disclosing of nature, except there be some allowance for expenses about experiments, whether they be experiments appertaining to Vulcanus or Dædalus, furnace or engine, or any other kind; and therefore as secretaries and spials* of princes and states bring in bills for intelligence, so you must allow the spials and intelligencers of nature to bring in their bills, or else you shall be ill advertised.*

spend his whole life in discharging and attending to his profession, and therefore [he] must have an income equivalent to the average salary or living wage, etc.

[18] I Samuel 30:24.

[19] consideration.

[20] "The puny offspring betray the feeble sire." *Georgics*, III.128.

[21] effective, productive.

[22] i.e., not the only instruments.

And if Alexander made such a liberal assignation to Aristotle of treasure for the allowance of hunters, fowlers, fishers, and the like, that he might compile an History of nature,[23] much better do they deserve it that travail* in Arts of nature.

Another defect which I note is an intermission or neglect in those which are governors in universities of consultation, and in princes or superior persons of visitation to enter into account and consideration, whether the readings, exercises, and other customs appertaining unto learning, anciently begun and since continued, be well instituted or no, and thereupon to ground an amendment or reformation in that which shall be found inconvenient.[24] For it is one of your Majesty's own most wise and princely maxims, *that in all usages and precedents, the times be considered wherein they first began, which if they were weak or ignorant, it derogateth from the authority of the usage, and leaveth it for suspect.* And therefore inasmuch as most of the usages and orders of the universities were derived from more obscure times, it is the more requisite they be re-examined. In this kind I will give an instance or two for example sake of things that are the most obvious and familiar. The one is a matter which though it be ancient and general, yet I hold to be an error, which is that scholars in universities come too soon and too unripe to logic and rhetoric, arts fitter for graduates than children and novices; for these two, rightly taken, are the gravest of sciences, being the arts of arts, the one for judgment, the other for ornament; and they be the rules and directions how to set forth and dispose matter; and therefore for minds empty and unfraught with matter, and which have not gathered that which Cicero calleth *sylva* and *supellex*,[25] stuff and variety, to begin with those arts (as if one should learn to weigh or to measure or to paint the wind) doth work but this effect, that the wisdom of those arts, which is great and universal, is almost made contemptible, and is degenerate into childish sophistry and ridiculous affectation. And further, the untimely learning of them hath drawn on by consequence the superficial and

---

[23] See Pliny, *Nat. Hist.*, VIII.17.
[24] unsuitable.

[25] *sylva: On the Orator*, III.26.103.
supellex: Orator, XXIV.80.

unprofitable teaching and writing of them, as fitteth indeed to the capacity of children. Another is a lack I find in the exercises used in the universities, which do make too great a divorce between invention and memory, for their speeches are either premeditate *in verbis conceptis*,[26] where nothing is left to invention, or merely *extemporal*, where little is left to memory, whereas in life and action there is least use of either of these, but rather of intermixtures of premeditation and invention, notes and memory; so as the exercise fitteth not the practice nor the image the life; and it is ever a true rule in exercises, that they be framed as near as may be to the life of practice, for otherwise they do pervert the motions and faculties of the mind, and not prepare them. The truth whereof is not obscure: when scholars come to the practices of professions or other actions of civil life, which when they set into, this want is soon found by themselves and sooner by others. But this part, touching the amendment of the institutions and orders of universities, I will conclude with the clause of Cæsar's letter to Oppius and Balbus, *Hoc quemadmodum fieri possit, nonnulla mihi in mentem veniunt, et multa reperiri possunt; de iis rebus rogo vos ut cogitationem suscipiatis.*[27]

Another defect which I note ascendeth a little higher than the precedent. For as the proficience* of learning consisteth much in the orders and institutions of universities in the same states and kingdoms, so it would be yet more advanced if there were more intelligence mutual between the universities of Europe than now there is. We see there be many orders and foundations, which though they be divided under several sovereignties and territories, yet they take themselves to have a kind of contract, fraternity, and correspondence one with the other, insomuch as they have Provincials and Generals.[28] And surely as nature createth brotherhood in families, and arts mechanical contract brotherhoods in communalties,[29] and the anointment

[26] "in prepared language".

[27] "How this may be done, some things come to mind and more may be thought of. I ask you to take these matters under consideration." *To Atticus*, IX.7. Oppius and Balbus: friends and advisers of Julius Caesar.

[28] local and general officers.

[29] communities, societies.

of God superinduceth a brotherhood in kings and bishops, so in like manner there cannot but be a fraternity in learning and illumination, relating to that paternity which is attributed to God, who is called the Father of illuminations or lights.[30]

The last defect which I will note is that there hath not been, or very rarely been, any public designation of writers or inquirers concerning such parts of knowledge as may appear not to have been already sufficiently laboured or undertaken, unto which point it is an inducement to enter into a view and examination what parts of learning have been prosecuted, and what omitted, for the opinion of plenty is amongst the causes of want, and the great quantity of books maketh a show rather of superfluity than lack, which surcharge nevertheless is not to be remedied by making no more books, but by making more good books, which, as the serpent of Moses, might devour the serpents of the enchanters.[31]

The removing of all the defects formerly enumerate except the last, and of the active part also of the last (which is the designation of writers), are *opera basilica*,[32] towards which the endeavours of a private man may be but as an image in a cross-way, that may point at the way but cannot go it. But the inducing[33] part of the latter (which is the survey of learning) may be set forward by private travel.* Wherefore I will now attempt to make a general and faithful perambulation of learning with an inquiry what parts thereof lie fresh and waste and not improved and converted by the industry of man, to the end that such a plot made and recorded to memory may both minister light to any public designation, and also serve to excite voluntary endeavours; wherein nevertheless my purpose is at this time to note only omissions and deficiencies, and not to make any redargution* of errors or incomplete prosecutions, for it is one thing to set forth what ground lieth unmanured, and another thing to correct ill husbandry in that which is manured.

In the handling and undertaking of which work I am not ignorant what it is that I do now move and attempt, nor in-

[30] See James 1:17.
[31] Not Moses but Aaron; see Exod. 7:12.
[32] "works for a king".
[33] introductory.

sensible of mine own weakness to sustain my purpose, but my hope is that if my extreme love to learning carry me too far, I may obtain the excuse of affection, for that *it is not granted to man to love and to be wise.*[34] But I know well I can use no other liberty of judgment than I must leave to others, and I for my part shall be indifferently* glad either to perform myself or accept from another that duty of humanity, *Nam qui erranti comiter monstrat viam*, etc.[35] I do foresee likewise that of those things which I shall enter and register as deficiencies and omissions, many will conceive and censure that some of them are already done and extant; others to be but curiosities and things of no great use; and others to be of too great difficulty and almost impossibility to be compassed and effected. But for the two first, I refer myself to the particulars. For the last, touching impossibility, I take it those things are to be held possible which may be done by some person, though not by every one; and which may be done by many, though not by any one; and which may be done in succession of ages, though not within the hourglass of one man's life; and which may be done by public designation, though not by private endeavour. But notwithstanding, if any man will take to himself rather that of Salomon, *Dicit piger, Leo est in via*,[36] than that of Virgil, *Possunt quia posse videntur*,[37] I shall be content that my labours be esteemed but as the better sort of wishes, for as it asketh some knowledge to demand a question not impertinent,* so it requireth some sense to make a wish not absurd.

[34] Publius Syrus, *Sent.*, 15; cf. Erasmus, *Adages*, II.ii.80 (476DE).

[35] "For he who kindly shows the wanderer the way, etc." Cicero, *On Duties*, I.16.

[36] "The slothful man saith there is a lion in the path." Cf. Prov. 22:13.

[37] "They can because they think they can." *Aeneid*, V.231.

De Sapientia Veterum

1609

The Wisdom of the Ancients

Preface

THE most ancient times (except what is preserved of them in the scriptures) are buried in oblivion and silence; to that silence succeeded the fables of the poets; to those fables the written records which have come down to us. Thus between the hidden depths of antiquity and the days of tradition and evidence that followed there is drawn a veil, as it were, of fables, which come in and occupy the middle region that separates what has perished from what survives.

Now I suppose most people will think I am but entertaining myself with a toy, and using much the same kind of licence in expounding the poets' fables which the poets themselves did in inventing them; and it is true that if I had a mind to vary and relieve my severer studies with some such exercise of pleasure for my own or my reader's recreation, I might very fairly indulge in it. But that is not my meaning. Not but that I know very well what pliant stuff fable is made of, how freely it will follow any way you please to draw it, and how easily with a little dexterity and discourse of wit meanings which it was never meant to bear may be plausibly put upon it. Neither have I forgotten that there has been old abuse of the thing in practice; that many, wishing only to gain the sanction and reverence of antiquity for doctrines and inventions of their own, have tried to twist the fables of the poets into that sense; and that this is neither a modern vanity nor a rare one, but old of standing and frequent in use; that Chrysippus[1] long ago, interpreting the oldest poets after the manner of an interpreter of dreams, made them out to be Stoics; and that the alchemists more absurdly still have discovered in the pleasant and sportive fic-

---

[1] Stoic philosopher (280-207 B.C.). Bacon seems here to be following Plutarch, *How a Young Man Ought to Hear Poems*, XIII, or Diogenes Laertius, X.

tions of the transformation of bodies, allusion to experiments of the furnace. All this I have duly examined and weighed, as well as all the levity and looseness with which people indulge their fancy in the matter of allegories; yet for all this I cannot change my mind. For in the first place, to let the follies and licence of a few detract from the honour of parables in general is not to be allowed, being indeed a boldness savouring of profanity, seeing that religion delights in such veils and shadows; and to take them away would be almost to interdict all communion between divinity and humanity. But passing that and speaking of human wisdom only, I do certainly for my own part (I freely and candidly confess) incline to this opinion, that beneath no small number of the fables of the ancient poets there lay from the very beginning a mystery and an allegory. It may be that my reverence for the primitive time carries me too far, but the truth is that in some of these fables, as well in the very frame and texture of the story as in the propriety of the names by which the persons that figure in it are distinguished, I find a conformity and connexion with the thing signified, so close and so evident that one cannot help believing such a signification to have been designed and meditated from the first, and purposely shadowed out. For who is there so impenetrable and that can so shut his eyes to a plain thing, but when he is told that after the *Giants* were put down *Fame** sprang up as their posthumous sister,[2] he will at once see that it is meant of those murmurs of parties and seditious rumours which always circulate for a time after the suppression of a rebellion? Or again who can hear that the *Giant Typhon* cut off and carried away *Jupiter's* sinews, and that *Mercury* stole them from Typhon and gave them back to Jupiter,[3] without at once perceiving that it relates to successful rebellions, by which kings have their sinews both of money and authority cut off; yet not so but that by fair words and wise edicts the minds of the subjects may be presently reconciled, and as it were stolen back,

[2] See Virgil, *Aeneid*, IV.178ff. Although Bacon appears to have depended in *The Wisdom of the Ancients* more upon Renaissance mythographers than upon the ancients, references will be given to the latter.

[3] See Hesiod, *Theog.*, 819ff., 869, etc.

and so kings recover their strength? Or who can hear that in that memorable expedition of the gods against the giants[4] the braying of *Silenus's ass* had a principal stroke in putting the giants to flight, and not be sure that the incident was invented in allusion to the vast attempts of rebels, dissipated as they commonly are by empty rumours and vain terrors? Then again there is a conformity and significancy in the very names, which must be clear to everybody. Metis, Jupiter's wife, plainly means counsel; Typhon, swelling; Pan, the universe; Nemesis, revenge; and the like. And what if we find here and there a bit of real history underneath, or some things added only for ornament, or times confounded, or part of one fable transferred to another and a new allegory introduced? Such things could not but occur in stories invented (as these were) by men who both lived in different ages and had different ends, some being more modern, some more ancient, some having in their thoughts natural philosophy, others civil affairs; and therefore they need not trouble us.

But there is yet another sign, and one of no small value, that these fables contain a hidden and involved meaning, which is that some of them are so absurd and stupid upon the face of the narrative taken by itself, that they may be said to give notice from afar and cry out that there is a parable below. For a fable that is probable may be thought to have been composed merely for pleasure, in imitation of history. But when a story is told which could never have entered any man's head either to conceive or relate on its own account, we must presume that it had some further reach. What a fiction (for instance) is that of Jupiter and Metis! Jupiter took Metis to wife: as soon as he saw that she was with child, he ate her up; whereupon he grew to be with child himself, and so brought forth out of his head Pallas in armour![5] Surely I think no man had ever a dream so monstrous and extravagant, and out of all natural ways of thinking.

But the consideration which has most weight with me is this,

[4] See Euripides, *Cyclops*, 5ff.; Virgil, *Eclogues*, VI.13f.

[5] See Hesiod, *Theog.*, 471, 886ff.; Pindar, *Olympian Odes*, VII.34ff. Metis is the personification of prudence.

that few of these fables were invented, as I take it, by those who recited and made them famous – Homer, Hesiod, and the rest. For had they been certainly the production of that age and of those authors by whose report they have come down to us, I should not have thought of looking for anything great or lofty from such a source. But it will appear upon an attentive examination that they are delivered not as new inventions then first published, but as stories already received and believed. And since they are told in different ways by writers nearly contemporaneous, it is easy to see that what all the versions have in common came from ancient tradition, while the parts in which they vary are the additions introduced by the several writers for embellishment – a circumstance which gives them in my eyes a much higher value: for so they must be regarded as neither being the inventions nor belonging to the age of the poets themselves, but as sacred relics and light airs breathing out of better times, that were caught from the traditions of more ancient nations and so received into the flutes and trumpets of the Greeks.

Nevertheless, if any one be determined to believe that the allegorical meaning of the fable was in no case original and genuine, but that always the fable was first and the allegory put in after, I will not press that point; but allowing him to enjoy that gravity of judgment (of the dull and leaden order though it be) which he affects, I will attack him, if indeed he be worth the pains, in another manner upon a fresh ground. Parables have been used in two ways, and (which is strange) for contrary purposes. For they serve to disguise and veil the meaning, and they serve also to clear and throw light upon it. To avoid dispute then, let us give up the former of these uses. Let us suppose that these fables were things without any definite purpose, made only for pleasure. Still there remains the latter use. No force of wit can deprive us of that. Nor is there any man of ordinary learning that will object to the reception of it as a thing grave and sober, and free from all vanity, of prime use to the sciences, and sometimes indispensable: I mean the employment of parables as a method of teaching, whereby inventions that are new and abstruse and remote from vulgar opinions may find an easier passage to the understanding. On this account it was that in the old times, when the inventions and conclusions of human reason (even those that are now trite and vulgar) were as yet new and strange, the world was full of all kinds of fables, and enigmas, and parables, and similitudes: and these were used not as a device for shadowing and concealing the meaning, but as a method of making it understood; the understandings of men being then rude and impatient of all subtleties that did not address themselves to the sense, indeed scarcely capable of them. For as hieroglyphics came before letters, so parables came before arguments. And even now if any one wish to let new light on any subject into men's minds, and that without offence or harshness, he must still go the same way and call in the aid of similitudes.

Upon the whole I conclude with this: the wisdom of the primitive ages was either great or lucky: great, if they knew what they were doing and invented the figure to shadow the meaning; lucky, if without meaning or intending it they fell upon matter which gives occasion to such worthy contemplations. My own pains, if there be any help in them, I shall think well bestowed either way: I shall be throwing light either upon antiquity or upon nature itself.

That the thing has been attempted by others I am of course aware, but if I may speak what I think freely without mincing it, I must say that the pains which have been hitherto taken that way, though great and laborious, have gone near to deprive the inquiry of all its beauty and worth; while men of no experience in affairs, nor any learning beyond a few commonplaces, have applied the sense of the parables to some generalities and vulgar observations, without attaining their true force, their genuine propriety, or their deeper reach. Here, on the other hand, it will be found (if I mistake not) that though the subjects be old, yet the matter is new; while leaving behind us the open and level parts, we bend our way towards the nobler heights that rise beyond.

VI. PAN,

OR NATURE

THE ancients have given under the person of Pan[1] an elaborate description of universal nature. His parentage they leave in doubt. Some call him the son of Mercury; others assign him an origin altogether different, saying that he was the offspring of a promiscuous intercourse between Penelope and all her suitors. But in this the name of Penelope has doubtless been foisted by some later author into the original fable. For it is no uncommon thing to find the more ancient narrations transferred to persons and names of later date, sometimes absurdly and stupidly, as in this instance; for Pan was one of the oldest gods, and long before the times of Ulysses; and Penelope was for her matronly chastity held in veneration by antiquity. But there is yet a third account of his birth, which must not be passed over; for some have called him the son of Jupiter and Hybris, or Insolence.

Whatever was his origin, the Fates are said to have been his sisters.

His person is described by ancient tradition as follows: with horns, and the tops of the horns reaching heaven; his whole body shaggy and hairy; his beard especially long. In figure, biform: human in the upper parts, the other half brute, ending in the feet of a goat. As emblems of his power he carried in his left hand a pipe compact of seven reeds, in his right a sheep-hook or staff crooked at the top; and he was clothed in a scarf made of panther's skin. The powers and offices assigned to him are these: he is the god of hunters, of shepherds, and generally of dwellers in the country; also he presides over mountains; and is (next to Mercury) the messenger of the gods. He was accounted moreover the captain and commander of the nymphs, who were always dancing and frisking about him; the Satyrs, and their elders, the Sileni, were also of his company. He had the power

---

[1] See the *Homeric Hymn to Pan*; Homer, *Odyssey*, VII.34; *Iliad*, I.603; Scholiast on Theocritus, I.3, 123; Cicero, *On the Nature of the Gods*, III.22, 56; Ovid, *Met.*, I. 691ff.; III.356ff.; XI.146ff.; Lucian, *Dialogues of the Gods*, 22; Apollodorus, I.v.1 and I.vi.3. An expanded version of this essay appears in the *De Augmentis*, II.xiii.

likewise of exciting sudden terrors – empty and superstitious ones especially – thence called Panics. The actions that are recorded of him are not many; the principal is that he challenged Cupid to wrestle, and was beaten by him. He also entangled and caught the giant Typhon in a net; and they say, besides, that when Ceres, out of grief and indignation at the rape of Proserpina, had hid herself, and all the gods were earnestly engaged in seeking her out, and had dispersed several ways in search of her, it was Pan's good fortune to light upon and discover her by accident while he was hunting. He had also the presumption to match himself against Apollo in music, and was by Midas's judgment pronounced victor; for which judgment Midas had to wear the ears of an ass, but not so as to be seen. There are no amours reported of Pan, or at least very few: which among a crowd of gods so excessively amorous may seem strange. The only thing imputed to him in this kind is a passion for Echo, who was also accounted his wife; and for one nymph called Syrinx, with love of whom he was smitten by Cupid in anger and revenge because of his presumption in challenging him to wrestle. Nor had he any issue (which is again strange, seeing that the gods, especially the males, were remarkably prolific) except one daughter, a little serving woman called Iambe, who used to amuse guests with ridiculous stories, and was supposed by some to be Pan's offspring by his wife Echo.

A noble fable this, if there be any such, and big almost to bursting with the secrets and mysteries of Nature.

Pan, as the very word declares, represents the universal frame of things, or Nature. About his origin there are and can be but two opinions: for Nature is either the offspring of Mercury – that is of the Divine Word (an opinion which the Scriptures establish beyond question, and which was entertained by all the more divine philosophers) – or else of the seeds of things mixed and confused together. For they who derive all things from a single principle, either take that principle to be God, or if they hold it to be a material principle, assert it to be though actually one yet potentially many; so that all difference of opinion on this point is reducible to one or other of these two heads – the world is sprung either from Mercury, or from all the suitors. He sang, says Virgil,

> How through the void of space the seeds of things
> Came first together; seeds of the sea, land, air,
> And the clear fire; how from these elements
> All embryos grew, and the great world itself
> Swelled by degrees and gathered in its globe.[2]

The third account of the generation of Pan might make one think that the Greeks had heard something, whether through the Egyptians or otherwise, concerning the Hebrew mysteries; for it applies to the state of the world, not at its very birth, but as it was after the fall of Adam, subject to death and corruption. For that state was the offspring of God and Sin, and so remains. So that all three stories of the birth of Pan (if they be understood with a proper distinction as to facts and times) may be accepted as indeed true. For true it is that this Pan, whom we behold and contemplate and worship only too much, is sprung from the Divine Word, through the medium of confused matter (which is itself God's creature), and with the help of sin and corruption entering in.

To the Nature of things, the Fates or destinies of things are truly represented as sisters.[3] For natural causes are the chain which draws after it the births and durations and deaths of all things, their fallings and risings, their labours and felicities — in short all the fates that can befall them.

That the world is represented with horns, and that such horns are broad at bottom and narrow at top, has relation to the fact that the whole frame of nature rises to a point like a pyramid. For individuals are infinite: these are collected into species, which are themselves also very numerous; the species are gathered up into genera, and these again into genera of a higher stage; till nature, contracting as it rises, seems to meet at last in one point. Nor need we wonder that Pan's horns touch heaven, since the summits, or universal forms, of nature do in

[2] *Eclogues*, VI.31f.
[3] See Hesiod, *Theog.*, 217ff.; Homer, *Iliad*, XXIV.49.

a manner reach up to God, the passage from metaphysic to natural theology being ready and short.

The body of Nature is most elegantly and truly represented as covered with hair, in allusion to the rays which all objects emit; for rays are like the hairs or bristles of nature, and there is scarcely anything which is not more or less radiant. This is very plainly seen in the power of vision, and not less so in all kinds of magnetic virtue, and in every effect which takes place at a distance. For whatever produces an effect at a distance may be truly said to emit rays. But Pan's hair is longest in the beard, because the rays of the celestial bodies operate and penetrate from a greater distance than any other; and we see also that the sun, when the upper part of him is veiled by a cloud and the rays break out below, has the appearance of a face with a beard.

Again, the body of Nature is most truly described as biform, on account of the difference between the bodies of the upper and the lower world. For the upper or heavenly bodies are for their beauty and the equability and constancy of their motion, as well as for the influence they have upon earth and all that belongs to it, fitly represented under the human figure: but the others, by reason of their perturbations and irregular motions, and because they are under the influence of the celestial bodies, may be content with the figure of a brute. The same description of Nature's body may be referred also to the mixture of one species with another. For there is no nature which can be regarded as simple, every one seeming to participate and be compounded of two. Man has something of the brute; the brute has something of the vegetable; the vegetable something of the inanimate body; and so all things are in truth biformed and made up of a higher species and a lower. There is also a very ingenious allegory involved in that attribute of the goat's feet, which has reference to the motion upwards of terrestrial bodies towards the regions of air and sky; for the goat is a climbing animal, and loves to hang from rocks and cling to the sides of precipices: a tendency which is also exhibited in a wonderful manner by substances that belong properly to the lower world – witness clouds and meteors.

The emblems in Pan's hands are of two kinds, one of harmony, the other of empire. The pipe compact of seven reeds evidently indicates that harmony and concent of things, that concord mixed with discord, which results from the motions of the seven planets. Also the sheep-hook is a noble metaphor, alluding to the mixture of straight and crooked in the ways of nature. But the staff is curved chiefly towards the top, because all the works of Divine Providence in the world are wrought by winding and roundabout ways – where one thing seems to be doing, and another is doing really – as in the selling of Joseph into Egypt, and the like. So also in all the wiser kinds of human government, they who sit at the helm can introduce and insinuate what they desire for the good of the people more successfully by pretexts and indirect ways than directly; so that every rod or staff of empire is truly crooked at the top. The scarf or mantle of Pan is very ingeniously feigned to be made of a panther's skin, on account of the spots scattered all over it. For the heavens are spotted with stars, the sea with islands, the earth with flowers; and even particular objects are generally variegated on the surface, which is as it were their mantle or scarf.

Now the office of Pan can in no way be more lively set forth and explained than by calling him god of hunters. For every natural action, every motion and process of nature, is nothing else than a hunt. For the sciences and arts hunt after their works, human counsels hunt after their ends, and all things in nature hunt either after their food, which is like hunting for prey, or after their pleasures, which is like hunting for recreation, and that too by methods skilful and sagacious.

> After the wolf the lion steals; the wolf the kid doth follow;
> The kid pursues the cytisus o'er hillock and thro' hollow.[4]

Also Pan is the god of country people in general, because they live more according to nature; whereas in courts and cities nature is corrupted by too much culture, till it is true what the poet said of his mistress, *The girl herself is the least part of the matter*.[5]

---

[4] Virgil, *Eclogues*, II.63f. cytisus: a spiny shrub of the pea family. [5] Ovid, *The Remedy of Love*, V.343.

Pan is likewise especially called president of mountains, because it is in mountains and elevated places that the nature of things is most spread abroad, and lies most open to view and study. As for Pan's being, next to Mercury, the messenger of the gods, that is an allegory plainly divine, seeing that next to the Word of God the image itself of the world is the great proclaimer of the divine wisdom and goodness. So sings the Psalmist: *The heavens declare the glory of God, and the firmament showeth his handiwork.*[6]

Again Pan takes delight in the nymphs, that is the souls; for the souls of the living are the delight of the world. And Pan is truly called their commander, since they follow the guidance each of her several nature, leaping and dancing about it with infinite variety, every one in her country's fashion, and with motion that never ceases. And in their company are ever found the Satyrs and the Sileni, that is old age and youth; for all things have their merry and dancing time, and likewise their heavy and tippling time. And yet to one who truly considers them, the pursuits of either age appear perhaps, as they did to Democritus, ridiculous and deformed,[7] like to a Satyr or Silenus.

In the Panic terrors there is set forth a very wise doctrine; for by the nature of things all living creatures are endued with a certain fear and dread, the office of which is to preserve their life and essence, and to avoid or repel approaching mischief. But the same nature knows not how to keep just measure, but together with salutary fears ever mingles vain and empty ones; insomuch that all things (if one could see into the heart of them) are quite full of Panic terrors, human things most of all, so infinitely tossed and troubled as they are with superstition (which is in truth nothing but a Panic terror), especially in seasons of hardship, anxiety, and adversity.

With regard to the audacity of Pan in challenging Cupid to fight, it refers to this, that matter is not without a certain inclination and appetite to dissolve the world and fall back into

---

[6] Psalms 19:1.

[7] See, for example, Seneca, *On Anger*, II.10; Juvenal, *Satires*, X.35f.; Horace, *Epist.*, II.i.194f.

the ancient chaos, but that the overswaying concord of things (which is represented by Cupid or Love) restrains its will and effort in that direction and reduces it to order. And therefore it is well for man and for the world that in that contest Pan was foiled. The same thing is alluded to in that other circumstance of the catching of Typhon in a net: because however it be that vast and strange swellings (for that is the meaning of Typhon) take place occasionally in nature – whether of the sea, or the clouds, or the earth, or any other body – nevertheless all such exuberancies and irregularities are by the nature of things caught and confined in an inextricable net, and bound down as with a chain of adamant.

As for the tale that the discovery of Ceres was reserved for this god, and that while he was hunting, and denied to the rest of the gods though diligently and specially engaged in seeking her, it contains a very true and wise admonition; namely that the discovery of things useful to life and the furniture of life, such as corn, is not to be looked for from the abstract philosophies, as it were the greater gods, no not though they devote their whole powers to that special end, but only from Pan; that is from sagacious experience and the universal knowledge of nature, which will often by a kind of accident, and as it were while engaged in hunting, stumble upon such discoveries.

Then again, that match in music and the result of it exhibits a wholesome doctrine, fit to restrain and reduce to sobriety the pride and overweening confidence of human reason and judgment. For it seems there are two kinds of harmony and music, one of divine providence, the other of human reason; and to the human judgment and the ears as it were of mortals, the government of the world and nature and the more secret judgments of God sound somewhat harsh and untunable; and though this be ignorance, such as deserves to be distinguished with the ears of an ass, yet those ears are worn secretly and not in the face of the world, for it is not a thing observed or noted as a deformity by the vulgar.

Lastly, it is not to be wondered at that no amours are attributed to Pan, except his marriage with Echo. For the world enjoys itself and in itself all things that are. Now he that is in love wants something, and where there is abundance of everything want can have no place. The world therefore can have no loves, nor any want (being content with itself) unless it be of discourse. Such is the nymph Echo, or, if it be of the more exact and measured kind, Syrinx. And it is excellently provided that of all discourses or voices Echo alone should be chosen for the world's wife. For that is in fact the true philosophy which echoes most faithfully the voice of the world itself, and is written as it were from the world's own dictation, being indeed nothing else than the image and reflexion of it, which it only repeats and echoes, but adds nothing of its own. That the world has no issue is another allusion to the sufficiency and perfection of it in itself. Generation goes on among the parts of the world, but how can the whole generate when no body exists out of itself? As for that little woman, Pan's putative daughter, it is an addition to the fable, with a great deal of wisdom in it; for by her are represented those vain babbling doctrines about the nature of things, which wander abroad in all times and fill the world – doctrines barren in fact, counterfeit in breed, but by reason of their garrulity sometimes entertaining, and sometimes again troublesome and annoying.

IX. THE SISTER OF THE GIANTS,

OR FAME

THE poets tell us that the Giants, being brought forth by Earth, made war upon Jupiter and the gods, and were routed and vanquished with thunderbolts, whereupon Earth, in rage at the wrath of the gods, to revenge her sons brought forth Fame,* youngest sister of the giants.[1]

The meaning of the fable appears to be this: by Earth is meant the nature of the common people, always swelling with

[1] See Homer, *Iliad*, XIV.279ff.; Hesiod, *Theog.*, 697ff.; 851ff.; Virgil, *Aeneid*, IV.178f.

malice towards their rulers, and hatching revolutions. This upon occasion given brings forth rebels and seditious persons, who with wicked audacity endeavour the overthrow of princes. And when these are suppressed, the same nature of the common people, still leaning to the worse party and impatient of tranquillity, gives birth to rumours and malignant whispers, and querulous fames, and defamatory libels, and the like, tending to bring envy upon the authorities of the land: so that seditious fames differ from acts of rebellion, not in race and parentage, but only in sex, the one being feminine and the other masculine.

XI. ORPHEUS,

OR PHILOSOPHY

THE story of Orpheus, which though so well known has not yet been in all points perfectly well interpreted, seems meant for a representation of universal Philosophy. For Orpheus himself – a man admirable and truly divine, who being master of all harmony subdued and drew all things after him by sweet and gentle measures – may pass by an easy metaphor for philosophy personified. For as the works of wisdom surpass in dignity and power the works of strength, so the labours of Orpheus surpass the labours of Hercules.

Orpheus, moved by affection for his wife, who had been snatched from him by an untimely death, resolved to go down to Hell and beg her back again of the Infernal Powers, trusting to his lyre. Nor was he disappointed. For so soothed and charmed were the infernal powers by the sweetness of his singing and playing, that they gave him leave to take her away with him; but upon one condition: she was to follow behind him, and he was not to look back until they had reached the confines of light. From this, however, in the impatience of love and anxiety, he could not refrain. Before he had quite reached the point of safety, he looked back; and so the covenant was broken, and she suddenly fell away from him and was hurried back into Hell. From that time Orpheus betook himself to solitary places, a melancholy man and averse from the sight of women; where by the same sweetness of his song and lyre he drew to him all kinds of wild beasts, in such manner that putting off their several natures, forgetting all their quarrels and ferocity, no longer driven by the stings and furies of lust, no longer caring to satisfy their hunger or to hunt their prey, they all stood about him gently and sociably, as in a theatre, listening only to the concords of his lyre. Nor was that all: for so great was the power of his music that it moved the woods and the very stones to shift themselves and take their stations decently and orderly about him. And all this went on for some time with happy success and great admiration; till at last certain Thracian women, under the stimulation and excitement of Bacchus, came where he was; and first they blew such a hoarse and hideous blast upon a horn that the sound of his music could no longer be heard for the din; whereupon, the charm being broken that had been the bond of that order and good fellowship, confusion began again; the beasts returned each to his several nature and preyed one upon the other as before; the stones and woods stayed no longer in their places; while Orpheus himself was torn to pieces by the women in their fury, and his limbs scattered about the fields: at whose death, Helicon (river sacred to the Muses) in grief and indignation buried his waters under the earth, to reappear elsewhere.[1]

The meaning of the fable appears to be this. The singing of Orpheus is of two kinds, one to propitiate the infernal powers, the other to draw the wild beasts and the woods. The former may be best understood as referring to natural philosophy, the latter to philosophy moral and civil. For natural philosophy proposes to itself, as its noblest work of all, nothing less than the restitution and renovation of things corruptible, and (what is indeed the same thing in a lower degree) the conservation of bodies in the state in which they are, and the retardation of dissolution and putrefaction. Now certainly if this can be effected at all, it cannot be otherwise than by due and exquisite attempering and

[1] See Plato, *Symposium*, 179D; Euripides, *Bacchae*, 561f.; Ovid, *Met.*,
X.1-112, 145ff. and XI.1-85.

adjustment of parts in nature, as by the harmony and perfect modulation of a lyre. And yet being a thing of all others the most difficult, it commonly fails of effect, and fails (it may be) from no cause more than from curious and premature meddling and impatience. Then Philosophy finding that her great work is too much for her, in sorrowful mood, as well becomes her, turns to human affairs, and, applying her powers of persuasion and eloquence to insinuate into men's minds the love of virtue and equity and peace, teaches the peoples to assemble and unite and take upon them the yoke of laws and submit to authority, and forget their ungoverned appetites, in listening and conforming to precepts and discipline; whereupon soon follows the building of houses, the founding of cities, the planting of fields and gardens with trees; insomuch that the stones and the woods are not unfitly said to leave their places and come about her. And this application of Philosophy to civil affairs is properly represented, and according to the true order of things, as subsequent to the diligent trial and final frustration of the experiment of restoring the dead body to life. For true it is that the clearer recognition of the inevitable necessity of death sets men upon seeking immortality by merit and renown. Also it is wisely added in the story that Orpheus was averse from women and from marriage; for the sweets of marriage and the dearness of children commonly draw men away from performing great and lofty services to the commonwealth, being content to be perpetuated in their race and stock, and not in their deeds.

But howsoever the works of wisdom are among human things the most excellent, yet they too have their periods and closes. For so it is that after kingdoms and commonwealths have flourished for a time, there arise perturbations and seditions and wars, amid the uproars of which, first the laws are put to silence, and then men return to the depraved conditions of their nature, and desolation is seen in the fields and cities. And if such troubles last, it is not long before letters also and philosophy are so torn in pieces that no traces of them can be found but a few fragments, scattered here and there like planks from a ship-wreck; and then a season of barbarism sets in, the waters of

Helicon being sunk under the ground, until, according to the appointed vicissitude of things, they break out and issue forth again, perhaps among other nations, and not in the places where they were before.

XIII. PROTEUS,

OR MATTER

PROTEUS, the poets tell us, was herdsman to Neptune. He was an old man and a prophet; a prophet moreover of the very first order, and indeed thrice excellent; for he knew all three, not the future only, but likewise the past and the present; insomuch that besides his power of divination, he was the messenger and interpreter of all antiquity and all secrets. His dwelling was under an immense cave. There it was his custom every day at noon to count his flock of seals and then go to sleep. And if any one wanted his help in any matter, the only way was first to secure his hands with handcuffs, and then to bind him with chains. Whereupon he on his part, in order to get free, would turn himself into all manner of strange shapes – fire, water, wild beasts, etc., till at last he returned again to his original shape.[1]

The sense of this fable relates, it would seem, to the secrets of nature and the conditions of matter. For under the person of Proteus, Matter – the most ancient of all things, next to God – is meant to be represented. Now matter has its habitation under the vault of heaven, as under a cave. And it may be called the servant of Neptune, inasmuch as all the operation and dispensation of matter is effected principally in liquids. The herd or flock of Proteus seems to be nothing else than the ordinary species of animals, plants, minerals, etc., in which matter may be said to diffuse and use itself up; insomuch that having once made up and finished those species it seems to sleep and rest, as if its task were done, without applying itself or attempting or preparing

[1] See Homer, *Odyssey*, IV.355ff.; Virgil, *Georgics*, IV.386f.; Ovid, *The Art of Love*, I.761.

to make any more. And this is what is meant by Proteus counting his herd and then going to sleep. Now this is said to take place not in the morning or in the evening, but at noon: that is to say, when the full and legitimate time has come for completing and bringing forth the species out of matter already duly prepared and predisposed, which is the middle point between the first rudiments of them and their declination. And this we know from the sacred history to have been in fact at the very time of the creation. For then it was that by virtue of the divine word *producat* matter came together at the command of the Creator, not by its own circuitous processes, but all at once, and brought its work to perfection on the instant, and constituted the species. And here the story is complete, as regards Proteus free and at large with his herd. For the universe with its several species according to their ordinary frame and structure, is merely the face of matter unconstrained and at liberty, with its flock of materiate[2] creatures. Nevertheless if any skilful servant of Nature shall bring force to bear on matter, and shall vex it and drive it to extremities as if with the purpose of reducing it to nothing, then will matter (since annihilation or true destruction is not possible except by the omnipotence of God), finding itself in these straits, turn and transform itself into strange shapes, passing from one change to another till it has gone through the whole circle and finished the period, when, if the force be continued, it returns at last to itself. And this constraint and binding will be more easily and expeditiously effected if matter be laid hold on and secured by the hands, that is, by its extremities. And whereas it is added in the fable that Proteus was a prophet and knew the three times, this agrees well with the nature of matter: for if a man knew the conditions, affections, and processes of matter, he would certainly comprehend the sum and general issue (for I do not say that his knowledge would extend to the parts and singularities) of all things past, present, and to come.

[2] of the nature of matter; material.

XVI. JUNO'S SUITOR,

OR DISHONOUR

THE poets tell us that Jupiter in pursuit of his loves assumed many different shapes – a bull, an eagle, a swan, a shower of gold – but that when he courted Juno, he turned himself into the ignoblest shape that could be, a very object of contempt and ridicule, that of a wretched cuckoo, drenched with rain and tempest, amazed, trembling, and half dead.[1]

It is a wise fable, derived from the depths of moral science. The meaning is that men are not to flatter themselves that an exhibition of their virtue and worth will win them estimation and favour with everybody. For that depends upon the nature and character of those to whom they apply themselves. If these be persons of no gifts or ornaments of their own, but only a proud and malignant disposition (the character represented by Juno), then they should know that they must put off everything about them that has the least show of honour or dignity, and that it is mere folly in them to proceed any other way; nay that it is not enough to descend to the baseness of flattery, unless they put on the outward show and character of abjectness and degeneracy.

Hypocrisy

XVII. CUPID,

OR THE ATOM

THE accounts given by the poets of Cupid, or Love, are not properly applicable to the same person; yet the discrepancy is such that one may see where the confusion is and where the similitude, and reject the one and receive the other.

They say then that Love was the most ancient of all the gods, the most ancient therefore of all things whatever, except Chaos, which is said to have been coeval with him; and Chaos is never

[1] See Homer, *Odyssey*, XI.299f.; *Iliad*, III.426 and XX.231f.; Ovid, *Met.*, II.834ff. and VI.113f.; Apol- lodorus, III.xii.6; Diodorus Siculus, V.72; Pausanias, II.xxxvi.2 and xvii.4.

distinguished by the ancients with divine honour or the name of a god. This Love is introduced without any parent at all; only, that some say he was an egg of Night. And himself out of Chaos begot all things, the gods included. The attributes which are assigned to him are in number four: he is always an infant; he is blind; he is naked; he is an archer. There was also another Love, the youngest of all the gods, son of Venus, to whom the attributes of the elder are transferred, and whom in a way they suit.[1]

The fable relates to the cradle and infancy of nature, and pierces deep. This Love I understand to be the appetite or instinct of primal matter, or to speak more plainly, *the natural motion of the atom*, which is indeed the original and unique force that constitutes and fashions all things out of matter. Now this is entirely without parent, that is, without cause. For the cause is as it were parent of the effect; and of this virtue there can be no cause in nature (God always excepted): there being nothing before it, therefore no efficient;[2] nor anything more original in nature, therefore neither kind nor form. Whatever it be therefore, it is a thing positive[3] and inexplicable. And even if it were possible to know the method and process of it, yet to know it by way of cause is not possible; it being, next to God, the cause of causes, itself without cause. That the method even of its operation should ever be brought within the range and comprehension of human inquiry, is hardly perhaps to be hoped; with good reason therefore it is represented as an egg hatched by night. Such certainly is the judgment of the sacred philosopher, when he says, *He hath made all things beautiful according to their seasons; also he hath submitted the world to man's inquiry, yet so that man cannot find out the work which God worketh from the beginning to the end.*[4] For the summary law of nature, that impulse of desire impressed by God upon the primary particles of matter which makes them come together, and which by repeti-

---

[1] See Hesiod, *Theog.*, 120; Aristotle, *Metaphysics*, I.4; Virgil, *Ciris*, 134; Cicero, *On the Nature of the Gods*, III.23.

[2] i.e., efficient cause.

[3] (law) dependent on authority or agreement.

[4] Cf. Eccles. 3:11.

tion and multiplication produces all the variety of nature, is a thing which mortal thought may glance at, but can hardly take in.

Now the philosophy of the Greeks, which in investigating the material principles of things is careful and acute, in inquiring the principles of motion, wherein lies all vigour of operation, is negligent and languid; and on the point now in question seems to be altogether blind and babbling; for that opinion of the Peripatetics which refers the original impulse of matter to privation,[5] is little more than words – a name for the thing rather than a description of it. And those who refer it to God, though they are quite right in that, yet they ascend by a leap and not by steps. For beyond all doubt there is a single and summary law in which nature centres and which is subject and subordinate to God, the same in fact which in the text just quoted is meant by the words, *The work which God worketh from the beginning to the end.* Democritus[6] considered the matter more deeply, and having first given the atom some dimension and shape, attributed to it a single desire or primary motion simply and absolutely, and a second by comparison. For he thought that all things move by their proper nature towards the centre of the world; but that that which has more matter, moving thither faster, strikes aside that which has less, and forces it to go the other way. This however was but a narrow theory, and framed with reference to too few particulars: for it does not appear that either the motion of the heavenly bodies in circle, or the phenomena of contraction and expansion, can be reduced to this principle, or reconciled with it. As for Epicurus's opinion of the declination and fortuitous agitation of the atom, it is a relapse to trifling and ignorance. So it is but too plain that the parentage of this Cupid is wrapped in night.

Let us now consider his attributes. He is described with great elegance as a little child, and a child forever; for things compounded are larger and are affected by age, whereas the primary

---

[5] Cf. Aristotle, *Physics*, III.1, 2 and VIII.1 (251^b f.).

[6] See Aristotle, *Physics*, II.2 (194^a);

Metaphysics, M(XIII).4; etc.; Sextus Empiricus, *Against the Philosophers*, VII.130ff.

seeds of things, or atoms, are minute and remain in perpetual infancy.

Most truly also is he represented as naked: for all compounds (to one that considers them rightly) are masked and clothed, and there is nothing properly naked except the primary particles of things.

The blindness likewise of Cupid has an allegorical meaning full of wisdom. For it seems that this Cupid, whatever he be, has very little providence, but directs his course, like a blind man groping, by whatever he finds nearest; which makes the supreme divine Providence all the more to be admired, as that which contrives out of subjects peculiarly empty and destitute of providence, and as it were blind, to educe by a fatal and necessary law all the order and beauty of the universe.

His last attribute is archery, meaning that this virtue is such as acts at a distance: for all operation at a distance is like shooting an arrow. Now whoever maintains the theory of the atom and the vacuum (even though he suppose the vacuum not to be collected by itself but intermingled through space), necessarily implies the action of the virtue of the atom at a distance: for without this no motion could be originated, by reason of the vacuum interposed, but all things would remain fixed and immovable.

As for that younger Cupid, it is with reason that he is reported to be the youngest of the gods, since until the species were constituted he could have no operation. In the description of him the allegory changes its aim and passes to morals. And yet there remains a certain conformity between him and the elder Cupid. For Venus excites the general appetite of conjunction[7] and procreation; Cupid, her son, applies the appetite to an individual object. From Venus therefore comes the general disposition, from Cupid the more exact sympathy. Now the general disposition depends upon causes near at hand, the particular sympathy upon principles more deep and fatal, and as if derived from that ancient Cupid, who is the source of all exquisite sympathy.

[7] sexual union.

Instauratio Magna

1620

The Great Instauration

Prœmium

FRANCIS OF VERULAM *Reasoned Thus With Himself And Judged It To Be For The Interest Of The Present And Future Generations That They Should Be Made Acquainted With His Thoughts.*

BEING convinced that the human intellect makes its own difficulties, not using the true helps which are at man's disposal soberly and judiciously, whence follows manifest ignorance of things, and by reason of that ignorance mischiefs innumerable, he thought all trial should be made, whether that commerce between the mind of man and the nature of things, which is more precious than anything on earth, or at least than anything that is of the earth, might by any means be restored to its perfect and original condition, or if that may not be, yet reduced to a better condition than that in which it now is. Now that the errors which have hitherto prevailed, and which will prevail for ever, should (if the mind be left to go its own way), either by the natural force of the understanding or by help of the aids and instruments of Logic, one by one correct themselves, was a thing not to be hoped for, because the primary notions of things which the mind readily and passively imbibes, stores up, and accumulates (and it is from them that all the rest flow) are false, confused, and overhastily abstracted from the facts; nor are the secondary and subsequent notions less arbitrary and inconstant; whence it follows that the entire fabric of human reason which we employ in the inquisition of nature is badly put together and built up, and like some magnificent structure without any foundation. For while men are occupied in admiring and applauding the false powers of the mind, they pass by and throw away those true powers which, if it be supplied with the proper aids and can itself be content to wait upon nature instead of vainly affecting* to overrule her, are within its reach. There was but one course left, therefore – to try the whole thing anew upon a better plan, and to commence a total reconstruction of sciences, arts, and all human knowledge, raised upon the proper foundations. And this, though in the project and undertaking it may seem a thing infinite and beyond the powers of man, yet when it comes to be dealt with, it will be found sound and sober, more so than what has been done hitherto. For of this there is some issue; whereas in what is now done in the matter of science there is only a whirling round about, and perpetual agitation, ending where it began. And although he was well aware how solitary an enterprise it is, and how hard a thing to win faith and credit for, nevertheless he was resolved not to abandon either it or himself, nor to be deterred from trying and entering upon that one path which is alone open to the human mind. For better it is to make a beginning of that which may lead to something, than to engage in a perpetual struggle and pursuit in courses which have no exit. And certainly the two ways of contemplation are much like those two ways of action, so much celebrated, in this – that the one, arduous and difficult in the beginning, leads out at last into the open country; while the other, seeming at first sight easy and free from obstruction, leads to pathless and precipitous places.

Moreover, because he knew not how long it might be before these things would occur to any one else, judging especially from this, that he has found no man hitherto who has applied his mind to the like, he resolved to publish at once so much as he has been able to complete. The cause of which haste was not ambition for himself, but solicitude for the work; that in case of his death there might remain some outline and project of that which he had conceived, and some evidence likewise of his honest mind and inclination towards the benefit of the human race. Certain it is that all other ambition whatsoever seemed poor in his eyes compared with the work which he had in hand, seeing that the matter at issue is either nothing, or a thing so great that it may well be content with its own merit, without seeking other recompense.

Epistle Dedicatory

Most Gracious and Mighty King,

Your Majesty may perhaps accuse me of larceny, having stolen from your affairs so much time as was required for this work. I know not what to say for myself. For of time there can be no restitution, unless it be that what has been abstracted from your business may perhaps go to the memory of your name and the honour of your age, if these things are indeed worth anything. Certainly they are quite new, totally new in their very kind; and yet they are copied from a very ancient model, even the world itself and the nature of things and of the mind. And to say truth, I am wont for my own part to regard this work as a child of time rather than of wit,* the only wonder being that the first notion of the thing and such great suspicions concerning matters long established should have come into any man's mind. All the rest follows readily enough. And no doubt there is something of accident (as we call it) and luck as well in what men think as in what they do or say. But for this accident which I speak of, I wish that if there be any good in what I have to offer, it may be ascribed to the infinite mercy and goodness of God, and to the felicity of your Majesty's times, to which as I have been an honest and affectionate servant in my life, so after my death I may yet perhaps, through the kindling of this new light in the darkness of philosophy, be the means of making this age famous to posterity; and surely to the times of the wisest and most learned of kings belongs of right the regeneration and restoration of the sciences. Lastly, I have a request to make, a request no way unworthy of your Majesty, and which especially concerns the work in hand; namely, that you who resemble Solomon in so many things – in the gravity of your judgments, in the peacefulness of your reign, in the largeness of your heart, in the noble variety of the books which you have composed – would further follow his example in taking order* for the collecting and perfecting of a Natural and Experimental History true and severe (unincumbered with literature and book-learning), such as philosophy may be built upon, such, in fact, as I shall in its proper place describe, that so at length, after the lapse of so many ages, philosophy and the sciences may no longer float in air, but rest on the solid foundation of experience of every kind, and the same well examined and weighed. I have provided the machine, but the stuff must be gathered from the facts of nature. May God Almighty long preserve your Majesty!

Your Majesty's Most bounden and devoted Servant,

Francis Verulam,
Chancellor.

Preface

That the state of knowledge is not prosperous nor greatly advancing; and that a way must be opened for the human understanding entirely different from any hitherto known, and other helps provided, in order that the mind may exercise over the nature of things the authority which properly belongs to it.

IT seems to me that men do not rightly understand either their store or their strength, but overrate the one and underrate the other. Hence it follows that either from an extravagant estimate of the value of the arts which they possess they seek no further, or else from too mean an estimate of their own powers they spend their strength in small matters and never put it fairly to the trial in those which go to the main. These are as the pillars of fate set in the path of knowledge, for men have neither desire nor hope to encourage them to penetrate further. And since opinion of store[1] is one of the chief causes of want, and satisfaction with the present induces neglect of provision for the future, it becomes a thing not only useful but absolutely necessary that the excess of honour and admiration with which our existing stock of inventions is regarded be in the very entrance and threshold of the work, and that frankly and without circumlocution, stripped off, and men be duly warned not to exaggerate or make too much of them. For let a man look carefully into all that variety of books with which the arts and sciences abound, he will find everywhere endless repetitions of the same thing, varying in the method of treatment but not new in substance, insomuch that the whole stock, numerous as it appears at first view, proves on examination to be but scanty. And for its value and utility it must be plainly avowed that that wisdom which we have derived principally from the Greeks is but like the boy-

[1] abundance.

hood of knowledge, and has the characteristic property of boys: it can talk, but it cannot generate, for it is fruitful of controversies but barren of works. So that the state of learning as it now is appears to be represented to the life in the old fable of Scylla, who had the head and face of a virgin, but her womb was hung round with barking monsters, from which she could not be delivered. For in like manner the sciences to which we are accustomed have certain general positions* which are specious and flattering, but as soon as they come to particulars, which are as the parts of generation, when they should produce fruit and works, then arise contentions and barking disputations, which are the end of the matter and all the issue they can yield. Observe also that if sciences of this kind had any life in them, that could never have come to pass which has been the case now for many ages – that they stand almost at a stay, without receiving any augmentations worthy of the human race; insomuch that many times not only what was asserted once is asserted still, but what was a question once is a question still, and instead of being resolved by discussion is only fixed and fed; and all the tradition and succession of schools is still a succession of masters and scholars, not of inventors and those who bring to further perfection the things invented. In the mechanical arts we do not find it so; they, on the contrary, as having in them some breath of life, are continually growing and becoming more perfect. As originally invented they are commonly rude, clumsy, and shapeless; afterwards they acquire new powers and more commodious arrangements and constructions; insofar that men shall sooner leave the study and pursuit of them and turn to something else, than they arrive at the ultimate perfection of which they are capable. Philosophy and the intellectual sciences, on the contrary, stand like statues, worshipped and celebrated but not moved or advanced. Nay, they sometimes flourish most in the hands of the first author, and afterwards degenerate. For when men have once made over their judgments to others' keeping, and (like those senators whom they called *Pedarii*[2]) have agreed to support some one person's opinion, from that time they make

[2] senators of inferior rank.

no enlargement of the sciences themselves, but fall to the servile office of embellishing certain individual authors and increasing their retinue. And let it not be said that the sciences have been growing gradually till they have at last reached their full stature, and so (their course being completed) have settled in the works of a few writers; and that there being now no room for the invention of better, all that remains is to embellish and cultivate those things which have been invented already. Would it were so! But the truth is that this appropriating[s] of the sciences has its origin in nothing better than the confidence of a few persons and the sloth and indolence of the rest. For after the sciences had been in several parts perhaps cultivated and handled diligently, there has risen up some man of bold disposition and famous for methods and short ways which people like, who has in appearance reduced them to an art, while he has in fact only spoiled all that the others have done. And yet this is what posterity like, because it makes the work short and easy, and saves further enquiry, of which they are weary and impatient. And if any one take this general acquiescence and consent for an argument of weight, as being the judgment of Time, let me tell him that the reasoning on which he relies is most fallacious and weak. For, first, we are far from knowing all that in the matter of sciences and arts has in various ages and places been brought to light and published, much less all that has been by private persons secretly attempted and stirred; so neither the births nor the miscarriages of Time are entered in our records. Nor, secondly, is the consent itself and the time it has continued a consideration of much worth. For however various are the forms of civil polities, there is but one form of polity in the sciences, and that always has been and always will be popular. Now the doctrines which find most favour with the populace are those which are either contentious and pugnacious or specious and empty, such, I say, as either entangle assent or tickle it. And therefore no doubt the greatest wits in each successive age have been forced out of their own course, men of capacity and intellect above the vulgar having been fain, for reputation's sake, to

[s] allotting or limiting.

bow to the judgment of the time and the multitude; and thus if any contemplations of a higher order took light anywhere, they were presently blown out by the winds of vulgar opinions. So that Time is like a river, which has brought down to us things light and puffed up, while those which are weighty and solid have sunk. Nay, those very authors who have usurped a kind of dictatorship in the sciences and taken upon them to lay down the law with such confidence, yet when from time to time they come to themselves again, they fall to complaints of the subtlety of nature, the hiding places of truth, the obscurity of things, the entanglement of causes, the weakness of the human mind; wherein nevertheless they show themselves never the more modest, seeing that they will rather lay the blame upon the common condition of men and nature than upon themselves. And then whatever any art fails to attain, they ever set it down upon the authority of that art itself as impossible of attainment; and how can art be found guilty when it is judge in its own cause? So it is but a device for exempting ignorance from ignominy. Now for those things which are delivered and received, this is their condition: barren of works, full of questions; in point of enlargement slow and languid; carrying a show of perfection in the whole, but in the parts ill filled up; in selection popular, and unsatisfactory even to those who propound them; and therefore fenced round and set forth with sundry artifices. And if there be any who have determined to make trial for themselves, and put their own strength to the work of advancing the boundaries of the sciences, yet have they not ventured to cast themselves completely loose from received opinions or to seek their knowledge at the fountain, but they think they have done some great thing if they do but add and introduce into the existing sum of science something of their own, prudently considering with themselves that by making the addition they can assert their liberty, while they retain the credit of modesty by assenting to the rest. But these mediocrities[4] and middle ways so much praised, in deferring to opinions and customs, turn to the great detriment of the sciences. For it is hardly possible at

[4] middle courses.

once to admire an author and to go beyond him, knowledge being as water, which will not rise above the level from which it fell. Men of this kind, therefore, amend some things, but advance little, and improve the condition of knowledge, but do not extend its range. Some, indeed, there have been who have gone more boldly to work, and taking it all for an open matter and giving their genius full play, have made a passage for themselves and their own opinions by pulling down and demolishing former ones; and yet all their stir has but little advanced the matter, since their aim has been not to extend philosophy and the arts in substance and value, but only to change doctrines and transfer the kingdom of opinions to themselves; whereby little has indeed been gained, for though the error be the opposite of the other, the causes of erring are the same in both. And if there have been any who, not binding themselves either to other men's opinions or to their own, but loving liberty, have desired to engage others along with themselves in search, these, though honest in intention, have been weak in endeavour. For they have been content to follow probable reasons, and are carried round in a whirl of arguments, and in the promiscuous liberty of search have relaxed the severity of inquiry. There is none who has dwelt upon experience and the facts of nature as long as is necessary. Some there are indeed who have committed themselves to the waves of experience, and almost turned mechanics; yet these again have in their very experiments pursued a kind of wandering inquiry without any regular system of operations. And besides they have mostly proposed to themselves certain petty tasks, taking it for a great matter to work out some single discovery — a course of proceeding at once poor in aim and unskilful in design. For no man can rightly and successfully investigate the nature of anything in the thing itself; let him vary his experiments as laboriously as he will, he never comes to a resting place, but still finds something to seek beyond. And there is another thing to be remembered; namely, that all industry in experimenting has begun with proposing to itself certain definite works to be accomplished, and has pursued them with premature and unseasonable eagerness; it has sought,

I say, experiments of Fruit, not experiments of Light, not imitating the divine procedure, which in its first day's work created
light only and assigned to it one entire day, on which day it
produced no material work, but proceeded to that on the days
following. As for those who have given the first place to Logic,
supposing that the surest helps to the sciences were to be found
in that, they have indeed most truly and excellently perceived
that the human intellect left to its own course is not to be
trusted; but then the remedy is altogether too weak for the
disease, nor is it without evil in itself. For the Logic which is
received, though it be very properly applied to civil business
and to those arts which rest in discourse and opinion, is not
nearly subtle enough to deal with nature, and in offering at
what it cannot master, has done more to establish and perpetuate
error than to open the way to truth.

Upon the whole, therefore, it seems that men have not been
happy hitherto either in the trust which they have placed in
others or in their own industry with regard to the sciences,
especially as neither the demonstrations nor the experiments as
yet known are much to be relied upon. But the universe to the
eye of the human understanding is framed like a labyrinth, presenting as it does on every side so many ambiguities of way, such
deceitful resemblances of objects and signs, natures so irregular
in their lines and so knotted and entangled. And then the way
is still to be made by the uncertain light of the sense, sometimes
shining out, sometimes clouded over, through the woods of experience and particulars, while those who offer themselves for
guides are (as was said) themselves also puzzled, and increase the
number of errors and wanderers. In circumstances so difficult
neither the natural force of man's judgment nor even any accidental felicity offers any chance of success. No excellence of wit,
no repetition of chance experiments, can overcome such difficulties as these. Our steps must be guided by a clue, and the
whole way from the very first perception of the senses must be
laid out upon a sure plan. Not that I would be understood to
mean that nothing whatever has been done in so many ages by
so great labours. We have no reason to be ashamed of the dis-

coveries which have been made, and no doubt the ancients
proved themselves in everything that turns on wit and abstract
meditation wonderful men. But as in former ages when men
sailed only by observation of the stars, they could indeed coast
along the shores of the old continent or cross a few small and
mediterranean seas, but before the ocean could be traversed and
the new world discovered, the use of the mariner's needle, as a
more faithful and certain guide, had to be found out; in like
manner the discoveries which have been hitherto made in the
arts and sciences are such as might be made by practice, meditation, observation, argumentation, for they lay near to the
senses and immediately beneath common notions; but before
we can reach the remoter and more hidden parts of nature, it is
necessary that a more perfect use and application of the human
mind and intellect be introduced.

For my own part at least, in obedience to the everlasting love
of truth, I have committed myself to the uncertainties and
difficulties and solitudes of the ways, and relying on the divine
assistance have upheld my mind both against the shocks and
embattled ranks of opinion, and against my own private and
inward hesitations and scruples, and against the fogs and clouds
of nature, and the phantoms flitting about on every side, in the
hope of providing at last for the present and future generations
guidance more faithful and secure. Wherein if I have made any
progress, the way has been opened to me by no other means than
the true and legitimate humiliation of the human spirit. For all
those who before me have applied themselves to the invention
of arts have but cast a glance or two upon facts and examples
and experience, and straightway proceeded, as if invention were
nothing more than an exercise of thought, to invoke their own
spirits to give them oracles. I, on the contrary, dwelling purely
and constantly among the facts of nature, withdraw my intellect
from them no further than may suffice to let the images and rays
of natural objects meet in a point, as they do in the sense of
vision; whence it follows that the strength and excellency of the
wit has but little to do in the matter. And the same humility
which I use in inventing I employ likewise in teaching. For I

do not endeavour either by triumphs of confutation, or pleadings of antiquity, or assumption of authority, or even by the veil of obscurity, to invest these inventions of mine with any majesty, which might easily be done by one who sought to give lustre to his own name rather than light to other men's minds. I have not sought (I say) nor do I seek either to force or ensnare men's judgments, but I lead them to things themselves and the concordances of things, that they may see for themselves what they have, what they can dispute, what they can add and contribute to the common stock. And for myself, if in anything I have been either too credulous or too little awake and attentive, or if I have fallen off by the way and left the inquiry incomplete, nevertheless I so present these things naked and open, that my errors can be marked and set aside before the mass of knowledge be further infected by them; and it will be easy also for others to continue and carry on my labours. And by these means I suppose that I have established forever a true and lawful marriage between the empirical and the rational faculty, the unkind and ill-starred divorce and separation of which has thrown into confusion all the affairs of the human family.

Wherefore, seeing that these things do not depend upon myself, at the outset of the work I most humbly and fervently pray to God the Father, God the Son, and God the Holy Ghost, that remembering the sorrows of mankind and the pilgrimage of this our life wherein we wear out days few and evil, they will vouchsafe through my hands to endow the human family with new mercies. This likewise I humbly pray, that things human may not interfere with things divine, and that from the opening of the ways of sense and the increase of natural light there may arise in our minds no incredulity or darkness with regard to the divine mysteries, but rather that the understanding being thereby purified and purged of fancies and vanity, and yet not the less subject and entirely submissive to the divine oracles, may give to faith that which is faith's. Lastly, that knowledge being now discharged of that venom which the serpent infused into it, and which makes the mind of man to swell, we may not be wise above measure and sobriety, but cultivate truth in charity.

And now having said my prayers I turn to men, to whom I have certain salutary admonitions to offer and certain fair requests to make. My first admonition (which was also my prayer) is that men confine the sense within the limits of duty in respect of things divine, for the sense is like the sun, which reveals the face of earth, but seals and shuts up the face of heaven. My next, that in flying from this evil they fall not into the opposite error, which they will surely do if they think that the inquisition of nature is in any part interdicted or forbidden. For it was not that pure and uncorrupted natural knowledge whereby Adam gave names to the creatures according to their propriety, which gave occasion to the fall: it was the ambitious and proud desire of moral knowledge to judge of good and evil, to the end that man may revolt from God and give laws to himself, which was the form and manner of the temptation. Whereas of the sciences which regard nature, the divine philosopher declares that "it is the glory of God to conceal a thing, but it is the glory of the King to find a thing out."[5] Even as though the divine nature took pleasure in the innocent and kindly sport of children playing at hide and seek, and vouchsafed of his kindness and goodness to admit the human spirit for his playfellow at that game. Lastly, I would address one general admonition to all, that they consider what are the true ends of knowledge, and that they seek it not either for pleasure of the mind, or for contention, or for superiority to others, or for profit, or fame, or power, or any of these inferior things, but for the benefit and use of life; and that they perfect and govern it in charity. For it was from lust of power that the angels fell, from lust of knowledge that man fell; but of charity there can be no excess, neither did angel or man ever come in danger by it.

The requests I have to make are these. Of myself I say nothing, but in behalf of the business which is in hand I entreat men to believe that it is not an opinion to be held but a work to be done; and to be well assured that I am labouring to lay the foundation, not of any sect or doctrine, but of human utility and power. Next, I ask them to deal fairly by their own interests,

[5] Prov. 25:2.

and laying aside all emulations and prejudices in favour of this or that opinion, to join in consultation for the common good, and being now freed and guarded by the securities and helps which I offer from the errors and impediments of the way, to come forward themselves and take part in that which remains to be done. Moreover, to be of good hope, nor to imagine that this Instauration of mine is a thing infinite and beyond the power of man, when it is in fact the true end and termination of infinite error; and seeing also that it is by no means forgetful of the conditions of mortality and humanity (for it does not suppose that the work can be altogether completed within one generation, but provides for its being taken up by another); and finally that it seeks for the sciences not arrogantly in the little cells of human wit but with reverence in the greater world. But it is the empty things that are vast; things solid are most contracted and lie in little room.[6] And now I have only one favour more to ask (else injustice to me may perhaps imperil the business itself) – that men will consider well how far, upon that which I must needs assert (if I am to be consistent with myself), they are entitled to judge and decide upon these doctrines of mine; inasmuch as all that premature human reasoning which anticipates inquiry, and is abstracted from the facts rashly and sooner than is fit, is by me rejected (so far as the inquisition of nature is concerned) as a thing uncertain, confused, and ill built up; and I cannot be fairly asked to abide by the decision of a tribunal which is itself on its trial.

[6] space.

The Plan of the Work

The work is in six Parts:

1. *The Divisions of the Sciences.*
2. *The New Organon; or Directions concerning the Interpretation of Nature.*
3. *The Phenomena of the Universe; or a Natural and Experimental History for the foundation of Philosophy.*
4. *The Ladder of the Intellect.*
5. *The Forerunners; or Anticipations of the New Philosophy.*
6. *The New Philosophy; or Active Science.*

THE ARGUMENTS OF THE SEVERAL PARTS

IT being part of my design to set everything forth, as far as may be, plainly and perspicuously (for nakedness of the mind is still, as nakedness of the body once was, the companion of innocence and simplicity), let me first explain the order and plan of the work. I distribute it into six parts.

The first part exhibits a summary or general description of the knowledge which the human race at present possesses. For I thought it good to make some pause upon that which is received, that thereby the old may be more easily made perfect and the new more easily approached. And I hold the improvement of that which we have to be as much an object as the acquisition of more. Besides which it will make me the better listened to, for "He that is ignorant (says the proverb) receives not the words of knowledge, unless thou first tell him that which is in his own heart."[1] We will therefore make a coasting voyage along the shores of the arts and sciences received, not without importing into them some useful things by the way.

[1] an unusual translation of the Vulgate, Prov. 18:2.

In laying out the divisions of the sciences, however, I take into account not only things already invented and known, but likewise things omitted which ought to be there. For there are found in the intellectual as in the terrestrial globe waste regions as well as cultivated ones. It is no wonder therefore if I am sometimes obliged to depart from the ordinary divisions. For in adding to the total you necessarily alter the parts and sections, and the received divisions of the sciences are fitted only to the received sum of them as it stands now.

With regard to those things which I shall mark as omitted, I intend not merely to set down a simple title or a concise argument of that which is wanted. For as often as I have occasion to report anything as deficient, the nature of which is at all obscure, so that men may not perhaps easily understand what I mean or what the work is which I have in my head, I shall always (provided it be a matter of any worth) take care to subjoin either directions for the execution of such work, or else a portion of the work itself executed by myself as a sample of the whole, thus giving assistance in every case either by work or by counsel. For if it were for the sake of my own reputation only and other men's interests were not concerned in it, I would not have any man think that in such cases merely some light and vague notion has crossed my mind, and that the things which I desire and offer at are no better than wishes, when they are in fact things which men may certainly command if they will, and of which I have formed in my own mind a clear and detailed conception. For I do not propose merely to survey these regions in my mind, like an augur taking auspices, but to enter them like a general who means to take possession. So much for the first part of the work.

Having thus coasted past the ancient arts, the next point is to equip the intellect for passing beyond. To the second part therefore belongs the doctrine concerning the better and more perfect use of human reason in the inquisition of things, and the true helps of the understanding, that thereby (as far as the condition of mortality and humanity allows) the intellect may be raised and exalted and made capable of overcoming the difficulties and obscurities of nature. The art which I introduce with this view (which I call *Interpretation of Nature*) is a kind of logic, though the difference between it and the ordinary logic is great, indeed immense. For the ordinary logic professes to contrive and prepare helps and guards for the understanding as mine does, and in this one point they agree. But mine differs from it in three points especially; viz., in the end aimed at; in the order of demonstration; and in the starting point of the inquiry.

practical end

For the end which this science of mine proposes is the invention not of arguments but of arts, not of things in accordance with principles but of principles themselves, not of probable reasons but of designations and directions for works. And as the intention is different, so accordingly is the effect, the effect of the one being to overcome an opponent in argument, of the other to command nature in action.

In accordance with this end is also the nature and order of the demonstrations. For in the ordinary logic almost all the work is spent about the syllogism. Of induction the logicians seem hardly to have taken any serious thought, but they pass it by with a slight notice, and hasten on to the formulae of disputation. I on the contrary reject demonstration by syllogism, as acting too confusedly and letting nature slip out of its hands. For although no one can doubt that things which agree in a middle term agree with one another (which is a proposition of mathematical certainty), yet it leaves an opening for deception, which is this: the syllogism consists of propositions, propositions of words, and words are the tokens and signs of notions. Now if the very notions of the mind (which are as the soul of words and the basis of the whole structure) be improperly and over-hastily abstracted from facts, vague, not sufficiently definite, faulty, in short, in many ways, the whole edifice tumbles. I

rejects deductive logic

therefore reject the syllogism; and that not only as regards principles (for to principles the logicians themselves do not apply it) but also as regards middle propositions, which, though obtainable no doubt by the syllogism, are, when so obtained, barren of works, remote from practice, and altogether unavailable for the active department of the sciences. Although therefore I leave to the syllogism and these famous and boasted modes of demonstration their jurisdiction over popular arts and such as are matter of opinion (in which department I leave all as it is), yet in dealing with the nature of things I use induction throughout, and that in the minor propositions as well as the major. For I consider induction to be that form of demonstration which upholds the sense, and closes with nature, and comes to the very brink of operation, if it does not actually deal with it.

Hence it follows that the order of demonstration is likewise inverted. For hitherto the proceeding has been to fly at once from the sense and particulars up to the most general propositions, as certain fixed poles for the argument to turn upon, and from these to derive the rest by middle terms: a short way, no doubt, but precipitate, and one which will never lead to nature, though it offers an easy and ready way to disputation. Now my plan is to proceed regularly and gradually from one axiom to another, so that the most general are not reached till the last, but then when you do come to them, you find them to be not empty notions but well defined, and such as nature would really recognize as her first principles, and such as lie at the heart and marrow of things.

But the greatest change I introduce is in the form itself of induction and the judgment made thereby. For the induction of which the logicians speak, which proceeds by simple enumeration, is a puerile thing; concludes at hazard; is always liable to be upset by a contradictory instance; takes into account only what is known and ordinary; and leads to no result.

Now what the sciences stand in need of is a form of induction which shall analyse experience and take it to pieces, and by a due process of exclusion and rejection lead to an inevitable conclusion. And if that ordinary mode of judgment practised by the logicians was so laborious, and found exercise for such great wits, how much more labour must we be prepared to bestow upon this other, which is extracted not merely out of the depths of the mind but out of the very bowels of nature.

Nor is this all. For I also sink the foundations of the sciences deeper and firmer; and I begin the inquiry nearer the source than men have done heretofore, submitting to examination those things which the common logic takes on trust. For first, the logicians borrow the principles of each science from the science itself; secondly, they hold in reverence the first notions of the mind; and lastly, they receive as conclusive the immediate informations of the sense, when well disposed. Now upon the first point, I hold that true logic ought to enter the several provinces of science armed with a higher authority than belongs to the principles of those sciences themselves, and ought to call those putative principles to account until they are fully established. Then with regard to the first notions of the intellect, there is not one of the impressions taken by the intellect when left to go its own way, but I hold it for suspected and no way established, until it has submitted to a new trial and a fresh judgment has been thereupon pronounced. And lastly, the information of the sense itself I sift and examine in many ways. For certain it is that the senses deceive, but then at the same time they supply the means of discovering their own errors; only the errors are here, the means of discovery are to seek.*

The sense fails in two ways. Sometimes it gives no information; sometimes it gives false information. For first, there are very many things which escape the sense, even when best disposed and no way obstructed, by reason either of the subtlety of the whole body, or the minuteness of the parts, or distance of place, or slowness or else swiftness of motion, or familiarity of the object, or other causes. And again, when the sense does apprehend a thing, its apprehension is not much to be relied upon. For the testimony and information of the sense has reference always to man, not to the universe; and it is a great error to assert that the sense is the measure of things.

To meet these difficulties, I have sought on all sides diligently and faithfully to provide helps for the sense — substitutes to supply its failures, rectifications to correct its errors; and this I endeavour to accomplish not so much by instruments as by experiments. For the subtlety of experiments is far greater than that of the sense itself, even when assisted by exquisite instruments; such experiments, I mean, as are skilfully and artificially devised for the express purpose of determining the point in question. To the immediate and proper perception of the sense therefore I do not give much weight, but I contrive that the office of the sense shall be only to judge of the experiment, and that the experiment itself shall judge of the thing. And thus I conceive that I perform the office of a true priest of the sense (from which all knowledge in nature must be sought, unless men mean to go mad) and a not unskilful interpreter of its oracles; and that while others only profess to uphold and culti-vate the sense, I do so in fact. Such then are the provisions I make for finding the genuine light of nature and kindling and bringing it to bear. And they would be sufficient of themselves if the human intellect were even and like a fair sheet of paper with no writing on it. But since the minds of men are strangely possessed and beset, so that there is no true and even surface left to reflect the genuine rays of things, it is necessary to seek a remedy for this also.

Now the idols, or phantoms, by which the mind is occupied are either adventitious or innate. The adventitious come into the mind from without; namely, either from the doctrines and sects of philosophers or from perverse rules of demonstration. But the innate are inherent in the very nature of the intellect, which is far more prone to error than the sense is. For let men please themselves as they will in admiring and almost adoring the human mind, this is certain, that as an uneven mirror distorts the rays of objects according to its own figure and section, so the mind, when it receives impressions of objects through the sense, cannot be trusted to report them truly, but in forming its notions mixes up its own nature with the nature of things.

And as the first two kinds of idols are hard to eradicate, so idols of this last kind cannot be eradicated at all. All that can be done is to point them out, so that this insidious action of the mind may be marked and reproved (else as fast as old errors are destroyed new ones will spring up out of the ill complexion of the mind itself, and so we shall have but a change of errors, and not a clearance), and to lay it down once for all as a fixed and established maxim that the intellect is not qualified to judge except by means of induction, and induction in its legitimate form. This doctrine then of the expurgation of the intellect to qualify it for dealing with truth is comprised in three refutations: the refutation of the Philosophies; the refutation of the Demonstrations; and the refutation of the Natural Human Reason. The explanation of which things, and of the true relation between the nature of things and the nature of the mind, is as the strewing and decoration of the bridal chamber of the Mind and the Universe, the Divine Goodness assisting; out of which marriage let us hope (and be this the prayer of the bridal song) there may spring helps to man, and a line and race of inventions that may in some degree subdue and overcome the necessities and miseries of humanity. This is the second part of the work.

But I design not only to indicate and mark out the ways, but also to enter them. And therefore the third part of the work embraces the Phenomena of the Universe; that is to say, experience of every kind, and such a natural history as may serve for a foundation to build philosophy upon. For a good method of demonstration or form of interpreting nature may keep the mind from going astray or stumbling, but it is not any excellence of method that can supply it with the material of knowledge. Those however who aspire not to guess and divine, but to discover and know, who propose not to devise mimic and fabulous worlds of their own, but to examine and dissect the nature of this very world itself, must go to facts themselves for everything. Nor can the place of this labour and search and worldwide perambulation be supplied by any genius or meditation or argumentation; no, not if all men's wits could meet in one. This therefore we must have, or the business must be forever abandoned. But up to this day such has been the condition of men in this matter that it is no wonder if nature will not give herself into their hands.

For first, the information of the sense itself, sometimes failing, sometimes false; observation, careless, irregular, and led by chance; tradition, vain and fed on rumour; practice, slavishly bent upon its work; experiment, blind, stupid, vague, and prematurely broken off; lastly, natural history trivial and poor – all these have contributed to supply the understanding with very bad materials for philosophy and the sciences.

Then an attempt is made to mend the matter by a preposterous subtlety and winnowing of argument. But this comes too late, the case being already past remedy, and is far from setting the business right or sifting away the errors. The only hope therefore of any greater increase or progress lies in a reconstruction of the sciences.

Of this reconstruction the foundation must be laid in natural history, and that of a new kind and gathered on a new principle. For it is in vain that you polish the mirror if there are no images to be reflected, and it is as necessary that the intellect should be supplied with fit matter to work upon, as with safeguards to guide its working. But my history differs from that in use (as my logic does) in many things: in end and office, in mass and composition, in subtlety, in selection also and setting forth, with a view to the operations which are to follow.

For first, the object of the natural history which I propose is not so much to delight with variety of matter or to help with present* use of experiments, as to give light to the discovery of causes and supply a suckling philosophy with its first food. For though it be true that I am principally in pursuit of works and the active department of the sciences, yet I wait for harvest time, and do not attempt to mow the moss or to reap the green corn. For I well know that axioms once rightly discovered will carry whole troops of works along with them, and produce them, not here and there one, but in clusters. And that unseasonable and puerile hurry to snatch by way of earnest at the first works which come within reach, I utterly condemn and reject, as an Atalanta's apple that hinders the race.[2] Such then is the office of this natural history of mine.

[2] Atalanta challenged every suitor for her hand to a race. If he won, she would marry him; if she won, he was to die. Hippomenes (Melanion) finally overcame her with the help of Aphrodite. During the race he dropped, one after the other, three golden apples; these Atalanta could not resist, and as she went out of her way to pick them up, she lost the contest. See, for example, Ovid, *Met.*, X.565ff.

Next, with regard to the mass and composition of it, I mean it to be a history not only of nature free and at large (when she is left to her own course and does her work her own way) – such as that of the heavenly bodies, meteors, earth and sea, minerals, plants, animals – but much more of nature under constraint and vexed; that is to say, when by art and the hand of man she is forced out of her natural state, and squeezed and moulded. Therefore I set down at length all experiments of the mechanical arts, of the operative part of the liberal arts, of the many crafts which have not yet grown into arts properly so called, so far as I have been able to examine them and as they conduce to the end in view. Nay (to say the plain truth) I do in fact (low and vulgar as men may think it) count more upon this part both for helps and safeguards than upon the other, seeing that the nature of things betrays itself more readily under the vexations of art than in its natural freedom.

Nor do I confine the history to Bodies, but I have thought it my duty besides to make a separate history of such Virtues as may be considered cardinal in nature. I mean those original passions or desires of matter which constitute the primary elements of nature, such as Dense and Rare, Hot and Cold, Solid and Fluid, Heavy and Light, and several others.

Then again, to speak of subtlety, I seek out and get together a kind of experiments much subtler and simpler than those which occur accidentally. For I drag into light many things which no one who was not proceeding by a regular and certain way to the discovery of causes would have thought of inquiring after, being indeed in themselves of no great use, which shows that they were not sought for on their own account, but having just the same relation to things and works which the letters of the alphabet have to speech and words – which, though in themselves useless, are the elements of which all discourse is made up.

Further, in the selection of the relations and experiments I conceive I have been a more cautious purveyor than those who have hitherto dealt with natural history. For I admit nothing but on the faith of eyes, or at least of careful and severe examination, so that nothing is exaggerated for wonder's sake, but what I state is sound and without mixture of fables or vanity. All received or current falsehoods also (which by strange negligence have been allowed for many ages to prevail and become established) I proscribe and brand by name, that the sciences may be no more troubled with them. For it has been well observed that the fables and superstitions and follies which nurses instil into children do serious injury to their minds; and the same consideration makes me anxious, having the management of the childhood as it were of philosophy in its course of natural history, not to let it accustom itself in the beginning to any vanity. Moreover, whenever I come to a new experiment of any subtlety (though it be in my own opinion certain and approved), I nevertheless subjoin a clear account of the manner in which I made it, that men knowing exactly how each point was made out, may see whether there be any error connected with it, and may arouse themselves to devise proofs more trustworthy and exquisite,* if such can be found; and finally, I interpose everywhere admonitions and scruples and cautions, with a religious care to eject, repress, and as it were exorcise every kind of phantasm.

Lastly, knowing how much the sight of man's mind is distracted by experience and history, and how hard it is at the first (especially for minds either tender or preoccupied) to become familiar with nature, I not unfrequently subjoin observations of my own, being as the first offers, inclinations, and as it were glances of history towards philosophy, both by way of an assurance to men that they will not be kept for ever tossing on the waves of experience, and also that when the time comes for the intellect to begin its work, it may find everything the more ready. By such a natural history then as I have described, I conceive that a safe and convenient approach may be made to nature, and matter supplied of good quality and well prepared for the understanding to work upon.

And now that we have surrounded the intellect with faithful helps and guards, and got together with most careful selection a regular army of divine works, it may seem that we have no more to do but to proceed to philosophy itself. And yet in a matter so difficult and doubtful there are still some things which it seems necessary to premise, partly for convenience of explanation, partly for present* use.

Of these the first is to set forth examples of inquiry and invention according to my method, exhibited by anticipation in some particular subjects, choosing such subjects as are at once the most noble in themselves among those under inquiry and most different one from another, that there may be an example in every kind. I do not speak of those examples which are joined to the several precepts and rules by way of illustration (for of these I have given plenty in the second part of the work), but I mean actual types and models, by which the entire process of the mind and the whole fabric and order of invention from the beginning to the end in certain subjects, and those various and remarkable, should be set as it were before the eyes. For I remember that in the mathematics it is easy to follow the demonstration when you have a machine beside you; whereas without that help all appears involved and more subtle than it really is. To examples of this kind – being in fact nothing more than an application of the second part in detail and at large – the fourth part of the work is devoted.

The fifth part is for temporary use only, pending the completion of the rest, like interest payable from time to time until the principal be forthcoming. For I do not make so blindly for the end of my journey as to neglect anything useful that may turn up by the way. And therefore I include in this fifth part such things as I have myself discovered, proved, or added – not however according to the true rules and methods of interpretation, but by the ordinary use of the understanding in inquiring and discovering. For besides that I hope my speculations may in virtue of my continual conversancy with nature have a value beyond the pretensions of my wit, they will serve in the meantime for wayside inns, in which the mind may rest and refresh itself on its journey to more certain conclusions. Nevertheless I wish it to be understood in the meantime that they are conclusions by which (as not being discovered and proved by the true form of interpretation) I do not at all mean to bind myself. Nor need any one be alarmed at such suspension of judgment in one who maintains not simply that nothing can be known, but only that nothing can be known except in a certain course and way; and yet establishes provisionally certain degrees of assurance for use and relief until the mind shall arrive at a knowledge of causes in which it can rest. For even those schools of philosophy which held the absolute impossibility of knowing anything were not inferior to those which took upon them to pronounce. But then they did not provide helps for the sense and understanding, as I have done, but simply took away all their authority, which is quite a different thing – almost the reverse.

The sixth part of my work (to which the rest is subservient and ministrant) discloses and sets forth that philosophy which by the legitimate, chaste, and severe course of inquiry which I have explained and provided is at length developed and established. The completion however of this last part is a thing both above my strength and beyond my hopes. I have made a beginning of the work – a beginning, as I hope, not unimportant; the fortune of the human race will give the issue – such an issue, it may be, as in the present condition of things and men's minds cannot easily be conceived or imagined. For the matter in hand is no mere felicity of speculation, but the real business and fortunes of the human race, and all power of operation. For man is but the servant and interpreter of nature: what he does and what he knows is only what he has observed of nature's order in fact or in thought; beyond this he knows nothing and can do nothing. For the chain of causes cannot by any force be loosed or broken, nor can nature be commanded except by being obeyed. And so those twin objects, human knowledge and human power, do really meet in one; and it is from ignorance of causes that operation fails.

And all depends on keeping the eye steadily fixed upon the facts of nature and so receiving their images simply as they are. For God forbid that we should give out a dream of our own imagination for a pattern of the world; rather may he graciously grant to us to write an apocalypse or true vision of the footsteps of the Creator imprinted on his creatures.

Therefore do thou, O Father, who gavest the visible light as the first fruits of creation, and didst breathe into the face of man the intellectual light as the crown and consummation thereof, guard and protect this work, which coming from thy goodness returneth to thy glory. Thou, when thou turnedst to look upon the works which thy hands had made, sawest that all was very good, and didst rest from thy labours. But man, when he turned to look upon the work which his hands had made, saw that all was vanity and vexation of spirit, and could find no rest therein. Wherefore if we labour in thy works with the sweat of our brows thou wilt make us partakers of thy vision and thy sabbath. Humbly we pray that this mind may be steadfast in us, and that through these our hands and the hands of others to whom thou shalt give the same spirit, thou wilt vouchsafe to endow the human family with new mercies.

Closing prayer; cf Herbert's "Pulley"

———

THE FIRST PART OF THE INSTAURATION,
WHICH COMPRISES THE
DIVISIONS OF THE SCIENCES,
IS WANTING.

But some account of them will be found in the Second Book of the "Proficience and Advancement of Learning, Divine and Human".

Next comes

THE SECOND PART OF THE INSTAURATION,
WHICH EXHIBITS
THE ART ITSELF OF INTERPRETING NATURE,
AND OF THE TRUER EXERCISE OF THE INTELLECT;

Not however in the form of a regular Treatise, but only a Summary digested into Aphorisms.

THE
SECOND PART OF THE WORK,
WHICH IS CALLED

The New Organon

OR

TRUE DIRECTIONS
CONCERNING
THE INTERPRETATION OF NATURE

Preface

THOSE who have taken upon them to lay down the law of nature as a thing already searched out and understood, whether they have spoken in simple assurance or professional affectation, have therein done philosophy and the sciences great injury. For as they have been successful in inducing belief, so they have been effective in quenching and stopping inquiry, and have done more harm by spoiling and putting an end to other men's efforts than good by their own. Those on the other hand who have taken a contrary course, and asserted that absolutely nothing can be known – whether it were from hatred of the ancient Sophists, or from uncertainty and fluctuation of mind, or even from a kind of fulness of learning, that they fell upon this opinion – have certainly advanced reasons for it that are not to be despised; but yet they have neither started from true principles nor rested in the just conclusion, zeal and affectation* having carried them much too far. The more ancient of the Greeks (whose writings are lost)[1] took up with better judgment a position between these two extremes – between the presumption of pronouncing on everything, and the despair of comprehending anything; and though frequently and bitterly complaining of the difficulty of inquiry and the obscurity of things, and like impatient horses champing the bit, they did not the less follow up their object and engage with Nature, thinking (it seems) that this very question, viz., whether or no anything can be known, was to be settled not by arguing, but by trying. And yet they too, trusting entirely to the force of their understanding, applied no rule, but made everything turn upon hard thinking and perpetual working and exercise of the mind.

[1] Bacon seems here to have in mind such philosophers as Pythagoras, Heraclitus, and Democritus.

Now my method, though hard to practise, is easy to explain, and it is this. I propose to establish progressive stages of certainty. The evidence of the sense, helped and guarded by a certain process of correction, I retain. But the mental operation which follows the act of sense I for the most part reject; and instead of it I open and lay out a new and certain path for the mind to proceed in, starting directly from the simple sensuous perception. The necessity of this was felt no doubt by those who attributed so much importance to Logic, showing thereby that they were in search of helps for the understanding, and had no confidence in the native and spontaneous process of the mind. But this remedy comes too late to do any good, when the mind is already, through the daily intercourse and conversation of life, occupied with unsound doctrines and beset on all sides by vain imaginations. And therefore that art of Logic coming (as I said) too late to the rescue, and no way able to set matters right again, has had the effect of fixing errors rather than disclosing truth. There remains but one course for the recovery of a sound and healthy condition; namely, that the entire work of the understanding be commenced afresh, and the mind itself be from the very outset not left to take its own course, but guided at every step, and the business be done as if by machinery. Certainly if in things mechanical men had set to work with their naked hands, without help or force of instruments, just as in things intellectual they have set to work with little else than the naked forces of the understanding, very small would the matters have been which, even with their best efforts applied in conjunction, they could have attempted or accomplished. Now (to pause awhile upon this example and look in it as in a glass) let us suppose that some vast obelisk were (for the decoration of a triumph* or some such magnificence) to be removed from its place, and that men should set to work upon it with their naked hands, would not any sober spectator think them mad? And if they should then send for more people, thinking that in that way they might manage it, would he not think them all the madder? And if they then proceed to make a selection, putting away the weaker hands, and using only the strong and vigorous, would he not think them madder than ever? And if lastly, not content with this, they resolved to call in aid the art of athletics, and required all their men to come with hands, arms, and sinews well anointed and medicated according to the rules of art, would he not cry out that they were only taking pains to show a kind of method and discretion in their madness? Yet just so it is that men proceed in matters intellectual – with just the same kind of mad effort and useless combination of forces – when they hope great things either from the number and co-operation or from the excellency and acuteness of individual wits; yea, and when they endeavour by Logic (which may be considered as a kind of athletic art) to strengthen the sinews of the understanding, and yet with all this study and endeavour it is apparent to any true judgment that they are but applying the naked intellect all the time; whereas in every great work to be done by the hand of man it is manifestly impossible, without instruments and machinery, either for the strength of each to be exerted or the strength of all to be united.

Upon these premises two things occur to me of which, that they may not be overlooked, I would have men reminded. First it falls out fortunately, as I think, for the allaying of contradictions and heart-burnings, that the honour and reverence due to the ancients remains untouched and undiminished, while I may carry out my designs and at the same time reap the fruit of my modesty. For if I should profess that I, going the same road as the ancients, have something better to produce, there must needs have been some comparison or rivalry between us (not to be avoided by any art of words) in respect of excellency or ability of wit; and though in this there would be nothing unlawful or new (for if there be anything misapprehended by them, or falsely laid down, why may not I, using a liberty common to all, take exception to it?) yet the contest, however just and allowable, would have been an unequal one perhaps, in respect of the measure of my own powers. As it is however (my object being to open a new way for the understanding, a way by them untried and unknown) the case is altered; party zeal and emulation are at an end, and I appear merely as a guide to point out the road, an office of small authority, and depending more upon a kind of luck than upon any ability or excellency. And thus much relates to the persons only. The other point of which I would have men reminded relates to the matter itself.

Be it remembered then that I am far from wishing to interfere with the philosophy which now flourishes, or with any other philosophy more correct and complete than this which has been or may hereafter be propounded. For I do not object to the use of this received philosophy, or others like it, for supplying matter for disputations or ornaments for discourse, for the professor's lecture and for the business of life. Nay more, I declare openly that for these uses the philosophy which I bring forward will not be much available. It does not lie in the way. It cannot be caught up in passage. It does not flatter the understanding by conformity with preconceived notions. Nor will it come down to the apprehension of the vulgar except by its utility and effects.

Let there be therefore (and may it be for the benefit of both) two streams and two dispensations of knowledge, and in like manner two tribes or kindreds of students in philosophy, tribes not hostile or alien to each other, but bound together by mutual services; let there in short be one method for the cultivation, another for the invention, of knowledge.

And for those who prefer the former, either from hurry or from considerations of business or for want of mental power to take in and embrace the other (which must needs be most men's case), I wish that they may succeed to their desire in what they are about, and obtain what they are pursuing. But if any man there be who, not content to rest in and use the knowledge which has already been discovered, aspires to penetrate further; to overcome, not an adversary in argument, but nature in action; to seek, not pretty and probable conjectures, but certain and demonstrable knowledge — I invite all such to join themselves, as true sons of knowledge, with me, that passing by the outer courts of nature, which numbers have trodden, we may find a way at length into her inner chambers. And to make my meaning clearer and to familiarize the thing by giving it a name, I have chosen to call one of these methods or ways *Anticipation of the Mind*, the other *Interpretation of Nature*.

Moreover I have one request to make. I have on my own part made it my care and study that the things which I shall propound should not only be true, but should also be presented to men's minds, how strangely soever preoccupied and obstructed, in a manner not harsh or unpleasant. It is but reasonable however (especially in so great a restoration of learning and knowledge) that I should claim of men one favour in return, which is this: if any one would form an opinion or judgment either out of his own observation, or out of the crowd of authorities, or out of the forms of demonstration (which have now acquired a sanction like that of judicial laws) concerning these speculations of mine, let him not hope that he can do it in passage or by the by; but let him examine the thing thoroughly; let him make some little trial for himself of the way which I describe and lay out; let him familiarize his thoughts with that subtlety of nature to which experience bears witness; let him correct by seasonable patience and due delay the depraved and deep-rooted habits of his mind; and when all this is done and he has begun to be his own master, let him (if he will) use his own judgment.

[BOOK I]

Aphorisms

THE INTERPRETATION OF NATURE

AND

THE KINGDOM OF MAN

I

MAN, being the servant and interpreter of Nature, can do and understand so much and so much only as he has observed in fact or in thought of the course of nature; beyond this he neither knows anything nor can do anything.

II

Neither the naked hand nor the understanding left to itself can effect much. It is by instruments and helps that the work is done, which are as much wanted for the understanding as for the hand. And as the instruments of the hand either give motion or guide it, so the instruments of the mind supply either suggestions for the understanding or cautions.

III

Human knowledge and human power meet in one, for where the cause is not known the effect cannot be produced. Nature to be commanded must be obeyed, and that which in contemplation is as the cause is in operation as the rule.

IV

Towards the effecting of works, all that man can do is to put together or put asunder natural bodies. The rest is done by nature working within.

V

The study of nature with a view to works is engaged in by the mechanic, the mathematician, the physician, the alchemist, and the magician, but by all (as things now are) with slight endeavour and scanty success.

VI

It would be an unsound fancy and self-contradictory to expect that things which have never yet been done can be done except by means which have never yet been tried.

VII

The productions of the mind and hand seem very numerous in books and manufactures. But all this variety lies in an exquisite subtlety and derivations from a few things already known, not in the number of axioms.

VIII

Moreover, the works already known are due to chance and experiment rather than to sciences; for the sciences we now possess are merely systems for the nice ordering and setting forth of things already invented, not methods of invention or directions for new works.

IX

The cause and root of nearly all evils in the sciences is this, that while we falsely admire and extol the powers of the human mind we neglect to seek for its true helps.

X

The subtlety of nature is greater many times over than the subtlety of the senses and understanding, so that all those specious meditations, speculations, and glosses in which men indulge are quite from the purpose, only there is no one by to observe it.

XI

As the sciences which we now have do not help us in finding out new works, so neither does the logic which we now have help us in finding out new sciences.

XII

The logic now in use serves rather to fix and give stability to the errors which have their foundation in commonly received notions than to help the search after truth. So it does more harm than good.

XIX

There are and can be only two ways of searching into and discovering truth. The one flies from the senses and particulars to the most general axioms, and from these principles, the truth of which it takes for settled and immovable, proceeds to judgment and to the discovery of middle axioms. And this way is now in fashion. The other derives axioms from the senses and particulars, rising by a gradual and unbroken ascent, so that it arrives at the most general axioms last of all. This is the true way, but as yet untried.

XXII

Both ways set out from the senses and particulars, and rest in the highest generalities, but the difference between them is infinite. For the one just glances at experiment and particulars in passing, the other dwells duly and orderly among them. The one, again, begins at once by establishing certain abstract and useless generalities, the other rises by gradual steps to that which is prior and better known in the order of nature.

XXIII

There is a great difference between the Idols[1] of the human mind and the Ideas of the divine. That is to say, between certain empty dogmas and the true signatures and marks set upon the works of creation as they are found in nature.

XXVI

The conclusions of human reason as ordinarily applied in matters of nature, I call for the sake of distinction *Anticipations of Nature* (as a thing rash or premature). That reason which is elicited from facts by a just and methodical process, I call *Interpretation of Nature*.

XXXI

It is idle to expect any great advancement in science from the superinducing and engrafting of new things upon old. We must begin anew from the very foundations, unless we would revolve for ever in a circle with mean and contemptible progress.

XXXII

The honour of the ancient authors, and indeed of all, remains untouched, since the comparison I challenge is not of wits or faculties, but of ways and methods, and the part I take upon myself is not that of a judge, but of a guide.

XXXIII

This must be plainly avowed: no judgment can be rightly formed either of my method or of the discoveries to which it leads, by means of anticipations (that is to say, of the reasoning

---

[1] unsubstantial images; phantoms.

which is now in use), since I cannot be called on to abide by the sentence of a tribunal which is itself on its trial.

XXXVI

One method of delivery alone remains to us, which is simply this: we must lead men to the particulars themselves, and their series and order, while men on their side must force themselves for awhile to lay their notions by and begin to familiarize themselves with facts.

XXXVII

The doctrine of those[2] who have denied that certainty could be attained at all has some agreement with my way of proceeding at the first setting out, but they end in being infinitely separated and opposed. For the holders of that doctrine assert simply that nothing can be known; I also assert that not much can be known in nature by the way which is now in use. But then they go on to destroy the authority of the senses and understanding; whereas I proceed to devise and supply helps for the same.

XXXVIII

The idols and false notions which are now in possession of the human understanding, and have taken deep root therein, not only so beset men's minds that truth can hardly find entrance, but even after entrance obtained, they will again in the very instauration of the sciences meet and trouble us, unless men being forewarned of the danger fortify themselves as far as may be against their assaults.

XXXIX

There are four classes of Idols which beset men's minds. To these for distinction's sake I have assigned names, calling the first class *Idols of the Tribe*; the second, *Idols of the Cave*; the third, *Idols of the Market Place*; the fourth, *Idols of the Theatre*.

[2] Sceptics (of the New Academy).

XL

The formation of ideas and axioms by true induction is no doubt the proper remedy to be applied for the keeping off and clearing away of idols. To point them out, however, is of great use, for the doctrine of Idols is to the Interpretation of Nature what the doctrine of the refutation of sophisms is to common logic.

XLI

The Idols of the Tribe have their foundation in human nature itself and in the tribe or race of men. For it is a false assertion that the sense of man is the measure of things. On the contrary, all perceptions as well of the sense as of the mind are according to the measure of the individual and not according to the measure of the universe. And the human understanding is like a false mirror, which, receiving rays irregularly, distorts and discolours the nature of things by mingling its own nature with it.

XLII

The Idols of the Cave are the idols of the individual man. For every one (besides the errors common to human nature in general) has a cave or den of his own, which refracts and discolours the light of nature, owing either to his own proper and peculiar nature, or to his education and conversation with others, or to the reading of books, and the authority of those whom he esteems and admires, or to the differences of impressions, accordingly as they take place in a mind preoccupied and predisposed or in a mind indifferent and settled, or the like. So that the spirit of man (according as it is meted out to different individuals) is in fact a thing variable and full of perturbation, and governed as it were by chance. Whence it was well observed by Heraclitus that men look for sciences in their own lesser worlds and not in the greater or common world.[3]

---

[3] See Sextus Empiricus, *Against the Logicians*, I.133.

XLIII

There are also Idols formed by the intercourse and association
of men with each other, which I call Idols of the Market Place
on account of the commerce and consort of men there. For it is
by discourse that men associate, and words are imposed according to the apprehension of the vulgar. And therefore the ill and
unfit choice of words wonderfully obstructs the understanding.
Nor do the definitions or explanations wherewith in some things
learned men are wont to guard and defend themselves, by any
means set the matter right. But words plainly force and overrule
the understanding, and throw all into confusion, and lead men
away into numberless empty controversies and idle fancies.

XLIV

Lastly, there are Idols which have immigrated into men's minds
from the various dogmas of philosophies and also from wrong
laws of demonstration. These I call Idols of the Theatre, because
in my judgment all the received systems are but so many stage
plays, representing worlds of their own creation after an unreal
and scenic fashion. Nor is it only of the systems now in vogue
or only of the ancient sects and philosophies that I speak, for
many more plays of the same kind may yet be composed and in
like artificial manner set forth, seeing that errors the most widely
different have nevertheless causes for the most part alike. Neither
again do I mean this only of entire systems, but also of many
principles and axioms in science, which by tradition, credulity,
and negligence have come to be received.

But of these several kinds of Idols I must speak more largely
and exactly, that the understanding may be duly cautioned.

XLV

The human understanding is of its own nature prone to suppose
the existence of more order and regularity in the world than it
finds. And though there be many things in nature which are
singular and unmatched, yet it devises for them parallels and

conjugates and relatives which do not exist. Hence the fiction that all celestial bodies move in perfect circles, spirals and dragons[4] being (except in name) utterly rejected. Hence too the element of fire with its orb[5] is brought in, to make up the square with the other three which the sense perceives. Hence also the ratio of density of the so-called elements is arbitrarily fixed at ten to one.[6] And so on of other dreams. And these fancies affect not dogmas only, but simple notions also.

XLIX

The human understanding is no dry light, but receives an infusion from the will and affections; whence proceed sciences which may be called "sciences as one would". For what a man had rather were true he more readily believes. Therefore he rejects difficult things from impatience of research; sober things because they narrow hope; the deeper things of nature from superstition; the light of experience for arrogance and pride, lest his mind should seem to be occupied with things mean and transitory; things not commonly believed, out of deference to the opinion of the vulgar. Numberless, in short, are the ways, and sometimes imperceptible, in which the affections colour and infect the understanding.

L

But by far the greatest hindrance and aberration of the human understanding proceeds from the dulness, incompetency, and deceptions of the senses; in that things which strike the sense outweigh things which do not immediately strike it, though they be more important. Hence it is that speculation commonly

---

[4] The Latin has *draco*, apparently a reference to certain helical movements of the moon and the planets. Bacon's meaning is obscure, but he seems to be criticizing (perhaps ironically) those who considered any movement of the heavenly bodies other than circular to be impossible and emanating from sacrilegious theorizing.

[5] In the old astronomy the four elements formed concentric spheres, with earth at the centre and the orbit of fire outside, just below that of the moon.

[6] See Aristotle, *On Generation and Corruption*, II.6 (333ᵃ); but Bacon may have come across the idea in the works of a mystical contemporary, Robert Fludd.

ceases where sight ceases; insomuch that of things invisible there is little or no observation. Hence all the working of the spirits[7] inclosed in tangible bodies lies hid and unobserved of men. So also all the more subtle changes of form in the parts of coarser substances (which they commonly call alteration, though it is in truth local motion through exceedingly small spaces) is in like manner unobserved. And yet, unless these two things just mentioned be searched out and brought to light, nothing great can be achieved in nature as far as the production of works is concerned. So again, the essential nature of our common air and of all bodies less dense than air (which are very many) is almost unknown. For the sense by itself is a thing infirm and erring; neither can instruments for enlarging or sharpening the senses do much; but all the truer kind of interpretation of nature is effected by instances and experiments fit and apposite, wherein the sense decides touching the experiment only, and the experiment touching the point in nature and the thing itself.

LI

The human understanding is of its own nature prone to abstractions and gives a substance and reality to things which are fleeting. But to resolve nature into abstractions is less to our purpose than to dissect her into parts, as did the school of Democritus,[8] which went further into nature than the rest. Matter rather than forms[9] should be the object of our attention, its configurations and changes of configuration, and simple action, and law of action or motion, for forms are figments of the human mind, unless you will call those laws of action forms.

[7] Bacon and his contemporaries distinguished three kinds of spirits or "subtle vapours" in the body: the natural (for the performance of instinctual or involuntary actions), the vital (for the support of life and provision of heat), and the animal (for direction of rational motions and the linking of body and soul). Here, however, the distinction is between gross and tangible parts of bodies and their volatile, intangible, invisible characters or operations.

[8] i.e., the Atomistic school.

[9] In Aristotelian philosophy a form was "that in a thing which determines it in its kind or species", its essence (what it can or ought to be as distinguished [by Bacon] from what it actually is).

LII

Such then are the idols which I call *Idols of the Tribe*, and which take their rise either from the homogeneity of the substance of the human spirit, or from its preoccupation, or from its narrowness, or from its restless motion, or from an infusion of the affections, or from the incompetency of the senses, or from the mode of impression.

LIII

The *Idols of the Cave* take their rise in the peculiar constitution, mental or bodily, of each individual, and also in education, habit, and accident. Of this kind there is a great number and variety, but I will instance those the pointing out of which contains the most important caution, and which have most effect in disturbing the clearness of the understanding.

LIV

Men become attached to certain particular sciences and speculations, either because they fancy themselves the authors and inventors thereof, or because they have bestowed the greatest pains upon them and become most habituated to them. But men of this kind, if they betake themselves to philosophy and contemplations of a general character, distort and colour them in obedience to their former fancies, a thing especially to be noticed in Aristotle, who made his natural philosophy a mere bondservant to his logic, thereby rendering it contentious and well nigh useless. The race of chemists again out of a few experiments of the furnace have built up a fantastic philosophy, framed with reference to a few things, and Gilbert also, after he had employed himself most laboriously in the study and observation of the loadstone, proceeded at once to construct an entire system in accordance with his favourite subject.

LV

There is one principal and as it were radical distinction between different minds in respect of philosophy and the sciences, which is this: that some minds are stronger and apter to mark the differences of things, others to mark their resemblances. The steady and acute mind can fix its contemplations and dwell and fasten on the subtlest distinctions; the lofty and discursive mind recognizes and puts together the finest and most general resemblances. Both kinds however easily err in excess, by catching the one at gradations, the other at shadows.

LVIII

Let such then be our provision and contemplative prudence for keeping off and dislodging the *Idols of the Cave*, which grow for the most part either out of the predominance of a favourite subject, or out of an excessive tendency to compare or to distinguish, or out of partiality for particular ages, or out of the largeness or minuteness of the objects contemplated. And generally let every student of nature take this as a rule, that whatever his mind seizes and dwells upon with peculiar satisfaction is to be held in suspicion, and that so much the more care is to be taken in dealing with such questions to keep the understanding even and clear.

LIX

But the *Idols of the Market Place* are the most troublesome of all – idols which have crept into the understanding through the alliances of words and names. For men believe that their reason governs words, but it is also true that words react on the understanding, and this it is that has rendered philosophy and the sciences sophistical and inactive. Now words, being commonly framed and applied according to the capacity of the vulgar, follow those lines of division which are most obvious to the vulgar understanding. And whenever an understanding of greater acuteness or a more diligent observation would alter those lines to suit the true divisions of nature, words stand in the way and resist the change. Whence it comes to pass that the high and formal discussions of learned men end oftentimes in disputes about words and names, with which (according to the use and wisdom of the mathematicians) it would be more prudent to begin, and so by means of definitions reduce them to order. Yet even definitions cannot cure this evil in dealing with natural and material things; since the definitions themselves consist of words, and those words beget others, so that it is necessary to recur to individual instances, and those in due series and order, as I shall say presently when I come to the method and scheme for the formation of notions and axioms.

LX

The idols imposed by words on the understanding are of two kinds. They are either names of things which do not exist (for as there are things left unnamed through lack of observation, so likewise are there names which result from fantastic suppositions and to which nothing in reality corresponds), or they are names of things which exist, but yet confused and ill defined and hastily and irregularly derived from realities. Of the former kind are Fortune, the Prime Mover, Planetary Orbits,[10] Element of Fire, and like fictions which owe their origin to false and idle theories. And this class of idols is more easily expelled, because to get rid of them it is only necessary that all theories should be steadily rejected and dismissed as obsolete.

But the other class, which springs out of a faulty and unskilful abstraction, is intricate and deeply rooted. Let us take for example such a word as *humid*, and see how far the several things which the word is used to signify agree with each other; and we shall find the word *humid* to be nothing else than a mark loosely and confusedly applied to denote a variety of actions which will not bear to be reduced to any constant meaning. For it both signifies that which easily spreads itself round any other body; and that which in itself is indeterminate and cannot solidize; and that which readily yields in every direction; and that which easily divides and scatters itself; and that which easily unites and collects itself; and that which readily flows and is put in motion; and that which readily clings to an-

[10] in the old astronomy, the spheres of the planets.

other body and wets it; and that which is easily reduced to a liquid, or being solid easily melts. Accordingly when you come to apply the word, if you take it in one sense, flame is humid; if in another, air is not humid; if in another, fine dust is humid; if in another, glass is humid. So that it is easy to see that the notion is taken by abstraction only from water and common and ordinary liquids without any due verification.

There are however in words certain degrees of distortion and error. One of the least faulty kinds is that of names of substances, especially of lowest species and well deduced (for the notion of *chalk* and of *mud* is good, of *earth* bad); a more faulty kind is that of actions, as *to generate, to corrupt, to alter*; the most faulty is of qualities (except such as are the immediate objects of the sense) as *heavy, light, rare, dense*, and the like. Yet in all these cases some notions are of necessity a little better than others, in proportion to the greater variety of subjects that fall within the range of the human sense.

LXI

But the *Idols of the Theatre* are not innate, nor do they steal into the understanding secretly, but are plainly impressed and received into the mind from the playbooks[11] of philosophical systems and the perverted rules of demonstration. To attempt refutations in this case would be merely inconsistent with what I have already said, for since we agree neither upon principles nor upon demonstrations there is no place for argument. And this is so far well, inasmuch as it leaves the honour of the ancients untouched. For they are no wise disparaged, the question between them and me being only as to the way. For as the saying is, the lame man who keeps the right road outstrips the runner who takes a wrong one.[12] Nay, it is obvious that when a man runs the wrong way, the more active and swift he is the further he will go astray.

But the course I propose for the discovery of sciences is such

[11] collections of dramas.
[12] St. Augustine, *Sermons*, CLXIX.

as leaves but little to the acuteness and strength of wits,* but places all wits and understandings nearly on a level. For as in the drawing of a straight line or a perfect circle much depends on the steadiness and practice of the hand, if it be done by aim of hand only, but if with the aid of rule or compass, little or nothing; so is it exactly with my plan. But though particular confutations would be of no avail, yet touching the sects and general divisions of such systems I must say something; something also touching the external signs which show that they are unsound; and finally something touching the causes of such great infelicity and of such lasting and general agreement in error: that so the access to truth may be made less difficult, and the human understanding may the more willingly submit to its purgation and dismiss its idols.

LXII

Idols of the Theatre, or of Systems, are many, and there can be and perhaps will be yet many more. For were it not that now for many ages men's minds have been busied with religion and theology, and were it not that civil governments, especially monarchies, have been averse to such novelties, even in matters speculative, so that men labour therein to the peril and harming of their fortunes, not only unrewarded but exposed also to contempt and envy, doubtless there would have arisen many other philosophical sects like to those which in great variety flourished once among the Greeks. For as on the phenomena of the heavens many hypotheses may be constructed, so likewise (and more also) many various dogmas may be set up and established on the phenomena of philosophy. And in the plays of this philosophical theatre you may observe the same thing which is found in the theatre of the poets, that stories invented for the stage are more compact and elegant, and more as one would wish them to be than true stories out of history.

In general however there is taken for the material of philosophy either a great deal out of a few things, or a very little out of many things, so that on both sides philosophy is based on too narrow a foundation of experiment and natural history, and decides on the authority of too few cases. For the Rational School of philosophers snatches from experience a variety of common instances, neither duly ascertained nor diligently examined and weighed, and leaves all the rest to meditation and agitation of wit.

There is also another class of philosophers, who having bestowed much diligent and careful labour on a few experiments, have thence made bold to educe and construct systems, wresting all other facts in a strange fashion to conformity therewith.

And there is yet a third class, consisting of those who out of faith and veneration mix their philosophy with theology and traditions, among whom the vanity of some has gone so far aside as to seek the origin of sciences among spirits and genii. So that this parent stock of errors – this false philosophy – is of three kinds: the Sophistical, the Empirical, and the Superstitious.

LXIII

The most conspicuous example of the first class was Aristotle, who corrupted natural philosophy by his logic: fashioning the world out of categories; assigning to the human soul, the noblest of substances, a genus from words of the second intention;[13] doing the business of density and rarity (which is to make bodies of greater or less dimensions, that is, occupy greater or less space) by the frigid distinction of act and power; asserting that single bodies have each a single and proper motion, and that if they participate in any other, then this results from an external cause; and imposing countless other arbitrary restrictions on the nature of things – being always more solicitous to provide an answer to the question and affirm something positive in words than about the inner truth of things; a failing best

[13] In his *Logic* Aristotle listed ten fundamental concepts or classifications (categories) into which all knowledge can be placed: substance, quantity, quality, relation, place, time, position, state, action, passion. In medieval logic, first intention was the conception of a thing formed by the first or direct application of the mind to an individual object; second intention was a conception abstracted or generalized from first intention, as species, genus, whiteness. See Aristotle's definition of the soul in *On the Soul*, II.1.

shown when his philosophy is compared with other systems of note among the Greeks. For the Homœomera of Anaxagoras, the Atoms of Leucippus and Democritus, the Heaven and Earth of Parmenides, the Strife and Friendship of Empedocles, Heraclitus's doctrine how bodies are resolved into the indifferent* nature of fire, and remoulded into solids[14] – have all of them some taste of the natural philosopher, some savour of the nature of things, and experience, and bodies; whereas in the physics of Aristotle you hear hardly anything but the words of logic, which in his metaphysics also, under a more imposing name, and more forsooth as a realist than a nominalist, he has handled over again. Nor let any weight be given to the fact that in his books on animals and his problems and other of his treatises there is frequent dealings with experiments. For he had come to his conclusion before; he did not consult experience, as he should have done, in order to the framing of his decisions and axioms; but having first determined the question according to his will, he then resorts to experience, and bending her into conformity with his placets leads her about like a captive in a procession, so that even on this count he is more guilty than his modern followers, the schoolmen, who have abandoned experience altogether.

LXIV

But the Empirical school of philosophy gives birth to dogmas more deformed and monstrous than the Sophistical or Rational school. For it has its foundations not in the light of common notions (which though it be a faint and superficial light, is yet in a manner universal, and has reference to many things) but

---

[14] Anaxagoras taught that there was an infinity of simple substances whose similar parts or seeds, *Homoeomera*, made up the universe. Leucippus and Democritus, the Atomists, believed that the universe is composed of indivisible, unchanging particles or atoms moving without direction or purpose in a void. Parmenides held that all things are composed of light (the fire of heaven) and dark (the night of earth). Empedocles taught that love and hate (attraction and repulsion) are the cause of motion and therefore of the mixing of the four elements. Heraclitus regarded the universe as being in constant, ceaseless flux, as an ever-living fire from which all derived and to which all returned.

in the narrowness and darkness of a few experiments. To those therefore who are daily busied with these experiments, and have infected their imagination with them, such a philosophy seems probable and all but certain; to all men else incredible and vain. Of this there is a notable instance in the alchemists and their dogmas, though it is hardly to be found elsewhere in these times, except perhaps in the philosophy of Gilbert. Nevertheless with regard to philosophies of this kind there is one caution not to be omitted; for I foresee that if ever men are roused by my admonitions to betake themselves seriously to experiment and bid farewell to sophistical doctrines, then indeed through the premature hurry of the understanding to leap or fly to universals and principles of things, great danger may be apprehended from philosophies of this kind, against which evil we ought even now to prepare.

LXV

But the corruption of philosophy by superstition and an admixture of theology is far more widely spread, and does the greatest harm, whether to entire systems or to their parts. For the human understanding is obnoxious* to the influence of the imagination no less than to the influence of common notions. For the contentious and sophistical kind of philosophy ensnares the understanding; but this kind, being fanciful and tumid and half poetical, misleads it more by flattery. For there is in man an ambition of the understanding, no less than of the will, especially in high and lofty spirits.

Of this kind we have among the Greeks a striking example in Pythagoras, though he united with it a coarser and more cumbrous superstition; another in Plato and his school, more dangerous and subtle. It shows itself likewise in parts of other philosophies, in the introduction of abstract forms and final causes and first causes, with the omission in most cases of causes intermediate, and the like. Upon this point the greatest caution should be used. For nothing is so mischievous as the apotheosis of error; and it is a very plague of the understanding for vanity to become the object of veneration. Yet in this vanity some of the moderns have with extreme levity indulged so far as to attempt to found a system of natural philosophy on the first chapter of Genesis, on the book of Job, and other parts of the sacred writings, seeking for the dead among the living; which also makes the inhibition and repression of it the more important, because from this unwholesome mixture of things human and divine there arises not only a fantastic philosophy but also an heretical religion. Very meet it is therefore that we be sober-minded, and give to faith that only which is faith's.

LXVIII

So much concerning the several classes of Idols, and their equipage: all of which must be renounced and put away with a fixed and solemn determination, and the understanding thoroughly freed and cleansed; the entrance into the kingdom of man, founded on the sciences, being not much other than the entrance into the kingdom of heaven, whereinto none may enter except as a little child.

LXIX

But vicious demonstrations are as the strongholds and defences of Idols; and those we have in logic do little else than make the world the bondslave of human thought, and human thought the bondslave of words. Demonstrations truly are in effect the philosophies themselves and the sciences. For such as *they* are, well or ill established, such are the systems of philosophy and the contemplations which follow. Now in the whole of the process which leads from the sense and objects to axioms and conclusions, the demonstrations which we use are deceptive and incompetent. This process consists of four parts, and has as many faults. In the first place, the impressions of the sense itself are faulty, for the sense both fails us and deceives us. But its shortcomings are to be supplied, and its deceptions to be corrected. Secondly, notions are ill drawn from the impressions of the senses, and are indefinite and confused, whereas they should be definite and distinctly bounded. Thirdly, the induction is amiss which infers the principles of sciences by simple enumeration, and does not, as it ought, employ exclusions and solutions (or separations) of nature. Lastly, that method of discovery and proof according to which the most general principles are first established, and then intermediate axioms are tried and proved by them, is the parent of error and the curse of all science. Of these things, however, which now I do but touch upon, I will speak more largely, when, having performed these expiations and purgings of the mind, I come to set forth the true way for the interpretation of nature.

LXX

But the best demonstration by far is experience, if it go not beyond the actual experiment. For if it be transferred to other cases which are deemed similar, unless such transfer be made by a just and orderly process, it is a fallacious thing. But the manner of making experiments which men now use is blind and stupid. And therefore, wandering and straying as they do with no settled course, and taking counsel only from things as they fall out, they fetch a wide circuit and meet with many matters, but make little progress, and sometimes are full of hope, sometimes are distracted, and always find that there is something beyond to be sought. For it generally happens that men make their trials carelessly, and as it were in play, slightly varying experiments already known, and, if the thing does not answer, growing weary and abandoning the attempt. And even if they apply themselves to experiments more seriously and earnestly and laboriously, still they spend their labour in working out some one experiment, as Gilbert with the magnet, and the chemists with gold, a course of proceeding not less unskilful in the design than small in the attempt. For no one successfully investigates the nature of a thing in the thing itself; the inquiry must be enlarged, so as to become more general.

And even when they seek to educe some science or theory from their experiments, they nevertheless almost always turn aside with overhasty and unseasonable eagerness to practice, not only for the sake of the uses and fruits of the practice, but from impatience to obtain in the shape of some new work an assurance for themselves that it is worth their while to go on, and also to show themselves off to the world, and so raise the credit of the business in which they are engaged. Thus, like Atalanta, they go aside to pick up the golden apple, but meanwhile they interrupt their course, and let the victory escape them. But in the true course of experience and in carrying it on to the effecting of new works, the divine wisdom and order must be our pattern. Now God on the first day of creation created light only, giving to that work an entire day, in which no material substance was created. So must we likewise from experience of every kind first endeavour to discover true causes and axioms, and seek for experiments of Light, not for experiments of Fruit. For axioms rightly discovered and established supply practice with its instruments, not one by one but in clusters, and draw after them trains and troops of works. Of the paths, however, of experience, which no less than the paths of judgment are impeded and beset, I will speak hereafter; here I have only mentioned ordinary experimental research as a bad kind of demonstration. But now the order of the matter in hand leads me to add something both as to those *signs* which I lately mentioned (signs that the systems of philosophy and contemplation in use are in a bad condition) and also as to the *causes* of what seems at first so strange and incredible. For a knowledge of the signs prepares assent; an explanation of the causes removes the marvel: which two things will do much to render the extirpation of Idols from the understanding more easy and gentle.

LXXIII

Of all signs there is none more certain or more noble than that taken from fruits. For fruits and works are as it were sponsors and sureties for the truth of philosophies. Now, from all these systems of the Greeks and their ramifications through particular sciences there can hardly after the lapse of so many years be

THE NEW ORGANON / 351

adduced a single experiment which tends to relieve and benefit the condition of man, and which can with truth be referred to the speculations and theories of philosophy. And Celsus ingenuously and wisely owns as much, when he tells us that the experimental part of medicine was first discovered, and that afterwards men philosophised about it, and hunted for and assigned causes; and not by an inverse process that philosophy and the knowledge of causes led to the discovery and development of the experimental part.[15] And therefore it was not strange that among the Egyptians, who rewarded inventors with divine honours and sacred rites, there were more images of brutes than of men; inasmuch as brutes by their natural instinct have produced many discoveries, whereas men by discussion and the conclusions of reason have given birth to few or none.

Some little has indeed been produced by the industry of chemists, but it has been produced accidentally and in passing, or else by a kind of variation of experiments, such as mechanics use, and not by any art or theory; for the theory which they have devised rather confuses the experiments than aids them. They too who have busied themselves with natural magic, as they call it, have but few discoveries to show, and those trifling and imposture-like. Wherefore, as in religion we are warned to show our faith by works, so in philosophy by the same rule the system should be judged of by its fruits, and pronounced frivolous if it be barren, more especially if, in place of fruits of grape and olive, it bear thorns and briars of dispute and contention.

LXXIV

Signs also are to be drawn from the increase and progress of systems and sciences. For what is founded on nature grows and increases, while what is founded on opinion varies but increases not. If therefore those doctrines had not plainly been like a plant torn up from its roots, but had remained attached to the

[15] See the Preface to Celsus, *On Medicine* (where, however, the view is held up to criticism).

womb of nature and continued to draw nourishment from her, that could never have come to pass which we have seen now for twice a thousand years; namely, that the sciences stand where they did and remain almost in the same condition, receiving no noticeable increase, but on the contrary, thriving most under their first founder, and then declining. Whereas in the mechanical arts, which are founded on nature and the light of experience, we see the contrary happen, for these (as long as they are popular) are continually thriving and growing, as having in them a breath of life, at first rude, then convenient, afterwards adorned, and at all times advancing.

LXXVIII

I now come to the *causes* of these errors, and of so long a continuance in them through so many ages, which are very many and very potent, that all wonder how these considerations which I bring forward should have escaped men's notice till now, may cease; and the only wonder be, how now at last they should have entered into any man's head and become the subject of his thoughts, which truly I myself esteem as the result of some happy accident rather than of any excellence of faculty in me, a birth of Time rather than a birth of Wit. Now, in the first place, those so many ages, if you weigh the case truly, shrink into a very small compass. For out of the five and twenty centuries over which the memory and learning of men extends, you can hardly pick out six that were fertile in sciences or favourable to their development. In times no less than in regions there are wastes and deserts. For only three revolutions and periods of learning can properly be reckoned: one among the Greeks, the second among the Romans, and the last among us, that is to say, the nations of Western Europe; and to each of these hardly two centuries can justly be assigned. The intervening ages of the world, in respect of any rich or flourishing growth of the sciences, were unprosperous. For neither the Arabians nor the Schoolmen need be mentioned, who in the intermediate times rather crushed the sciences with a multitude of treatises than increased their weight. And therefore the first cause of so meagre a progress in the sciences is duly and orderly referred to the narrow limits of the time that has been favourable to them.

LXXX

To this it may be added that natural philosophy, even among those who have attended to it, has scarcely ever possessed, especially in these later times, a disengaged and whole man (unless it were some monk studying in his cell, or some gentleman in his country-house), but that it has been made merely a passage and bridge to something else. And so this great mother of the sciences has with strange indignity been degraded to the offices of a servant, having to attend on the business of medicine or mathematics, and likewise to wash and imbue youthful and unripe wits with a sort of first dye, in order that they may be the fitter to receive another afterwards. Meanwhile let no man look for much progress in the sciences – especially in the practical part of them – unless natural philosophy be carried on and applied to particular sciences, and particular sciences be carried back again to natural philosophy. For want of this, astronomy, optics, music, a number of mechanical arts, medicine itself – nay, what one might more wonder at, moral and political philosophy, and the logical sciences – altogether lack profoundness, and merely glide along the surface and variety of things; because after these particular sciences have been once distributed and established, they are no more nourished by natural philosophy; which might have drawn out of the true contemplation of motions, rays, sounds, texture and configuration of bodies, affections, and intellectual perceptions, the means of imparting to them fresh strength and growth. And therefore it is nothing strange if the sciences grow not, seeing they are parted from their roots.

LXXXI

Again there is another great and powerful cause why the sciences have made but little progress, which is this. It is not possible to run a course aright when the goal itself has not been rightly placed. Now the true and lawful goal of the sciences is none other than this: that human life be endowed with new discoveries and powers. But of this the great majority have no feeling, but are merely hireling and professorial, except when it occasionally happens that some workman of acuter wit and covetous of honour applies himself to a new invention, which he mostly does at the expense of his fortunes. But in general, so far are men from proposing to themselves to augment the mass of arts and sciences, that from the mass already at hand they neither take nor look for anything more than what they may turn to use in their lectures, or to gain, or to reputation, or to some similar advantage. And if any one out of all the multitude court science with honest affection and for her own sake, yet even with him the object will be found to be rather the variety of contemplations and doctrines than the severe and rigid search after truth. And if by chance there be one who seeks after truth in earnest, yet even he will propose to himself such a kind of truth as shall yield satisfaction to the mind and understanding in rendering causes for things long since discovered, and not the truth which shall lead to new assurance of works and new light of axioms. If then the end of the sciences has not as yet been well placed, it is not strange that men have erred as to the means.

LXXXII

And as men have misplaced the end and goal of the sciences, so again, even if they had placed it right, yet they have chosen a way to it which is altogether erroneous and impassable. And an astonishing thing it is to one who rightly considers the matter, that no mortal should have seriously applied himself to the opening and laying out of a road for the human understanding direct from the sense by a course of experiment orderly conducted and well built up, but that all has been left either to the mist of tradition or the whirl and eddy of argument or the fluctuations and mazes of chance and of vague and ill-digested experience. Now let any man soberly and diligently consider what the way is by which men have been accustomed to proceed in the investigation and discovery of things, and in the first place he will no doubt remark a method of discovery very simple and inartificial, which is the most ordinary method, and is no more than this. When a man addresses himself to discover something, he first seeks out and sets before him all that has been said about it by others; then he begins to meditate for himself, and so by much agitation and working of the wit solicits and as it were evokes his own spirit to give him oracles – which method has no foundation at all, but rests only upon opinions and is carried about with them.

Another may perhaps call in logic to discover it for him, but that has no relation to the matter except in name. For logical invention does not discover principles and chief axioms, of which arts are composed, but only such things as appear to be consistent with them. For if you grow more curious and importunate and busy, and question her of probations* and invention of principles or primary axioms, her answer is well known: she refers you to the faith you are bound to give to the principles of each separate art.

There remains simple experience, which, if taken as it comes, is called accident, if sought for, experiment. But this kind of experience is no better than a broom without its band, as the saying is, a mere groping, as of men in the dark that feel all round them for the chance of finding their way, when they had much better wait for daylight, or light a candle, and then go. But the true method of experience on the contrary first lights the candle, and then by means of the candle shows the way, commencing as it does with experience duly ordered and digested, not bungling or erratic, and from it educing axioms, and from established axioms again new experiments; even as it was not without order and method that the divine word operated on the created mass. Let men therefore cease to wonder that the course of science is not yet wholly run, seeing that they have gone altogether astray, either leaving and abandoning experience entirely, or losing their way in it and wandering round and

round as in a labyrinth; whereas a method rightly ordered leads
by an unbroken route through the woods of experience to the
open ground of axioms.

LXXXIII

This evil however has been strangely increased by an opinion
or conceit, which though of long standing is vain and hurtful;
namely, that the dignity of the human mind is impaired by long
and close intercourse with experiments and particulars, subject
to sense and bound in matter; especially as they are laborious
to search, ignoble to meditate, harsh to deliver, illiberal to practise, infinite in number, and minute in subtlety. So that it has
come at length to this, that the true way is not merely deserted,
but shut out and stopped up, experience being, I do not say
abandoned or badly managed, but rejected with disdain.

LXXXIV

Again, men have been kept back as by a kind of enchantment
from progress in the sciences by reverence for antiquity, by the
authority of men accounted great in philosophy, and then by
general consent. Of the last I have spoken above.

As for antiquity, the opinion touching it which men entertain is quite a negligent one, and scarcely consonant with the
word itself. For the old age of the world is to be accounted the
true antiquity; and this is the attribute of our own times, not
of that earlier age of the world in which the ancients lived, and
which, though in respect of us it was the elder, yet in respect
of the world it was the younger. And truly as we look for greater
knowledge of human things and a riper judgment in the old
man than in the young, because of his experience and of the
number and variety of the things which he has seen and heard
and thought of, so in like manner from our age: if it but knew
its own strength and chose to essay and exert it, much more
might fairly be expected than from the ancient times, inasmuch
as it is a more advanced age of the world, and stored and stocked
with infinite experiments and observations.

Nor must it go for nothing that by the distant voyages and travels which have become frequent in our times, many things in nature have been laid open and discovered which may let in new light upon philosophy. And surely it would be disgraceful if, while the regions of the material globe – that is, of the earth, of the sea, and of the stars – have been in our times laid widely open and revealed, the intellectual globe should remain shut up within the narrow limits of old discoveries.

And with regard to authority, it shows a feeble mind to grant so much to authors and yet deny time his rights, who is the author of authors, nay rather of all authority. For rightly is truth called the daughter of time,[16] not of authority. It is no wonder therefore if those enchantments of antiquity and authority and consent have so bound up men's powers that they have been made impotent (like persons bewitched) to accompany with the nature of things.

XC

Again, in the customs and institutions of schools, academies, colleges, and similar bodies destined for the abode of learned men and the cultivation of learning, everything is found adverse to the progress of science. For the lectures and exercises there are so ordered that to think or speculate on anything out of the common way can hardly occur to any man. And if one or two have the boldness to use any liberty of judgment, they must undertake the task all by themselves; they can have no advantage from the company of others. And if they can endure this also, they will find their industry and largeness of mind no slight hindrance to their fortune. For the studies of men in these places are confined and as it were imprisoned in the writings of certain authors, from whom if any man dissent he is straightway arraigned as a turbulent person and an innovator. But surely there is a great distinction between matters of state and the arts, for the danger from new motion and from new light is not the same. In matters of state a change even for the better is dis-

[16] See Aulus Gellius, *Attic Nights*, XII.11.

trusted, because it unsettles what is established, these things resting on authority, consent, fame and opinion, not on demontration. But arts and sciences should be like mines, where the noise of new works and further advances is heard on every side. But though the matter be so according to right reason, it is not so acted on in practice; and the points above mentioned in the administration and government of learning put a severe restraint upon the advancement of the sciences.

XCI

Nay, even if that jealousy were to cease, still it is enough to check the growth of science, that efforts and labours in this field go unrewarded. For it does not rest with the same persons to cultivate sciences and to reward them. The growth of them comes from great wits; the prizes and rewards of them are in the hands of the people or of great persons, who are but in very few cases even moderately learned. Moreover this kind of progress is not only unrewarded with prizes and substantial benefits; it has not even the advantage of popular applause. For it is a greater matter than the generality of men can take in, and is apt to be overwhelmed and extinguished by the gales of popular opinions. And it is nothing strange if a thing not held in honour does not prosper.

XCII

But by far the greatest obstacle to the progress of science and to the undertaking of new tasks and provinces therein is found in this – that men despair and think things impossible. For wise and serious men are wont in these matters to be altogether distrustful, considering with themselves the obscurity of nature, the shortness of life, the deceitfulness of the senses, the weakness of the judgment, the difficulty of experiment and the like; and so supposing that in the revolution of time and of the ages of the world the sciences have their ebbs and flows; that at one season they grow and flourish, at another wither and decay, yet in such sort that when they have reached a certain point and condition they can advance no further. If therefore any one believes or promises more, they think this comes of an ungoverned and unripened mind, and that such attempts have prosperous beginnings, become difficult as they go on, and end in confusion. Now since these are thoughts which naturally present themselves to grave men and of great judgment, we must take good heed that we be not led away by our love for a most fair and excellent object to relax or diminish the severity of our judgment; we must observe diligently what encouragement dawns upon us and from what quarter; and, putting aside the lighter breezes of hope, we must thoroughly sift and examine those which promise greater steadiness and constancy. Nay, and we must take state-prudence too into our counsels, whose rule is to distrust and to take the less favourable view of human affairs. I am now therefore to speak touching Hope, especially as I am not a dealer in promises, and wish neither to force nor to ensnare men's judgments, but to lead them by the hand with their good will. And though the strongest means of inspiring hope will be to bring men to particulars, especially to particulars digested and arranged in my Tables of Discovery (the subject partly of the second, but much more of the fourth part of my Instauration), since this is not merely the promise of the thing but the thing itself; nevertheless that everything may be done with gentleness, I will proceed with my plan of preparing men's minds, of which preparation to give hope is no unimportant part. For without it the rest tends rather to make men sad (by giving them a worse and a meaner opinion of things as they are than they now have, and making them more fully to feel and know the unhappiness of their own condition) than to induce any alacrity or to whet their industry in making trial. And therefore it is fit that I publish and set forth those conjectures of mine which make hope in this matter reasonable, just as Columbus did before that wonderful voyage of his across the Atlantic, when he gave the reasons for his conviction that new lands and continents might be discovered besides those which were known before; which reasons, though rejected at first, were afterwards made good by experience, and were the causes and beginnings of great events.

XCV

Those who have handled sciences have been either men of experiment or men of dogmas. The men of experiment are like the ant: they only collect and use; the reasoners resemble spiders, who make cobwebs out of their own substance.[17] But the bee takes a middle course: it gathers its material from the flowers of the garden and of the field, but transforms and digests it by a power of its own. Not unlike this is the true business of philosophy, for it neither relies solely or chiefly on the powers of the mind, nor does it take the matter which it gathers from natural history and mechanical experiments and lay it up in the memory whole, as it finds it, but lays it up in the understanding altered and digested. Therefore from a closer and purer league between these two faculties, the experimental and the rational (such as has never yet been made), much may be hoped.

XCVII

No one has yet been found so firm of mind and purpose as resolutely to compel himself to sweep away all theories and common notions, and to apply the understanding, thus made fair and even, to a fresh examination of particulars. Thus it happens that human knowledge, as we have it, is a mere medley and ill-digested mass, made up of much credulity and much accident, and also of the childish notions which we at first imbibed.

Now if any one of ripe age, unimpaired senses, and well-purged mind apply himself anew to experience and particulars, better hopes may be entertained of that man. In which point I promise to myself a like fortune to that of Alexander the Great; and let no man tax me with vanity till he have heard the end, for the thing which I mean tends to the putting off of all vanity. For of Alexander and his deeds Æschines spake thus: "Assuredly we do not live the life of mortal men; but to this end were we born, that in after ages wonders might be told of

[17] See Stobaeus, *Florilegium*, LXXXII.

us;"[18] as if what Alexander had done seemed to him miraculous. But in the next age Titus Livius took a better and a deeper view of the matter, saying in effect that Alexander "had done no more than take courage to despise vain apprehensions".[19] And a like judgment I suppose may be passed on myself in future ages: that I did no great things, but simply made less account of things that were accounted great. In the meanwhile, as I have already said, there is no hope except in a new birth of science; that is, in raising it regularly up from experience and building it afresh, which no one (I think) will say has yet been done or thought of.

XCIX

Again, even in the great plenty of mechanical experiments there is yet a great scarcity of those which are of most use for the information of the understanding. For the mechanic, not troubling himself with the investigation of truth, confines his attention to those things which bear upon his particular work, and will not either raise his mind or stretch out his hand for anything else. But then only will there be good ground of hope for the further advance of knowledge, when there shall be received and gathered together into natural history a variety of experiments, which are of no use in themselves, but simply serve to discover causes and axioms, which I call *Experimenta lucifera*, experiments of *light*, to distinguish them from those which I call *fructifera*, experiments of *fruit*.

Now experiments of this kind have one admirable property and condition: they never miss or fail. For since they are applied, not for the purpose of producing any particular effect, but only of discovering the natural cause of some effect, they answer the end equally well whichever way they turn out; for they settle the question.

---

[18] Aeschines, *On the Crown.*
[19] Livy, IX.17.

C

But not only is a greater abundance of experiments to be sought for and procured, and that too of a different kind from those hitherto tried; an entirely different method, order, and process for carrying on and advancing experience must also be introduced. For experience, when it wanders in its own track, is, as I have already remarked, mere groping in the dark, and confounds men rather than instructs them. But when it shall proceed in accordance with a fixed law, in regular order, and without interruption, then may better things be hoped of knowledge.

CI

But even after such a store of natural history and experience as is required for the work of the understanding, or of philosophy, shall be ready at hand, still the understanding is by no means competent to deal with it offhand and by memory alone; no more than if a man should hope by force of memory to retain and make himself master of the computation of an ephemeris. And yet hitherto more has been done in matter of invention by thinking than by writing; and experience has not yet learned her letters. Now no course of invention can be satisfactory unless it be carried on in writing. But when this is brought into use, and experience has been taught to read and write, better things may be hoped.

CII

Moreover, since there is so great a number and army of particulars, and that army so scattered and dispersed as to distract and confound the understanding, little is to be hoped for from the skirmishings and slight attacks and desultory movements of the intellect, unless all the particulars which pertain to the subject of inquiry shall, by means of Tables of Discovery, apt, well arranged, and, as it were, animate, be drawn up and marshalled; and the mind be set to work upon the helps duly prepared and digested which these tables supply.

CIII

But after this store of particulars has been set out duly and in order before our eyes, we are not to pass at once to the investigation and discovery of new particulars or works; or at any rate if we do so we must not stop there. For although I do not deny that when all the experiments of all the arts shall have been collected and digested, and brought within one man's knowledge and judgment, the mere transferring of the experiments of one art to others may lead, by means of that experience which I term *literate*,[20] to the discovery of many new things of service to the life and state of man, yet it is no great matter that can be hoped from that; but from the new light of axioms, which, having been educed from those particulars by a certain method and rule, shall in their turn point out the way again to new particulars, greater things may be looked for. For our road does not lie on a level, but ascends and descends, first ascending to axioms, then descending to works.

CIV

The understanding must not however be allowed to jump and fly from particulars to remote axioms and of almost the highest generality (such as the first principles, as they are called, of arts and things), and taking stand upon them as truths that cannot be shaken, proceed to prove and frame the middle axioms by reference to them, which has been the practice hitherto, the understanding being not only carried that way by a natural impulse but also by the use of syllogistic demonstration trained and inured to it. But then, and then only, may we hope well of the sciences, when in a just scale of ascent and by successive steps not interrupted or broken, we rise from particulars to lesser axioms, and then to middle axioms, one above the other, and last of all to the most general. For the lowest axioms differ but slightly from bare experience, while the highest and most general (which we now have) are notional and abstract and

[20] apparently, pertaining to the ability to arrange disparate things into a meaningful combination.

without solidity. But the middle are the true and solid and living axioms, on which depend the affairs and fortunes of men; and above them again, last of all, those which are indeed the most general, such I mean as are not abstract, but of which those intermediate axioms are really limitations.[21]

The understanding must not therefore be supplied with wings, but rather hung with weights to keep it from leaping and flying. Now this has never yet been done; when it is done, we may entertain better hopes of the sciences.

CV

In establishing axioms another form of induction must be devised than has hitherto been employed, and it must be used for proving and discovering not first principles (as they are called) only, but also the lesser axioms, and the middle, and indeed all. For the induction which proceeds by simple enumeration is childish: its conclusions are precarious and exposed to peril from a contradictory instance, and it generally decides on too small a number of facts, and on those only which are at hand. But the induction which is to be available for the discovery and demonstration of sciences and arts must analyse nature by proper rejections and exclusions, and then, after a sufficient number of negatives, come to a conclusion on the affirmative instances; which has not yet been done or even attempted, save only by Plato, who does indeed employ this form of induction to a certain extent for the purpose of discussing definitions and ideas. But in order to furnish this induction or demonstration well and duly for its work, very many things are to be provided which no mortal has yet thought of; insomuch that greater labour will have to be spent in it than has hitherto been spent on the syllogism. And this induction must be used not only to discover axioms, but also in the formation of notions. And it is in this induction that our chief hope lies.

21 i.e., particular instances.

CVI

But in establishing axioms by this kind of induction, we must also examine and try whether the axiom so established be framed to the measure of those particulars only from which it is derived, or whether it be larger and wider. And if it be larger and wider, we must observe whether by indicating to us new particulars it confirm that wideness and largeness as by a collateral security, that we may not either stick fast in things already known, or loosely grasp at shadows and abstract forms, not at things solid and realised in matter. And when this process shall have come into use, then at last shall we see the dawn of a solid hope.

CVIII

So much then for the removing of despair and the raising of hope through the dismissal or rectification of the errors of past time. We must now see what else there is to ground hope upon. And this consideration occurs at once, that if many useful discoveries have been made by accident or upon occasion, when men were not seeking for them but were busy about other things, no one can doubt but that when they apply themselves to seek and make this their business, and that too by method and in order and not by desultory impulses, they will discover far more. For although it may happen once or twice that a man shall stumble on a thing by accident which, when taking great pains to search for it, he could not find, yet upon the whole it unquestionably falls out the other way. And therefore far better things, and more of them, and at shorter intervals, are to be expected from man's reason and industry and direction and fixed application than from accident and animal instinct and the like, in which inventions have hitherto had their origin.

CXI

There is another ground of hope that must not be omitted. Let men but think over their infinite expenditure of understanding, time, and means on matters and pursuits of far less use and value; whereof if but a small part were directed to sound and solid studies, there is no difficulty that might not be overcome. This I thought good to add, because I plainly confess that a collection of history natural and experimental, such as I conceive it and as it ought to be, is a great, I may say a royal, work, and of much labour and expense.

CXII

Meantime, let no man be alarmed at the multitude of particulars, but let this rather encourage him to hope. For the particular phenomena of art and nature are but a handful to the inventions of the wit, when disjoined and separated from the evidence of things. Moreover this road has an issue in the open ground and not far off; the other has no issue at all, but endless entanglement. For men hitherto have made but short stay with experience, but passing her lightly by, have wasted an infinity of time on meditations and glosses of the wit. But if some one were by that could answer our questions and tell us in each case what the fact in nature is, the discovery of all causes and sciences would be but the work of a few years.

CXV

Concerning the grounds then for putting away despair, which has been one of the most powerful causes of delay and hindrance to the progress of knowledge, I have now spoken. And this also concludes what I had to say touching the *signs* and *causes* of the errors, sluggishness, and ignorance which have prevailed, especially since the more subtle causes, which do not fall under popular judgment and observation, must be referred to what has been said on the Idols of the human mind.

And here likewise should close that part of my Instauration which is devoted to pulling down, which part is performed by three refutations: first, by the refutation of the *natural human reason*, left to itself; secondly, by the refutation of the *demonstrations*; and thirdly, by the refutation of the *theories*, or the received systems of philosophy and doctrine. And the refutation of these has been such as alone it could be, that is to say, by signs and the evidence of causes, since no other kind of confutation was open to me, differing as I do from others both on first principles and on rules of demonstration.

It is time therefore to proceed to the art itself and rule of interpreting nature; still, however, there remains something to be premised. For whereas in this first book of aphorisms I proposed to prepare men's minds as well for understanding as for receiving what is to follow; now that I have purged and swept and levelled the floor of the mind, it remains that I place the mind in a good position and as it were in a favourable aspect towards what I have to lay before it. For in a new matter it is not only the strong preoccupation of some old opinion that tends to create a prejudice, but also a false preconception or prefiguration of the new thing which is presented. I will endeavour therefore to impart sound and true opinions as to the things I propose, although they are to serve only for the time, and by way of interest (so to speak), till the thing itself, which is the principal, be fully known.

CXVI

First, then, I must request men not to suppose that after the fashion of ancient Greeks and of certain moderns, as Telesius, Patricius, Severinus,[22] I wish to found a new sect in philosophy. For this is not what I am about; nor do I think that it matters much to the fortunes of men what abstract notions one may entertain concerning nature and the principles of things; and no doubt many old theories of this kind can be revived and many new ones introduced, just as many theories of the heavens may be supposed, which agree well enough with the phenomena and yet differ with each other.

But for my part I do not trouble myself with any such speculative and withal unprofitable matters. My purpose, on the con-

---

[22] all anti-Aristotelian system-builders. Bernardino Telesio (1509-88): Italian empiricist, with whose work *On the Nature of Things* Bacon was very familiar. Fran- cisco Patrizzi (*c.* 1529-97): Italian physicist. Peter Severinus (d. 1602): Danish physician, follower of Paracelsus.

trary, is to try whether I cannot in very fact lay more firmly the foundations, and extend more widely the limits of the power and greatness of man. And although on some special subjects and in an incomplete form I am in possession of results which I take to be far more true and more certain and withal more fruitful than those now received (and these I have collected into the fifth part of my Instauration), yet I have no entire or universal theory to propound. For it does not seem that the time is come for such an attempt. Neither can I hope to live to complete the sixth part of the Instauration (which is destined for the philosophy discovered by the legitimate interpretation of nature), but hold it enough if in the intermediate business I bear myself soberly and profitably, sowing in the meantime for future ages the seeds of a purer truth, and performing my part towards the commencement of the great undertaking.

CXXII

It may be thought also a strange and a harsh thing that we should at once and with one blow set aside all sciences and all authors, and that too without calling in any of the ancients to our aid and support, but relying on our own strength.

And I know that if I had chosen to deal less sincerely, I might easily have found authority for my suggestions by referring them either to the old times before the Greeks (when natural science was perhaps more flourishing, though it made less noise, not having yet passed into the pipes and trumpets of the Greeks) or even, in part at least, to some of the Greeks themselves; and so gained for them both support and honour, as men of no family devise for themselves by the good help of genealogies the nobility of a descent from some ancient stock. But for my part, relying on the evidence and truth of things, I reject all forms of fiction and imposture; nor do I think that it matters any more to the business in hand whether the discoveries that shall now be made were long ago known to the ancients, and have their settings and their risings according to the vicissitude of things and course of ages, than it matters to mankind whether the new world be that island of Atlantis[23] with which the ancients were acquainted, or now discovered for the first time. For new discoveries must be sought from the light of nature, not fetched back out of the darkness of antiquity.

And as for the universality of the censure, certainly if the matter be truly considered, such a censure is not only more probable but more modest, too, than a partial one would be. For if the errors had not been rooted in primary notions, there must have been some true discoveries to correct the false. But the errors being fundamental, and not so much of false judgment as of inattention and oversight, it is no wonder that men have not obtained what they have not tried for, nor reached a mark which they never set up, nor finished a course which they never entered on or kept.

And as for the presumption implied in it, certainly if a man undertakes by steadiness of hand and power of eye to describe a straighter line or more perfect circle than any one else, he challenges a comparison of abilities; but if he only says that he with the help of a rule or a pair of compasses can draw a straighter line or a more perfect circle than any one else can by eye and hand alone, he makes no great boast. And this remark, be it observed, applies not merely to this first and inceptive attempt of mine, but to all that shall take the work in hand hereafter. For my way of discovering sciences goes far to level men's wits, and leaves but little to individual excellence, because it performs everything by the surest rules and demonstrations. And therefore I attribute my part in all this, as I have often said, rather to good luck than to ability, and account it a birth of time rather than of wit. For certainly chance has something to do with men's thoughts, as well as with their works and deeds.

CXXIV

Again, it will be thought, no doubt, that the goal and mark of knowledge which I myself set up (the very point which I object

[23] See Plato, *Timaeus*, 25; *Critias*, 113C to end.

to in others) is not the true or the best; for that the contemplation of truth is a thing worthier and loftier than all utility and magnitude of works, and that this long and anxious dwelling with experience and matter and the fluctuations of individual things drags down the mind to earth, or rather sinks it to a very Tartarus of turmoil and confusion, removing and withdrawing it from the serene tranquillity of abstract wisdom, a condition far more heavenly. Now to this I readily assent; and indeed this which they point at as so much to be preferred is the very thing of all others which I am about. For I am building in the human understanding a true model of the world, such as it is in fact, not such as a man's own reason would have it to be; a thing which cannot be done without a very diligent dissection and anatomy of the world. But I say that those foolish and apish images of worlds which the fancies of men have created in philosophical systems must be utterly scattered to the winds. Be it known then how vast a difference there is (as I said above) between the Idols of the human mind and the Ideas of the divine. The former are nothing more than arbitrary abstractions; the latter are the creator's own stamp upon creation, impressed and defined in matter by true and exquisite lines. Truth, therefore, and utility are here the very same things, and works themselves are of greater value as pledges of truth than as contributing to the comforts of life.

CXXVI

It will also be thought that by forbidding men to pronounce and to set down principles as established until they have duly arrived through the intermediate steps at the highest generalities, I maintain a sort of suspension of the judgment, and bring it to what the Greeks call *Acatalepsia*, a denial of the capacity of the mind to comprehend truth. But in reality that which I meditate and propound is not *Acatalepsia* but *Eucatalepsia*, not denial of the capacity to understand but provision for understanding truly; for I do not take away authority from the senses, but supply them with helps; I do not slight the understanding, but govern it. And better surely it is that we should know all we need to know, and yet think our knowledge imperfect, than that we should think our knowledge perfect, and yet know anything we need to know.

CXXVII

It may also be asked (in the way of doubt rather than objection) whether I speak of natural philosophy only, or whether I mean that the other sciences, logic, ethics, and politics, should be carried on by this method. Now I certainly mean what I have said to be understood of them all; and as the common logic, which governs by the syllogism, extends not only to natural but to all sciences, so does mine also, which proceeds by induction, embrace everything. For I form a history and tables of discovery for anger, fear, shame, and the like; for matters political; and again for the mental operations of memory, composition and division,[24] judgment, and the rest; not less than for heat and cold, or light, or vegetation, or the like. But nevertheless since my method of interpretation, after the history has been prepared and duly arranged, regards not the working and discourse of the mind only (as the common logic does) but the nature of things also, I supply the mind with such rules and guidance that it may in every case apply itself aptly to the nature of things. And therefore I deliver many and diverse precepts in the doctrine of Interpretation, which in some measure modify the method of invention according to the quality and condition of the subject of the inquiry.

CXXVIII

On one point not even a doubt ought to be entertained; namely, whether I desire to pull down and destroy the philosophy and arts and sciences which are at present in use. So far from that, I am most glad to see them used, cultivated, and honoured. There is no reason why the arts which are now in fashion should

[24] probably "affirmation and negation", following Aristotelian usage. [Fowler]

not continue to supply matter for disputation and ornaments for discourse, to be employed for the convenience of professors and men of business, to be in short like current coin, which passes among men by consent. Nay, I frankly declare that what I am introducing will be but little fitted for such purposes as these, since it cannot be brought down to common apprehension, save by effects and works only. But how sincere I am in my professions of affection and good will towards the received sciences, my published writings, especially the books on the Advancement of Learning, sufficiently show; and therefore I will not attempt to prove it further by words. Meanwhile I give constant and distinct warning that by the methods now in use neither can any great progress be made in the doctrines and contemplative part of sciences, nor can they be carried out to any magnitude of works.

CXXIX

It remains for me to say a few words touching the excellency of the end in view. Had they been uttered earlier, they might have seemed like idle wishes, but now that hopes have been raised and unfair prejudices removed, they may perhaps have greater weight. Also if I had finished all myself, and had no occasion to call in others to help and take part in the work, I should even now have abstained from such language lest it might be taken as a proclamation of my own deserts. But since I want to quicken the industry and rouse and kindle the zeal of others, it is fitting that I put men in mind of some things.

In the first place, then, the introduction of famous discoveries appears to hold by far the first place among human actions; and this was the judgment of the former ages. For to the authors of inventions they awarded divine honours; while to those who did good service in the state (such as founders of cities and empires, legislators, saviours of their country from long endured evils, quellers of tyrannies, and the like) they decreed no higher honours than heroic. And certainly if a man rightly compare the two, he will find that this judgment of antiquity was just.

For the benefits of discoveries may extend to the whole race of man, civil benefits only to particular places; the latter last not beyond a few ages, the former through all time. Moreover, the reformation of a state in civil matters is seldom brought in without violence and confusion; but discoveries carry blessings with them, and confer benefits without causing harm or sorrow to any.

Again, discoveries are as it were new creations, and imitations of God's works, as well sang the poet:

> To man's frail race great Athens long ago
> First gave the seed whence waving harvests grow,
> And *re-created* all our life below.[25]

And it appears worthy of remark in Solomon that, though mighty in empire and in gold, in the magnificence of his works, his court, his household, and his fleet, in the lustre of his name and the worship of mankind, yet he took none of these to glory in, but pronounced that "The glory of God is to conceal a thing; the glory of the king to search it out."[26]

Again, let a man only consider what a difference there is between the life of men in the most civilized province of Europe, and in the wildest and most barbarous districts of New India; he will feel it be great enough to justify the saying that "man is a god to man",[27] not only in regard to aid and benefit, but also by a comparison of condition. And this difference comes not from soil, not from climate, not from race, but from the arts.

Again, it is well to observe the force and virtue and consequences of discoveries, and these are to be seen nowhere more conspicuously than in those three which were unknown to the ancients, and of which the origin, though recent, is obscure and inglorious; namely, printing, gunpowder, and the magnet. For these three have changed the whole face and state of things throughout the world: the first in literature, the second in warfare, the third in navigation; whence have followed innumer-

---

[25] Lucretius, *On the Nature of Things*, VI.1-3.

[26] Prov. 25:2.

[27] There is a Latin proverb that says, "Man is to man either a god or a wolf." But cf. Caecilius: "Man is a god to man, if he knows how to do his duty." New India: West Indies.

able changes, insomuch that no empire, no sect, no star seems to have exerted greater power and influence in human affairs than these mechanical discoveries.

Further, it will not be amiss to distinguish the three kinds and, as it were, grades of ambition in mankind. The first is of those who desire to extend their own power in their native country, which kind is vulgar and degenerate. The second is of those who labour to extend the power of their country and its dominion among men. This certainly has more dignity, though not less covetousness. But if a man endeavour to establish and extend the power and dominion of the human race itself over the universe, his ambition (if ambition it can be called) is without doubt both a more wholesome thing and a more noble than the other two. Now the empire of man over things depends wholly on the arts and sciences. For we cannot command nature except by obeying her.

Again, if men have thought so much of some one particular discovery as to regard him as more than man who has been able by some benefit to make the whole human race his debtor, how much higher a thing to discover that by means of which all things else shall be discovered with ease! And yet (to speak the whole truth), as the uses of light are infinite in enabling us to walk, to ply our arts, to read, to recognize one another – and nevertheless the very beholding of the light is itself a more excellent and a fairer thing than all the uses of it – so assuredly the very contemplation of things as they are, without superstition or imposture, error or confusion, is in itself more worthy than all the fruit of inventions.

Lastly, if the debasement of arts and sciences to purposes of wickedness, luxury, and the like, be made a ground of objection, let no one be moved thereby. For the same may be said of all earthly goods: of wit, courage, strength, beauty, wealth, light itself, and the rest. Only let the human race recover that right over nature which belongs to it by divine bequest, and let power be given it: the exercise thereof will be governed by sound reason and true religion.

CXXX

And now it is time for me to propound the art itself of interpreting nature, in which, although I conceive that I have given true and most useful precepts, yet I do not say either that it is absolutely necessary (as if nothing could be done without it) or that it is perfect. For I am of opinion that if men had ready at hand a just history of nature and experience, and laboured diligently thereon, and if they could bind themselves to two rules – the first, to lay aside received opinions and notions, and the second, to refrain the mind for a time from the highest generalizations, and those next to them – they would be able by the native and genuine force of the mind, without any other art, to fall into my form of interpretation. For interpretation is the true and natural work of the mind when freed from impediments. It is true however that by my precepts everything will be in more readiness, and much more sure.

Nor again do I mean to say that no improvement can be made upon these. On the contrary, I, that regard the mind not only in its own faculties but in its connection with things, must needs hold that the art of discovery may advance as discoveries advance.

[BOOK II]

Aphorisms

THE INTERPRETATION OF NATURE

AND

THE KINGDOM OF MAN

I

ON a given body to generate and superinduce a new nature or new natures is the work and aim of Human Power. Of a given nature to discover the form, or true specific difference, or nature-engendering nature,[1] or source of emanation (for these are the terms which come nearest to a description of the thing) is the work and aim of Human Knowledge. Subordinate to these primary works are two others that are secondary and of inferior mark: to the former, the transformation of concrete bodies, so far as as this is possible; to the latter, the discovery, in every case of generation and motion, of the *latent process* carried on from the manifest efficient and the manifest material to the form which is engendered; and in like manner the discovery of the *latent configuration* of bodies at rest and not in motion.

II

In what an ill condition human knowledge is at the present time is apparent even from the commonly received maxims. It is a correct position* that "true knowledge is knowledge by

[1] See Aquinas, *Summa Theologica*, II¹.Q.LXXV.6; Aristotle, *Metaphysics*, III.4 (999ª-1001ᵇ). In this and the next aphorism Bacon uses the Aristotelian terminology, although "form" means for him (usually) a law of nature or universal principle governing bodies or phenomena, "the very thing itself", its particular reality independent of human cognition or senses.

causes". And causes again are not improperly distributed into four kinds: the material, the formal, the efficient, and the final. But of these the final cause rather corrupts than advances the sciences, except such as have to do with human action. The discovery of the formal is despaired of. The efficient and the material (as they are investigated and received, that is, as remote causes, without reference to the latent process leading to the form) are but slight and superficial, and contribute little, if anything, to true and active science. Nor have I forgotten that in a former passage I noted and corrected as an error of the human mind the opinion that Forms give existence. For though in nature nothing really exists beside individual bodies performing pure individual acts according to a fixed law, yet in philosophy this very law and the investigation, discovery, and explanation of it is the foundation as well of knowledge as of operation. And it is this law, with its clauses, that I mean when I speak of *Forms*, a name which I the rather adopt because it has grown into use and become familiar.

III

If a man be acquainted with the cause of any nature (as whiteness or heat) in certain subjects only, his knowledge is imperfect, and if he be able to superinduce an effect on certain substances only (of those susceptible of such effect), his power is in like manner imperfect. Now if a man's knowledge be confined to the efficient and material causes (which are unstable causes, and merely vehicles or causes which convey the form in certain cases), he may arrive at new discoveries in reference to substances in some degree similar to one another, and selected beforehand, but he does not touch the deeper boundaries of things. But whosoever is acquainted with Forms embraces the unity of nature in substances the most unlike, and is able therefore to detect and bring to light things never yet done, and such as neither the vicissitudes of nature, nor industry in experimenting, nor accident itself would ever have brought into act, and which would never have occurred to the thought of man. From the discovery of Forms therefore result truth in speculation and freedom in operation.

IV

Although the roads to human power and to human knowledge lie close together and are nearly the same, nevertheless on account of the pernicious and inveterate habit of dwelling on abstractions, it is safer to begin and raise the sciences from those foundations which have relation to practice, and to let the active part itself be as the seal which prints and determines the contemplative counterpart. We must therefore consider, if a man wanted to generate and superinduce any nature upon a given body, what kind of rule or direction or guidance he would most wish for, and express the same in the simplest and least abstruse language. For instance, if a man wishes to superinduce upon silver the yellow colour of gold or an increase of weight (observing the laws of matter), or transparency on an opaque stone, or tenacity on glass, or vegetation on some substance that is not vegetable, we must consider, I say, what kind of rule or guidance he would most desire. And in the first place, he will undoubtedly wish to be directed to something which will not deceive him in the result, nor fail him in the trial. Secondly, he will wish for such a rule as shall not tie him down to certain means and particular modes of operation. For perhaps he may not have those means, nor be able conveniently to procure them. And if there be other means and other methods for producing the required nature (beside the one prescribed) these may perhaps be within his reach, and yet he shall be excluded by the narrowness of the rule, and get no good from them. Thirdly, he will desire something to be shown him, which is not as difficult as the thing proposed to be done, but comes nearer to practice.

For a true and perfect rule of operation, then, the direction will be *that it be certain, free, and disposing or leading to action*. And this is the same thing with the discovery of the true Form. For the Form of a nature is such that given the Form the nature infallibly follows. Therefore it is always present when the nature is present, and universally implies it, and is constantly inherent in it. Again, the Form is such that if it be taken away the nature infallibly vanishes. Therefore it is always absent when the nature is absent, and implies its absence, and inheres in nothing else. Lastly, the true Form is such that it deduces the given nature from some source of being which is inherent in more natures, and which is better known in the natural order of things than the Form itself. For a true and perfect axiom of knowledge, then, the direction and precept will be, *that another nature be discovered which is convertible with the given nature, and yet is a limitation of a more general nature, as of a true and real genus.* Now these two directions, the one active the other contemplative, are one and the same thing; and what in operation is most useful, that in knowledge is most true.

V

The rule or axiom for the transformation of bodies is of two kinds. The first regards a body as a troop or collection of simple natures. In gold, for example, the following properties meet. It is yellow in colour; heavy up to a certain weight; malleable or ductile to a certain degree of extension; it is not volatile, and loses none of its substance by the action of fire; it turns into a liquid with a certain degree of fluidity; it is separated and dissolved by particular means; and so on for the other natures which meet in gold. This kind of axiom, therefore, deduces the thing from the forms of simple natures. For he who knows the forms of yellow, weight, ductility, fixity, fluidity, solution, and so on, and the methods of superinducing them, and their gradations and modes, will make it his care to have them joined together in some body, whence may follow the transformation of that body into gold. And this kind of operation pertains to the first kind of action. For the principle of generating some one simple nature is the same as that of generating many, only that a man is more fettered and tied down in operation, if more are required, by reason of the difficulty of combining into one so many natures, which do not readily meet, except in the beaten and ordinary paths of nature. It must be said however that this mode of operation (which looks to simple natures though in a compound body) proceeds from what in nature is constant and eternal and universal, and opens broad roads to human power, such as (in the present state of things) human thought can scarcely comprehend or anticipate.

The second kind of axiom, which is concerned with the discovery of the *latent process*, proceeds not by simple natures, but by compound bodies, as they are found in nature in its ordinary course. As, for instance, when inquiry is made from what beginnings and by what method and by what process gold or any other metal or stone is generated, from its first menstrua[2] and rudiments up to the perfect mineral; or in like manner by what process herbs are generated, from the first concretion of juices in the ground or from seeds up to the formed plant, with all the successive motions and diverse and continued efforts of nature. So also in the inquiry concerning the process of development in the generation of animals, from coition to birth; and in like manner of other bodies.

It is not however only to the generations of bodies that this investigation extends, but also to other motions and operations of nature. As, for instance, when inquiry is made concerning the whole course and continued action of nutrition, from the first reception of the food to its complete assimilation; or again, concerning the voluntary motion of animals, from the first impression on the imagination and the continued efforts of the spirit up to the bendings and movements of the limbs; or concerning the motion of the tongue and lips and other instruments, and the changes through which it passes till it comes to the utterance of articulate sounds. For these inquiries also relate to natures concrete or combined into one structure, and have regard to what may be called particular and special habits of nature, not to her fundamental and universal laws which constitute Forms. And yet it must be confessed that this plan appears to be readier and to lie nearer at hand and to give more ground for hope than the primary one.

[2] liquid state. Menstruum means solvent.

In like manner the operative which answers to this speculative part, starting from the ordinary incidents of nature, extends its operation to things immediately adjoining, or at least not far removed. But as for any profound and radical operations on nature, they depend entirely on the primary axioms. And in those things too, where man has no means of operating but only of knowing, as in the heavenly bodies (for these he cannot operate upon or change or transform), the investigation of the fact itself or truth of the thing, no less than the knowledge of the causes and consents,* must come from those primary and catholic axioms concerning simple natures, such as the nature of spontaneous rotation, of attraction or magnetism, and of many others which are of a more general form than the heavenly bodies themselves. For let no one hope to decide the question whether it is the earth or heaven that really revolves in the diurnal motion, until he has first comprehended the nature of spontaneous rotation.

VI

But this Latent Process of which I speak is quite another thing than men, preoccupied as their minds now are, will easily conceive. For what I understand by it is not certain measures or signs or successive steps of process in bodies, which can be seen, but a process perfectly continuous, which for the most part escapes the sense.

For instance, in all generation and transformation of bodies, we must inquire what is lost and escapes; what remains, what is added; what is expanded, what contracted; what is united, what separated; what is continued, what cut off; what propels, what hinders; what predominates, what yields; and a variety of other particulars.

Again, not only in the generation or transformation of bodies are these points to be ascertained, but also in all other alterations and motions it should in like manner be inquired what goes before, what comes after; what is quicker, what more tardy; what produces, what governs motion; and like points – all which nevertheless in the present state of the sciences (the texture of which is as rude as possible and good for nothing) are unknown and unhandled. For seeing that every natural action depends on things infinitely small, or at least too small to strike the sense, no one can hope to govern or change nature until he has duly comprehended and observed them.

VII

In like manner the investigation and discovery of the *latent configuration* in bodies is a new thing, no less than the discovery of the Latent Process and of the Form. For as yet we are but lingering in the outer courts of nature, nor are we preparing ourselves a way into her inner chambers. Yet no one can endow a given body with a new nature, or successfully and aptly transmute it into a new body, unless he has attained a competent knowledge of the body so to be altered or transformed. Otherwise he will run into methods which, if not useless, are at any rate difficult and perverse and unsuitable to the nature of the body on which he is operating. It is clear therefore that to this also a way must be opened and laid out.

And it is true that upon the anatomy of organized bodies (as of man and animals) some pains have been well bestowed and with good effect; and a subtle thing it seems to be, and a good scrutiny of nature. Yet this kind of anatomy is subject to sight and sense, and has place only in organized bodies. And besides it is a thing obvious and easy when compared with the true anatomy of the Latent Configuration in bodies which are thought to be of uniform structure, especially in things that have a specific character and their parts, as iron, stone, and again in parts of uniform structure in plants and animals, as the root, the leaf, the flower, flesh, blood, and bones. But even in this kind, human industry has not been altogether wanting; for this is the very thing aimed at in the separation of bodies of uniform structure by means of distillations and other modes of analysis: that the complex structure of the compound may be made apparent by bringing together its several homogeneous parts. And this is of use too, and conduces to the object we are seeking, although too often fallacious in its results, because many natures which are in fact newly brought out and super-induced by fire and heat and other modes of solution are taken to be the effect of separation merely, and to have subsisted in the compound before. And after all, this is but a small part of the work of discovering the true Configuration in the compound body; which Configuration is a thing far more subtle and exact, and such as the operation of fire rather confounds than brings out and makes distinct.

Therefore a separation and solution of bodies must be effected, not by fire indeed, but by reasoning and true induction, with experiments to aid, and by a comparison with other bodies, and a reduction to simple natures and their Forms, which meet and mix in the compound. In a word we must pass from Vulcan to Minerva if we intend to bring to light the true textures and configurations of bodies, on which all the occult and, as they are called, specific properties and virtues in things depend, and from which too the rule of every powerful alteration and trans-formation is derived.

For example, we must inquire what amount of spirit* there is in every body, what of tangible essence; and of the spirit, whether it be copious and turgid, or meagre and scarce, whether it be fine or coarse, akin to air or to fire, brisk or sluggish, weak or strong, progressive or retrograde, interrupted or continuous, agreeing with external and surrounding objects or disagreeing, etc. In like manner we must inquire into the tangible essence (which admits of no fewer differences than the spirit), into its coats, its fibres, its kinds of texture. Moreover the disposition of the spirit throughout the corporeal frame, with its pores, passages, veins and cells, and the rudiments or first essays of the organized body, fall under the same investigation. But on these inquiries also, and I may say on all the discovery of the Latent Configura-tion, a true and clear light is shed by the primary axioms, which entirely dispels all darkness and subtlety.

VIII

Nor shall we thus be led to the doctrine of atoms, which implies the hypothesis of a vacuum and that of the unchangeableness of matter (both false assumptions); we shall be led only to real particles, such as really exist. Nor again is there any reason to be alarmed at the subtlety of the investigation, as if it could not be disentangled; on the contrary, the nearer it approaches to simple natures, the easier and plainer will everything become, the business being transferred from the complicated to the simple, from the incommensurable to the commensurable, from surds to rational quantities, from the infinite and vague to the finite and certain, as in the case of the letters of the alphabet and the notes of music. And inquiries into nature have the best result when they begin with physics and end in mathematics. Again, let no one be afraid of high numbers or minute fractions. For in dealing with numbers it is as easy to set down or conceive a thousand as one, or the thousandth part of an integer as an integer itself.

IX

From the two kinds of axioms which have been spoken of, arises a just division of philosophy and the sciences, taking the received terms (which come nearest to express the thing) in a sense agreeable to my own views. Thus, let the investigation of Forms, which are (in the eye of reason at least, and in their essential law) eternal and immutable, constitute *Metaphysics*; and let the investigation of the Efficient Cause, and of Matter, and of the Latent Process, and the Latent Configuration (all of which have reference to the common and ordinary course of nature, not to her eternal and fundamental laws) constitute *Physics*. And to these let there be subordinate two practical divisions: to Physics, *Mechanics*; to Metaphysics, what (in a purer sense of the word) I call *Magic*, on account of the broadness of the ways it moves in, and its greater command over nature.

X

Having thus set up the mark of knowledge, we must go on to precepts, and that in the most direct and obvious order. Now my directions for the interpretation of nature embrace two generic divisions, the one how to educe and form axioms from experience, the other how to deduce and derive new experiments from axioms. The former again is divided into three ministrations, a ministration to the sense, a ministration to the memory, and a ministration to the mind or reason.

For first of all we must prepare a *Natural and Experimental History*, sufficient and good, and this is the foundation of all; for we are not to imagine or suppose, but to discover, what nature does or may be made to do.

But natural and experimental history is so various and diffuse that it confounds and distracts the understanding, unless it be ranged and presented to view in a suitable order. We must therefore form *Tables and Arrangements of Instances*, in such a method and order that the understanding may be able to deal with them.

And even when this is done, still the understanding, if left to itself and its own spontaneous movements, is incompetent and unfit to form axioms, unless it be directed and guarded. Therefore in the third place we must use *Induction*, true and legitimate induction, which is the very key of interpretation. But of this, which is the last, I must speak first, and then go back to the other ministrations.

XI

The investigation of Forms proceeds thus: a nature being given, we must first of all have a muster or presentation before the understanding of all known instances which agree in the same nature, though in substances the most unlike. And such collection must be made in the manner of a history, without premature speculation, or any great amount of subtlety. For example, let the investigation be into the Form of Heat.[3]

[3] There follows a "Table of Essence and Presence" providing twenty-seven "instances agreeing in the nature of heat" such as the rays of the sun, fiery meteors, bodies rubbed violently, fresh horse dung, etc.

XII

Secondly, we must make a presentation to the understanding of instances in which the given nature is wanting, because the Form, as stated above, ought no less to be absent when the given nature is absent, than present when it is present. But to note all these would be endless.

The negatives should therefore be subjoined to the affirmatives, and the absence of the given nature inquired of in those subjects only that are most akin to the others in which it is present and forthcoming. This I call the *Table of Deviation, or of Absence in Proximity*.[4]

XIII

Thirdly, we must make a presentation to the understanding of instances in which the nature under inquiry is found in different degrees, more or less, which must be done by making a comparison either of its increase and decrease in the same subject, or of its amount in different subjects, as compared one with another. For since the Form of a thing is the very thing itself, and the thing differs from the form no otherwise than as the apparent differs from the real, or the external from the internal, or the thing in reference to man from the thing in reference to the universe, it necessarily follows that no nature can be taken as the true form unless it always decrease when the nature in question decreases, and in like manner always increase when the nature in question increases. This Table therefore I call the *Table of Degrees* or the *Table of Comparison*.[5]

XIV

How poor we are in history any one may see from the foregoing tables, where I not only insert sometimes mere traditions and reports (though never without a note of doubtful credit and

---

[4] There follow twenty-seven "instances in proximity where the nature of heat is absent"; these parallel the preceding instances, as Bacon examines conditions under which the sun's rays, meteors, rubbed bodies, etc. do not or may not produce heat.

[5] The Table gives forty-one instances of different degrees of heat.

authority) in place of history proved and instances certain, but am also frequently forced to use the words "Let trial be made," or "Let it be further inquired."

XV

The work and office of these three tables I call the Presentation of Instances to the Understanding. Which presentation having been made, Induction itself must be set at work; for the problem is, upon a review of the instances, all and each, to find such a nature as is always present or absent with the given nature, and always increases and decreases with it, and which is, as I have said, a particular case of a more general nature. Now if the mind attempt this affirmatively from the first, as when left to itself it is always wont to do, the result will be fancies and guesses and notions ill defined, and axioms that must be mended every day, unless like the schoolmen we have a mind to fight for what is false, though doubtless these will be better or worse according to the faculties and strength of the understanding which is at work. To God, truly, the Giver and Architect of Forms, and it may be to the angels and higher intelligences, it belongs to have an affirmative knowledge of forms immediately and from the first contemplation. But this assuredly is more than man can do, to whom it is granted only to proceed at first by negatives, and at last to end in affirmatives, after exclusion has been exhausted.

XVI

We must make therefore a complete solution and separation of nature, not indeed by fire, but by the mind, which is a kind of divine fire. The first work therefore of true induction (as far as regards the discovery of Forms) is the rejection or exclusion of the several natures which are not found in some instance where the given nature is present, or are found in some instance where the given nature is absent, or are found to increase in some instance when the given nature decreases, or to decrease when the given nature increases. Then indeed after the rejection and exclusion has been duly made, there will remain at the bottom, all light opinions vanishing into smoke, a Form affirmative, solid and true and well defined. This is quickly said, but the way to come at it is winding and intricate. I will endeavour however not to overlook any of the points which may help us towards it.

XVII

But when I assign so prominent a part to Forms, I cannot too often warn and admonish men against applying what I say to those forms to which their thoughts and contemplations have hitherto been accustomed.

For in the first place I do not at present speak of Compound Forms, which are, as I have remarked, combinations of simple natures according to the common course of the universe, as of the lion, eagle, rose, gold, and the like. It will be time to treat of these when we come to the Latent Processes and Latent Configurations, and the discovery of them, as they are found in what are called substances or natures concrete.

And even in the case of simple natures I would not be understood to speak of abstract forms and ideas, either not defined in matter at all, or ill defined. For when I speak of Forms, I mean nothing more than those laws and determinations of absolute actuality which govern and constitute any simple nature, as heat, light, weight, in every kind of matter and subject that is susceptible of them. Thus the Form of Heat or the Form of Light is the same thing as the Law of Heat or the Law of Light. Nor indeed do I ever allow myself to be drawn away from things themselves and the operative part. And therefore when I say (for instance) in the investigation of the form of heat, "reject rarity," or "rarity does not belong to the form of heat," it is the same as if I said, "It is possible to superinduce heat on a dense body," or "It is possible to take away or keep out heat from a rare body."

But if any one conceive that my Forms too are of a somewhat abstract nature, because they mix and combine things heterogeneous (for the heat of heavenly bodies and the heat of fire seem to be very heterogeneous; so do the fixed red of the rose or the like, and the apparent red in the rainbow, the opal, or the diamond; so again do the different kinds of death: death by drowning, by hanging, by stabbing, by apoplexy, by atrophy; and yet they agree severally in the nature of heat, redness, death); if any one, I say, be of this opinion, he may be assured that his mind is held in captivity by custom, by the gross appearance of things, and by men's opinions. For it is most certain that these things, however heterogeneous and alien from each other, agree in the Form or Law which governs heat, redness, and death, and that the power of man cannot possibly be emancipated and freed from the common course of nature, and expanded and exalted to new efficients and new modes of operation, except by the revelation and discovery of Forms of this kind. And yet, when I have spoken of this union of nature, which is the point of most importance, I shall proceed to the divisions and veins* of nature, as well the ordinary as those that are more inward and exact, and speak of them in their place.

XVIII

I must now give an example of the Exclusion or Rejection of natures which by the Tables of Presentation are found not to belong to the Form of Heat, observing in the meantime that not only each table suffices for the rejection of any nature, but even any one of the particular instances contained in any of the tables. For it is manifest from what has been said that any one contradictory instance overthrows a conjecture as to the Form. But nevertheless, for clearness' sake and that the use of the tables may be more plainly shown, I sometimes double or multiply an exclusion.[6]

---

[6] Bacon gives fourteen examples of rejection of natures (i.e., characteristics) not belonging to the Form ("laws and determinations of absolute actuality") of heat; for example, he rejects "rarity" because gold, which is dense, may be ignited, and air, which is rarefied, is usually cold.

XIX

In the process of Exclusion are laid the foundations of true Induction, which however is not completed till it arrives at an Affirmative. Nor is the Exclusive part itself at all complete, nor indeed can it possibly be so at first. For Exclusion is evidently the rejection of simple natures; and if we do not yet possess sound and true notions of simple natures, how can the process of Exclusion be made accurate? Now some of the above-mentioned notions (as that of the nature of the elements, of the nature of heavenly bodies, of rarity) are vague and ill-defined. I, therefore, well knowing and nowise forgetting how great a work I am about (viz., that of rendering the human understanding a match for things and nature), do not rest satisfied with the precepts I have laid down, but proceed further to devise and supply more powerful aids for the use of the understanding, which I shall now subjoin. And assuredly in the Interpretation of Nature the mind should by all means be so prepared and disposed that while it rests and finds footing in due stages and degrees of certainty, it may remember withal (especially at the beginning) that what it has before it depends in great measure upon what remains behind.

XX

And yet since truth will sooner come out from error than from confusion, I think it expedient that the understanding should have permission, after the three Tables of First Presentation (such as I have exhibited) have been made and weighed, to make an essay of the Interpretation of Nature in the affirmative way; on the strength both of the instances given in the tables, and of any others it may meet with elsewhere. Which kind of essay I call the *Indulgence of the Understanding*, or the *Commencement of Interpretation*, or the *First Vintage*.[7]

---

[7] After a lengthy consideration of the different instances of heat in the three Tables of First Presentation, Bacon arrives at the following definition: "*Heat is a motion, expansive, restrained, and acting in its strife upon the smaller particles of bodies.* But the expansion is thus modified: *while it expands all ways, it has at the same time an inclination upwards.* And the struggle in the particles is modified also: *it is not sluggish, but hurried and with violence.*"

XXI

The Tables of First Presentation and the Rejection or process of Exclusion being completed, and also the First Vintage being made thereupon, we are to proceed to the other helps of the understanding in the Interpretation of Nature and true and perfect Induction. In propounding which, I mean, when Tables are necessary, to proceed upon the Instances of Heat and Cold, but when a smaller number of examples will suffice, I shall proceed at large; so that the inquiry may be kept clear, and yet more room be left for the exposition of the system.

I propose to treat then, in the first place, of *Prerogative Instances*; secondly, of the *Supports of Induction*; thirdly, of the *Rectification of Induction*; fourthly, of *Varying the Investigation according to the nature of the Subject*; fifthly, of *Prerogative Natures* with respect to Investigation, or of what should be inquired first and what last; sixthly, of the *Limits of Investigation*, or a Synopsis of all Natures in the Universe; seventhly, of the *Application to Practice*, or of things in their relation to Man; eighthly, of *Preparations for Investigation*; and lastly, of the *Ascending and Descending Scale of Axioms*.[8]

LII

So much then for the Dignities or Prerogatives of Instances. It must be remembered however that in this Organum of mine I am handling logic, not philosophy. But since my logic aims to teach and instruct the understanding, not that it may with the slender tendrils of the mind snatch at and lay hold of abstract notions (as the common logic does), but that it may in very truth dissect nature, and discover the virtues and actions of bodies, with their laws as determined in matter − so that this science flows not merely from the nature of the mind, but also from the nature of things − no wonder that it is everywhere

---

[8] Bacon goes on to consider the first, Prerogative Instances (generalized categories of phenomena), at considerable length. The others, however, he never recorded, except for the eighth, which appeared, in part at least, as the *Parasceve* or *Preparative towards a Natural and Experimental History*.

sprinkled and illustrated with speculations and experiments in nature, as examples of the art I teach. . . .

But now I must proceed to the supports and rectifications of Induction, and then to concretes, and Latent Processes, and Latent Configurations, and the rest, as set forth in order in the twenty-first Aphorism, that at length (like an honest and faithful guardian) I may hand over to men their fortunes, now their understanding is emancipated and come as it were of age; whence there cannot but follow an improvement in man's estate and an enlargement of his power over nature. For man by the fall fell at the same time from his state of innocency and from his dominion over creation. Both of these losses however can even in this life be in some part repaired, the former by religion and faith, the latter by arts and sciences. For creation was not by the curse made altogether and for ever a rebel, but in virtue of that charter "In the sweat of thy face shalt thou eat bread," it is now by various labours (not certainly by disputations or idle magical ceremonies, but by various labours) at length and in some measure subdued to the supplying of man with bread, that is, to the uses of human life.

END OF THE SECOND BOOK OF THE NEW ORGANUM

De Dignitate et Augmentis

Scientiarum Libri IX

1623

Nine Books of the Dignity and

Advancement of Learning

BOOK II[1]

Chapter I

The Division of all Human Learning into History, Poesy, Philosophy; *with reference to the three Intellectual Faculties* — Memory, Imagination, *and* Reason; *and that the same division holds good likewise in* Theology.

THE best division of human learning is that derived from the three faculties of the rational soul, which is the seat of learning. History has reference to the Memory, poesy to the Imagination, and philosophy to the Reason. And by poesy here I mean nothing else than feigned history or fables, for verse is but a character of style, and belongs to the arts of speech, whereof I will treat in its proper place.

History is properly concerned with individuals, which are circumscribed by place and time. For though Natural History may seem to deal with species, yet this is only because of the general resemblance which in most cases natural objects of the same species bear to another, so that when you know one, you know all. And if individuals are found which are either unique in their species, like the sun and moon, or notable deviations from their species, like monsters, the description of these has as fit a place in Natural History as that of remarkable men has in Civil History. All this relates to the Memory.

Poesy, in the sense in which I have defined the word, is also concerned with individuals; that is, with individuals invented in imitation of those which are the subject of true history, yet with this difference: that it commonly exceeds the measure of nature, joining at pleasure things which in nature would never have come together, and introducing things which in nature

[1] For the first book, see Book I of the *Advancement of Learning.*

would never have come to pass, just as Painting likewise does. This is the work of Imagination.

Philosophy discards individuals; neither does it deal with the impressions immediately received from them, but with abstract notions derived from these impressions, in the composition and division whereof, according to the law of nature and fact, its business lies. And this is the office and work of Reason.

That these things are so, may be easily seen by observing the commencements of the intellectual process. The sense, which is the door of the intellect, is affected by individuals only. The images of those individuals – that is, the impressions which they make on the sense – fix themselves in the memory, and pass into it in the first instance entire as it were, just as they come. These the human mind proceeds to review and ruminate, and thereupon either simply rehearses them, or makes fanciful imitations of them, or analyses and classifies them. Wherefore from these three fountains, Memory, Imagination, and Reason, flow these three emanations, History, Poesy, and Philosophy; and there can be no others. For I consider history and experience to be the same thing, as also philosophy and the sciences.

Nor do I think that any other division is wanted for Theology. The information derived from revelation and the information derived from the sense differ no doubt both in the matter and in the manner of conveyance, but the human mind is the same, and its repositories and cells the same. It is only like different liquids poured through different funnels into one and the same vessel. Theology therefore in like manner consists either of Sacred History or of Parables, which are a divine poesy, or of Doctrines and Precepts, which are a perennial philosophy. For as for that part which seems supernumerary, which is Prophecy, it is but a kind of history, for divine history has this prerogative over human, that the narration may be before the event as well as after.

Chapter II

The Division of History into Natural *and* Civil, Ecclesiastical *and* Literary *History being included in Civil. Division of Natural History into* History of Generations, Pretergenerations, *and* Arts.

HISTORY is either Natural or Civil. Natural History treats of the deeds and works of nature, Civil History of those of men. Matter of Divinity shows itself no doubt in both, but principally in the latter, so much so as to form a species of history proper to itself, which I call Sacred or Ecclesiastical. And a similar distinction is in my opinion also due to Learning and the Arts – their importance being such as to entitle them to a separate history of their own. And this (as well as the Ecclesiastical) I mean to be included in Civil History.

The division which I will make of Natural History is founded upon the state and condition of nature herself. For I find nature in three different states, and subject to three different conditions of existence. She is either free, and follows her ordinary course of development, as in the heavens, in the animal and vegetable creation, and in the general array of the universe; or she is driven out of her ordinary course by the perverseness, insolence, and frowardness of matter, and violence of impediments, as in the case of monsters; or lastly, she is put in constraint, moulded, and made as it were new by art and the hand of man, as in things artificial. Let Natural History therefore be divided into the History of Generations, of Pretergenerations, and of Arts, which last I also call Mechanical and Experimental History. Of these the first treats of the Freedom of Nature, the second of her Errors, the third of her Bonds. And I am the more induced to set down the History of the Arts as a species of Natural History, because an opinion has long been prevalent that art is something different from nature, and things artificial different from things natural; whence this evil has arisen, that

most writers of Natural History think they have done enough
when they have given an account of animals or plants or minerals, omitting all mention of the experiments of mechanical
arts. But there is likewise another and more subtle error which
has crept into the human mind; namely, that of considering art
as merely an assistant to nature, having the power indeed to finish what nature has begun, to correct her when lapsing into error,
or to set her free when in bondage, but by no means to change,
transmute, or fundamentally alter nature. And this has bred
a premature despair in human enterprises. Whereas men ought
on the contrary to be surely persuaded of this: that the artificial
does not differ from the natural in form or essence but only
in the efficient, in that man has no power over nature except
that of motion; he can put natural bodies together, and he can
separate them; and therefore that wherever the case admits of
the uniting or disuniting of natural bodies, by joining (as they
say) actives with passives, man can do everything; where the
case does not admit this, he can do nothing. Nor matters it,
provided things are put in the way to produce an effect, whether
it be done by human means or otherwise. Gold is sometimes
refined in the fire and sometimes found pure in the sands, nature
having done the work for herself. So also the rainbow is made
in the sky out of a dripping cloud; it is also made here below
with a jet of water. Still, therefore, it is nature which governs
everything; but under nature are included these three: the
course of nature, the *wanderings* of nature, and *art*, or nature
with man to help; which three must therefore all be included
in Natural History, as indeed they are in great measure by Pliny,
the only person who ever undertook a Natural History according to the dignity of it, though he was far from carrying out his
undertaking in a manner worthy of the conception.

The first of these, the history of nature in course, is extant,
and that in moderate perfection, but the two latter are so
weakly and unprofitably handled that they may be set down as
deficient. For you will find no sufficient and competent collection of those works of nature which have a digression and
deflexion from the ordinary course of generations, productions,

and motions; whether they be singularities of place and region, or the strange events of time, or *casuum ingenia* (as they have been called) – devices of chance, or the effects of hidden properties, or productions of nature singular in their kind. It is true, I find books more than enough filled with fabulous experiments, idle secrets, and frivolous impostures, for pleasure and novelty, but a substantial and methodical collection of the Heteroclites or Irregulars of nature well examined and described I find not, especially not with due rejection and as it were public proscription of fables and popular errors. For as things now are, if an untruth in nature once get a footing and be made common, what by reason of men's reverence for antiquity, what by reason of the troublesomeness of putting it to the test anew, and what by reason of the use of the opinion in similitudes and ornaments of speech, it is never overthrown or retracted.

The end of this work, honoured with a precedent in Aristotle, is nothing less than to gratify the appetite of curious and vain wits, as the manner of mirabilaries[1] is to do, but for two reasons, both of great weight: the one to correct the partiality[2] of axioms and opinions, which are framed for the most part upon common and familiar examples; the other, because from the wonders of nature is the most clear and open passage to the wonders of art. For you have but to follow and as it were hound nature in her wanderings, and you will be able, when you like, to lead and drive her afterwards to the same place again. Neither am I of opinion in this history of marvels that superstitious narratives of sorceries, witchcrafts, charms, dreams, divinations, and the like, where there is an assurance and clear evidence of the fact, should be altogether excluded. For it is not yet known in what cases and how far effects attributed to superstition participate of natural causes; and therefore, howsoever the use and practice of such arts is to be condemned, yet from the speculation and consideration of them (if they be diligently unravelled) a useful light may be gained, not only for the true judgment of the offences of persons charged with such practices, but likewise

[1] dealers in wonders or marvels. (The *De Mirabilibus Auscultationibus* that Bacon evokes here is no longer attributed to Aristotle.)
[2] limited nature.

for the further disclosing of the secrets of nature. Neither ought a man to make scruple of entering and penetrating into these holes and corners, when the inquisition of truth is his sole object – as your Majesty has shown in your own example,[3] who with the two clear and acute eyes of religion and natural philosophy have looked deeply and wisely into those shadows, and yet proved yourself to be truly of the nature of the sun, which passes through pollutions and is not defiled. I would recommend, however, that those narrations which are tinctured with superstition be sorted by themselves, and not mingled with those which are purely and sincerely natural. But as for narrations touching the prodigies and miracles of religions, they are either not true or not natural, and therefore impertinent* for the story of nature.

For History of Nature Wrought, or Mechanical as I also call it, I find some collections made of agriculture and likewise of many manual arts, but always (which is a great detriment in this kind of learning) with a neglect and rejection of experiments familiar and vulgar, which yet in the interpretation of nature are of equal, if not of more value than those which are less common. For it is esteemed a kind of dishonour upon learning for learned men to descend to inquiry or meditation upon matters mechanical, except they be such as may be thought secrets of art or rarities and special subtleties. Which humour of vain and supercilious arrogancy is justly derided in Plato, where he brings in Hippias,[4] a vaunting Sophist, disputing with Socrates, a true and unfeigned inquisitor of truth; where, the discourse being touching beauty, Socrates, after his loose and wandering manner of inductions, put first an example of a fair virgin, then of a fair horse, then of a fair pot well glazed. Whereat Hippias was offended, and said, "Were it not for courtesy's sake, I should be loth to dispute with one that did allege such base and sordid instances." Whereunto Socrates answered, "You have reason, and it becomes you well, being a man so trim in your vestments, and so fairly shod," and so goes on

[3] King James had written a book on demonology (1597).

[4] See the *Hippias Major*, 290ff.

in irony. But the truth is that they are not the highest instances which give the best or securest information, as is expressed not inelegantly in the common story of the philosopher[5] who, while he gazed upwards to the stars, fell into the water, for if he had looked down he might have seen the stars in the water, but looking aloft he could not see the water in the stars. So it often comes to pass that mean and small things discover great better than great can discover small, and therefore it was well observed by Aristotle "that the nature of everything is best seen in its smallest portions".[6] For which cause he inquires the nature of a commonwealth first in a family and the simplest conjugations of society – man and wife, parent and child, master and servant – which are present in every cottage. Even so likewise the nature of this great city of the world and the policy thereof must be first sought in its primary concordances[7] and smallest portions; as we see that that secret of nature (esteemed one of the great mysteries) of the turning of iron touched with the loadstone towards the north, was found out not in bars of iron but in needles.

But if my judgment be of any weight, the use of History Mechanical is, of all others, the most radical and fundamental towards natural philosophy; such natural philosophy I mean as shall not vanish in the fumes of subtle or sublime speculations, but such as shall be operative to relieve the inconveniences of man's estate. For it will not only be of immediate benefit by connecting and transferring the observations of one art to the use of others, and thereby discovering new commodities, a result which must needs follow when the experience of different arts shall fall under the observation and consideration of one man's mind; but further, it will give a more true and real illumination concerning the investigation of causes of things and axioms of arts than has hitherto shone upon mankind. For like as a man's disposition is never well known or proved till he be crossed, nor Proteus ever changed shapes till he was straitened and held fast,[8]

[5] Thales. See Plato, *Theaetetus*, 174A; Diogenes Laertius, I.34.

[6] *Politics*, I.1 (1252ᵃ), I.3 (1253ᵇ), etc.; *Physics*, I.1 (184ᵃ).

[7] i.e., basic or primitive relationships.

[8] See, for example, Virgil, *Georgics*, IV.387ff.

so nature exhibits herself more clearly under the trials and vexations of art than when left to herself.

Before I dismiss this part of Natural History (which I call mechanical and experimental) I must add that the body of this kind of history should not be made up from the mechanical arts alone, but also from the operative part of the liberal sciences, as well as from many other practices which have not as yet grown up into arts, so as to omit nothing which may tend to inform the intellect. And this is the first division of Natural History.

Chapter III

The Second Division of Natural History, according to its Use and End, into Narrative *and* Inductive, *and that the noblest end of Natural History is to minister and be in order for the Foundation of Philosophy, which is the end aimed at in* Induction. *The Division of the History of Generations into the History of the* Heavenly Bodies, *the History of* Meteors, *the History of the* Globe of Earth and Sea, *the History of the* Masses *or* Greater Colleges, *and the History of the* Species *or* Lesser Colleges.

NATURAL History, which is threefold (as I said) in subject, is in use twofold. For it is used either for the sake of the knowledge of the things themselves that are committed to the history, or as the primary matter of philosophy. Now the first kind, which aims either to please by the agreeableness of the narrative or to help by the use of experiments, and is pursued for the sake of such pleasure or such profit, I account as far inferior in importance to that which is the stuff and material of a solid and lawful Induction, and may be called the nursing-mother of philosophy. Accordingly I shall now make a second division of Natural History into Narrative and Inductive, the latter whereof I set down as wanting. But let not any one be dazzled either by the great names of ancient philosophers or the great volumes of modern. For I well know that a natural history is extant, larger in its bulk, pleasing in its variety, curious often in its diligence, but yet weed it of fables, antiquities, quotations, idle controversies, philology, and ornaments (which are more fitted for table talk and the *noctes*[1] of learned men than for the instauration of philosophy), and it will shrink into a small compass. Certainly it is very different from that kind of history which I have in view. For in the first place there are wanting those two parts of natural history which I have just mentioned, Pretergenerations and Arts, of which I make great account; and next, in the third and remaining part, that of Generations, only one out of five parts is sufficiently handled. For the history of Generations is composed of five subordinate parts. First, a history of the *Celestial Bodies*, exhibiting the actual phenomena simply and apart from theories. Second, a history of *Meteors* (including comets), and what they call the *Regions of the Air*, for there is no history of comets, fiery meteors, winds, rains, storms, and the like, which is of any value. Third, a history of the *Earth and Sea* (considered as integral parts of the universe), mountains, rivers, tides, sands, woods, islands, and the shapes of continents as they lie, in all these inquiring and observing rather the laws of nature than cosmography. Fourth, a history of the *Common Masses of Matter*, which I call the *Greater Colleges* (commonly called the *Elements*), for I find there are no accounts of fire, air, earth, and water, with their natures, motions, operations, and impressions, such as to form a just body of history. Fifth and last, a history of the *Exquisite Collections of Matter*, which I call the *Lesser Colleges*, but which are generally called *Species*. Now it is only in this last that writers have shown any conspicuous industry, and yet in such sort that they have rather filled it with things superfluous (as figures of animals, plants, and the like) than enriched it with sound and careful observations, which should ever be annexed to natural history. And in a word all the natural history we have, whether in the mode of inquiry or in the matter collected, is quite unfit for the end which I have

---

[1] "night sessions". The natural history is Pliny's, but, perhaps because this chapter is an addition to the *Advancement of Learning*, Bacon seems to have forgotten his mention of Pliny in Chapter II.

mentioned, namely, the Foundation of Philosophy. Wherefore I set down Inductive History as wanting. And so much for Natural History.

Chapter IV

The Division of Civil History into Ecclesiastical, Literary, *and* Civil *(which retains the name of the Genus) and that the History of* Literature *is wanting. Precepts for the Construction of it.*

CIVIL History may rightly be divided into three species. First, *Sacred* or *Ecclesiastical*; next, that which we call *Civil History* (using the generic name specially); lastly, the History of *Learning* and *the Arts*. I will begin with the kind last mentioned, for the two former are extant, while the latter – the History of Learning (without which the history of the world seems to me as the statue of Polyphemus without the eye, that very feature being left out which most marks the spirit and life of the person) – I set down as wanting. Not but I know that in the particular sciences of the jurisconsults, mathematicians, rhetoricians, philosophers we have some slight mention or some barren narrations about the sects, schools, books, authors, and successions belonging to them; also that there exist some meagre and unprofitable memoirs of the inventors of arts and usages; but I say that a complete and universal History of Learning is yet wanting. Of this therefore I will now proceed to set forth the argument, the method of construction, and the use.

The *argument* is no other than to inquire and collect out of the records of all time what particular kinds of learning and arts have flourished in what ages and regions of the world, their antiquities, their progresses, their migrations (for sciences migrate like nations) over the different parts of the globe, and again their decays, disappearances, and revivals. The occasion and origin of the invention of each art should likewise be observed, the manner and system of transmission, and the plan and order of study and practice. To these should be added a history of the sects and the principal controversies in which learned men have been engaged, the calumnies to which they have been exposed, the praises and honours by which they have been rewarded; an account of the principal authors, books, schools, successions, academies, societies, colleges, orders – in a word, everything which relates to the state of learning. Above all things (for this is the ornament and life of Civil History) I wish events to be coupled with their causes. I mean that an account should be given of the characters of the several regions and peoples; their natural disposition, whether apt and suited for the study of learning, or unfitted and indifferent to it; the accidents of the times, whether adverse or propitious to science; the emulations and infusions of different religions; the enmity or partiality of laws; the eminent virtues and services of individual persons in the promotion of learning; and the like. Now all this I would have handled in a historical way, not wasting time after the manner of critics in praise and blame, but simply narrating the fact historically with but slight intermixture of private judgment.

For the *manner* of compiling such a history I particularly advise that the matter and provision of it be not drawn from histories and commentaries alone, but that the principal books written in each century, or perhaps in shorter periods, proceeding in regular order from the earliest ages, be themselves taken into consultation, that so (I do not say by a complete perusal, for that would be an endless labour, but) by tasting them here and there and observing their argument, style, and method, the Literary Spirit of each age may be charmed as it were from the dead.

With regard to the *use* of the work, it is not so much to swell the honour and pomp of learning with a profusion of images, nor because out of my exceeding love for learning I wish the inquiry, knowledge, and preservation of everything that relates thereto to be pursued even to curiosity, but chiefly for a purpose more serious and important, which, in a word, is this: I consider that such a history as I have described would very greatly assist the wisdom and skill of learned men in the use and administration of learning; that it would exhibit the movements and perturbations, the virtues and vices, which take place no less in intellectual than in civil matters; and that from the observation of these the best system of government might be derived and established. For the works of St. Ambrose or St. Augustine will not make so wise a bishop or divine as a diligent examination and study of Ecclesiastical History, and the History of Learning would be of like service to learned men. For everything is subject to chance and error which is not supported by examples and experience. And so much for the History of Learning.

Chapter V

On the Dignity and Difficulty of Civil History.

I COME next to *Civil History*, properly so called, whereof the dignity and authority are pre-eminent among human writings. For to its fidelity are entrusted the examples of our ancestors, the vicissitudes of things, the foundations of civil policy, and the name and reputation of men. But the difficulty is no less than the dignity. For to carry the mind in writing back into the past, and bring it into sympathy with antiquity, diligently to examine, freely and faithfully to report, and by the light of words to place as it were before the eyes the revolutions of times, the characters of persons, the fluctuations of counsels, the courses and currents of actions, the bottoms of pretences, and the secrets of governments is a task of great labour and judgment – the rather because in ancient transactions the truth is difficult to ascertain, and in modern it is dangerous to tell. Hence Civil History is beset on all sides with faults: some (and these are the greater part) write only barren and commonplace narratives, a very reproach to history; others hastily and disorderly string together a few particular relations and trifling memoirs; others merely run over the heads of events; others, on the contrary, go into all the minutest particularities. and such as have no relation to the main action; some indulge their imaginations in bold inventions; while others impress on their works the image not so much of their minds as of their passions, ever thinking of their party, but no good witnesses as to facts; some are always inculcating their favourite political doctrines, and idly interrupting the narrative by going out of the way to display them; others are injudiciously prolix in reporting orations and harangues and even in relating the actions themselves – so that, among all the writings of men there is nothing rarer than a true and perfect Civil History. But my present purpose in this division of learning is to mark omissions, and not to censure faults. I will now pursue the divisions of Civil History, and those of the different kinds; for the species will be exhibited more clearly under several heads than under one head curiously* traced through all its members.

Chapter XIII

On the second principal part of Learning, namely, Poesy. The Division of Poesy into Narrative, Dramatic, *and* Parabolical. *Three Examples of Parabolical Poesy are propounded.*

I NOW come to Poesy, which is a part of learning in measure of words for the most part restrained, but in all other points extremely free and licensed; and therefore (as I said at first) it is referred to the Imagination, which may at pleasure make unlawful matches and divorces of things. Now Poesy (as I have already observed) is taken in two senses, in respect of words or matter. In the first sense it is but a character of speech, for verse is only a kind of style and a certain form of elocution, and has nothing to do with the matter, for both true history may be written in verse and feigned history in prose. But in the latter sense, I have set it down from the first as one of the principal branches of learning, and placed it by the side of history, being indeed nothing else but an imitation of history at pleasure. And therefore, endeavouring as I do in these divisions to trace out and pursue the true veins of learning, without (in many points) following custom and the divisions which are received, I dismiss from the present discourse Satires, Elegies, Epigrams, Odes, and the like, and refer them to philosophy and arts of speech. And under the name of Poesy I treat only of feigned history.

The division of Poesy which is aptest and most according to the propriety thereof, besides those divisions which it has in common with History (for there are feigned Chronicles, feigned Lives, and feigned Relations) is into Poesy *Narrative*, *Dramatic*, and *Parabolical*. Narrative Poesy is a mere imitation of History, such as might pass for real, only that it commonly exaggerates things beyond probability. Dramatic Poesy is as History made visible, for it represents actions as if they were present, whereas History represents them as past. Parabolical Poesy is typical[1] History, by which ideas that are objects of the intellect are represented in forms that are objects of the sense.

As for Narrative Poesy – or Heroical, if you like so to call it (understanding it of the matter, not of the verse) – the foundation of it is truly noble, and has a special relation to the dignity of human nature. For as the sensible world is inferior in dignity to the rational soul, Poesy seems to bestow upon human nature those things which history denies to it, and to satisfy the mind with the shadows of things when the substance cannot be obtained. For if the matter be attentively considered, a sound argument may be drawn from Poesy to show that there is agreeable to the spirit of man a more ample greatness, a more perfect order, and a more beautiful variety than it can anywhere (since the Fall) find in nature. And therefore, since the acts and events which are the subjects of real history are not of sufficient grandeur to satisfy the human mind, Poesy is at hand to feign acts more heroical; since the successes and issues of actions as related in true history are far from being agreeable to the merits of virtue and vice, Poesy corrects it, exhibiting events and fortunes as according to merit and the law of providence; since true history wearies the mind with satiety of ordinary events, one like

[1] of the nature of a type; emblematic.

another, Poesy refreshes it by reciting things unexpected and various and full of vicissitudes. So that this Poesy conduces not only to delight but also to magnanimity and morality. Whence it may be fairly thought to partake somewhat of a divine nature, because it raises the mind and carries it aloft, accommodating the shows of things to the desires of the mind, not (like reason and history) buckling and bowing down the mind to the nature of things. And by these charms and that agreeable congruity which it has with man's nature, accompanied also with music, to gain more sweet access, it has so won its way as to have been held in honour even in the rudest ages and among barbarous peoples, when other kinds of learning were utterly excluded.

Dramatic Poesy, which has the theatre for its world, would be of excellent use if well directed. For the stage is capable of no small influence both of discipline and of corruption. Now of corruptions in this kind we have enough, but the discipline has in our times been plainly neglected. And though in modern states play-acting is esteemed but as a toy, except when it is too satirical and biting, yet among the ancients it was used as a means of educating men's minds to virtue. Nay, it has been regarded by learned men and great philosophers as a kind of musician's bow by which men's minds may be played upon. And certainly it is most true, and one of the great secrets of nature, that the minds of men are more open to impressions and affections when many are gathered together than when they are alone.

But Parabolical Poesy is of higher character than the others, and appears to be something sacred and venerable, especially as religion itself commonly uses its aid as a means of communication between divinity and humanity. But this too is corrupted by the levity and idleness of wits in dealing with allegory. It is of double use and serves for contrary purposes; for it serves for an infoldment,[2] and it likewise serves for illustration. In the latter case the object is a certain method of teaching, in the former an artifice for concealment. Now this method of teach-

[2] concealment (as the next sentence indicates).

ing, used for illustration, was very much in use in the ancient times. For the inventions and conclusions of human reason (even those that are now common and trite) being then new and strange, the minds of men were hardly subtle enough to conceive them, unless they were brought nearer to the sense by this kind of resemblances and examples. And hence the ancient times are full of all kinds of fables, parables, enigmas, and similitudes, as may appear by the numbers of Pythagoras, the enigmas of the Sphinx, the fables of Æsop, and the like. The Apophthegms too of the ancient sages commonly explained the matter by similitudes. Thus Menenius Agrippa among the Romans (a nation at that time by no means learned) quelled a sedition by a fable.[3] In a word, as hieroglyphics were before letters, so parables were before arguments. And even now, and at all times, the force of parables is and has been excellent, because arguments cannot be made so perspicuous nor true examples so apt.

But there remains yet another use of Poesy Parabolical, opposite to the former, wherein it serves (as I said) for an infoldment; for such things, I mean, the dignity whereof requires that they should be seen as it were through a veil, that is, when the secrets and mysteries of religion, policy, and philosophy are involved in fables or parables. Now whether any mystic meaning be concealed beneath the fables of the ancient poets is a matter of some doubt. For my own part I must confess that I am inclined to think that a mystery is involved in no small number of them. Nor does the fact that they are left commonly to boys and grammarians, and held in slight repute make me despise them; but rather, since it is evident that the writings in which these fables are related are, next to sacred story, the most ancient of human writings, and the fables themselves still more ancient (for they are related not as being invented by the writers, but as things believed and received from of old), I take them to be a kind of breath from the traditions of more ancient nations, which fell into the pipes of the Greeks. But since that which

[3] See Shakespeare, *Coriolanus*, I.i.
100ff., and Shakespeare's source,
Plutarch, *Coriolanus*, 6.

has hitherto been done in the interpretation of these parables, being the work of unskilful men not learned beyond commonplaces, does not by any means satisfy me, I think fit to set down Philosophy according to the Ancient Parables among the *desiderata*. Of which work I will subjoin one or two examples, not so much perhaps for the value of the thing as for the sake of carrying out my principle, which is this: whenever I set down a work among the desiderata (if there be anything obscure about it), I intend always to set forth either instructions for the execution of it or an example of the thing, else it might be thought that it was merely some light notion that had glanced through my mind, or that I am like an augur measuring countries in thought without knowing the way to enter them. I can report no other deficiency in Poesy, for being as a plant which comes from the lust of the earth without a formal seed, it has sprung up and spread abroad more than any other kind of learning. But I will now propound the examples, only three in number, one taken from things Natural, one from things Political, and one from things Moral.[4]

---

[4] There follow three lengthy interpretations of the fables of Pan (on nature – an expanded version of the treatment in *The Wisdom of the Ancients*), of Perseus (on war), and of Dionysus (on desire).

BOOK III

Chapter I

Division of Science into Theology *and* Philosophy. *Division of* Philosophy *into three doctrines, concerning the* Deity, *concerning* Nature, *and concerning* Man. *Constitution of* Primary Philosophy, *as the common mother of all.*

ALL History, excellent King, walks upon the earth, and performs the office rather of a guide than of a light; whereas Poesy is as a dream of learning, a thing sweet and varied, and that would be thought to have in it something divine, a character which dreams likewise affect. But now it is time for me to awake, and rising above the earth, to wing my way through the clear air of Philosophy and the Sciences.

The knowledge of man is as the waters. Some waters descend from above, and some spring from beneath; and in like manner the primary division of sciences is to be drawn from their sources, of which some are above in the heavens, and some here below. For all knowledge admits of two kinds of information, the one inspired by divine revelation, the other arising from the senses. For as to that knowledge which man receives by teaching, it is cumulative and not original; as it is likewise in waters, which beside their own springheads, are fed with other springs and streams. I will therefore divide knowledge into Divinity and Philosophy, meaning by Divinity Sacred or Inspired, not Natural Divinity, of which I will speak hereafter. But this (namely, Inspired Divinity) I will reserve to the end, that with it I may conclude my discourse, being as it is the haven and sabbath of all human contemplations.

The object of philosophy is threefold: God, Nature, and Man; as there are likewise three kinds of ray: direct, refracted, and reflected. For nature strikes the understanding with a ray direct; God, by reason of the unequal medium (viz., his creatures), with a ray refracted; man, as shown and exhibited to himself, with a ray reflected. Philosophy may therefore be conveniently divided into three branches of knowledge: knowledge of God, knowledge of Nature, and knowledge of Man, or Humanity. But since the divisions of knowledge are not like several lines that meet in one angle, but are rather like branches of a tree that meet in one stem (which stem grows for some distance entire and continuous, before it divide itself into arms and boughs), therefore it is necessary before we enter into the branches of the former division, to erect and constitute one universal science, to be as the mother of the rest, and to be regarded in the progress of knowledge as portion of the main and common way, before we come where the ways part and divide themselves. This science I distinguish by the name of *Philosophia Prima,* primitive or summary philosophy, or *Sapience,* which was formerly defined as the knowledge of things divine and human. To this no other is opposed; for it differs from the rest rather in the limits within which it ranges than in the subject matter, treating only of the highest stages of things. Which science whether I should report as deficient or not, I stand doubtful, though I rather incline to do so. For I find a certain rhapsody and incongruous mass of Natural Theology, of Logic, and of some parts of Natural Philosophy (as those concerning First Principles and the Soul), all mixed up and confused, and in the lofty language of men who take delight in admiring themselves advanced as it were to the pinnacle of the sciences. But setting all high conceits* aside, my meaning is simply this: that a science be constituted, which may be a receptacle for all such axioms as are not peculiar to any of the particular sciences, but belong to several of them in common.

Now that there are very many axioms of that kind need not be doubted. For example, "If equals be added to unequals the wholes will be unequal" is a rule of mathematics. The same holds in ethics, as regards distributive justice; for in commutative justice the rule of equity requires that equals be given to unequals; whereas in distributive, if unequals be not given to unequals there is the greatest injustice.[1] Again, "Things that are equal to the same are equal to one another" is likewise a rule of mathematics; but it is at the same time so potent in logic as to be the basis of the syllogism. "The nature of everything is best seen in its smallest portions" is a rule in Physics of such force that it produced the atoms of Democritus; and yet Aristotle made good use of it in his Politics, where he commences his inquiry of the nature of a commonwealth with a family.[2] "All things are changed and nothing is lost"[3] is in like manner a rule in Physics, exhibited thus, "The Quantum of nature is neither diminished nor increased." The same holds in Natural Theology, with this variation, "It is the work of omnipotence to make somewhat nothing, and to make nothing somewhat;" which likewise the Scripture testifies: "I know that whatsoever God doeth, it shall be for ever; nothing can be put to it, nor anything taken from it."[4] "Things are preserved from destruction by bringing them back to their first principles" is a rule in Physics; the same holds good in Politics (as Machiavelli rightly observed), for there is scarcely anything which preserves states from destruction more than the reformation and reduction of them to their ancient manners.[5] "Putrefaction is more contagious before than after maturity" is a rule in Physics; the same is eminently true in Morals, for the men who are most wicked and profligate produce less corruption in the public manners than those who appear to have some soundness and virtue in them, and are only partly evil. "Whatever is preservative of a greater Form is more powerful in action" is a rule in Physics; for that the connexion of things should not be severed, nor a vacuum (as they call it) admitted, tends to preserve the fabric of the universe, whereas the collection of heavy bodies towards the mass of the earth tends to preserve only the region of dense bodies, and therefore the first motion overcomes the last. The same holds in Politics; for whatsoever contributes to preserve

[1] Cf. Aristotle, *Nicomachean Ethics*, V.3,4,5 (1131ᵃ-1134ᵃ). [Spedding]

[2] See Aristotle, *Politics*, I.1 (1252ᵃ); *Physics*, I.1 (184ᵃ); Diogenes Laertius, IX.44,45.

[3] Ovid, *Met.*, XV.165.

[4] Eccles. 3:14.

[5] Machiavelli, *Disc. on Livy*, III.1.

the whole state in its own nature, has greater power than that which only benefits the particular members of that state. It holds likewise in Theology; for of the theological virtues, charity, which is the virtue most communicative of good, excels all the rest. "The force of an agent is increased by the reaction of a contrary"[6] is a rule in Physics. The same has wonderful efficacy in Politics, since every faction is violently irritated by the encroachment of a contrary faction. "A discord ending immediately in a concord sets off the harmony" is a rule in Music. The same holds in Ethics and in the affections. The trope of Music, to glide gently from the close or cadence (as they call it) when you seem to be on the point of it, resembles the trope of Rhetoric, of deceiving expectation. The quavering upon a stop in music gives the same pleasure to the ear as the playing of light on water or a diamond gives to the eye:

Splendet tremulo sub lumine pontus.[7]

"The organs of the senses resemble the organs of reflexions" is a rule in Perspective; for the eye is like to a glass, or to water; and it is the same in Acoustics, for the instrument of hearing is like an obstruction in a cavern. These few cases are enough by way of examples. But indeed the chief business of the Persian magic (so much celebrated) was to note the correspondences between the architectures and fabrics of things natural and things civil. Neither are all these which I have mentioned, and others of this kind, only similitudes (as men of narrow observation may perhaps conceive them to be), but plainly the same footsteps of nature treading or printing upon different subjects and matters. And it is a thing which has not as yet been carefully handled. You may perhaps find in the writings of the profounder sort of wits such axioms here and there sparingly inserted for the use of the argument they have in hand; but for any body of such axioms, which should tend primitively and summarily to the advancement of the sciences, no one has as yet

---

[6] See Aristotle, *Meteorology*, I.12 (348b); *Physics*, VIII.7 (260a).

[7] "Beneath the trembling light glit-ters the sea." Virgil, *Aeneid*, VII. 9.

collected one, though it is a thing of excellent use for displaying the unity of nature, which is supposed to be the true office of Primitive Philosophy.

There is also another part of this philosophy, which, if you look to the terms, is ancient, if to the thing which I mean, is new. It is an inquiry with regard to the Adventitious Conditions of Essences (which we may call Transcendentals), as Much, Little; Like, Unlike; Possible, Impossible; likewise Being and Not-Being, and the like. For since these do not properly come under Physic, and the logical discussion concerning them belongs rather to the laws of reasoning than to the existence of things, it is very proper that the consideration of them (wherein there is no little dignity and profit) should not be altogether neglected, but should find at least some place in the divisions of the sciences. Nevertheless I mean that it should be handled in a way very different from the common. For example, no one who has treated of Much and Little has endeavoured to assign a reason why some things in nature are and can be so numerous and plentiful, others so few and scanty; for it certainly cannot be that in the nature of things there should be as much gold as iron, that roses should be as abundant as grass, and that there should be as great variety of the specific as of the non-specific. In like manner no one in handling Similitude and Diversity has sufficiently explained why betwixt different species there almost always lie certain individuals which partake of the nature of both: as moss between corruption and a plant; fishes that stick to rocks and cannot move away, between a plant and an animal; rats and mice, and some other things, between animals generated of putrefaction and of seed; bats, between birds and beasts; flying-fish (which are now well known), between birds and fishes; seals, between fishes and quadrupeds; and the like. Nor has any one inquired the reason why, seeing that likes delight in likes, iron does not attract iron, which the magnet does, nor why gold does not attract gold, though it does attract quicksilver. With regard to these and similar things in the discussion of Transcendentals there is a deep silence; for men have aimed rather at height of speech than at the subtleties of things. Wherefore I wish the real and solid inquiry, according to the laws of nature and not of language, concerning these Transcendentals or Adventitious Conditions of Essences, to have a place in Primitive or Summary Philosophy. And so much for *Philosophia Prima* (or Sapience), which I have with reason set down as deficient,

New Atlantis

A WORK UNFINISHED

1627

See Introd., pp. 11-12

To the Reader

THIS fable my Lord devised, to the end that he might exhibit therein a model or description of a college instituted for the interpreting of nature and the producing of great and marvellous works for the benefit of men, under the name of Salomon's House, or the College of the Six Days Works. And even so far his Lordship hath proceeded, as to finish that part. Certainly the model is more vast and high than can possibly be imitated in all things; notwithstanding most things therein are within men's power to effect. His Lordship thought also in this present fable to have composed a frame of Laws, or of the best state or mould of a commonwealth; but foreseeing it would be a long work, his desire of collecting the Natural History diverted him, which he preferred many degrees before it.

This work of the *New Atlantis* (as much as concerneth the English edition) his Lordship designed for this place;[1] in regard it hath so near affinity (in one part of it) with the preceding Natural History.

W. RAWLEY[2]

---

[1] It was published at the end of the volume containing the *Sylva Sylvarum*.

[2] William Rawley (1588-1667): Bacon's "learned chaplain", his amanuensis, and his first biographer.

WE sailed from Peru (where we had continued by the space of one whole year) for China and Japan by the South Sea,[3] taking with us victuals for twelve months, and had good winds from the east, though soft and weak, for five months' space and more. But then the wind came about and settled in the west for many days, so as we could make little or no way, and were sometimes in purpose to turn back. But then again there arose strong and great winds from the south with a point east, which carried us up (for all that we could do) towards the north, by which time our victuals failed us, though we had made good spare[4] of them. So that finding ourselves in the midst of the greatest wilderness of waters in the world without victual, we gave ourselves for lost men, and prepared for death. Yet we did lift up our hearts and voices to God above, who *showeth his wonders in the deep*,[5] beseeching him of his mercy that as in the beginning he discovered* the face of the deep, and brought forth dry land, so he would now discover land to us, that we might not perish. And it came to pass that the next day about evening, we saw within a kenning[6] before us, towards the north, as it were thick clouds, which did put us in some hope of land, knowing how that part of the South Sea was utterly unknown, and might have islands or continents that hitherto were not come to light. Wherefore we bent our course thither, where we saw the appearance of land all that night, and in the dawning of the next day we might plainly discern that it was a land, flat to our sight and full of boscage, which made it show the more dark. And after an hour and a half's sailing we entered into a good haven, being the port of a fair city, not great indeed, but well built, and that gave a pleasant view from the sea; and we thinking every minute long till we were on land, came close to the shore and offered to land. But straightways we saw divers of the people with bastons[7] in their hands as it were forbidding us to land, yet

[3] Pacific Ocean.
[4] frugal use.
[5] Psalms 107:24.
[6] the distance within which land or

ships may ordinarily be discerned; about twenty or twenty-one miles.
[7] cudgels.

without any cries or fierceness, but only as warning us off by signs that they made. Whereupon being not a little discomforted, we were advising with ourselves what we should do. During which time there made forth to us a small boat with about eight persons in it, whereof one of them had in his hand a tipstaff of a yellow cane, tipped at both ends with blue, who came aboard our ship without any show of distrust at all. And when he saw one of our number present himself somewhat afore the rest, he drew forth a little scroll of parchment (somewhat yellower than our parchment, and shining like the leaves of writing tables,* but otherwise soft and flexible) and delivered it to our foremost man. In which scroll were written in ancient Hebrew and in ancient Greek and in good Latin of the School[8] and in Spanish these words: "Land ye not, none of you; and provide to be gone from this coast within sixteen days, except you have further time given you. Meanwhile, if you want fresh water, or victual, or help for your sick, or that your ship needeth repair, write down your wants, and you shall have that which belongeth to mercy." This scroll was signed with a stamp of cherubins' wings, not spread but hanging downwards, and by them a cross. This being delivered, the officer returned, and left only a servant with us to receive our answer. Consulting hereupon amongst ourselves, we were much perplexed. The denial of landing and hasty warning us away troubled us much; on the other side, to find that the people had languages and were so full of humanity did comfort us not a little. And above all, the sign of the cross to that instrument was to us a great rejoicing, and as it were a certain presage of good. Our answer was in the Spanish tongue: That for our ship, it was well, for we had rather met with calms and contrary winds than any tempests. For our sick, they were many, and in very ill case, so that if they were not permitted to land, they ran danger of their lives. Our other wants we set down in particular, adding that we had some little store of merchandise, which if it pleased them to deal for, it might supply our wants without being

[8] i.e., correct classical Latin.

chargeable unto them. We offered some reward in pistolets[9] unto the servant, and a piece of crimson velvet to be presented to the officer, but the servant took them not, nor would scarce look upon them, and so left us and went back in another little boat which was sent for him.

About three hours after we had dispatched our answer, there came towards us a person (as it seemed) of place. He had on him a gown with wide sleeves, of a kind of water chamolet,[10] of an excellent azure colour, far more glossy than ours; his under apparel was green, and so was his hat, being in the form of a turban, daintily made, and not so huge as the Turkish turbans, and the locks of his hair came down below the brims of it. A reverend man was he to behold. He came in a boat, gilt in some part of it, with four persons more only in that boat, and was followed by another boat, wherein were some twenty. When he was come within a flightshot[11] of our ship, signs were made to us that we should send forth some to meet him upon the water, which we presently* did in our ship-boat, sending the principal man amongst us save one, and four of our number with him. When we were come within six yards of their boat, they called to us to stay, and not to approach farther, which we did. And thereupon the man whom I before described stood up, and with a loud voice in Spanish asked, "Are ye Christians?" We answered we were, fearing the less because of the cross we had seen in the subscription. At which answer the said person lifted up his right hand towards heaven, and drew it softly to his mouth (which is the gesture they use when they thank God) and then said: "If ye will swear (all of you) by the merits of the Saviour that ye are no pirates, nor have shed blood lawfully nor unlawfully within forty days past, you may have licence to come on land." We said we were all ready to take that oath. Whereupon one of those that were with him, being (as it seemed) a notary, made an entry of this act. Which done, another of the attendants of the great person, which was with him in the same boat, after

[9] pistoles.
[10] camlet: a costly fabric of satin weave made of camel's hair.
[11] bowshot.

water: wavy and shiny.

his lord had spoken a little to him, said aloud: "My lord would have you know that it is not of pride or greatness that he cometh not aboard your ship; but for that[12] in your answer you declare that you have many sick amongst you, he was warned by the Conservator of Health of the city that he should keep a distance." We bowed ourselves towards him, and answered we were his humble servants, and accounted for great honour and singular humanity towards us that which was already done, but hoped well that the nature of the sickness of our men was not infectious. So he returned, and a while after came the notary to us aboard our ship, holding in his hand a fruit of that country, like an orange but of colour between orange-tawny and scarlet, which cast a most excellent odour. He used it (as it seemeth) for a preservative against infection. He gave us our oath, "By the name of Jesus and his merits," and after told us that the next day by six of the clock in the morning we should be sent to and brought to the Strangers' House (so he called it), where we should be accommodated of things both for our whole and for our sick. So he left us; and when we offered him some pistolets, he smiling said, he must not be twice paid for one labour, meaning (as I take it) that he had salary sufficient of the state for his service. For (as I after learned) they call an officer that taketh rewards *twice paid*.

The next morning early there came to us the same officer that came to us at first with his cane, and told us he came to conduct us to the Strangers' House, and that he had prevented* the hour, because we might have the whole day before us for our business. "For," said he, "if you will follow my advice, there shall first go with me some few of you, and see the place, and how it may be made convenient for you; and then you may send for your sick and the rest of your number, which ye will bring on land." We thanked him, and said that this care which he took of desolate strangers God would reward. And so six of us went on land with him, and when we were on land, he went before us, and turned to us, and said he was but our servant and our guide. He led us through three fair streets, and all the

² because.

way we went there were gathered some people on both sides standing in a row, but in so civil a fashion as if it had been not to wonder at us but to welcome us; and divers of them, as we passed by them, put their arms a little abroad, which is their gesture when they bid any welcome. The Strangers' House is a fair and spacious house, built of brick of somewhat a bluer colour than our brick, and with handsome windows, some of glass, some of a kind of cambric oiled. He brought us first into a fair parlour above stairs, and then asked us what number of persons we were? And how many sick? We answered we were in all (sick and whole) one and fifty persons, whereof our sick were seventeen. He desired us to have patience a little, and to stay till he came back to us, which was about an hour after; and then he led us to see the chambers which were provided for us, being in number nineteen, they having cast* it (as it seemeth) that four of those chambers, which were better than the rest, might receive four of the principal men of our company, and lodge them alone by themselves, and the other fifteen chambers were to lodge us, two and two together. The chambers were handsome and cheerful chambers and furnished civilly. Then he led us to a long gallery, like a dorture,[13] where he showed us all along the one side (for the other side was but wall and window) seventeen cells, very neat ones, having partitions of cedar wood. Which gallery and cells, being in all forty (many more than we needed), were instituted as an infirmary for sick persons. And he told us withal that as any of our sick waxed well, he might be removed from his cell to a chamber, for which purpose there were set forth ten spare chambers, besides the number we spake of before. This done, he brought us back to the parlour, and lifting up his cane a little (as they do when they give any charge or command), said to us, "Ye are to know that the custom of the land requireth that after this day and tomorrow (which we give you for removing of your people from your ship) you are to keep within doors for three days. But let it not trouble you, nor do not think yourselves restrained, but rather left to your rest and ease. You shall want nothing, and

[13] dormitory.

there are six of our people appointed to attend you for any business you may have abroad." We gave him thanks with all affection and respect, and said, "God surely is manifested in this land." We offered him also twenty pistolets, but he smiled, and only said, "What? twice paid!" And so he left us. Soon after our dinner was served in, which was right good viands, both for bread and meat, better than any collegiate diet that I have known in Europe. We had also drink of three sorts, all wholesome and good: wine of the grape; a drink of grain, such as is with us our ale, but more clear; and a kind of cider made of a fruit of that country, a wonderful pleasing and refreshing drink. Besides, there were brought in to us great store* of those scarlet oranges for our sick, which (they said) were an assured remedy for sickness taken at sea. There was given us also a box of small grey or whitish pills, which they wished our sick should take, one of the pills every night before sleep, which (they said) would hasten their recovery. The next day, after that our trouble of carriage and removing of our men and goods out of our ship was somewhat settled and quiet, I thought good to call our company together, and when they were assembled said unto them, "My dear friends, let us know ourselves, and how it standeth with us. We are men cast on land, as Jonas was out of the whale's belly, when we were as buried in the deep; and now we are on land, we are but between death and life, for we are beyond both the old world and the new, and whether ever we shall see Europe, God only knoweth. It is a kind of miracle hath brought us hither, and it must be little less that shall bring us hence. Therefore in regard of our deliverance past, and our danger present and to come, let us look up to God, and every man reform his own ways. Besides, we are come here amongst a Christian people, full of piety and humanity; let us not bring that confusion of face upon ourselves as to show our vices or unworthiness before them. Yet there is more. For they have by commandment (though in form of courtesy) cloistered us within these walls for three days; who knoweth whether it be not to take some taste of our manners and conditions, and if they find them bad, to banish us straightways; if good, to give us further

time? For these men that they have given us for attendance may
withal have an eye upon us. Therefore for God's love, and as
we love the weal of our souls and bodies, let us so behave ourselves as we may be at peace with God, and may find grace in the
eyes of this people." Our company with one voice thanked me
for my good admonition, and promised me to live soberly and
civilly and without giving any the least occasion of offence. So
we spent our three days joyfully and without care, in expectation what would be done with us when they were expired. During which time, we had every hour joy of the amendment of
our sick, who thought themselves cast into some divine pool of
healing, they mended so kindly[14] and so fast.

The morrow after our three days were past, there came to us
a new man that we had not seen before, clothed in blue as the
former was, save that his turban was white with a small red cross
on the top. He had also a tippet of fine linen. At his coming in
he did bend to us a little, and put his arms abroad. We of our
parts saluted him in a very lowly and submissive manner, as
looking that from him we should receive sentence of life and
death. He desired to speak with some few of us; whereupon
six of us only stayed, and the rest avoided[15] the room. He said,
"I am by office governor of this House of Strangers, and by
vocation I am a Christian priest, and therefore am come to you
to offer you my service, both as strangers and chiefly as Christians. Some things I may tell you, which I think you will not be
unwilling to hear. The state hath given you licence to stay on
land for the space of six weeks; and let it not trouble you if your
occasions ask further time, for the law in this point is not precise, and I do not doubt but myself shall be able to obtain for
you such further time as may be convenient. Ye shall also understand that the Strangers' House is at this time rich and much
aforehand,[16] for it hath laid up revenue these thirty-seven years,
for so long it is since any stranger arrived in this part: and therefore take ye no care: the state will defray you all the time you

---

[14] naturally, readily, thoroughly.
Bacon here evokes John 5:1-9.
[15] left.

[16] beforehand: in comfortable circumstances.

stay; neither shall you stay one day the less for that. As for any merchandise ye have brought, ye shall be well used, and have your return either in merchandise or in gold and silver, for to us it is all one. And if you have any other request to make, hide it not. For ye shall find we will not make your countenance to fall by the answer ye shall receive. Only this I must tell you, that none of you must go above a *karan* [that is with them a mile and an half] from the walls of the city without especial leave." We answered, after we had looked awhile one upon another, admiring[17] this gracious and parentlike usage, that we could not tell what to say, for we wanted words to express our thanks, and his noble free offers left us nothing to ask. It seemed to us that we had before us a picture of our salvation in heaven, for we that were awhile since in the jaws of death were now brought into a place where we found nothing but consolations. For the commandment laid upon us, we would not fail to obey it, though it was impossible but our hearts should be inflamed to tread further upon this happy and holy ground. We added that our tongues should first cleave to the roofs of our mouths, ere we should forget either his reverend person or this whole nation in our prayers. We also most humbly besought him to accept of us as his true servants by as just a right as ever men on earth were bounden, laying and presenting both our persons and all we had at his feet. He said he was a priest, and looked for a priest's reward, which was our brotherly love and the good of our souls and bodies. So he went from us, not without tears of tenderness in his eyes, and left us also confused with joy and kindness, saying amongst ourselves that we were come into a land of angels, which did appear to us daily and present us with comforts, which we thought not of, much less expected.

The next day, about ten of the clock, the governor came to us again, and after salutations said familiarly that he was come to visit us, and called for a chair, and sat him down, and we, being some ten of us (the rest were of the meaner sort, or else gone abroad) sat down with him. And when we were set, he began thus: "We of this island of Bensalem [for so they call it in their

[17] wondering at.

N. B.

language] have this, that by means of our solitary situation and of the laws of secrecy which we have for our travellers, and our rare admission of strangers, we know well most part of the habitable world, and are ourselves unknown. Therefore because he that knoweth least is fittest to ask questions, it is more reason for the entertainment of the time that ye ask me questions than that I ask you." We answered that we humbly thanked him that he would give us leave so to do, and that we conceived by the taste we had already, that there was no worldly thing on earth more worthy to be known than the state of that happy land. But above all, we said, since that we were met from the several ends of the world, and hoped assuredly that we should meet one day in the kingdom of heaven (for that we were both parts Christians), we desired to know (in respect* that land was so remote, and so divided by vast and unknown seas from the land where our Saviour walked on earth) who was the apostle of that nation, and how it was converted to the faith. It appeared in his face that he took great contentment in this our question; he said, "Ye knit my heart to you by asking this question in the first place, for it _showeth that you first seek the kingdom_ of _heaven;_[18] and I shall gladly and briefly satisfy your demand.

"About twenty years after the ascension of our Saviour, it came to pass that there was seen by the people of Renfusa (a city upon the eastern coast of our island) within night (the night was cloudy and calm), as it might be some mile into the sea, a great pillar of light, not sharp but in form of a column or cylinder, rising from the sea a great way up towards heaven, and on the top of it was seen a large cross of light more bright and resplendent than the body of the pillar. Upon which so strange a spectacle the people of the city gathered apace together upon the sands to wonder; and so after put themselves into a number of small boats to go nearer to this marvellous sight. But when the boats were come within about sixty yards of the pillar, they found themselves all bound, and could go no further; yet so as they might move to go about, but might not approach nearer, so as the boats stood all as in a theatre, beholding this light as

[18] Cf. Matt. 6:33 and Luke 12:31.

an heavenly sign. It so fell out that there was in one of the boats one of the wise men of the society of Salomon's House, which house or college (my good brethren) is the very eye of this kingdom, who having awhile attentively and devoutly viewed and contemplated this pillar and cross, fell down upon his face, and then raised himself upon his knees, and lifting up his hands to heaven, made his prayers in this manner:

" 'Lord God of heaven and earth, thou hast vouchsafed of thy grace to those of our order to know thy works of creation and the secrets of them, and to discern (as far as appertaineth to the generations of men) between divine miracles, works of nature, works of art, and impostures and illusions of all sorts. I do here acknowledge and testify before this people that the thing which we now see before our eyes is thy Finger and a true Miracle; and forasmuch as we learn in our books that thou never workest miracles but to a divine and excellent end (for the laws of nature are thine own laws, and thou exceedest them not but upon great cause), we most humbly beseech thee to prosper this great sign, and to give us the interpretation and use of it in mercy, which thou dost in some part secretly promise by sending it unto us.'

"When he had made his prayer, he presently found the boat he was in movable and unbound, whereas all the rest remained still fast, and taking that for an assurance of leave to approach, he caused the boat to be softly and with silence rowed towards the pillar. But ere he came near it, the pillar and cross of light brake up, and cast itself abroad, as it were, into a firmament of many stars, which also vanished soon after, and there was nothing left to be seen but a small ark or chest of cedar, dry and not wet at all with water, though it swam. And in the fore-end of it, which was towards him, grew a small green branch of palm; and when the wise man had taken it with all reverence into his boat, it opened of itself, and there were found in it a Book and a Letter, both written in fine parchment and wrapped in sindons[19] of linen. The Book contained all the canonical books of the Old and New Testament according as you have

[19] pieces.

them (for we know well what the Churches with you receive), and the Apocalypse itself and some other books of the New Testament, which were not at that time written, were nevertheless in the Book. And for the Letter, it was in these words:

" 'I Bartholomew, a servant of the Highest and Apostle of Jesus Christ, was warned by an angel that appeared to me in a vision of glory, that I should commit this ark to the floods of the sea. Therefore I do testify and declare unto that people where God shall ordain this ark to come to land that in the same day is come unto them salvation and peace and goodwill from the Father and from the Lord Jesus.'

"There was also in both these writings, as well the Book as the Letter, wrought a great miracle, conform[20] to that of the Apostles in the original Gift of Tongues. For there being at that time in this land Hebrews, Persians, and Indians, besides the natives, every one read upon the Book and Letter as if they had been written in his own language. And thus was this land saved from infidelity (as the remain[21] of the old world was from water) by an ark, through the apostolical and miraculous evangelism of St. Bartholomew." And here he paused, and a messenger came and called him from us. So this was all that passed in that conference.

The next day the same governor came again to us immediately after dinner, and excused himself, saying that the day before he was called from us somewhat abruptly, but now he would make us amends, and spend time with us, if we held his company and conference agreeable. We answered that we held it so agreeable and pleasing to us as we forgot both dangers past and fears to come for the time we heard him speak, and that we thought an hour spent with him was worth years of our former life. He bowed himself a little to us, and after we were set again, he said, "Well, the questions are on your part." One of our number said, after a little pause, that there was a matter we were no less desirous to know than fearful to ask, lest we might presume too far. But encouraged by his rare humanity towards

fine compliment

[20] corresponding.
[21] remnant.

us (that could scarce think ourselves strangers, being his vowed and professed servants) we would take the hardiness to propound it, humbly beseeching him, if he thought it not fit to be answered, that he would pardon it, though he rejected it. We said we well observed those his words which he formerly spake, that this happy island where we now stood was known to few, and yet knew most of the nations of the world, which we found to be true, considering they had the languages of Europe, and knew much of our state and business, and yet we in Europe (notwithstanding all the remote discoveries and navigations of this last age) never heard any of the least inkling or glimpse of this island. This we found wonderful strange, for that all nations have interknowledge[22] one of another either by voyage into foreign parts or by strangers that come to them, and though the traveller into a foreign country doth commonly know more by the eye than he that stayeth at home can by relation of the traveller, yet both ways suffice to make a mutual knowledge in some degree on both parts. But for this island, we never heard tell of any ship of theirs that had been seen to arrive upon any shore of Europe, no, nor of either the East or West Indies, nor yet of any ship of any other part of the world that had made return from them. And yet the marvel rested not in this. For the situation of it (as his lordship said) in the secret conclave of such a vast sea might cause it. But then that they should have knowledge of the languages, books, affairs of those that lie such a distance from them, it was a thing we could not tell what to make of, for that it seemed to us a condition and propriety* of divine powers and beings to be hidden and unseen to others and yet to have others open and as in a light to them. At this speech the governor gave a gracious smile, and said that we did well to ask pardon for this question we now asked, for that it imported as if we thought this land a land of magicians, that sent forth spirits of the air into all parts to bring them news and intelligence of other countries. It was answered by us all, in all possible humbleness, but yet with a countenance taking

[22] mutual knowledge.

knowledge[23] that we knew that he spake it but merrily, that we were apt enough to think there was somewhat supernatural in this island, but yet rather as angelical than magical. But to let his lordship know truly what it was that made us tender and doubtful to ask this question, it was not any such conceit,* but because we remembered he had given a touch in his former speech that this land had laws of secrecy touching strangers. To this he said, "You remember it aright; and therefore in that I shall say to you I must reserve some particulars, which it is not lawful for me to reveal, but there will be enough left to give you satisfaction.

"You shall understand (that which perhaps you will scarce think credible) that about three thousand years ago, or somewhat more, the navigation of the world (specially for remote voyages) was greater than at this day. Do not think with yourselves that I know not how much it is increased with you within these six-score years; I know it well, and yet I say greater then than now; whether it was that the example of the ark, that saved the remnant of men from the universal deluge, gave men confidence to adventure upon the waters, or what it was, but such is the truth. The Phoenicians, and especially the Tyrians, had great fleets. So had the Carthaginians their colony, which is yet further west. Toward the east, the shipping of Egypt and of Palestina was likewise great. China also and the great Atlantis (that you call America), which have now but junks and canoes, abounded then in tall ships. This island (as appeareth by faithful registers of those times) had then fifteen hundred strong ships of great content. Of all this there is with you sparing memory or none, but we have large knowledge thereof.

"At that time this land was known and frequented by the ships and vessels of all the nations before named. And (as it cometh to pass) they had many times men of other countries, that were no sailors, that came with them, as Persians, Chaldeans, Arabians; so as almost all nations of might and fame resorted hither, of whom we have some stirps and little tribes with us at this day. And for our own ships, they went sundry voyages,

[23] cognizance (revealing recognition).

as well to your Straits which you call the Pillars of Hercules, as to other parts in the Atlantic and Mediterrane Seas; as to Paguin (which is the same with Cambaline) and Quinzy upon the Oriental Seas, as far as to the borders of the East Tartary.[24]

"At the same time and an age after or more, the inhabitants of the great Atlantis did flourish. For though the narration and description which is made by a great man[25] with you, that the *Plato* descendants of Neptune planted there; and of the magnificent temple, palace, city, and hill; and the manifold streams of goodly navigable rivers (which, as so many chains, environed the same site and temple); and the several degrees of ascent whereby men did climb up to the same, as if it had been a *scala cœli*,[26] be all poetical and fabulous, yet so much is true, that the said country of Atlantis, as well that of Peru, then called Coya, as that of Mexico, then named Tyrambel, were mighty and proud kingdoms in arms, shipping, and riches, so mighty as at one time (or at least within the space of ten years) they both made two great expeditions: they of Tyrambel through the Atlantic to the Mediterrane Sea; and they of Coya through the South Sea upon this our island. And for the former of these, which was into Europe, the same author amongst you (as it seemeth) had some relation from the Egyptian priest whom he citeth. For assuredly such a thing there was. But whether it were the ancient Athenians that had the glory of the repulse and resistance of those forces, I can say nothing, but certain it is, there never came back either ship or man from that voyage. Neither had the other voyage of those of Coya upon us had better fortune, if they had not met with enemies of greater clemency. For the king of this island (by name Altabin) a wise man and a great warrior, knowing well both his own strength and that of his enemies, handled the matter so, as he cut off their land forces from their ships, and entoiled both their navy and their camp with a greater power than theirs, both by sea

Fact & fable in Atlantis tradition

---

[24] Paguin: Peking. Cambaline (or Cambalu, as Marco Polo called it): the Tartar name for Peking. Quinzy: the Quinsai of Marco Polo, now Hangchow. [Ellis]

[25] Plato in *Critias* and *Timaeus*.

[26] "a ladder to heaven". See Gen. 28: 12.

and land, and compelled them to render themselves without striking stroke, and after they were at his mercy, contenting himself only with their oath that they should no more bear arms against him, dismissed them all in safety. But the Divine Revenge overtook not long after those proud enterprises. For within less than the space of one hundred years, the great Atlantis was utterly lost and destroyed, not by a great earthquake, as your man saith (for that whole tract is little subject to earthquakes) but by a particular* deluge or inundation, those countries having at this day far greater rivers and far higher mountains to pour down waters than any part of the old world. But it is true that the same inundation was not deep, not past forty foot in most places from the ground, so that although it destroyed man and beast generally, yet some few wild inhabitants of the wood escaped. Birds also were saved by flying to the high trees and woods. For as for men, although they had buildings in many places higher than the depth of the water, yet that inundation, though it were shallow, had a long continuance, whereby they of the vale that were not drowned perished for want of food and other things necessary. So as marvel you not at the thin population of America, nor at the rudeness and ignorance of the people, for you must account your inhabitants of America as a young people, younger a thousand years at the least than the rest of the world, for that there was so much time between the universal flood and their particular inundation. For the poor remnant of human seed which remained in their mountains peopled the country again slowly, by little and little; and being simple and savage people (not like Noah and his sons, which was the chief family of the earth) they were not able to leave letters, arts, and civility* to their posterity; and having likewise in their mountainous habitations been used (in respect of the extreme cold of those regions) to clothe themselves with the skins of tigers, bears, and great hairy goats, that they have in those parts, when after they came down into the valley, and found the intolerable heats which are there, and knew no means of lighter apparel, they were forced to begin the custom of going naked, which continueth at this day.

Only they take great pride and delight in the feathers of birds, and this also they took from those their ancestors of the mountains, who were invited unto it by the infinite flights of birds that came up to the high grounds, while the waters stood below. So you see, by this main accident of time we lost our traffic with the Americans, with whom of all others, in regard they lay nearest to us, we had most commerce. As for the other parts of the world, it is most manifest that in the ages following (whether it were in respect of* wars or by a natural revolution of time) navigation did everywhere greatly decay, and specially far voyages (the rather by the use of galleys and such vessels as could hardly brook the ocean) were altogether left and omitted. So then, that part of intercourse which could be from other nations to sail to us, you see how it hath long since ceased, except it were by some rare accident, as this of yours. But now of the cessation of that other part of intercourse, which might be by our sailing to other nations, I must yield you some other cause. For I cannot say (if I shall say truly) but our shipping, for number, strength, mariners, pilots, and all things that appertain to navigation, is as great as ever; and therefore why we should sit at home, I shall now give you an account by itself, and it will draw nearer to give you satisfaction to your principal question.

"There reigned in this island, about nineteen hundred years ago, a king, whose memory of all others we most adore, not superstitiously, but as a divine instrument, though a mortal man; his name was Solamona, and we esteem him as the lawgiver of our nation. This king had a *large heart*,[27] inscrutable for good, and was wholly bent to make his kingdom and people happy. He, therefore – taking into consideration how sufficient and substantive this land was to maintain itself without any aid at all of the foreigner, being five thousand six hundred miles in circuit and of rare fertility of soil in the greatest part thereof; and finding also the shipping of this country might be plentifully set on work both by fishing and by transportations from

---

[27] See I Kings 4:29. inscrutable: unfathomable, beyond measure (dedicated).

port to port, and likewise by sailing unto some small islands that are not far from us and are under the crown and laws of this state; and recalling into his memory the happy and flourishing estate wherein this land then was, so as it might be a thousand ways altered to the worse, but scarce any one way to the better – thought nothing wanted to his noble and heroical intentions but only (as far as human foresight might reach) to give perpetuity to that which was in his time so happily established. Therefore amongst his other fundamental laws of this kingdom, he did ordain the interdicts and prohibitions which we have touching entrance of strangers, which at that time (though it was after the calamity of America) was frequent, doubting* novelties and commixture of manners. It is true, the like law against the admission of strangers without licence is an ancient law in the kingdom of China, and yet continued in use. But there it is a poor thing and hath made them a curious, ignorant, fearful, foolish nation. But our lawgiver made his law of another temper. For first, he hath preserved all points of humanity in taking order* and making provision for the relief of strangers distressed, whereof you have tasted." At which speech (as reason* was) we all rose up, and bowed ourselves. He went on. "That king also, still desiring to join humanity and policy together, and thinking it against humanity to detain strangers here against their wills, and against policy that they should return and discover their knowledge of this estate, he took this course: he did ordain that of the strangers that should be permitted to land, as many (at all times) might depart as would; but as many as would stay should have very good conditions and means to live from the state. Wherein he saw so far that now in so many ages since the prohibition, we have memory not of one ship that ever returned, and but of thirteen persons only at several times that chose to return in our bottoms.[28] What those few that returned may have reported abroad I know not. But you must think, whatsoever they have said could be taken where they came but for a dream. Now for our travelling from hence into parts abroad, our Lawgiver thought fit altogether

[28] vessels.

to restrain it. So is it not in China. For the Chineses sail where they will or can, which showeth that their law of keeping out strangers is a law of pusillanimity and fear. But this restraint of ours hath one only exception, which is admirable, preserving the good which cometh by communicating with strangers, and avoiding the hurt; and I will now open it to you. And here I shall seem a little to digress, but you will by and by find it pertinent. Ye shall understand (my dear friends) that amongst the excellent acts of that king, one above all hath the pre-eminence. It was the erection and institution of an Order or Society which we call *Salomon's House*, the noblest foundation (as we think) that ever was upon the earth, and the lanthorn of this kingdom. It is dedicated to the study of the Works and Creatures of God. Some think it beareth the founder's name a little corrupted, as if it should be Solamona's House. But the records write it as it is spoken. So as I take it to be denominate of[29] the King of the Hebrews, which is famous with you and no stranger to us. For we have some parts of his works which with you are lost; namely, that Natural History which he wrote, of all plants from the *cedar of Libanus* to the *moss that groweth out of the wall*, and of all *things that have life and motion*.[30] This maketh me think that our king, finding himself to symbolize[31] in many things with that king of the Hebrews (which lived many years before him), honoured him with the title of this foundation. And I am the rather induced to be of this opinion, for that I find in ancient records this Order or Society is sometimes called Salomon's House and sometimes the College of the Six Days Works; whereby I am satisfied that our excellent king had learned from the Hebrews that God had created the world and all that therein is within six days; and therefore he, instituting that House for the finding out of the true nature of all things (whereby God might have the more glory in the workmanship of them, and men the more fruit in the use of them), did give it also that second name. But now to come to our present purpose.

Salomon's House

[29] named after.
[30] I Kings 4:33.
[31] resemble, agree, be alike.

When the king had forbidden to all his people navigation into any part that was not under his crown, he made nevertheless this ordinance: that every twelve years there should be set forth out of this kingdom two ships, appointed to several* voyages; that in either of these ships there should be a mission of three of the Fellows or Brethren of Salomon's House, whose errand was only to give us knowledge of the affairs and state of those countries to which they were designed,[32] and especially of the sciences, arts, manufactures, and inventions of all the world, and withal to bring unto us books, instruments, and patterns in every kind; that the ships, after they had landed the brethren, should return, and that the brethren should stay abroad till the new mission. These ships are not otherwise fraught than with store of victuals and good quantity of treasure to remain with the brethren for the buying of such things and rewarding of such persons as they should think fit. Now for me to tell you how the vulgar sort of mariners are contained from being discovered at land; and how they that must be put on shore for any time colour themselves under the names of other nations; and to what places these voyages have been designed; and what places of *rendezvous* are appointed for the new missions; and the like circumstances of the practique,[33] I may not do it; neither is it much to your desire. But thus, you see, we maintain a trade, not for gold, silver, or jewels, nor for silks, nor for spices, nor any other commodity of matter, but only for God's first creature, which was *Light*, to have *light* (I say) of the growth of all parts of the world." And when he had said this, he was silent, and so were we all. For indeed we were all astonished to hear so strange things so probably told. And he, perceiving that we were willing to say somewhat but had it not ready, in great courtesy took us off,[34] and descended to ask us questions of our voyage and fortunes, and in the end concluded that we might do well to think with ourselves what time of stay we would demand of the state, and bade us not to scant ourselves, for he would procure such time as we desired.

[32] destined, directed.

[33] practice.

[34] i.e., changed the subject.

Whereupon we all rose up, and presented ourselves to kiss the skirt of his tippet, but he would not suffer us and so took his leave. But when it came once amongst our people that the state used* to offer conditions to strangers that would stay, we had work enough to get any of our men to look to our ship, and to keep them from going presently* to the governor to crave conditions. But with much ado we refrained them, till we might agree what course to take.

We took ourselves now for free men, seeing there was no danger of our utter perdition, and lived most joyfully, going abroad and seeing what was to be seen in the city and places adjacent within our tedder,[35] and obtaining acquaintance with many of the city, not of the meanest quality, at whose hands we found such humanity and such a freedom and desire to take strangers, as it were, into their bosom as was enough to make us forget all that was dear to us in our own countries; and continually we met with many things right worthy of observation and relation, as indeed, if there be a mirror in the world worthy to hold men's eyes, it is that country. One day there were two of our company bidden to a Feast of the Family, as they call it. A most natural, pious, and reverend custom it is, showing that nation to be compounded of all goodness. This is the manner of it. It is granted to any man that shall live to see thirty persons descended of his body alive together, and all above three years old, to make this feast, which is done at the cost of the state. The Father of the Family, whom they call the *Tirsan*, two days before the feast taketh to him three of such friends as he liketh to choose, and is assisted also by the governor of the city or place where the feast is celebrated; and all the persons of the family, of both sexes, are summoned to attend him. These two days the Tirsan sitteth in consultation concerning the good estate of the family. There, if there be any discord or suits between any of the family, they are compounded and appeased. There, if any of the family be distressed or decayed, order is taken for their relief and competent means to live. There, if any be subject to vice or take ill courses, they are reproved and censured. So likewise

[35] tether.

direction is given touching marriages and the courses of life which any of them should take, with divers other the like orders and advices. The governor assisteth, to the end to put in execution by his public authority the decrees and orders of the Tirsan, if they should be disobeyed, though that seldom needeth,[36] such reverence and obedience they give to the order of nature. The Tirsan doth also then ever choose one man from amongst his sons to live in house with him, who is called ever after the Son of the Vine. The reason will hereafter appear. On the feast day the Father or Tirsan cometh forth after divine service into a large room where the feast is celebrated, which room hath an half-pace[37] at the upper end. Against the wall, in the middle of the half-pace, is a chair placed for him, with a table and carpet before it. Over the chair is a state,[38] made round or oval, and it is of ivy, an ivy somewhat whiter than ours, like the leaf of a silver asp, but more shining, for it is green all winter. And the state is curiously wrought with silver and silk of divers colours, broiding[39] or binding in the ivy, and is ever of the work of some of the daughters of the family, and veiled over at the top with a fine net of silk and silver. But the substance of it is true ivy, whereof, after it is taken down, the friends of the family are desirous to have some leaf or sprig to keep. The Tirsan cometh forth with all his generation or lineage, the males before him and the females following him; and if there be a mother from whose body the whole lineage is descended, there is a traverse[40] placed in a loft above on the right hand of the chair, with a privy door and a carved window of glass, leaded with gold and blue, where she sitteth but is not seen. When the Tirsan is come forth, he sitteth down in the chair, and all the lineage place themselves against the wall, both at his back and upon the return* of the half-pace, in order of their years without difference of sex, and stand upon their feet. When he is set, the room being always full of company, but well kept and without disorder, after some pause there cometh in from the lower end of the room a *Taratan*

NB ←

Sex discrimination

---

[36] is necessary.
[37] a raised floor or dais.
[38] canopy.

[39] braiding, interweaving.
[40] movable screen or partition.

(which is as much as an herald) and on either side of him two young lads, whereof one carrieth a scroll of their shining yellow parchment, and the other a cluster of grapes of gold with a long foot or stalk. The herald and children are clothed with mantles of sea-water green satin, but the herald's mantle is streamed with gold, and hath a train. Then the herald with three courtesies, or rather inclinations, cometh up as far as the half-pace, and there first taketh into his hand the scroll. This scroll is the King's Charter, containing gift of revenue and many privileges, exemptions, and points of honour granted to the Father of the Family, and is ever styled and directed, *To such an one our well-beloved friend and creditor*, which is a title proper only to this case. For they say the king is debtor to no man but for propagation of his subjects. The seal set to the king's charter is the king's image, imbossed or moulded in gold; and though such charters be expedited of course and as of right,[41] yet they are varied by discretion according to the number and dignity of the family. This charter the herald readeth aloud, and while it is read, the father or Tirsan standeth up, supported by two of his sons, such as he chooseth. Then the herald mounteth the half-pace, and delivereth the charter into his hand, and with that there is an acclamation by all that are present in their language, which is thus much: *Happy are the people of Bensalem*. Then the herald taketh into his hand from the other child the cluster of grapes, which is of gold, both the stalk and the grapes. But the grapes are daintily enamelled; and if the males of the family be the greater number, the grapes are enamelled purple, with a little sun set on the top; if the females, then they are enamelled into a greenish yellow, with a crescent on the top. The grapes are in number as many as there are descendants of the family. This golden cluster the herald delivereth also to the Tirsan, who presently* delivereth it over to that son that he had formerly chosen to be in house with him, who beareth it before his father as an ensign of honour when he goeth in public, ever after, and is thereupon called the Son of the Vine. After this ceremony

Rent or life.

----

[41] i.e., are issued as matters of course and of right.

ended, the father or Tirsan retireth, and after some time cometh forth again to dinner, where he sitteth alone under the state as before; and none of his descendants sit with him, of what degree or dignity soever, except he hap to be of Salomon's House. He is served only by his own children, such as are male, who perform unto him all service of the table upon the knee, and the women only stand about him, leaning against the wall. The room below the half-pace hath tables on the sides for the guests that are bidden, who are served with great and comely order; and towards the end of dinner (which in the greatest feasts with them lasteth never above an hour and an half) there is an hymn sung, varied according to the invention of him that composeth it (for they have excellent poesy), but the subject of it is (always) the praises of Adam and Noah and Abraham, whereof the former two peopled the world, and the last was the Father of the Faithful, concluding ever with a thanksgiving for the nativity of our Saviour, in whose birth the births of all are only blessed. Dinner being done, the Tirsan retireth again, and having withdrawn himself alone into a place where he maketh some private prayers, he cometh forth the third time, to give the blessing, with all his descendants, who stand about him as at the first. Then he calleth them forth by one and by one, by name, as he pleaseth, though seldom the order of age be inverted. The person that is called (the table being before removed) kneeleth down before the chair, and the father layeth his hand upon his head, or her head, and giveth the blessing in these words: *Son of Bensalem* (or *Daughter of Bensalem*), *thy father saith it, the man by whom thou hast breath and life speaketh the word: the blessing of the everlasting Father, the Prince of Peace, and the Holy Dove be upon thee, and make the days of thy pilgrimage good and many.* This he saith to every of them; and that done, if there be any of his sons of eminent merit and virtue (so they be not above two), he calleth for them again, and saith, laying his arm over their shoulders, they standing, *Sons, it is well ye are born, give God the praise, and persevere to the end.* And withal delivereth to either of them a jewel made in the figure of an ear of wheat, which they ever after wear in the front of their turban or hat. This done, they fall to music and dances and other recreations, after their manner, for the rest of the day. This is the full order of that feast.

By that time six or seven days were spent, I was fallen into strait[42] acquaintance with a merchant of that city, whose name was Joabin. He was a Jew, and circumcised, for they have some few stirps of Jews yet remaining among them, whom they leave to their own religion. Which they may the better do, because they are of a far differing disposition from the Jews in other parts. For whereas they hate the name of Christ, and have a secret inbred rancour against the people amongst whom they live, these (contrariwise) give unto our Saviour many high attributes, and love the nation of Bensalem extremely. Surely this man of whom I speak would ever acknowledge that Christ was born of a Virgin, and that he was more than a man, and he would tell how God made him ruler of the Seraphims which guard his throne; and they call him also the *Milken Way* and the *Eliah*[43] of the *Messiah*, and many other high names, which though they be inferior to his divine Majesty, yet they are far from the language of other Jews. And for the country of Bensalem, this man would make no end of commending it, being desirous, by tradition among the Jews there, to have it believed that the people thereof were of the generations of Abraham by another son, whom they call Nachoran, and that Moses by a secret cabala ordained the laws of Bensalem which they now use, and that when the Messiah should come, and sit in his throne at Hierusalem, the king of Bensalem should sit at his feet, whereas other kings should keep a great distance. But yet setting aside these Jewish dreams, the man was a wise man, and learned, and of great policy, and excellently seen* in the laws and customs of that nation. Amongst other discourses, one day I told him I was much affected with the relation I had from some of the company, of their custom in holding the Feast of the Family, for that (methought) I had never heard of a solemnity wherein nature did so much preside.

[42] close, intimate.
[43] Elijah, the promised forerunner of Christ. See Malachi 4:5.

And because propagation of families proceedeth from nuptial copulation, I desired to know of him what laws and customs they had concerning marriage, and whether they kept marriage well, and whether they were tied to one wife? For that where population is so much affected,* and such as with them it seemed to be, there is commonly permission of plurality of wives. To this he said, "You have reason for to commend that excellent institution of the Feast of the Family. And indeed we have experience that those families that are partakers of the blessing of that feast do flourish and prosper ever after in an extraordinary manner. But hear me now, and I will tell you what I know. You shall understand that there is not under the heavens so chaste a nation as this of Bensalem, nor so free from all pollution or foulness. It is the virgin of the world. I remember I have read in one of your European books of an holy hermit amongst you that desired to see the Spirit of Fornication, and there appeared to him a little foul ugly Ethiop.[44] But if he had desired to see the Spirit of Chastity of Bensalem, it would have appeared to him in the likeness of a fair beautiful Cherubin. For there is nothing amongst mortal men more fair and admirable than the chaste minds of this people. Know therefore that with them there are no stews, no dissolute houses, no courtesans, nor any thing of that kind. Nay they wonder (with detestation) at you in Europe, which permit such things. They say ye have put marriage out of office, for marriage is ordained a remedy for unlawful concupiscence, and natural concupiscence seemeth as a spur to marriage. But when men have at hand a remedy more agreeable to their corrupt will, marriage is almost expulsed.* And therefore there are with you seen infinite men that marry not, but choose rather a libertine and impure single life than to be yoked in marriage; and many that do marry, marry late, when the prime and strength of their years is past. And when they do marry, what is marriage to them but a very bargain, wherein is sought alliance or portion or reputation, with some desire (almost in-

---

[44] Ethiopian: the Klein Meister of La Motte Fouqué's *Sintram*. [Ellis]

different) of issue, and not the faithful nuptial union of man and wife, that was first instituted? Neither is it possible that those that have cast away so basely so much of their strength should greatly esteem children (being of the same matter) as chaste men do. So likewise during marriage is the case much amended, as it ought to be if those things were tolerated only for necessity? No, but they remain still as a very affront to marriage. The haunting of those dissolute places or resort to courtesans are no more punished in married men than in bachelors. And the depraved custom of change, and the delight in meretricious embracements (where sin is turned into art) maketh marriage a dull thing, and a kind of imposition or tax. They hear you defend these things, as done to avoid greater evils, as advoutries,[45] deflowering of virgins, unnatural lust, and the like. But they say this is a preposterous wisdom, and they call it *Lot's offer*, who to save his guests from abusing, offered his daughters;[46] nay, they say farther that there is little gained in this, for that the same vices and appetites do still remain and abound, unlawful lust being like a furnace, that if you stop the flames altogether, it will quench, but if you give it any vent, it will rage. As for masculine love, they have no touch of it, and yet there are not so faithful and inviolate friendships in the world again as are there; and to speak generally (as I said before) I have not read of any such chastity in any people as theirs. And their usual saying is *That whosoever is unchaste cannot reverence himself*; and they say *That the reverence of a man's self is, next religion, the chiefest bridle of all vices*." And when he had said this, the good Jew paused a little; whereupon I, far more willing to hear him speak on than to speak myself, yet thinking it decent that upon his pause of speech I should not be altogether silent, said only this: that I would say to him, as the widow of Sarepta said to Elias, that he was come to bring to memory our sins;[47] and that I confess the righteousness of Bensalem was greater than the righteousness of Europe. At which speech he bowed his head, and went on in this manner: "They have also many wise and excellent laws touching

[45] adulteries.
[46] See Gen. 19:8.
[47] See I Kings 17:8.

marriage. They allow no polygamy. They have ordained that none do intermarry or contract, until a month be passed from their first interview. Marriage without consent of parents they do not make void, but they mulct it in the inheritors, for the children of such marriages are not admitted to inherit above a third part of their parents' inheritance. I have read in a book of one of your men, of a Feigned Commonwealth, where the married couple are permitted, before they contract, to see one another naked.[48] This they dislike, for they think it a scorn to give a refusal after so familiar knowledge; but because of many hidden defects in men and women's bodies, they have a more civil way, for they have near every town a couple of pools (which they call *Adam and Eve's pools*) where it is permitted to one of the friends of the man, and another of the friends of the woman, to see them severally bathe naked."

And as we were thus in conference, there came one that seemed to be a messenger, in a rich huke,[49] that spake with the Jew; whereupon he turned to me and said, "You will pardon me, for I am commanded away in haste." The next morning he came to me again, joyful as it seemed, and said, "There is word come to the governor of the city that one of the Fathers of Salomon's House will be here this day seven-night; we have seen none of them this dozen years. His coming is in state, but the cause of his coming is secret. I will provide you and your fellows of a good standing to see his entry." I thanked him, and told him I was most glad of the news. The day being come, he made his entry. He was a man of middle stature and age, comely of person, and had an aspect as if he pitied men. He was clothed in a robe of fine black cloth with wide sleeves and a cape. His under garment was of excellent white linen down to the foot, girt with a girdle of the same, and a sindon* or tippet of the same about his neck. He had gloves that were curious* and set with stone, and shoes of peach-coloured velvet. His neck was bare to the shoulders. His hat was like a helmet or Spanish montero, and his locks curled below it decently; they were of colour brown. His beard was cut

---

[48] Sir Thomas More, *Utopia*, Bk. II.
[49] hooded cape.

round, and of the same colour with his hair, somewhat lighter. He was carried in a rich chariot without wheels, litterwise, with two horses at either end, richly trapped in blue velvet embroidered, and two footmen on each side in the like attire. The chariot was all of cedar, gilt and adorned with crystal, save that the fore-end had panels of sapphires set in borders of gold, and the hinder-end the like of emeralds of the Peru colour.[50] There was also a sun of gold, radiant, upon the top, in the midst, and on the top before, a small cherub of gold, with wings displayed.[51] The chariot was covered with cloth of gold tissued[52] upon blue. He had before him fifty attendants, young men all, in white satin loose coats to the mid-leg, and stockings of white silk, and shoes of blue velvet, and hats of blue velvet, with fine plumes of divers colours, set round like hatbands. Next before the chariot went two men, bare-headed, in linen garments down to the foot, girt, and shoes of blue velvet, who carried the one a crosier, the other a pastoral staff like a sheep-hook, neither of them of metal, but the crosier of balm-wood, the pastoral staff of cedar. Horsemen he had none neither before nor behind his chariot: as it seemeth, to avoid all tumult and trouble. Behind his chariot went all the officers and principals of the Companies of the City. He sat alone upon cushions of a kind of excellent plush, blue, and under his foot curious* carpets of silk of divers colours, like the Persian but far finer. He held up his bare hand as he went, as blessing the people, but in silence. The street was wonderfully well kept, so that there was never any army had their men stand in better battle array than the people stood. The windows likewise were not crowded, but every one stood in them as if they had been placed. When the show was past, the Jew said to me, "I shall not be able to attend you as I would, in regard* of some charge the city hath laid upon me for the entertaining of this great person." Three days after the Jew came to me again, and said, "Ye are happy men; for the Father of Salomon's House taketh knowledge of your being here, and commanded me to tell you that he will

---

[50] emerald green.
[51] outspread.
[52] interwoven.

admit all your company to his presence, and have private conference with one of you that ye shall choose, and for this hath
appointed the next day after tomorrow. And because he meaneth
to give you his blessing, he hath appointed it in the forenoon."
We came at our day and hour, and I was chosen by my fellows
for the private access. We found him in a fair chamber, richly
hanged and carpeted under foot, without any degrees to the
state.[53] He was set upon a low throne richly adorned, and a rich
cloth of state over his head, of blue satin embroidered. He was
alone, save that he had two pages of honour, on either hand one,
finely attired in white. His under garments were the like that we
saw him wear in the chariot, but instead of his gown he had on
him a mantle with a cape of the same fine black, fastened about
him. When we came in, as we were taught, we bowed low at our
first entrance, and when we were come near his chair, he stood
up, holding forth his hand ungloved and in posture of blessing;
and we every one of us stooped down, and kissed the hem of his
tippet. That done, the rest departed and I remained. Then he
warned the pages forth of the room, and caused me to sit down
beside him, and spake to me thus in the Spanish tongue:

"God bless thee, my son; I will give thee the greatest jewel I
have. For I will impart unto thee, for the love of God and men,
a relation of the true state of Salomon's House. Son, to make you
know the true state of Salomon's House, I will keep this order.
First, I will set forth unto you the end of our foundation. Secondly, the preparations and instruments we have for our works.
Thirdly, the several employments and functions whereto our
fellows are assigned. And fourthly, the ordinances and rites
which we observe.

"The End of our Foundation is the knowledge of Causes and
secret motions of things, and the enlarging of the bounds of
Human Empire, to the effecting of all things possible.

"The Preparations and Instruments are these. We have large
and deep caves of several depths; the deepest are sunk six hundred fathom, and some of them are digged and made under great

[53] i.e., without any steps leading up
to the canopy.

Cave
Laboratories

hills and mountains, so that if you reckon together the depth of the hill and the depth of the cave, they are (some of them) above three miles deep. For we find that the depth of a hill and the depth of a cave from the flat is the same thing, both remote alike from the sun and heaven's beams and from the open air. These caves we call the Lower Region. And we use them for all coagulations, indurations, refrigerations, and conservations of bodies. We use them likewise for the imitation of natural mines and the producing also of new artificial metals by compositions and materials which we use, and lay there for many years. We use them also sometimes (which may seem strange) for curing of some diseases and for prolongation of life in some hermits that choose to live there, well accommodated of[54] all things necessary; and indeed live very long, by whom also we learn many things.

"We have burials in several earths, where we put divers cements, as the Chineses do their porcelain. But we have them in greater variety, and some of them more fine. We have also great variety of composts and soils for the making of the earth fruitful.

Towers

"We have high towers, the highest about half a mile in height, and some of them likewise set upon high mountains, so that the vantage of the hill with the tower is in the highest of them three miles at least. And these places we call the Upper Region, accounting the air between the high places and the low as a Middle Region. We use these towers, according to their several heights and situations, for insolation, refrigeration, conservation, and for the view of divers meteors,[55] as winds, rain, snow, hail, and some of the fiery meteors also. And upon them, in some places, are dwellings of hermits, whom we visit sometimes, and instruct what to observe.

"We have great lakes both salt and fresh, whereof we have use for the fish and fowl. We use them also for burials of some natural bodies, for we find a difference in things buried in earth or in air below the earth and things buried in water. We have also pools, of which some do strain fresh water out of salt, and

[54] with.
[55] meteorological phenomena.

others by art do turn fresh water into salt. We have also some rocks in the midst of the sea, and some bays upon the shore, for some works wherein is required the air and vapour of the sea. We have likewise violent streams and cataracts, which serve us for many motions, and likewise engines for multiplying and enforcing[56] of winds, to set also on going divers motions.

"We have also a number of artificial wells and fountains, made in imitation of the natural sources and baths, as tincted upon[57] vitriol, sulphur, steel, brass, lead, nitre, and other minerals. And again we have little wells for infusions of many things, where the waters take the virtue[58] quicker and better than in vessels or basons. And amongst them we have a water which we call Water of Paradise, being, by that we do to it, made very sovereign for health and prolongation of life.

"We have also great and spacious houses, where we imitate and demonstrate meteors, as snow, hail, rain, some artificial rains of bodies and not of water, thunders, lightnings, also generations of bodies in air, as frogs, flies, and divers others.

"We have also fair and large baths of several mixtures for the cure of diseases and the restoring of man's body from arefaction,[59] and others for the confirming of it in strength of sinews, vital parts, and the very juice and substance of the body.

"We have also large and various orchards and gardens, wherein we do not so much respect beauty as variety of ground and soil, proper for divers trees and herbs, and some very spacious, where trees and berries are set whereof we make divers kinds of drinks, besides the vineyards. In these we practise likewise all conclusions[60] of grafting and inoculating, as well of wild trees as fruit trees, which produceth many effects. And we make (by art) in the same orchards and gardens trees and flowers to come earlier or later than their seasons, and to come up and bear more speedily than by their natural course they do. We make them also by art greater much than their nature, and their fruit greater and sweeter and of differing taste, smell, colour, and figure, from

[56] giving force to, strengthening.
[57] tinctured with.
[58] i.e., absorb or dissolve the main property of the substance.
[59] drying up.
[60] experiments.

their nature. And many of them we so order as they become of medicinal use.

Botany

"We have also means to make divers plants rise by mixtures of earths without seeds, and likewise to make divers new plants differing from the vulgar, and to make one tree or plant turn into another.

Zoology

"We have also parks and inclosures of all sorts of beasts and birds, which we use not only for view or rareness but likewise for dissections and trials, that thereby we may take light[61] what may be wrought upon the body of man. Wherein we find many strange effects: as continuing life in them, though divers parts, which you account vital, be perished and taken forth; resuscitating of some that seem dead in appearance; and the like. We try also all poisons and other medicines upon them, as well of chirurgery as physic. By art likewise we make them greater or taller than their kind is, and contrariwise dwarf them, and stay their growth; we make them more fruitful and bearing than their kind is, and contrariwise barren and not generative. Also we make them differ in colour, shape, activity, many ways. We find means to make commixtures and copulations of different kinds, which have produced many new kinds, and them not barren, as the general opinion is. We make a number of kinds of serpents, worms, flies, fishes, of putrefaction, whereof some are advanced (in effect) to be perfect creatures, like beasts or birds, and have sexes, and do propagate. Neither do we this by chance, but we know beforehand of what matter and commixture what kind of those creatures will arise.

Medical Surgical Experiment

Create life

"We have also particular pools, where we make trials upon fishes, as we have said before of beasts and birds.

"We have also places for breed and generation of those kinds of worms and flies which are of special use, such as are with you your silkworms and bees.

"I will not hold you long with recounting of our brew-houses, bakehouses, and kitchens, where are made divers drinks, breads, and meats, rare and of special effects. Wines we have of grapes,

---

[61] gain enlightenment or understanding.

and drinks of other juice of fruits, of grains, and of roots, and of mixtures with honey, sugar, manna, and fruits dried and decocted. Also of the tears or woundings of trees and of the pulp of canes. And these drinks are of several ages, some to the age or last[62] of forty years. We have drinks also brewed with several herbs and roots and spices, yea with several fleshes and white meats,[63] whereof some of the drinks are such as they are in effect *food* meat and drink both, so that divers, especially in age, do desire to live with[64] them, with little or no meat or bread. And above all, we strive to have drinks of extreme thin parts to insinuate into the body, and yet without all biting, sharpness, or fretting, insomuch as some of them put upon the back of your hand will, *drinks* with a little stay, pass through to the palm, and yet taste mild to the mouth. We have also waters which we ripen in that fashion, as they become nourishing, so that they are indeed excellent drink, and many will use no other. Breads we have of several grains, roots, and kernels; yea and some of flesh and fish dried, with divers kinds of leavenings and seasonings, so that some do extremely move appetites; some do nourish so, as divers do live of them without any other meat, who live very long. So for meats: we have some of them so beaten and made tender and mortified, yet without all corrupting, as a weak heat of the stomach will turn them into good chylus,[65] as well as a strong heat would meat otherwise prepared. We have some meats also and breads and drinks, which taken by men enable them to fast long after, and some other that, used, make the very flesh of men's bodies sensibly more hard and tough, and their strength far greater than otherwise it would be.

"We have dispensatories, or shops of medicines. Wherein you may easily think, if we have such variety of plants and living creatures more than you have in Europe (for we know what you have), the simples, drugs, and ingredients of medicines must likewise be in so much the greater variety. We have them likewise

[62] duration.

[63] either food (as butter, cheese, etc.) derived from animal products such as milk and eggs, or any light-coloured flesh, as veal, poultry, rabbits, etc.

[64] on.

[65] chyle. mortified: aged (to the point of putrefaction).

Medicine

of divers ages and long fermentations. And for their preparations, we have not only all manner of exquisite* distillations and separations, and especially by gentle heats and percolations through divers strainers, yea and substances, but also exact forms of composition, whereby they incorporate almost, as they were natural simples.

Consumer goods

"We have also divers mechanical arts, which you have not, and stuffs made by them, as papers, linen, silks, tissues, dainty works of feathers of wonderful lustre, excellent dyes, and many others; and shops likewise as well for such as are not brought into vulgar use amongst us as for those that are. For you must know that of the things before recited, many of them are grown into use throughout the kingdom, but yet if they did flow from our invention, we have of them also for patterns and principals.[66]

practical application

"We have also furnaces of great diversities and that keep great diversity of heats: fierce and quick; strong and constant; soft and mild; blown, quiet; dry, moist; and the like. But above all, we have heats in imitation of the sun's and heavenly bodies' heats, that pass divers inequalities and (as it were) orbs, progresses, and returns,[67] whereby we produce admirable effects. Besides, we have heats of dungs, and of bellies and maws of living creatures, and of their bloods and bodies, and of hays and herbs laid up moist, of lime unquenched,[68] and such like. Instruments also which generate heat only by motion. And farther, places for strong insolations; and again, places under the earth, which by nature or art yield heat. These divers heats we use, as the nature of the operation which we intend requireth.

Diverse heats

"We have also perspective-houses, where we make demonstrations of all lights and radiations, and of all colours; and out of things uncoloured and transparent we can represent unto you all several colours, not in rainbows, as it is in gems and prisms, but of themselves single. We represent also all multiplications of light, which we carry to great distance, and make so sharp as to discern small points and lines; also all colorations of light, all

light and sight

---

[66] originals from which copies are made, models.
[67] movements of the heavenly bodies in their orbits.
[68] i.e., unslaked.

delusions and deceits of the sight in figures, magnitudes, motions, colours, all demonstrations of shadows. We find also divers means, yet unknown to you, of producing of light originally from divers bodies. We procure means of seeing objects afar off, as in the heaven and remote places, and represent things near as afar off and things afar off as near, making feigned distances. We have also helps for the sight, far above spectacles and glasses in use. We have also glasses and means to see small and minute bodies perfectly and distinctly, as the shapes and colours of small flies and worms, grains and flaws in gems, which cannot otherwise be seen, observations in urine and blood, not otherwise to be seen. We make artificial rainbows, haloes, and circles about light. We represent also all manner of reflexions, refractions, and multiplications of visual beams of objects.

"We have also precious stones of all kinds, many of them of great beauty and to you unknown; crystals likewise; and glasses of divers kinds; and amongst them some of metals vitrificated, and other materials besides those of which you make glass. Also a number of fossils and imperfect minerals,[69] which you have not. Likewise loadstones of prodigious virtue and other rare stones, both natural and artificial.

"We have also sound-houses, where we practise and demonstrate all sounds and their generation. We have harmonies, which you have not, of quarter-sounds and lesser slides of sounds. Divers instruments of music likewise to you unknown, some sweeter than any you have, together with bells and rings that are dainty and sweet. We represent small sounds as great and deep, likewise great sounds extenuate[70] and sharp; we make divers tremblings and warblings of sounds, which in their original are entire. We represent and imitate all articulate sounds and letters, and the voices and notes of beasts and birds. We have certain helps which set to the ear do further the hearing greatly. We have also divers strange and artificial echoes, reflecting the voice many times, and as it were tossing it, and some that give back the voice louder than it came, some shriller and some deeper;

[69] i.e., mineral ores.
[70] extenuated, thin.

yea, some rendering the voice differing in the letters or articulate sound from that they receive. We have also means to convey sounds in trunks[71] and pipes, in strange lines and distances.

telephone?

"We have also perfume-houses, wherewith we join also practices of taste. We multiply smells, which may seem strange. We imitate smells, making all smells to breathe out of other mixtures than those that give them. We make divers imitations of taste likewise, so that they will deceive any man's taste. And in this house we contain also a confiture-house, where we make all sweetmeats, dry and moist, and divers pleasant wines, milks, broths, and sallets,[72] far in greater variety than you have.

Smell & taste

Experiment

"We have also engine-houses, where are prepared engines and instruments for all sorts of motions. There we imitate and practise to make swifter motions than any you have, either out of your muskets or any engine that you have; and to make them and multiply them more easily and with small force by wheels and other means, and to make them stronger and more violent than yours are, exceeding your greatest cannons and basilisks.[73] We represent also ordnance and instruments of war, and engines of all kinds, and likewise new mixtures and compositions of gunpowder, wildfires burning in water and unquenchable. Also fireworks of all variety both for pleasure and use. We imitate also flights of birds; we have some degrees of flying in the air; we have ships and boats for going under water, and brooking of seas, also swimming-girdles and supporters. We have divers curious clocks and other like motions of return[74] and some perpetual motions. We imitate also motions of living creatures by images of men, beasts, birds, fishes, and serpents. We have also a great number of other various motions, strange for equality, fineness, and subtilty.

Engines & machines

airplanes & submarines

"We have also a mathematical house, where are represented all instruments, as well of geometry as astronomy, exquisitely made.

math (Bacon's weakness)

"We have also houses of deceits of the senses, where we represent all manner of feats of juggling, false apparitions, impostures,

[71] tubes.
[72] salads.

[73] stone-shooting cannon.
[74] oscillation.

and illusions, and their fallacies. And surely you will easily believe that we that have so many things truly natural which induce admiration* could in a world of particulars deceive the senses, if we would disguise those things and labour to make them seem more miraculous. But we do hate all impostures and lies; insomuch as we have severely forbidden it to all our fellows, under pain of ignominy and fines, that they do not show any natural work or thing adorned or swelling, but only pure as it is, and without all affectation of strangeness.

"These are, my son, the riches of Salomon's House.

"For the several employments and offices of our fellows, we have twelve that sail into foreign countries, under the names of other nations (for our own we conceal), who bring us the books and abstracts and patterns of experiments of all other parts. These we call Merchants of Light.

"We have three that collect the experiments which are in all books. These we call Depredators.

"We have three that collect the experiments of all mechanical arts, and also of liberal sciences, and also of practices which are not brought into arts. These we call Mystery Men.

"We have three that try new experiments, such as themselves think good. These we call Pioneers or Miners.

"We have three that draw the experiments of the former four into titles and tables, to give the better light for the drawing of observations and axioms out of them. These we call Compilers.

"We have three that bend[75] themselves, looking into the experiments of their fellows, and cast about how to draw out of them things of use and practice for man's life, and knowledge as well for works as for plain demonstration of causes, means of natural divinations, and the easy and clear discovery of the virtues and parts of bodies. These we call Dowry Men or Benefactors.

"Then, after divers meetings and consults of our whole number to consider of the former labours and collections, we have three that take care, out of them, to direct new experiments of a

[75] apply.

higher light, more penetrating into nature than the former. These we call Lamps.

"We have three others that do execute the experiments so directed, and report them. These we call Inoculators.

"Lastly, we have three that raise the former discoveries by experiments into greater observations, axioms, and aphorisms. These we call Interpreters of Nature.

"We have also, as you must think, novices and apprentices, that the succession of the former employed men do not fail, besides a great number of servants and attendants, men and women. And this we do also: we have consultations, which of the inventions and experiences which we have discovered shall be published, and which not; and take all an oath of secrecy for the concealing of those which we think fit to keep secret, though some of those we do reveal sometimes to the state, and some not.

"For our ordinances and rites, we have two very long and fair galleries: in one of these we place patterns and samples of all manner of the more rare and excellent inventions, in the other we place the statuas of all principal inventors. There we have the statua of your Columbus, that discovered the West Indies; also the inventor of ships; your monk[76] that was the inventor of ordnance and of gunpowder; the inventor of music; the inventor of letters; the inventor of printing; the inventor of observations of astronomy; the inventor of works in metal; the inventor of glass; the inventor of silk of the worm; the inventor of wine; the inventor of corn and bread; the inventor of sugars; and all these by more certain tradition than you have. Then have we divers inventors of our own, of excellent works, which since you have not seen, it were too long to make descriptions of them; and besides, in the right understanding of those descriptions you might easily err. For upon every invention of value we erect a statua to the inventor, and give him a liberal and honourable reward. These statuas are some of brass, some of marble and touchstone, some of cedar and other special woods gilt and adorned, some of iron, some of silver, some of gold.

"We have certain hymns and services, which we say daily, of

[76] Roger Bacon.

laud and thanks to God for his marvellous works, and forms of *Prayer* prayers imploring his aid and blessing for the illumination of our labours and the turning of them into good and holy uses.

"Lastly, we have circuits or visits of divers principal cities of the kingdom, where, as it cometh to pass, we do publish such new profitable inventions as we think good. And we do also declare natural divinations[77] of diseases, plagues, swarms of hurtful creatures, scarcity, tempests, earthquakes, great inundations, comets, temperature of the year, and divers other things; and we give counsel thereupon what the people shall do for the prevention and remedy of them."

And when he had said this, he stood up, and I, as I had been taught, kneeled down, and he laid his right hand upon my head, and said, "God bless thee, my son, and God bless this relation which I have made. I give thee leave to publish it for the good of other nations, for we here are in God's bosom, a land unknown." And so he left me, having assigned a value of about two thousand ducats for a bounty to me and my fellows. For they give great largesses where they come upon all occasions.

[THE REST WAS NOT PERFECTED]

---

[77] i.e., make scientific forecasts.

Letters

To my Lord Treasurer Burghley[1]

My Lord,

With as much confidence as mine own honest and faithful devotion unto your service and your honourable correspondence unto me and my poor estate can breed in a man, do I commend myself unto your Lordship. I wax now somewhat ancient; one and thirty years is a great deal of sand in the hour-glass. My health, I thank God, I find confirmed; and I do not fear that action shall impair it, because I account my ordinary course of study and meditation to be more painful than most parts of action are. I ever bare a mind (in some middle place that I could discharge) to serve her Majesty; not as a man born under Sol, that loveth honour; nor under Jupiter, that loveth business (for the contemplative planet carrieth me away wholly); but as a man born under an excellent Sovereign, that deserveth the dedication of all men's abilities. Besides, I do not find in myself so much self-love, but that the greater parts of my thoughts are to deserve well (if I were able) of my friends, and namely of your Lordship; who being the Atlas of this commonwealth, the honour of my house, and the second founder of my poor estate, I am tied by all duties, both of a good patriot, and of an unworthy kinsman, and of an obliged servant, to employ whatsoever I am to do you service. Again, the meanness of my estate doth somewhat move me: for though I cannot accuse myself that I am either prodigal or slothful, yet my health is not to spend, nor my course to get. Lastly, I confess that I have as vast contemplative ends, as I have moderate civil ends: for I have taken all knowledge to be my province; and if I could purge it of two sorts of rovers, whereof the one with frivolous disputations,

[1] William Cecil (1520-98): Bacon's uncle, Secretary of State and first minister to Elizabeth.

confutations, and verbosities, the other with blind experiments and auricular traditions and impostures, hath committed so many spoils, I hope I should bring in industrious observations, grounded conclusions, and profitable inventions and discoveries; the best state of that province. This, whether it be curiosity, or vain glory, or nature, or (if one take it favourably) *philanthropia*, is so fixed in my mind as it cannot be removed. And I do easily see, that place of any reasonable countenance doth bring commandment of more wits than of a man's own; which is the thing I greatly affect. And for your Lordship, perhaps you shall not find more strength and less encounter in any other. And if your Lordship shall find now, or at any time, that I do seek or affect any place whereunto any that is nearer unto your Lordship shall be concurrent, say then that I am a most dishonest man. And if your Lordship will not carry me on, I will not do as Anaxagoras did, who reduced himself with contemplation unto voluntary poverty: but this I will do; I will sell the inheritance that I have, and purchase some lease of quick revenue, or some office of gain that shall be executed by deputy, and so give over all care of service, and become some sorry book-maker, or a true pioner in that mine of truth, which (he said) lay so deep. This which I have writ unto your Lordship is rather thoughts than words, being set down without all art, disguising, or reservation. Wherein I have done honour both to your Lordship's wisdom, in judging that that will be best believed of your Lordship which is truest, and to your Lordship's good nature, in retaining nothing from you. And even so I wish your Lordship all happiness, and to myself means and occasion to be added to my faithful desire to do you service. From my lodging at Gray's Inn.

[1592]

To the Queen

Madam,

Remembering that your Majesty had been gracious to me both in countenancing me and conferring upon me the reversion of a good place, and perceiving your Majesty had taken some displeasure towards me, both these were arguments to move me to offer unto your Majesty my service, to the end to have means to deserve your benefit and to repair my error.[1] Upon this ground I affected myself to no great matter, but only a place of my profession, such as I do see divers younger in proceeding to myself, and men of no great note, do without blame aspire unto. But if any of my friends do press this matter, I do assure your Majesty my spirit is not with them. It sufficeth me that I have let your Majesty know that I am ready to do that for your service which I never would do for mine own gain. And if your Majesty like others better, I shall with the Lacedemonian be glad that there is such choice of abler men than myself. Your Majesty's favour indeed, and access to your royal person, I did ever, encouraged by your own speeches, seek and desire; and I would be very glad to be reintegrate in that. But I will not wrong mine own good mind so much as to stand upon it now, when your Majesty may conceive I do it but to make my profit of it. But my mind turneth upon other wheels than those of profit. The conclusion shall be that I wish your Majesty served answerable to yourself. *Principis est virtus maxima nosse suos.*[2] Thus I most humbly crave pardon of my boldness and plainness. God preserve your Majesty.

[1593]

Francis Bacon to the Earl of Essex

My Lord,

I thank your Lordship very much for your kind and comfortable letter, which I hope will be followed at hand with another of more assurance. And I must confess this very delay hath gone so near me, as it hath almost overthrown my health. For when I revolved the good memory of my father, the near degree of

---

[1] Bacon had angered Elizabeth by attacking in the House of Commons her plans to have a large levy ratified by rather questionable means.

[2] "The chief virtue of a prince is to know his followers." Martial, *Epigrams*, VIII.xv.8.

alliance I stand in to my Lord Treasurer, your Lordship's so signalled and declared favour, the honourable testimony of so many counsellors, the commendation unlaboured and in sort offered by my Lords the Judges and the Master of the Rolls elect; that I was voiced with great expectation, and (though I say it myself) with the wishes of most men, to the higher place; that I am a man that the Queen hath already done for; and princes, especially her Majesty, loveth to make an end where they begin; and then add hereunto the obscureness and many exceptions to my competitors; when (I say) I revolve all this, I cannot but conclude with myself that no man ever received a more exquisite disgrace. And therefore truly, my Lord, I was determined, and am determined, if her Majesty reject me, this to do. My nature can take no evil ply; but I will by God's assistance, with this disgrace of my fortune, and yet with that comfort of the good opinion of so many honourable and worthy persons, retire myself with a couple of men to Cambridge, and there spend my life in my studies and contemplations, without looking back. I humbly pray your Lordship to pardon me for troubling you with my melancholy. For the matter itself, I commend it to your love. Only I pray you communicate afresh this day with my Lord Treasurer and Sir Robert Cecil;[1] and if you esteem my fortune, remember the point of precedency. The objections to my competitors your Lordship knoweth partly. I pray spare them not, not over the Queen, but to the great ones, to show your confidence and to work their distaste. Thus longing exceedingly to exchange troubling your Lordship with serving you, I rest

Your Lordship's,

In most entire and faithful duty,

F. B.

[March 30, 1593][2]

I humbly pray your Lordship I may hear from you sometime this day.

---

[1] Lord Salisbury (1563-1612): son of Burghley, Secretary of State, Lord Treasurer, Chancellor of the University of Cambridge.

[2] This is the date docketed on the manuscript, but it probably should have read 1594. The new year had just come in (March 25, old style).

To Robert, Lord Cecil

It may please your good Lordship,

They say late thanks are ever best. But the reason was, I thought to have seen your Lordship ere this. Howsoever I shall never forget this your last favour amongst others; and it grieveth me not a little, that I find myself of no use to such an honourable and kind friend.

For that matter, I think I shall desire your assistance for the punishment of the contempt; not that I would use the privilege in future time, but because I would not have the dignity of the King's service prejudiced in my instance. But herein I will be ruled by your Lordship.

It is fit likewise, though much against my mind, that I let your Lordship know that I shall not be able to pay the money within the time by your Lordship undertaken, which was a fortnight. Nay money I find so hard to come by at this time, as I thought to have become an humble suitor to your Honour to have sustained me with your credit for the present from urgent debts, with taking up 300*l*. till I can put away some land. But I am so forward with some sales, as this request I hope I may forbear.

For my estate (because your Honour hath care of it), it is thus: I shall be able with selling the skirts of my living in Hertfordshire to preserve the body; and to leave myself, being clearly out of debt, and having some money in my pocket, 300*l*. land *per annum*, with a fair house, and the ground well timbered. This is now my labour.

For my purpose or course, I desire to meddle as little as I can in the King's causes, his Majesty now abounding in counsel; and to follow my private thrift and practice, and to marry with some convenient advancement. For as for any ambition, I do assure your Honour mine is quenched. In the Queen's, my excellent Mistress's, time the *quorum* was small: her service was a kind of freehold, and it was a more solemn time. All those points agreed with my nature and judgment. My ambition now I shall only put upon my pen, whereby I shall be able to maintain memory and merit of the times succeeding.

Lastly, for this divulged and almost prostituted title of knighthood, I could without charge, by your Honour's mean, be content to have it, both because of this late disgrace, and because I have three new knights in my mess in Gray's-Inn commons; and because I have found out an alderman's daughter, an handsome maiden, to my liking. So as if your Honour will find the time, I will come to the court from Gorhambury upon any warning.

How my sales go forward, your Lordship shall in a few days hear. Mean while, if you will not be pleased to take further day with this lewd fellow, I hope your Lordship will not suffer him to take any part of the penalty, but principal, interest, and costs.

So I remain your Lordship's most bounden,

Fr. Bacon.

3 July, 1603.

*To Sir Thomas Bodley,[1] upon sending him his Book of
the Advancement of Learning*

Sir,

I think no man may more truly say with the Psalm *Multum incola fuit anima mea*,[2] than myself. For I do confess, since I was of any understanding, my mind hath in effect been absent from that I have done; and in absence are many errors which I do willingly acknowledge; and amongst the rest this great one that led the rest; that knowing myself by inward calling to be fitter to hold a book than to play a part, I have led my life in civil causes; for which I was not very fit by nature, and more unfit by the preoccupation of my mind. Therefore calling myself home, I have now for a time enjoyed myself; whereof likewise I desire to make the world partaker. My labours (if I may so term that which was the comfort of my other labours) I have

[1] (1545-1613): founder of the Bodleian Library at Oxford.

[2] "My soul has long been a sojourner" [with him that hateth peace]. Cf. Psalms 120:6.

dedicated to the King; desirous, if there be any good in them, it may be as the fat of a sacrifice, incensed to his honour: and the second copy I have sent unto you, not only in good affection, but in a kind of congruity, in regard of your great and rare desert of learning. For books are the shrines where the Saint is, or is believed to be: and you having built an Ark to save learning from deluge, deserve propriety in any new instrument or engine, whereby learning should be improved or advanced.

[1605]

To the Earl of Salisbury, upon sending him one of his Books of Advancement of Learning

It may please your good Lordship,

I present your Lordship with a work of my vacant time, which if it had been more, the work had been better. It appertaineth to your Lordship (besides my particular respects) in some propriety, in regard you are a great governor in a province of learning, and (that which is more) you have added to your place affection towards learning, and to your affection judgment; of which the last I could be content were (for the time) less, that you might the less exquisitely censure that which I offer to you. But sure I am the argument is good, if it had lighted upon a good author. But I shall content myself to awake better spirits, like a bell-ringer, which is first up to call others to church. So with my humble desire of your Lordship's good acceptation, I remain.

[1605]

To Mr. Matthew[1]

Sir,

I perceive you have some time when you can be content to think of your friends; from whom since you have borrowed

---

[1] Sir Tobie Matthew (1577-1655): friend and confidant of Bacon's.

yourself, you do well, not paying the principal, to send the interest at six months day. The relation[2] which here I send you inclosed, carries the truth of that which is public; and though my little leisure might have required a briefer, yet the matter would have endured and asked a larger.

I have now at last taught that child to go, at the swadling whereof you were. My work touching the *Proficiency* and *Advancement* of *Learning*, I have put into two books; whereof the former, which you saw, I count but as a Page to the latter. I have now published them both; whereof I thought it a small adventure to send you a copy, who have more right to it than any man, except Bishop Andrews,[3] who was my inquisitor.

The death of the late great Judge concerned not me, because the other was not removed. I write this in answer to your good wishes; which I return not as flowers of Florence, but as you mean them; whom I conceive place cannot alter, no more than time shall me, except it to be the better.

[Nov., 1605]

A Letter to Sir Tho: Bodley, after he had imparted to Sir Tho: a writing entituled Cogitata et Visa

Sir,

In respect of my going down to my house in the country, I shall have miss of my papers; which I pray you therefore to return unto me. You are, I bear you witness, slothful, and you help me nothing; so as I am half in conceit that you affect not the argument; for myself I know well you love and affect. I can say no more to you, but *non canimus surdis, respondent omnia sylvæ*.[1] If you be not of the lodgings chalked up (whereof I speak in my preface) I am but to pass by your door. But if I had you but a fortnight at Gorhambury, I would make you tell me an-

---

[2] This "relation" is lost, but it must have dealt with the Gunpowder Plot.

[3] Dr. Lancelot Andrewes (1555-1626): Dean of Westminster,

Bishop of Chichester.

---

[1] "We sing not to deaf ears, for all the woods reply." Virgil, *Eclogues*, X.8.

other tale; or else I would add a Cogitation against Libraries, and be revenged on you that way. I pray send me some good news of Sir Thomas Smith, and commend me very kindly to him. So I rest.

[1607]

A Letter to Mr. Matthew, upon sending to him Part of "Instauratio Magna"

Mr. Matthew,

I plainly perceive by your affectionate writing touching my work, that one and the same thing affecteth us both; which is the good end to which it is dedicate; for as to any ability of mine, it cannot merit that degree of approbation. For your caution for church-men and church-matters, as for any impediment it might be to the applause and celebrity of my work, it moveth me not; but as it may hinder the fruit and good which may come of a quiet and calm passage to the good port to which it is bound, I hold it a just respect; so as to fetch a fair wind I go not too far about. But the troth is, I shall have no occasion to meet them in my way, except it be as they will needs confederate themselves with Aristotle, who, you know, is intemperately magnified with the schoolmen; and is also allied (as I take it) to the Jesuits, by Faber,[1] who was a companion of Loyola, and a great Aristotelian. I send you at this time the only part which hath any harshness; and yet I framed to myself an opinion, that whosoever allowed well of that preface which you so much commend, will not dislike, or at least ought not to dislike, this other speech of preparation; for it is written out of the same spirit, and out of the same necessity. Nay it doth more fully lay open that the question between me and the ancients is not of the virtue of the race, but of the rightness of the way. And to speak truth, it is to the other but as *palma* to *pugnus*,[2] part of the same thing more large. You conceive aright

---

[1] Johannes Faber (1478-1541): "The Hammer of Heretics", German Roman Catholic bishop.

[2] "the hand" to "the fist".

that in this and the other you have commission to impart and communicate them to others according to your discretion. Other matters I write not of. Myself am like the miller of Huntingdon, that was wont to pray for peace amongst the willows; for while the winds blew, the wind-mills wrought, and the water-mill was less customed. So I see that controversies of religion must hinder the advancement of sciences. Let me conclude with my perpetual wish towards yourself, that the approbation of yourself, by your own discreet and temperate carriage, may restore you to your country, and your friends to your society. And so I commend you to God's goodness.

Gray's-Inn, this 10th of October, 1609.

A Letter to Mr. Matthew, upon sending his book "De sapientia veterum"

Mr. Matthew,

I do heartily thank you for your letter of the 24th of August from Salamanca; and in recompence thereof, I send you a little work of mine that hath begun to pass the world. They tell me my latin is turned into silver, and become current. Had you been here, you should have been my inquisitor before it came forth: but I think the greatest inquisitor in Spain will allow it. But one thing you must pardon me if I make no haste to believe, that the world should be grown to such an ecstasy as to reject truth in philosophy, because the author dissenteth in religion; no more than they do by Aristotle or Averroes. My great work goeth forward; and after my manner, I alter ever when I add. So that nothing is finished till all be finished. This I have written in the midst of a term and parliament; thinking no time so precious, but that I should talk of these matters with so good and dear a friend. And so with my wonted wishes I leave you to God's goodness.

From Gray's-Inn, the 17th of Febr., 1610. [1611 N.S.]

To the King

It may please your most excellent Majesty,

Having understood of the death of the Lord Chief Justice,[1] I do ground in all humbleness and assured hope, that your Majesty will not think of any other but your poor servants, your attorney and your solicitor (one of them) for that place. Else we shall be like Noah's dove, not knowing where to rest our foot. For the places of rest after the extreme painful places wherein we serve have used to be, either the Lord Chancellor's place, or the mastership of the Rolls, or the places of the two chief justices: whereof, for the first, I would be almost loth to live to see this worthy counsellor fail. The mastership of the Rolls is blocked with a reversion. My lord Coke is like to outlive us both. So as if this turn fail, I for my part know not whither to look. I have served your Majesty above a prenticehood, full seven years and more, as your solicitor, which is, I think, one of the painfulest places in your kingdom, specially as my employments have been; and God hath brought mine own years to fifty-two, which I think is older than ever any solicitor continued unpreferred. My suit is principally that you would remove Mr. Attorney to the place; if he refuse, then I hope your Majesty will seek no furder than myself, that I may at last, out of your Majesty's grace and favour, step forwards to a place either of more comfort or more ease. Besides how necessary it is for your Majesty to strengthen your service amongst the Judges by a Chief Justice which is sure to your prerogative, your Majesty knoweth. Therefore I cease furder to trouble your Majesty, humbly craving pardon, and relying wholly upon your goodness and remembrance, and resting in all true humbleness,

Your Majesty's most devoted
and faithful subject and servant,

Fr. Bacon.

[c. Aug. 7, 1613]

[1] Sir Thomas Fleming (1544-1613).

To the Earl of Buckingham[1]

My very good Lord,

This day I have made even with the business of the kingdom for common justice. Not one cause unheard. The lawyers drawn dry of all the motions they were to make. Not one petition unanswered. And this I think could not be said in our age before. This I speak not out of ostentation, but out of gladness, when I have done my duty. I know men think I cannot continue, if I should thus oppress myself with business. But that account is made. The duties of life are more than life. And if I die now I shall die before the world be weary of me, which in our times is somewhat rare. And all this while I have been a little unperfect in my foot. But I have taken pains more like the beast with four legs, than like a man with scarce two legs. But if it be a gout (which I do neither acknowledge nor much disclaim) it is a good-natured gout; for I have no rage of it, and it goeth away quickly. I have hope it is but an accident of changing from a field-air to a Thames-air; or rather, I think, it is the distance of the King and your Lordship from me that doth congeal my humours and spirits.

When I had written this letter, I received your Lordship's letter of the third of this present, wherein your Lordship sheweth your solicitous care of my health, which did wonderfully comfort me. And it is true, that at this present I am very well, and my supposed gout quite vanished.

I humbly pray you to commend my service, infinite in desire, howsoever limited in ability, to his Majesty, to hear of whose health and good disposition is to me the greatest beatitude which I can receive in this world. And I humbly beseech his Majesty to pardon me that I do not now send him my account of council business, and other his royal commands, till within these four days; because this flood of business of justice did hitherto wholly possess me; which I know worketh this effect, as it contenteth his subjects, and knitteth their hearts more and

[1] George Villiers (1592-1628): courtier, Lord High Admiral, favourite of James I.

more to his Majesty; though I must confess my mind is upon
other matters, as his Majesty shall know, by the grace of God,
at his return. God ever bless and prosper you.

Your Lordship's true and most
devoted friend and servant,
Fr. Bacon.

Whitehall, this 8th
of June, 1617.

To the Marquis of Buckingham

My very good Lord,

I am much bounden to his Majesty, and likewise to your
Lordship. I see by the late accesses I have had with his Majesty,
and now by his royal and real favour,[1] that he loveth me, and
knowledgeth me for the servant that I am, or desire to be. This
in me must turn to a great alacrity to honour and serve him with
a mind less troubled and divided. And for your Lordship, my
affection may and doth daily receive addition, but cannot, nor
never could, receive alteration. I pray present my humble thanks
to his Majesty; and I am very glad his health confirmeth; and
I hope to see him this summer at Gorhambury. There is sweet
air as any is. God preserve and prosper you both. I ever rest

Your Lordship's most obliged friend,
and faithful servant,
Fr. Verulam, Canc.

May 9, 1619.

To the King's Most Excellent Matie

It may please your most excellent Majesty,

It being one thing to speak or write, specially to a King, in
public, another in private, although I have dedicated a work,

---

[1] The King had just made him a
grant of £1500 a year for life.

or rather a portion of a work, which at last I have overcome, to your Majesty by a public epistle, where I speak to you in the hearing of others; yet I thought fit also humbly to seek access for the same, not so much to your person as to your judgment, by these private lines.

The work, in what colours soever it may be set forth, is no more but a new logic, teaching to invent and judge by induction (as finding syllogism incompetent for sciences of nature), and thereby to make philosophy and sciences both more true and more active.

This, tending to enlarge the bounds of Reason and to endow man's estate with new value, was no improper oblation to your Majesty, who, of men, is the greatest master of reason, and author of beneficence.

There be two of your council, and one other bishop of this land, that know I have been about some such work near thirty years; so as I made no haste. And the reason why I have published it now, specially being unperfect, is, to speak plainly, because I number my days, and would have it saved. There is another reason of my so doing, which is to try whether I can get help in one intended part of this work, namely the compiling of a natural and experimental history, which must be the main foundation of a true and active philosophy.

This work is but a new body of clay, whereinto your Majesty by your countenance and protection, may breathe life. And, to tell your Majesty truly what I think, I account your favour may be to this work as much as an hundred years' time: for I am persuaded the work will gain upon men's minds in ages, but your gracing it may make it take hold more swiftly; which I would be glad of, it being a work meant not for praise or glory, but for practice, and the good of men. One thing, I confess, I am ambitious of, with hope, which is, that after these beginnings, and the wheel once set on going, men shall suck more truth out of Christian pens, than hitherto they have done out of heathen. I say with hope; because I hear my former book of the Advancement of Learning is well tasted in the universities here, and the

English colleges abroad: and this is the same argument sunk deeper.

And so I ever humbly rest in prayers and all other duties,

Your Majesty's most bounden

and devoted servant,

Fr. Verulam, Canc.

York-house, this 12th
of October, 1620.

To the Marquis of Buckingham

My very good Lord,

Your Lordship spake of purgatory. I am now in it, but my mind is in a calm; for my fortune is not my felicity. I know I have clean hands and a clean heart; and I hope a clean house for friends or servants. But Job himself, or whosoever was the justest judge, by such hunting for matters against him as hath been used against me, may for a time seem foul, specially in a time when greatness is the mark and accusation is the game. And if this be to be a Chancellor, I think if the great seal lay upon Hounslow Heath, nobody would take it up. But the King and your Lordship will, I hope, put an end to these miseries one way or other. And in troth that which I fear most is lest continual attendance and business, together with these cares, and want of time to do my weak body right this spring by diet and physic, will cast me down; and then it will be thought feigning or fainting. But I hope in God I shall hold out. God prosper you.

[March 14, 1620 (1621 N.S.)]

*To the Right Honourable his very good Lords,
the Lords Spiritual and Temporal
in the Upper House of Parliament assembled*

My very good Lords,

I humbly pray your Lordships all to make a favourable and true construction of my absence. It is no feigning nor fainting, but sickness both of my heart and of my back, though joined with that comfort of mind, that perswadeth me that I am not far from heaven, whereof I feel the first fruits. And because, whether I live or die, I would be glad to preserve my honour and fame, as far as I am worthy; hearing that some complaints of base bribery are come before your Lordships, my requests unto your Lordships are: first, that you will maintain me in your good opinion, without prejudice, until my cause be heard; secondly, that, in regard I have sequestred my mind at this time in great part from worldly matters, thinking of my account and answer in a higher court, your Lordships would give me some convenient time, according to the course of other courts, to advise with my counsel, and to make my answer; wherein nevertheless my counsel's part will be the least; for I shall not, by the grace of God, trick up an innocency with cavillations; but plainly and ingenuously (as your Lordships know my manner is) declare what I know or remember; thirdly, that, according to the course of justice, I may be allowed to except to the witnesses brought against me, and to move questions to your Lordships for their cross-examination, and likewise to produce my own witnesses for discovery of the truth: and lastly, if there come any more petitions of like nature, that your Lordships would be pleased not to take any prejudice or apprehension of any number or muster of them, especially against a Judge that makes two thousand decrees and orders in a year (not to speak of the courses that have been taken for hunting out complaints against me); but that I may answer them, according to the rules of justice, severally and respectively. These requests I hope appear to your Lordships no other than just. And so, thinking myself happy to have so noble Peers and reverend Prelates to discern of my cause, and desiring no privilege of greatness for subterfuge of guiltiness, but meaning (as I said) to deal fairly and plainly with your Lordships, and to put myself upon your honours and favours, I pray God to bless your counsels and your persons; and rest

Your Lordships' humble servant,
Fr. St. Alban, Canc.

19th March, 1620. [1621 N.S.]

To the King's Most Excellent Majesty

It may please your Majesty,

It hath pleased God for these three days past, to visit me with such extremity of head-ach, upon the hinder part of my head, fixed in one place, that I thought verily it had been some imposthumation. And then the little physic that I have told me, that either it must grow to a congelation, and so to a lethargy, or to break, and so to a mortal fever or sudden death. Which apprehension (and chiefly the anguish of the pain) made me unable to think of any business. But now that the pain itself is assuaged to be tolerable, I resume the care of my business, and therein prostrate myself again, by my letter, at your Majesty's feet.

Your Majesty can bear me witness, that at my last so comfortable access I did not so much as move your Majesty, by your absolute power of pardon or otherwise, to take my cause into your hands and to interpose between the sentence of the House; and according to mine own desire your Majesty left it to the sentence of the House, and so was reported by my Lord Treasurer.

But now if not *per omnipotentiam* (as the divines speak) but *per potestatem suaviter disponentem*,[1] your Majesty will graciously save me from a sentence with the good liking of the

---

[1] not "by means of supreme force" but "by means of force gently applied".

House, and that cup may pass from me; it is the utmost of my desires.

This I move with the more belief, because I assure myself that if it be reformation that is sought, the very taking away the seal, upon my general submission, will be as much in example for these four hundred years, as any furder severity.

The means of this I most humbly leave unto your Majesty. But surely I conceive, that your Majesty opening yourself in this kind to the Lords Counsellors, and a motion from the Prince after my submission, and my Lord Marquis using his interest with his friends in the House, may effect the sparing of a sentence; I making my humble suit to the House for that purpose, joined with the delivery of the seal into your Majesty's hands.

This is the last suit I shall make to your Majesty in this business, prostrating myself at your mercy-seat, after fifteen years' service, wherein I have served your Majesty in my poor endeavours with an entire heart, and as I presumed to say unto your Majesty, and still a virgin for matters that concern your person or crown; and now only craving that after eight steps of honour I be not precipitated altogether.

But because he that hath taken bribes is apt to give bribes, I will go furder, and present your Majesty with a bribe. For if your Majesty give me peace and leisure, and God give me life, I will present your Majesty with a good history of England, and a better digest of your laws. And so concluding with my prayers, I rest

> Your Majesty's afflicted,
> but ever devoted servant,
> Fr. St. Alban, Canc.

21 April, 1621.

To the Marquis of Buckingham

Good my Lord,

Procure the warrant for my discharge this day. Death, I thank God, is so far from being unwelcome to me, as I have called for it (as Christian resolution would permit) any time these two months. But to die before the time of his Majesty's grace, and in this disgraceful place, is even the worst that could be; and when I am dead, he is gone that was always in one tenor, a true and perfect servant to his master, and one that was never author of any immoderate, no, nor unsafe, no (I will say it) not unfortunate counsel; and one that no temptation could ever make other than a trusty, and honest, and thrice loving friend to your Lordship; and howsoever I acknowledge the sentence just, and for reformation sake fit, the justest Chancellor that hath been in the five changes since Sir Nicholas Bacon's time. God bless and prosper your Lordship, whatsoever become of me.

Your Lordship's true friend, living and dying,

Fr. St. Alban.

Tower, 31st May, 1621.

To the Right Reverend Father in God,
Lancelot Andrewes, Lord Bishop of Winchester,
and Counsellor of Estate to his Majesty

My Lord,

Amongst consolations, it is not the least to represent to a man's self like examples of calamity in others. For examples give a quicker impression than arguments; and besides they certify us that which the Scripture also tendereth for satisfaction, *that no new thing is happened unto us.*[1] This they do the better, by how much the examples are liker in circumstances to our own case; and more especially if they fall upon persons that are greater and worthier than ourselves. For as it savoureth of vanity to match ourselves highly in our own conceit; so on the other side it is a good sound conclusion, that if our betters have sustained the like events, we have the less cause to be grieved.

In this kind of consolation I have not been wanting to myself, though as a Christian I have tasted (through God's great goodness) of higher remedies. Having therefore, through the variety

[1] Cf. Eccles. 1:10.

of my reading, set before me many examples both of ancient and later times, my thoughts (I confess) have chiefly stayed upon three particulars, as the most eminent and the most resembling. All three, persons that had held chief place of authority in their countries; all three ruined, not by war, or by any other disaster, but by justice and sentence, as delinquents and criminals; all three famous writers, insomuch as the remembrance of their calamity is now as to posterity but as a little picture of night-work, remaining amongst the fair and excellent tables of their acts and works: and all three (if that were any thing to the matter) fit examples to quench any man's ambition of rising again; for that they were every one of them restored with great glory, but to their further ruin and destruction, ending in a violent death. The men were Demosthenes, Cicero, and Seneca; persons that I durst not claim affinity with, except the similitude of our fortunes had contracted it. When I had cast mine eyes upon these examples, I was carried on further to observe, how they did bear their fortunes, and principally how they did employ their times, being banished and disabled for public business: to the end that I might learn by them; and that they might be as well my counsellors as my comforters. Whereupon I happened to note, how diversly their fortunes wrought upon them; especially in that point at which I did most aim, which was the employing of their times and pens. In Cicero, I saw that during his banishment (which was almost two years) he was so softened and dejected, as he wrote nothing but a few womanish epistles. And yet, in mine opinion, he had least reason of the three to be discouraged: for that although it was judged, and judged by the highest kind of judgment, in form of a statute or law, that he should be banished, and his whole estate confiscated and seized, and his houses pulled down, and that it should be highly penal for any man to propound his repeal; yet his case even then had no great blot of ignominy; but it was thought but a tempest of popularity which overthrew him. Demosthenes contrariwise, though his case was foul, being condemned for bribery, and not simple bribery, but bribery in the nature of treason and disloyalty; yet nevertheless took so little knowledge of his fortune, as during his banishment he did much busy himself, and intermeddle with matters of state; and took upon him to counsel the state (as if he had been still at the helm) by letters; as appears by some epistles of his which are extant. Seneca indeed, who was condemned for many corruptions and crimes, and banished into a solitary island, kept a mean; and though his pen did not freeze, yet he abstained from intruding into matters of business; but spent his time in writing books of excellent argument and use for all ages; though he might have made better choice (sometimes) of his dedications.

These examples confirmed me much in a resolution (whereunto I was otherwise inclined) to spend my time wholly in writing; and to put forth that poor talent, or half talent, or what it is, that God hath given me, not as heretofore to particular exchanges, but to banks or mounts of perpetuity, which will not break. Therefore having not long since set forth a part of my *Instauration*; which is the work that in mine own judgment (*si nunquam fallit imago*[2]) I do most esteem; I think to proceed in some new parts thereof. And although I have received from many parts beyond the seas, testimonies touching that work, such as beyond which I could not expect at the first in so abstruse an argument; yet nevertheless I have just cause to doubt that it flies too high over men's heads. I have a purpose therefore (though I break the order of time) to draw it down to the sense, by some patterns of a *Natural Story* and *Inquisition*. And again, for that my book of *Advancement of Learning* may be some preparative, or key, for the better opening of the *Instauration*; because it exhibits a mixture of new conceits and old; whereas the *Instauration* gives the new unmixed, otherwise than with some little aspersion of the old for taste's sake; I have thought good to procure a translation of that book into the general language, not without great and ample additions, and enrichment thereof; especially in the second book, which handleth the *Partition of Sciences*; in such sort, as I hold it may serve in lieu of the first part of the *Instauration*, and acquit my promise

[2] "if the mirror does not lie". Virgil, *Eclogues*, II.27.

in that part. Again, because I cannot altogether desert the civil person that I have borne, which if I should forget, enough would remember; I have also entered into a work touching *Laws*, propounding a character of justice in a middle term, between the speculative and reverend discourses of philosophers, and the writings of lawyers, which are tied and obnoxious to their particular laws. And although it be true that I had a purpose to make a particular digest or recompilement of the laws of mine own nation; yet because it is a work of assistance, and that that I cannot master by my own forces and pen, I have laid it aside. Now having in the work of my *Instauration* had in contemplation the general good of men in their very being, and the dowries of nature; and in my work of laws, the general good of men likewise in society, and the dowries of government; I thought in duty I owed somewhat unto mine own country, which I ever loved; insomuch as although my place hath been far above my desert, yet my thoughts and cares concerning the good therefore were beyond, and over, and above my place: so now being (as I am) no more able to do my country service, it remained unto me [to] do it honour: which I have endeavoured to do in my work of *The Reign of King Henry the Seventh*. As for my *Essays*, and some other particulars of that nature, I count them but as the recreations of my other studies, and in that sort purpose to continue them; though I am not ignorant that those kind of writings would, with less pains and embracement (perhaps), yield more lustre and reputation to my name, than those other which I have in hand. But I account the use that a man should seek of the publishing of his own writings before his death, to be but an untimely anticipation of that which is proper to follow a man, and not to go along with him.

But revolving with myself my writings, as well those which I have published, as those which I had in hand, methought they went all into the City, and none into the Temple; where, because I have found so great consolation, I desire likewise to make some poor oblation. Therefore I have chosen an argument, mixt of religious and civil considerations; and likewise mixt between contemplative and active. For who can tell whether there may not be an *exoriere aliquis?*[8] Great matters (especially if they be religious) have (many times) small beginnings: and the platform may draw on the building. This work, because I was ever an enemy to flattering dedications, I have dedicated to your Lordship, in respect of our ancient and private acquaintance; and because amongst the men of our times I hold you in especial reverence.

Your Lordship's loving friend,
Fr. St. Alban.

[1622]

To the Duke of Buckingham

Excellent Lord,

There is a suit whereunto I may as it were claim kindred, and may be of credit and profit unto me. And it is an old arrear, which is called upon, from Sir Ni. Bacon, my eldest brother. It may be worth to me perhaps two thousand pounds, and yet I may deal kindly with my brother, and also reward liberally (as I mean to do) the officers of the Exchequer which have brought it to light. Good my Lord, obtain it of the King, and be earnest in it for me. It will acquit the King somewhat of his promise that he would have care of my wants. For hitherto since my misfortunes I have tasted of his Majesty's mercy, but not of his bounty. But your Lordship may be pleased in this to clear the coast with my Lord Treasurer; else there it will have a stop. I am almost at last cast for means, and yet it grieveth me most, that at such a time as this I should not be rather serviceable to your Grace than troublesome.

God preserve and prosper your Grace,

Your Grace's most obliged
and faithful servant,
Fr. St. Alban.

This 23 of January,
1623. [1624 N.S.]

---

⁸ Some avenger (or judge) to come(?). Cf. Virgil, *Aeneid,* IV. 625: "Exoriare aliquis nostris ex ossibus ultor": "May some avenger arise one day from my bones."

To the Duke of Buckingham

My Lord,

I am now full three years old in misery, neither hath there been any thing done for me, whereby I might die out of ignominy or live out of want. But now that your Grace (God's name be praised for it) hath recovered your health, and are comen to the court, and the parliament business hath also intermission, I firmly hope your Grace will deal with his Majesty, that as I have tasted of his mercy I may also taste of his bounty. Your Grace, I know, for a business of a private man, cannot win yourself more honour; and I hope I shall yet live to do you service. For my fortune hath (I thank God) made no alteration in my mind but to the better. I ever humbly rest

Your Grace's most obliged,
and faithful servant,
Fr. St. Alban.

[June 19, 1624]

If I may know by two or three words from your Grace, that you will set in for me, I will propound somewhat that shall be modest, and leave it to your Grace whether you will move his Majesty yourself or recommend it to some of your Lordship's friends that wish me well; as my Lord of Arundel, or Secretary Conway, or Mr. James Maxwell.

An humble petition of the Lord St. Albans to his Majesty

That whereas your supplicant is now three years old in misery, during which time he hath tasted of your Majesty's mercy, but not of your bounty, which his services past and necessity present may implore,

Your Majesty of your grace will so far compassionate your supplicant as to give order that he may have three years' payment of his pension beforehand; which in effect is but a borrowing.

And this may enable him to overcome his debts, but then because he shall want for his present maintenance, your Majesty will also be pleased during those three years, till his pension run again, to discharge him of the rent of 1,000*l.* reserved upon his farm of petty writs.

And your supplicant shall (as ever) pray for your Majesty's health and happiness.

[June, 1624]

Glossary

ABSTRACT: pertaining to one withdrawn from the world; hermitic
ABSURD: stupid, unreasonable
ABUSE: *v.* deceive, mislead; *n.* deception
ACCIDENTS: symptoms
ACCUMULATE: accumulated
ACQUAINTING: accustoming
ADAMANT: magnet
ADMIRATION: wonder
ADMIRING: wondering at
ADVANCEMENT: gift
ADVENTURES: dangers, risks; remarkable events
ADVERTISED: informed, advised
ADVISED: deliberate, cautious
ADVISETH: informs (himself)
ADVOUTERIES: adulteries
ADVOUTRESSES: adulteresses
AFFECT: desire, like
AFFECTED: strongly desired
AFFECTING: aiming at, striving for, desiring, liking
AFFECTION: inclination, liking for, zeal, enthusiasm
AFFECTIONATE: zealous, over-eager
AFTER: according
AGE: BEAR ITS AGE: remain fresh
AGREEABLY: suitably
ALL: any
ALLAY: alloy
ALLEY: bowling alley
ALLOW: approve
ALLOWANCE: approval
ALMOST: generally, for the most part

AMBASSAGE, EMBASSAGE: embassy
AMPLIFICATION: rhetorical flourish, exaggeration
APPARENT: evident, conspicuous
APPETITE: IN APPETITE: desiring something, with (unsatisfied) ambition
APPLIED: devoted (oneself) to
APPLY: suit, accommodate
APPOSED: questioned, have questions posed
APPREHENDETH: knows how; inclines himself
APPROPRIATING: allotting or limiting
ARBITREMENT: settlement, arbitration
AREFACTION: drying up
ARIETATIONS: assaults with battering-rams
ARTIFICIAL: skilful, with artifice
ASPERSION: intermixture
ASSURED: trustworthy
ATTEMPERED: moderated, softened
AUDITS: revenue, income
AVERSATION: aversion
AVOIDANCES: outlets for water
AVOIDED: left

BASILISKS: stone-shooting cannon
BASTONS: cudgels, staves
BATTLES: bodies of troops, forces
BEAT OVER: treat comprehensively, synthesize
BECOME: betake (oneself)
BEFORE HAND: ahead of another, having the advantage over
BEHOLDING: beholden
BELIKE: probably

BEND: apply

BENT: crafty

BLANCH: shrink back, be evasive, avoid

BORE: pipe

BORNE OUT: compensated for

BOTTOMS: vessels

BRAVE: *v.* challenge, insult, outface; *adj.* fine, excellent

BRAVERY: ostentation, show, finery; bravado, boastfulness

BREAKETH: subdues, disciplines

BROIDING: braiding, interweaving

BROKE: deal, do business (with)

BUCKLING (TOWARD): preparing (for)

BULLACE: small wild plum

BUSY: elaborate; meddling

CABINET COUNCILS: (unofficial) secret councils

CAN: *inf.* be able

CAPABLE (OF): able to receive

CARD: chart or map

CARE NOT: be hasty or careless

CAREFULNESS: anxiety

CARRY: spread abroad

CARRY THINGS AGAINST: prevail against, be preferred before

CAST: plan, arrange

CASTETH: makes the balance sink, decides

CASUALTY: instability, uncertainty

CATCHING: greedy

CAVILLATION: cavil

CERTAIN: fixed

CERTIFY OVER: report to

CESSIONS: concessions, yieldings to others

CHALLENGE: claim

CHAMAÏRIS: a kind of iris

CHAMOLET: camlet, a costly fabric of satin weave made of camel's hair

CHARGE: *v.* put a burden on; *n.* expense

CHECK: interfere, block

CHOP: bargain, argue

CIVIL: public; seemly, befitting a citizen

CIVILITY: civilization, refinement

CLAMOUR: shout down

CLARIFY: become clear

CLEAN: polished (style)

CLEAR: prove, justify

CLEAR AND ROUND: honest and straightforward

CLEARING: freeing from debt

CLEARNESS: openness

CLOSE: secret, hidden

COARCTATION: restriction

COEMPTION: cornering (of markets)

COLLEGIATE: corporate

COMFORTETH: strengthens

COMMANDED: dominated, overtopped

COMMANDING GROUND: vantage ground

COMMANDMENT: authority

COMMISERABLE: worthy of pity

COMMODITY: advantage

COMMONALTIES: corporations; communities, societies

COMMONPLACE: subject (for discussion)

COMMUNALTIES: commonalties

COMPLEXION: constitution

COMPOSITION: nature, temperament (mixture of humours)

COMPOUND: settle

CONCEIT: thought, idea, concept; mind, intelligence, comprehension; unrestrained fancies

CONCENT: harmony, accord

CONCLUSIONS: experiments

CONFORM: corresponding

CONJUNCTION: sexual union; ILL CONJUNCTION: lack of co-operation or co-ordination

CONSENT: agreement

CONSEQUENCE: inference

CONSTRUCTION: interpretation

CONTENT: give pleasure

CONTENTATION: satisfaction

CONTINENT: container

CONVENIENCE: TO HAVE CONVENIENCE: to be fitting

CONVERSANT IN, ABOUT: concerned with

CONVERSATION: social graces, society

CONVERSE IN: be engaged in

COPIE: copiousness, fluency

CORRESPONDENCE: WITH CORRESPONDENCE TO: in a manner suitable to; HOLD GOOD CORRESPONDENCE WITH: be equally matched with

CORROBORATE: full-grown

COURAGES: spirits

COURSE: OUT OF COURSE: out of bounds; irregularly

CRUDITIES: indigestible matter

CURIOSITY: subtlety (fine point recognized by "curious" persons); hence ingenuity, elegance

CURIOUS: observant, attentive, careful; critical, fastidious; complex, elaborate, carefully made, subtle

CURIOUSLY: in a complex way, elaborately

CURRENTLY: smoothly, uninterruptedly

DAINTILY: elegantly

DECEIVABLE: deceptive

DECENT: becoming, attractive, suitable

DECLARING: making clear

DECLINE: avoid, turn aside

DEGREES: steps

DELIVERIES: escapes, ways of getting out of difficulties

DENOMINATE OF: denominated of, named after

DEPENDENCES: retainers, followers, dependants

DEPRAVATION: slander

DEPRAVE: depreciate

DEPRAVING: injuring the reputation of, slandering

DERIVATION: subsidiary channel, contributing means

DERIVE: divert, change the course of

DESIGNED: assigned, destined, directed

DESIGNMENTS: designs, aims

DESTITUTE: desert

DIFFERENCE: distinguishing mark

DIFFICILENESS: obstinacy

DIGLADIATION: wrangling, disputing

DISABLE: disparage

DISADVANTAGEABLE: disadvantageous

DISALLOWED: disapproved

DISCHARGE: free, rid (oneself) of charges; prove (oneself) innocent

DISCLAIM IN: renounce

DISCOMMODITY: disadvantage, inconvenience

DISCOURSING WITS: rambling or talkative minds

DISCOVER: reveal, uncover

DISCOVERY: making disclosures, giving confidences

DISPENSE WITH: excuse; make up for

DISPLAYED: outspread

DISREPUTATION: disrepute

DISTASTES: annoyances

DOCTORS: learned men

DOLOURS: pains

DORTURE: dormitory

DOUBT: fear

EDGE: stimulate

EJACULATION: emission, a darting out

ELABORATE: elaborated

EMBASSAGE: embassy

ENABLE: qualify

ENABLEMENT: qualifying

ENDANGERETH: runs the risk of

ENFORCING: giving force to, strengthening

ENGAGED: bound

ENTERTAINMENT: preliminary, introduction; consideration

ENTIRE: continuous, unbroken; honest; undistracted

EPHEMERIDES: calendar

ESPIALS: spyings, spies

ESTATE: state; condition; order; station

EVEN: AT EVEN HAND: to be equal (to), even (with)

EXALTATION: (astrology) highest point, point of greatest influence

EXCUSATIONS: excuses, apologies

EXERCISED: achieved with difficulty

EXHAUST: exhausted

EXPECT: wait for

EXPERT MEN: men of experience

EXPOSTULATION: demand

EXPRESSING: demonstrating

EXPULSE: expel, drive out

EXQUISITE: careful, painstaking, exact

EXTENSIVE: extendible

EXTENUATE: depreciate; extenuated, thin

EXTERN: external

EXTIRPER: extirpator, destroyer

EXULCERATIONS: ulcerations

FACILE: easily worked upon, ready to comply, complaisant

FACILITY: complaisance, desire to please, pliancy

FAIN: obliged, forced

FAIR: simply

FALL UPON: note

FALLS UNDER: admits of

FAME: rumour; reputation

FASHIONS: habits

FAST: tenacious

FAVOUR: face; facial expression, countenance

FETCH ABOUT: go (round) about

FETCHING: striking, reaching

FLASHY: insipid, flat

FLIGHTSHOT: bowshot

FOOT-PACE: dais

FOR: as regards

FOR THAT: because

FORESEE: provide

FORMALISTS: pretenders to wisdom

FORWARDS: AND SO FORWARDS: and so forth

FREE: liberal

FRONT: GO IN FRONT UPON: advance towards

FUME: smoke; foolish idea

FUTILE: talkative

GAME: playfulness

GENITINGS: jennetings, early apples

GIDDINESS: inconstancy of opinion

GINGLES: rattles

GIVEN OVER: passed by

GLANCE: glancing reference, hint

GLOBE: collection, compendium

GLORIOUS: ostentatious, glory-seeking, boastful

GLORY: vanity

GOOD: MAKE GOOD: be true to

GRACE: condescension; favour

GRACIOUS: graceful; something to be thankful for, a positive favour

GRAVELLED: baffled

GRAZE: be turfed

HALFPACE: raised floor or dais

HAND: IN HAND WITH: concerned, dealing with

HANDSOMELY: dexterously, skilfully

HEATH: garden left wild

HIGH: high-flown, presumptuous

HOLD: uphold, support (a thesis or argument)

HOLDING OF THE SUBJECT: lacking in originality

HOLPEN: remedied, improved

HUKE: hooded cape

HUMOROUS: eccentric, odd, capricious

HUMOUR: caprice

HURT: unfit

IMBARRED: stopped

IMBASED: debased

IMPERTINENCE: matter of no importance, irrelevancy

IMPERTINENT: irrelevant

IMPORTUNE: importunate, troublesome

IMPOSETH: makes an impression (on)

IMPOSTHUMATION: abscess

IMPRINTING: impressive

IMPROPRIATE: *v.* appropriate

INBOWED: bowed, bay

INCENSED: burned

INCOMMODITIES: disadvantages

INCONVENIENT: unsuitable

INCURRETH: runs

INDIFFERENT: neutral, impartial

INDIFFERENTLY: equally

INDUCING: introductory

INDUSTRIOUSLY: purposely

INFAMED: branded with infamy, infamous

INFOLDED: compressed

INFORTUNATE: unfortunate

INGROSSING: engrossing

INQUISITION: inquiry

INSCRUTABLE: unfathomable, beyond measure

INSTRUMENTALS: instruments

INTELLIGENCE: HAVE INTELLIGENCE WITH: be in league with; ILL INTELLIGENCE: misunderstanding

INTEND: devote attention to

INTERESSED: interested

INTEREST IN: influence over

INTERKNOWLEDGE: mutual knowledge

INTERLACE: intermix

INTRINSIC: hidden

INVOCATE: invoke

INWARD: intimate; secret

JADE: ride

KENNING: distance within which land or ships may ordinarily be discerned, about twenty or thirty miles

KIND: manner, way

KINDLY: naturally, readily, thoroughly

KNEE TIMBER: timber with natural knees or angles in it

KNIT: become compact, set (said of limbs)

KNOTS: beds, earth plots

LAST: duration

LATITUDE: area, extent

LAUDATIVE: panegyric

LAY IT AS IF: imply, let on that

LEESE: lose, cause the loss of

LEGEND: legendary

LETTING: hindering, blocking

LIGHTLY: easily

LIMITATIONS: particular instances

LITERATE: pertaining to the ability to arrange disparate things into a meaningful combination

LOADING: TO BE ON THE LOADING PART: to aggravate

LOOK PRECISELY FOR: be strict regarding

LOOSE: excuse; escape; the flight of an arrow

LURCH: swallow up, absorb

MAINLY: strongly, greatly

MAKETH: FOR WHOM IT MAKETH: to whose advantage it is

MANAGED: trained

MANIABLE: manageable, tractable

MANNERS: morals, ethics; character

MARISH: marshy, swampy

MASTERIES: curings of disease

MATERIAL: matter-of-fact, to the point

MATERIATE: of the nature of matter; material

MATTER: UPON THE MATTER: on the whole

MEAN: means; IN A MEAN: moderately

MEDIOCRITIES: middle courses

MELOCOTONES: fruit of a peach grafted on a quince

MENSTRUUM: solvent

MERELY: entirely

MERE-STONE: boundary stone

METEORS: meteorological phenomena

METHODS: systems

MODERATE: control, limit

MORIGERATION: obsequiousness

MOUGHT: might, may

MUNITING: strengthening

NAME: BY NAME: for example; NAME OF: reputation for

NAUGHT: bad, worthless

NEAR HAND: near at hand

NEEDETH: is necessary

NICE: fastidious

NOSE: LED BY THE NOSE: deceived

NOTE: mark, sign

OBLIGED: bound

OBNOXIOUS TO: liable to, exposed to, influenced by; submissive to, dependent upon

OCCASION: GIVE THE OCCASION: suggest the subject (of conversation)

OF: amongst; for; by; with

OFFENCE OF: harm in

OFFICIOUS: ready to serve, dutiful, obliging

OPERATIVE: effective, productive

OPINION: reputation

ORACULOUS: oracular; obscure, enigmatical

ORDAINMENT: ordination, appointed condition

ORDER: TAKE ORDER: try, take measures, prepare

OVERCOME: win, complete

PACK: stack (arrange cards to win)

PAINTED OUT: depicted

PARABLE: figurative observation or saying

PARCEL: part

PARDON: BY PARDON: through allowances

PARTICULAR: partial, restricted to one place; private or personal consideration, self

PASSABLE: commonplace, ordinary; PASSABLE WITH: acceptable to

PASSAGE: transition; acceptance, belief; road; crossing (of a river); GIVE PASSAGE TO: accept; IN PASSAGE: in passing, incidentally

PASSPORT: GIVE A PASSPORT TO: release from

PEREMPTORY: destructive

PERIOD: completion, conclusion

PERSUADED: inculcated

PIECE: patch

PISTOLETS: pistoles

PLACE: TAKE LITTLE PLACE: be of little weight

PLANTATIONS: colonies

PLATFORM: pattern

PLAUSIBLE: deserving of applause, laudable

PLAYBOOK: book with plays in it

PLEASING: indulgent

PLY: TAKE THE PLY: be bent in any direction

POINT: appoint

POLICY: politics

POLITIC (PERSON), POLITIQUE: politician

POLLING: avaricious, predatory

POPULAR: democratic; courting esteem and favour with the people

POPULARITY: desire to gain esteem

POSER: examiner

POSITION: principle, proposition, maxim

POSITIVE: (law) dependent on authority or agreement

PRACTICE: intrigue, negotiation

PRAY IN AID: claim or call in the aid

PREFER: promote

PREOCCUPATE: anticipate, forestall

PRESCRIPTION: reputation, right to a title

PRESENT: *n.* writ; *adj.* immediate, ready

PRESENTLY: at once, immediately

PREST: ready, eager

PREVENT: anticipate, come before

PRICK: plant

PRINCIPALS: originals from which copies are made, models

PRINCIPIAL: initial

PRIVATE: oneself

PRIVATENESS: privacy

PROBATION: proof, experimentation, probing

PROCEEDING UPON: arising, resulting from

PROFESSION: livelihood

PROFICIENCE: progress, advancement

PROPER: belonging or peculiar to the species; personal, private, one's own

PROPORTIONABLE: adequate

PROPRIETY: peculiarity; characteristic; PROPRIETY INHERENT: property (in logic), i.e., an essential quality common to all members of a species or class and peculiar to them

PROSECUTIONS: methods

PROSPECTIVES: perspectives, optical instruments

PROYNING: pruning

PURCHASE: gain, advantage

PURPRISE: enclosure

PUSH: pimple

PUT ABROAD: unfold (of cloth)

PUT HIMSELF FORTH: strive his utmost

PUT IN EXPERIENCE: attempted, tried out, experimented

QUADLINGS: codlings

QUARREL: reasons, grounds for complaint

QUARTER: KEEP QUARTER: keep within bounds, be on friendly terms

QUECH: flinch, stir

QUICKNESS: vividness, liveliness, vigour

QUIT: renounce

RACE: extent

RAISED: desirous

READERS: lecturers

REAL: material, impersonal; realistic

REASON: right, reasonable

RECEIPT: receptacle

RECEIT: receipt, power of receiving; prescription, medicine

RECIPROQUE: reciprocal, mutual

REDARGUTION: refutation

REDUCE: lead, take back again

REDUCED: kept within bounds

REDUCTION: interpretation

RE-EDIFY: rebuild

REFERENDARIES: referees

REGARD: IN REGARD OF: because of; on account of; in view of

REGIMENT: management; education; mode of living; government

REGULAR: hide-bound, rigid in following rules

REIGLEMENT: regulation

RELATION: (law) a retroactive application (of an act or judicial decree)

RELUCTATION: struggle, effort

REMEMBERING: mindful

REMOVER: restless man

REPOSED: calm

REPREHENSION: demonstration of falsity, censure

RESEMBLANCE: comparison

RESPECT: consideration, preference; HAVE RESPECT TO: concern oneself with, have regard to; IN RESPECT:

in case; considering; IN RESPECT OF: because of; in comparison to

RESPECTIVE: having reference to, relative to

RESPECTS: regard for rank

REST: SET UP REST UPON: risk everything on; REST UPON: depend upon

RESTETH TO: (it) remains to

RETIRING: retirement

RETURN: side of building; oscillation; movement of heavenly body in its orbit

RIBES: currants

RID: dispose of

RISE: source

ROUND: direct, straightforward; swiftly

ROUNDETH ABOUT: wanders about

ROW OF RETURN: whole side of a court

RUDIMENT: a half-way form or stage between two species

SALLETS: salads

SARZA: sarsaparilla

SCANTLING: limit, measure

SCRIVENER: money broker

SEASON: TO BE IN SEASON: to flourish

SECOND: inferior, secondary

SEEK: TO SEEK: at a loss (for); deficient, lacking (in)

SEEN: versed

SENSUAL: sensuous

SENTENCE: opinion, judgment

SERVICES: battles

SEVERAL: separate, different

SEVERALLY: variously, in different forms

SHREWD: mischievous

SINDONS: pieces or wrappings (of linen)

SIT: be settled

SLUG: hindrance

SO: provided

SOBERLY: THINK SOBERLY OF: have only a small opinion of

SOLITUDE: solitary position; vacuum, deficiency

SOLUTION OF CONTINUITY: a cut

SORT: suit, fit, agree; consort, go out (with); arrange

SORTABLE: suitable

SORTETH TO: results in

SPARE: frugal use

SPECULATIVE: prying

SPEECH OF TOUCH: malicious speech

SPIALS: espials, spies

STADDLES: young trees left standing after the underbrush has been cleared away

STALE: stalemate

STAND: remain safe, survive; STAND WITH: be consistent with

STATE: canopy

STEAL: do by stealth

STICK: hesitate

STILL: always

STOND: hindrance, obstacle

STOOD UPON: dwelt upon

STORE: abundance

STOVED: kept warm (in a hot-house)

STRAIT: close, intimate

SUBJECT: HOLDING OF THE SUBJECT: lacking in originality

SUBSISTENCE: substance

SUCCESS: result

SUFFICIENCY: ability

SUFFICIENT: able, capable

SUIT: succession, order

SUMMARY: efficacious, important

SUPPLIETH: assists

SYMBOLIZE WITH: resemble, agree with, be alike

TABLE: picture, tableau; small wax-covered tablet of wood for writing upon

TAKING HIMSELF UP: checking himself

TARRASSES: terraces

TAXATION: censure

TAXING: censuring

TEDDER: tether

TEMPER: mixing, i.e., blending of temperament or qualities

TEMPERATURE: temperament (blending of humours), disposition

TENDER: delicate, touchy, critical, sensitive

TENDERING: care

THAT: some that; that which, what

TISSUED: interwoven

TOUCH: SPEECH OF TOUCH; malicious speech

TRACTS: traits, features

TRADITION: delivery, passing on (of knowledge)

TRADUCED (TO CONTEMPT): held up to (contempt), paraded so as to excite contempt

TRADUCEMENT: misrepresentation; calumny

TRANSCENDENCES: flights of the imagination

TRAVEL: travail, labour

TRAVERSE: movable screen or partition

TREATY: treatise

TRENCH TO: encroach upon

TRIBUNITIOUS: overbearing

TRIUMPH: show, parade, celebration, party

TRIVIAL: common; trite

TRUNKS: tubes

TURQUET: a player in Turkish attire

UNDER FOOT: too low

UNDERTAKERS: contractors, projectors

UNDERTAKING: opportunistically enterprising

UNDERVALUES: shortcomings

UNEQUAL: uneven

UNIVERSALITY: study of general principles

URE: use

USE: usury, interest; need

USE TO (BE, HAVE): generally (is, has); is accustomed to (be, have)

VALUE: represent as solvent

VAPOROUS: boastful

VEIN: natural disposition, inclination, course of action, procedure

VENTOSITY: windiness

VIRTUE: courage; the main property or essential character

VOICING: reporting, proclaiming

VOUCH: quote as evidence

WAIT UPON: observe, watch

WATCH CANDLE: night light

WAY: HOLD WAY WITH: equal

WELTS: edges, edging generally used for borders of gowns

WHITE MEATS: food (such as butter, cheese, etc.) derived from such animal products as milk and eggs; or any light-coloured flesh, as veal, poultry, rabbit, etc.

WIT: mind; native ability, ingenuity

WITTY: clever, ingenious

WONDERMENTS: surprises

WORK: manipulate, influence

WOULD: should, ought to

ZELANTS: zealots

Selected Bibliography

ADAMS, Robert P., "The Social Responsibility of Science in *Utopia, New Atlantis* and After", *Journal of the History of Ideas*, X (1949), pp. 374-98.

ANDERSON, F. H., "Bacon on Platonism", *University of Toronto Quarterly*, XI (1942), pp. 154-66.

——, *Francis Bacon, His Career and His Thought*, Los Angeles, University of Southern California Press, 1962.

——, *The Philosophy of Francis Bacon*, University of Chicago Press, 1948.

BROAD, C. D., *The Philosophy of Francis Bacon*, Cambridge University Press, 1926.

BULLOUGH, Geoffrey, "Bacon and the Defence of Learning", in *Seventeenth-Century Studies Presented to Sir Herbert Grierson*, Oxford University Press, 1938, pp. 1-20.

BUNDY, M. W., "Bacon's True Opinion of Poetry", *Studies in Philology*, XXVII (1930), pp. 480-508.

BURTT, E. A., *The Metaphysical Foundations of Modern Physical Science*, New York, Harcourt, Brace, 1925.

BURY, J. B., *The Idea of Progress*, London, Macmillan, 1920.

COCHRANE, Rexmond C., "Francis Bacon and the Architect of Fortune", *Studies in the Renaissance*, V (1958), pp. 176-95.

CRANE, R. S., "The Relation of Bacon's *Essays* to His Program for the Advancement of Learning", in *Schelling Anniversary Papers*, New York, Century Co., 1923, pp. 87-106.

CRANE, W. G., *Wit and Rhetoric in the Renaissance*, New York, Peter Smith, 1937.

CRESSON, A., *Francis Bacon: sa vie, son oeuvre*, Paris, Presses universitaires de France, 1948.

CROWTHER, J. G., *Francis Bacon, the First Statesman of Science*, London, Cresset Press, 1960.

EISELEY, Loren, *Francis Bacon and the Modern Dilemma*, Lincoln, University of Nebraska Press, 1962.

FARRINGTON, Benjamin, *Sir Francis Bacon: Philosopher of Industrial Science*, New York, Schuman, 1949.

GREEN, A. W., *Bacon: His Life and Works*, Denver, Swallow, 1952.

HALL, Marie Boas, "In Defense of Bacon's Views on the Reform of Science", *The Personalist*, XLIV (1964), pp. 437-53.

HARRISON, J. L., "Bacon's View of Rhetoric, Poetry, and Imagination", *Huntington Library Quarterly*, XX (1957), pp. 107-25.

HAYDN, Hiram, *The Counterrenaissance*, New York, S. J. Reginald Saunders, 1950.

JAMES, David G., *The Dream of Learning*, Oxford University Press, 1951.

JONES, Richard Foster, *Ancients and Moderns*, St. Louis, Mo., Washington University Press, 1936.

KNIGHTS, L. C., "Bacon and the Seventeenth-Century Dissociation of Sensibility", in *Explorations*, London, Chatto & Windus, 1946, pp. 92-111.

LEMMI, Charles W., *The Classic Deities in Bacon*, Baltimore, Johns Hopkins University Press, 1933.

LEVI, Adolfo, *Il Pensiero di Francesco Bacone*, Turin, E. Loescher, 1925.

MCRAE, R. F., "The Unity of the Sciences: Bacon, Descartes, and Leibniz", *Journal of the History of Ideas*, XVIII (1957), pp. 27-48.

METZ, Rudolph, "Bacon's Part in the Intellectual Life of His Time", in *Seventeenth-Century Studies Presented to Sir Herbert Grierson*, Oxford University Press, 1938, pp. 21-32.

PATRICK, J. Max, *Francis Bacon*, London, Longmans, 1961.

PRIOR, Moody E., "Bacon's Man of Science", *Journal of the History of Ideas*, XV (1954), pp. 348-70.

RÉMUSAT, Charles de, *Bacon, sa vie, son temps, sa philosophie*, Paris, Didier et Cie, 1858.

TAYLOR, A. E., "Francis Bacon", in *Proceedings of the British Academy*, XII (1926), pp. 273-94.

WALLACE, Karl R., *Francis Bacon on Communication and Rhetoric*, Chapel Hill, University of North Carolina Press, 1943.

WHITAKER, Virgil K., *Francis Bacon's Intellectual Milieu*, Los Angeles, University of California Press, 1962.

WHITEHEAD, Alfred North, *Science and the Modern World*, Lowell Lectures, New York, Macmillan, 1925.

WILLEY, Basil, *The Seventeenth Century Background*, London, Chatto & Windus, 1934.

WILLIAMSON, George, *The Senecan Amble*, University of Chicago Press, 1951.

WILSON, F. P., *Elizabethan and Jacobean*, Oxford University Press, 1945.

ZEITLIN, J., "The Development of Bacon's Essays", *Journal of English and Germanic Philology*, XXVII (1928), pp. 496-519.